Political Demography

Political Demography
How Population Changes Are Reshaping
International Security and National Politics

Edited by

Jack A. Goldstone
Eric P. Kaufmann
Monica Duffy Toft

OXFORD
UNIVERSITY PRESS

OXFORD
UNIVERSITY PRESS

Oxford University Press, Inc., publishes works that further
Oxford University's objective of excellence in research, scholarship,
and education.

Oxford New York
Auckland Cape Town Dar es Salaam Hong Kong Karachi
Kuala Lumpur Madrid Melbourne Mexico City Nairobi
New Delhi Shanghai Taipei Toronto

With offices in
Argentina Austria Brazil Chile Czech Republic France Greece
Guatemala Hungary Italy Japan Poland Portugal Singapore
South Korea Switzerland Thailand Turkey Ukraine Vietnam

Copyright © 2012 by Paradigm Publishers

First published by Paradigm Publishers
Published by Oxford University Press,
198 Madison Avenue, New York, New York 10016
http://www.oup.com

Oxford is a registered trademark of Oxford University Press

Library of Congress Cataloging-in-Publication Data available

ISBN 978-0-19-994596-2

Contents

Part I

Political Demography and Political Science

1

Introduction

Eric P. Kaufmann and Monica Duffy Toft

THE FIELD OF POLITICAL DEMOGRAPHY, DEFINED AS "the study of the size, composition, and distribution of population in relation to both government and politics," is dramatically under-represented in political science (Weiner and Teitelbaum 2001, pp. 11–12). This neglect is especially glaring in the field of international relations, where it contrasts markedly with the rising interest coming from policymakers. "Ten years ago, [demography] was hardly on the radar screen," remark Neil Howe and Richard Jackson of the Center for Strategic and International Studies, two contributors to this volume. They continue: "Today, it dominates almost any discussion of America's long-term fiscal, economic, or foreign-policy direction," (Jackson, Howe et al. 2008, p. 17).

Recently, two past presidents of the American Political Science Association, Robert Putnam and M. Kent Jennings, pointed to rapid demographic change as one of the most predictable future trends, yet one of the least studied by political scientists (Hochschild 2005). One could add that demographers and political scientists seem to exist in parallel disciplinary universes. Migration studies—one aspect of demography—occupies an academic archipelago, isolated from associated questions on the political impact of migration on the sending and receiving societies. At the same time, those working in international relations or comparative politics repeatedly encounter issues of political demography, yet have no forum for sharing common ideas. It is our hope that this book will crystallize and systematize the disparate insights that have so far floated quite loosely across the fields of demography and political science.

We claim that demography must be considered a major driver of politics alongside classic materialist, idealist, and institutional perspectives. Just as no credible political scientist can afford to ignore the role of economic incentives, institutions, or culture, we believe the chapters in this volume demonstrate that political scientists cannot afford to ignore demography in seeking to understand patterns of political identities, conflict, and change. This is better recognized in studies of long-term history, as when considering the role of demographic change in the origins of revolutions (Goldstone 1991), or in the rise and collapse of societies (Diamond 1997). Yet demographic factors also powerfully influence current geopolitics, fiscal politics, ethnic and religious conflicts, and voting patterns.

Population change needs to be considered as a political force in its own right—one that is on the rise today due to unprecedented global demographic turbulence that is likely to crest around 2050. Jack Goldstone, arguably a "founding father" of the discipline, points out in his chapter in this volume that the next four decades will present unprecedented changes in long-term demographic trends, including the shrinkage of Europe's labor force, the extreme aging of the advanced industrial societies, a global shift from mainly rural to mainly urban habitation, and a substantial turn in global economic growth toward the developing world (where 9 out of every 10 of the world's children under 15 now live).

Demographic shifts caused by the uneven global demographic transition will intensify by the 2020s and continue up through 2050. Political effects will arise from growing demographic disparities between: (a) *nation-states,* e.g., a declining Russia versus a rising Pakistan; (b) *age groups,* e.g., the growing proportion of young versus old people in Afghanistan; (c) *rural-urban groups,* e.g., urbanization in the Middle East; and (d) *ethnic* or *religious* groups within states, e.g., Hindus versus Muslims in India, or evangelicals versus seculars in the United States.

Each form of demographic disparity is associated with distinct political dilemmas: Interstate changes in population size and age structure affect the global balance of power. Unbalanced age (and sex) ratios tend to alter rates of economic growth, unemployment, instability, and violence. Urbanization creates dislocations that have traditionally been associated with religious, ethnic, class, or nationalist movements. And differential ethno-religious population growth may set the stage for ethnic, religious, and nationalist violence, value conflict, or challenges to the unity of what are often fragile states.

Consider global power dynamics. Whether looking at economic power or military capacity, population increase and decrease have always been identified as vital to a state's security and war-making capabilities. Though identified as critical by classical thinkers like Polybius, Cicero, and Ibn Khaldun, the importance of raw population as an increment of state power has waxed and waned over time, often in response to changes in the technology of war and the sources of military recruits (de Bliokh 1977; Mearsheimer 2001; Howe and Jackson, this volume).

Beginning with the American Civil War and continuing in World War I and World War II, the dominant role of machines in warfare appeared to make populations more vulnerable and at the same time less relevant to fighting power. Yet since the 1970s, population as a key component of national security again began to rise after a series of asymmetric wars in which high-tech, capital-intensive militaries lost bitter contests to relatively backward, labor-intensive militaries in Asia and Africa, such as the United States in Vietnam or the Soviet Union in Afghanistan (Arreguín-Toft 2005). Moreover, interstate wars between major industrialized powers—the type of conflict that had appeared to relegate people to insignificance from the 1880s to the 1940s—ceased to exist, while civil wars became the norm insofar as large-scale political violence is concerned. Iraq and Afghanistan provide further examples of this logic: Asymmetric warfare within these states between foreign troops or central governments and insurgents places the accent on labor-intensive, longer-term counterinsurgency operations. As a result, a large military recruitment pool and a sufficient tax base to finance costly campaigns are again becoming vital for great power projection. The demographic trends of the twenty-first century—aging great powers with shrinking labor forces alongside youthful and rapidly growing developing nations home to terrorism and turbulence—thus mark new challenges for geopolitical order.

If demography matters for war, it matters just as much in shaping politics in peace. This is especially the case due to another long-term trend following World War II: the increasing democratization of states, including Eastern

Europe, Latin America, and even more so, in Africa and Asia. Because democracy has as its foundation the principle of majority rule, states adopting democratic forms of government will find themselves keenly interested in the proportions of the politically active groups that inhabit their territories (Toft 2003). Shifts in population composition can affect who wins and loses in political battles, leading to party realignments (as argued in William Frey's article in this volume), or fueling violent conflict in fragile and transitional states (Goldstone 2002).

Nonetheless, mainstream political science research has devoted surprisingly little attention to the impact of population on politics. A search of the major journals devoted to war and conflict reveals that in the last 15 years only a handful of articles have been dedicated to understanding how demographic shifts contribute to large-scale violence both within states and beyond them.

The shifting nature of war and the so-called third wave of democratization are only part of the reason why demography is emerging as a critical issue in policy circles. Another is the demographic revolution that is sweeping across the globe. Unprecedented population aging in East Asia and Europe will see many developed countries' over-60 populations approach 40 percent of the national total by 2050. Because it is historically without precedent, we do not know what to expect from a state with over one-third of its population over 60, nor how its economic growth and finances will be impacted (see Howe and Jackson, this volume).

Meanwhile, many parts of the developing world will be transitioning through equally historic population booms. While Europe's improved sanitation and medical technology helped to cut infant mortality and generate a population explosion after 1750, the technical improvements were nowhere near as effective during the West's (and Japan's) population boom as they are today. The typical European population expanded three to five times during its demographic transition from 1750 to 1950, but today's developing countries—which are benefitting from the latest medical technology—can expect to see their populations expand 8 to 24 times before their demographic transition runs its course (Skirbekk 2009).

The young populations of the growing global South will strain at the seams of an economy and infrastructure that is not only underdeveloped, but designed for a much smaller population. This "youth bulge" is already having political repercussions. Youth bulges occur when there is an exceptionally large proportion of young people aged 15 to 29 among the adult population. The existence of a youth bulge—especially when it is dominated by unemployed young males—is associated with a higher incidence of violence and revolution, and may retard the onset of democracy (Huntington 1996; Urdal, this volume; Cincotta, this volume).

In both population growth and age structure, the contrast between the rich and poor worlds is glaring. It could well lead to enhanced North-South conflict over resources, migration, and climate change, while making developed-country military interventions even more problematic than they are today. The first two sections of this volume explore questions linked to changing age structures and population sizes between states. Neil Howe and Richard Jackson discuss how population aging and uneven population growth between regions impacts international politics. They pay particular attention to the history of political concerns over demography and the "softer" dimension of political consciousness that accompanies younger or older populations. In the chapters that follow, Mark Haas and Jennifer Sciubba address contemporary security concerns that accompany aging populations. Whereas Haas explores the impact of an aging society on U.S. national security, finding major effects on its economic development and military might, Sciubba broadens the lens, introducing a theoretical framework using power transition theory for understanding the implications of some of the dynamics that might be at play as societies age.

The next section looks at age structure in terms of development, democracy, and violence. Elizabeth Leahy Madsen provides a global analysis of different types of age structures and the implications for policy responses in the countries experiencing them. In contrast, both Richard Cincotta and Henrik Urdal take up the question of whether a particular age distribution—a high proportion of youths—influences the development of liberal democracy or violence. Richard Matthew then looks at the complex but increasingly pressing relations among population change, climate change, and conflict.

The next two parts of the book consider social and political conflicts arising from the changing ethnic and religious composition of states in an era of soaring domestic and international migration and widening fertility gaps.

We begin with American politics. William Frey shows the role of the decline of the white majority in the United States and the importance of minority ethnic groups in electing the nation's first nonwhite president. As Frey points out, in 2008 almost one in four voters were minorities, up from just over one in five in 2004. Moreover, shifts in minority populations were concentrated in electorally crucial "battleground" states. Frey demonstrates how both demographic change and differential ethnic voter turnout will have major implications for the future of American politics. Brian Gratton's chapter then steps back to look at American ethno-political demography in historical perspective. Against the prevailing view that anti-immigrant "nativism" takes the form of irrational outbursts whipped up during crises, Gratton shows how both rational interests (notably business pressure) and concrete demographic changes wrought by immigration hold the key to explaining the ebb and flow of American immigration politics.

David Coleman turns our attention to today's Europe and how ethno-demographic change is raising burning questions of identity, multiculturalism, security, and freedom of expression. The rapid rise of the non-European-origin population in Europe and the United States may herald what Coleman calls a "third demographic transition" in which differences between demographically mature host populations and youthful immigrants reconfigure domestic culture, identity, and power.

Eric Kaufmann and Vegard Skirbekk then discuss how demography underpins the growth of Islam in the world and in Europe in particular. They point to specific features of major world religions, such as pronatalism and traditional gender roles, which are precipitating the long-term demographic rise of religious fundamentalism while placing demographically weak seculars at a disadvantage.

The essays in Part V then look more closely at religious and ethnic conflict. Monica Duffy Toft examines how differential fertility can be seen as a "weapon" used by certain groups to increase their social power relative to others. Toft refers to this as "wombfare." In Christian Leuprecht's cases, Northern Ireland and Israel-Palestine, Leuprecht convincingly argues that demographic changes alter the incentives for ethnic groups to engage in violence or embrace peace negotiations. When Northern Ireland's Catholics enjoyed rapid population growth and a young age structure, they found the costs of violent conflict to be lower. As their age structure matured, peace became more attractive. Unionists likewise felt less threatened as the pace of demographic change slackened. In Israel-Palestine, however, the rising Arab demographic advantage over Jews portends continued difficulty in clinching a peace deal.

Elliott Green also considers the effects of differential ethnic population growth, but shifts our perspective from the developed to the developing world. Instead of examining changes generated by international migration between states, he directs us to the importance of intranational population movements from one ethnic region to another within African countries. Intranational migratory movements began in colonial times, encouraged by colonizers in the context of uneven population density. The collision of settlers from over-populated ethnic source regions with "sons of the soil" natives in sparsely populated destination regions mimics the process of North-South immigration. The difference is that in an environment of land scarcity, subsistence agriculture, and weak state legitimacy, violent conflict is more likely, as he shows in Uganda and Kenya.

From Uganda and Kenya in the east, we head west to Côte D'Ivoire on the Atlantic coast, where Ragnhild Nordas considers a conflict that combines religious (Muslim-Christian), ethnic (North-South), and nationalist (Ivoirian-foreigner) dimensions. The demographic ascent of the Muslim north is undeniable, but Nordas emphasizes that demography alone cannot explain why and when conflict erupted. Shifts in the salience of varied ethnic, regional, and national identities built on demographic changes but depended on deliberate political mobilization as well.

This raises a key theoretical point. States have demarcated boundaries and therefore behave more like the biological populations that demographers and epidemiologists study. But what about social groups defined by ethnic identities and religions? If their boundaries are tight and they change little over time, we may surmise that differential ethnic growth inevitably produces conflict (Vanhanen 1999). The opposing perspective in nationalism theory is that ethnic boundaries are socially constructed: sensitive to political manipulation and therefore relatively impervious to population shifts (Laitin 2007). In reality, the tightness or looseness of ethnic boundaries differs greatly, ranging from endogamous and rigidly defined South Asia and Northern Ireland to the more fluid contexts of sub–Saharan Africa, the Caribbean, and the Americas (Wimmer 2007). Future research will need to explore the interactions between the pace of demographic change and the nature of identity boundary mechanisms.

In varying ways and in a wide variety of settings, all of our contributors demonstrate that demography is a vital ingredient in shaping the political process. Its effect can be proximate or remote; first, second, or third order; necessary, but rarely sufficient; it can serve as a precipitant or a conditioning factor (Hout 2006; Horowitz 1985, pp. 258–259). But regardless of how it operates, demography in all its facets—population size, age structure, fertility, migration, mortality—urgently needs to be brought into the mainstream of political science. Especially in our age of demographic turbulence, the study of international security and global politics cannot go forward without grasping how the key concepts and data on population change bear on these issues.

2

A Theory of Political Demography

Human and Institutional Reproduction

Jack A. Goldstone

Rethinking Politics and Population Change

For most of the last two hundred-odd years, since the work of Thomas Malthus, debates regarding population have focused on a single issue: Will population growth and its effects (including pollution and consumption of natural resources) outrun the carrying capacity of local or global ecosystems, leading to widespread poverty? Or will technological progress outrun population increases, providing sufficient resources for continued income growth, so that only the distribution of resources is a valid concern? Although this debate continues today, it is remarkable that the discussion of how population affects

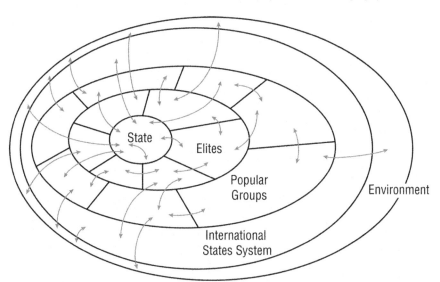

Figure 2.1 Society as a Nested Hierarchy of Structures and Processes

political systems has persisted so long in terms of simple aggregates: the ratio of total population versus total amounts of resources.

Political society is a set of nested and connected social groups and institutions—state administration, elites, and popular groups, all drawing from the natural environment and interacting with other societies—that is sustained by a continuous, ongoing set of processes involving flows and exchanges of resources and actions. Those flows and exchanges support states and elites, maintain varied popular groups in diverse economic and political roles, and allow administration, coordination, and security for the whole. I call this system a "nested hierarchy," and depict it roughly as shown in Figure 2.1.

Rather like a fishing net, this nested hierarchy can function even with some tears or disruptions in the overall set of flows. However, if the disruption of flows is too numerous, so that the state is starved of resources, or intra-elite competition becomes too great and violent, or widespread shortages occur in cities or in substantial rural areas, the system as whole starts to tear, and rebellion, state breakdown, and revolutions can arise (Goldstone 1991).

The point of this diagramming exercise is to illustrate that the dichotomy between problems of total population-resource ratios vs. problems in the distribution of resources that dominates the traditional discourse on population and politics is fundamentally wrongheaded. Because political systems are constantly in the act of distributing and redistributing resources across the various levels and segments of society, any significant changes in population—not only in the overall size of the population relative to environmental resources, but in the size and resources of any subgroups, including the state and elites—will likely affect the dynamic distribution of resources, and hence have political impacts.

In recent decades, political scientists and political sociologists have incorporated this fundamental insight into their work, helping to create the emerging field of *political demography*. This new political demography often begins by asking what the relationship is between the population of a society and its natural resource base and what the relevant trends are in the ratio of total population to overall resources. But that is just a basic starting point. Political demography goes on to study what changes in the distribution of resources and political power are likely to arise from changes in the absolute and relative sizes of various population subgroups: urban or rural populations; groups bearing various religious, regional, or ethnic identities; various elite groups or political factions; and different age groups.

During periods when populations are growing fairly slowly, or when most societies have populations that are fairly homogenous and growing at a reasonably constant and steady fashion over time, these questions may not seem pressing for current politics. Yet we no longer live in such a world. The twenty-first century—following a century of global and regional intermixing borne by technological change and economic integration—is a time when diverse and rapid population shifts are taking place across the globe. Around the world, very young and very old age groups are increasing rapidly, and urban populations are dramatically expanding. At the same time, migration and the political boundaries left from the days of imperialism and colonialism have produced numerous multiethnic societies with shifting ethnic or religious compositions. In short, whether we look at issues of governance in the United States or the European Union, the impact of the BRIC nations (Brazil, Russia, India, China) on global economic and political affairs, or problems of governance and instability in Africa, the Middle East, Latin America, and Asia, the challenge of understanding the political impacts of demographic factors is inescapable.

A Primer in Demography

Demography, much like studies of economic behavior or social mobility, has evolved into a highly specialized and technical field, requiring advanced mathematics and the analysis of enormous amounts of data. The goal of this advanced work is to identify and plot the causes and patterns of population dynamics—that is, why and how populations change over time. Political scientists thus have some reason for steering clear of the field.

Yet the consequences of demographic change are too important to be left solely to the demographers. While demographers and their research are crucial to identifying the factors that produce various kinds of population change—from voluntary changes in behavior to patterns of nutrition and climate and disease—and to estimating how the current and future size and distribution of various populations and groups is likely to vary depending on those factors, demographers usually cannot tell us how people and social institutions will react to those changes. That is the task of political demography. Fortunately it requires only a very basic understanding of key demographic concepts to grasp the various dimensions of population change. But such an understanding must then be coupled with a sophisticated and empirically sound understanding of political behavior and social institutions to draw out the consequences of how various kinds of population change will likely affect political relations.

The following paragraphs provide an introduction to the main demographic concepts that are critical for political demography.

Births, Deaths, Migration

The key elements of population change are straightforward; people enter or leave populations by three routes: births, deaths, and net migration (immigrants minus emigrants). Thus the growth rate of a population is easily determined: It is the crude birth rate (CBR, births per 1,000 population per year) minus the crude death rate (CDR, deaths per 1,000 population), plus the net migration rate (NMR, net migrants per 1,000 population). Adding these three rates gives the annual change in population per 1,000 people. So if in a country the rate of births minus deaths plus migrants is 10, the annual growth rate would be 10/1,000, which equals .01 or 1 percent.

For a typical developed country, such as France, these figures for 2010 were 12.4 births per 1,000 population, 8.9 deaths per 1,000, and 1.6 net migrants per 1,000. When we add these up, we find there was a total excess of births and migrants over deaths of 5.1 per 1,000 population. That means France had an annual growth rate of 0.51 percent, that is, about one-half percent per year.

For a poorer developing country, such as Ethiopia, while the principle is exactly the same, these numbers look very different (although developing countries vary widely, so none is truly typical). In 2010 Ethiopia had a CBR of 30.0, a CDR of 9.1, and a net migration rate of -0.2 (mainly refugees), for an annual growth rate of 2.07 percent. Thus, while its death rate was about the same as that of France, its birth rate was almost three times higher. These differences result in an annual growth rate that is *four times* higher.[1]

Many of the most interesting results of demography come from the power of exponential growth—that is, from sustaining positive annual growth rates over time. In 1995 France and Ethiopia were similar-sized countries: France had 58 million people; Ethiopia had 57 million. Just 15 years later, after growth in Ethiopia that averaged 2.5 percent per year but growth in France that was only one-half a percent per year, France had increased to 63 million, while Ethiopia had 83 million people! If France and Ethiopia continue to grow at these annual rates for another 25 years, they will be completely different in size. In 2035 France will reach 71 million, but Ethiopia's population will have increased to 154 million.

Will France continue to grow so slowly, and Ethiopia to grow so rapidly? Actually, these estimates may be conservative; if we look in more detail at the age structure of their populations, the growth rate in France seems likely to decline, while Ethiopia's growth rate may increase.

Cohorts and Age Structure

When people are born, they enter a population in a particular age group—those under one year of age. Demographers speak of those people who are born during a certain period—a one-year, five-year, or other period—as a *birth cohort*, or just "cohort" for short. Thus, all those babies born in France between 1960 and 1969 constitute the 1960–1969 birth cohort. Today, the survivors of that cohort are all aged 41 to 50, and because death rates for infants, children, and young adults are low in a developed country such as France, most of that cohort is still alive in 2010. Coming after the end of World War II, this was an unusually large cohort—bigger than the cohorts of the 1940s or 1970s, and thus part of what is known as the "baby boom." As this cohort passes into retirement, France's labor force will decline. Meanwhile, the smaller cohorts now entering their twenties and thirties will have smaller numbers of women in the prime child-bearing years; thus France's overall birth rate may decline unless these women decide, for whatever reason, to have more children than their baby boom predecessors.

By contrast, in Ethiopia, with its very high birth rates, the younger cohorts will continue to be much larger than the cohorts born before them. That means each new cohort has more women of child-bearing age than the cohorts born before them. Thus, even if the number of children born to each mother should slightly decline, the fact that there are more potential mothers entering the child-bearing years means that births per thousand population, the CBR, can continue to grow.

Moreover, to examine total population growth, we also need to look at deaths. Unlike with births, people can exit the population by death at any age. Indeed, in poor countries, most of those dying are not older people, but are infants and children. In Ethiopia, in 1995–2000 over 160 out of every 1,000 live-born children died before the age of 5. By 2005–2010, that figure had been cut by almost one-third, to 113 deaths by age 5 (United Nations Population Division 2011). Yet this progress not only cuts the crude death rate, but because those being saved are young, they can now survive to adulthood and have children themselves. Reductions in death rates among the very young therefore mean higher birth rates in the future.

By contrast, in a developed country like France there are relatively few child deaths (only 4 per 1,000 live births, or around 4 percent as high as in Ethiopia). That means that in France, any reductions in death rates come mostly from extending the life of the elderly, those who are not going to have any more children. So while in Ethiopia, gains in health and reductions in death rates will almost certainly translate into higher birth rates and higher rates of population growth, the opposite may be true in France—reductions in death rates will likely mean seniors living longer, having to be supported by higher taxes on working families, who therefore may choose to have fewer children. In sum, we might therefore expect France's rate of population growth to slow down in the near future, while Ethiopia's might well increase further (and indeed in 2008–2010, Ethiopia's crude birth rate was substantially higher than in 2003–2007).[2]

The relative size of a country's age cohorts can easily be seen by graphing the cohorts in a "stack" or "age pyramid." Figure 2.2 shows the age pyramids for France and Ethiopia in 2005; the very different shapes immediately indicate the relative proportions of different age groups. In France, the population is mostly middle-aged; between the small cohorts born in the Depression and World War II (now aged 60–80+), and recent smaller cohorts, is the "baby boom" bulge in the middle (though there is also an unusually high-surviving group of women over age 80). In Ethiopia, the population is mostly very young; the large base and small top of the age pyramid indicate that the overall population distribution is dominated by ever-larger young and very young cohorts.

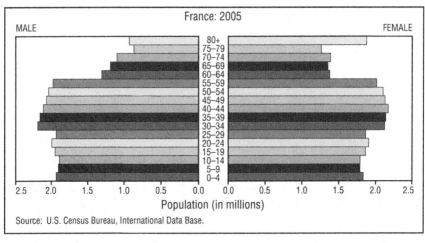

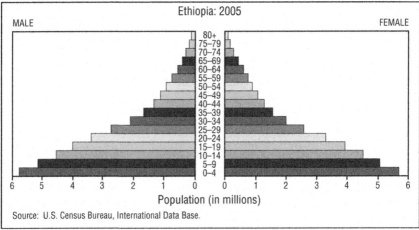

Figure 2.2 Age Pyramids for France and Ethiopia, 2005

Fertility and Life Expectancy

Because societies can differ so greatly in age structure, the crude birth and death rates, which only indicate the total of births or deaths per 1,000 total population, do not really tell us what is happening to specific age cohorts. Demographers thus have developed measures that try to better capture the varying experience of different cohorts.

In regard to births, demographers commonly speak of the *total fertility rate* of a society. This is arrived at by looking at the number of children born to women in each birth cohort. Demographers collect data on age-specific fertility: How many children were born in this year, on average, to women 22 years old, 23 years old, 24 years old, and so on? Then the *total fertility rate* is the sum of all the average age-specific fertility levels. Another, perhaps easier way to look at this is to say that *total fertility* is the total number of children that a woman would be expected to have if she lived out her entire child-bearing years and had the average number of children at each stage of her life as the overall average experience of all women in her society. In France, for example, where most women have few children, the total fertility rate in 1995–2000 was 1.76; in Ethiopia it was 6.48 (United Nations Population Division 2011).

Because some people will die before reaching adulthood, it is usually considered that a total fertility rate of 2.1 (just over two children for each woman) is needed to prevent a population from naturally declining. This means that in a country like France, the current fertility rate is not quite enough to assure replacement of the current population, and so France would not be able to keep growing without the positive contribution of net migration. In Ethiopia, however, if all children survived, then each generation would be roughly three times as large as the parent's generation. As we noted, Ethiopia's child mortality rates remain high, but the potential for growth remains enormous if fertility does not decline (although it does seem to have declined sharply in just the last few years).

A similar adjustment for cohort rates is made for deaths and is called *life expectancy*. As with fertility, demographers collect data on age-specific death rates: how many deaths were there per person in this age group for those aged zero to one this year, how many for those aged one, aged two, aged three, and so on. *Life expectancy*—or more accurately, life expectancy at birth—is then the average number of years that a group of infants would live if they died at the rate of each age-specific death rate summed over their entire lifetimes. To choose a very simple example, let us say that half the children born in a society die before age 1, but the others all live until age 60, and then die. The average life span in this society—hence the life expectancy at birth—is 30 years. So in this society, even though a typical adult lives to age 60 if he or she survives childhood, for demographers the life expectancy is still only 30—because half of all children die before reaching 1 year of age.

Demographers also calculate age-specific life expectancies by starting at different ages. This is particularly relevant for the elderly. Even in societies where average life expectancy at birth is 75, we would expect to see a large number of people living beyond that age. So we would want to know what is the life expectancy for people who reach age 75; in modern developed countries it can be substantial. In the United States in 2004, life expectancy at age 75 was 11.9 years; so the average person who reached 75 could expect to live to be 86.

In poorer countries, where child death rates are very high, life expectancies are lower; in Ethiopia it is 57 years. In most rich countries, life expectancies are in the upper 70s; in France it is 81 years. But that is not mainly because adults live longer in France than in Ethiopia; most of the 26-year difference in life expectancies is because children in France survive in far greater numbers than they do in Ethiopia (United Nations Population Division 2011).

The Demographic Transition

Fertility, life expectancy, and cohort experiences all come together in the phenomenon known as the *demographic transition*. In this process, societies move from having a combination of low life expectancy and high fertility to the opposite condition, with high life expectancy and low fertility.

For most of human history, with food supplies uncertain, minimal sanitation, and few medicines to halt the spread and impact of disease, death rates were very high. Infant mortality was particularly severe. As a result, even as late as the eighteenth century, life expectancy at birth in societies from Europe to China was very low, usually only around 30 years. Mothers therefore had to bear many children just to ensure that two or more survived to adulthood and could reproduce. It was common in preindustrial societies for fertility levels to range from four to six children per married woman, of whom only two, or very occasionally three, would survive to bear children of their own. High child mortality was thus balanced by high fertility, with the overall result that population grew only very slowly. Up to 1800, long-term historical population growth rates in most societies were only about one-tenth of one percent per year.

As societies grew richer, however, this situation changed. Small investments in sanitation and cleaner water supplies, better nutrition, and a bit of cheap medical care (just understanding that infants suffering stomach infections needed to be given lots of clean water to drink, or having access to generic antibiotics to treat infections) drastically lowered the death rate, especially for children. This had huge and immediate impacts on population growth and age structure. If women continued to have four or five children each, but now three rather than only two usually survived to adulthood, the population growth rate would rise from being negligible to a gain of 50 percent every generation, or an annual rate of roughly 1 percent per year. If four children survived, on average, then the population would double every generation, for an annual population growth rate of over 2 percent per year.

In this initial stage of demographic transition, with life expectancy growing mainly due to steep falls in infant mortality, but fertility remaining high, populations experience a huge surge in growth. From the long-term historical growth rate of perhaps one-tenth of a percent per year, growth rates increase by ten- or twentyfold! Populations go from remaining nearly stable for centuries to doubling in 60 or even in 30 years. It is this phenomenon—the onset of the demographic transition, which began in Europe in the eighteenth century and has since spread throughout the world—that has driven global population growth over the last two centuries. The world's population was only about 250 million people in 0 AD, and was still less than 1 billion almost 2,000 years later in 1800 AD. However, as the demographic transition spread to Asia, Africa, and Latin America, the world's population suddenly leaped to 6 billion by 2000 AD (Livi-Bacci 2007, p. 26).

At the same time, because this growth was driven by greater survival among the young, the increase in population is concentrated among the younger age cohorts. It is this situation that gives rise to age pyramids like that of Ethiopia, where each new younger generation (as those aged 10–24) is twice as numerous as the generation before them (those aged 25–39).

As societies grow richer still, there are further changes in their demographic behavior. As societies become more industrial and service oriented, more people move to cities, where living space is expensive. As education becomes a more important way to get ahead, parents want to invest more in the education of their children, which is also costly. Most important, parents may gain confidence that nearly all of their children will survive to adulthood, and thus do not need to ensure that outcome by giving birth to so many. As a result of all of these trends, women usually prefer to have fewer children than before.

Of course, there is a time lag for changes in preferences for children to spread through society. Moreover, even though preferences may change, it requires both access to birth control and education in how to use it for women to effectively limit the number of children they bear. As these become available and preferences change, the next stage in the demographic transition is a decline in fertility, as women have fewer children in the course of their married and child-bearing years.

For a considerable while, the increased survival of children tends to stay ahead of changes in fertility. That is, infant mortality tends to fall rapidly and stay low, while fertility falls more gradually. The result is a sustained period in which societies face rapid population growth and very young populations. However, in recent years, countries have seen fertility dropping more rapidly. It took 130 years for fertility to fall from 5 children per family to 2 in Great

Britain, one of the first countries to begin the transition, from 1800 to 1930. It took only 20 years, from 1965 to 1985, for the same change to occur in South Korea. In Iran, it took only 22 years, from 1984 to 2006, for fertility to drop from 7 to under 2, perhaps the most rapid decline in fertility in any society (*The Economist* 2009, p. 15). We can say the fertility transition is completed when fertility has fallen to the level where even with almost all children surviving to adulthood, a society's natural population growth again is at negligible levels. As we noted, demographers estimate this is usually the case when fertility is at 2.1 children born per woman. Most of the rich countries of the world reached this level, and thus completed their demographic transition, by the last quarter of the twentieth century. In countries that have made this transition, total population growth rates are minimal, or depend mainly on migration. Moreover, successive cohorts are all roughly the same size, as shown in the age pyramid of France in Figure 2.2.

While some countries have been moving rapidly through the demographic transition, it must be noted that other countries are moving more slowly, or even getting stuck at the first stage. Ethiopia is one of 45 countries around the world, mostly in the Middle East and Africa, with population still increasing at 2.0 percent per year or more. In Ethiopia, life expectancy is still rising—it grew from 51 in 2000 to 56 in 2010—but fertility is not declining very much; it declined only from 6.4 to 6.1 over the same period. Ethiopia's growth rate thus increased from 3.0 percent per year in 2000 to 3.2 percent per year in 2010 (U.S. Census Bureau 2011).

Even if fertility in such countries were to start declining tomorrow, so many young women will enter their child-bearing years in the next 20 years—nearly twice as many as those who were in their child-bearing years in the last 2 decades—that the number of total births will stay very high for another generation. This is called *demographic momentum;* and it means that even some countries where fertility rates have fallen below 2.0, such as China, will still continue to increase in overall size for years to come, due to both continuing increases in life expectancy and to the high fertility they experienced—and hence, the very large cohorts of young women who were born—in the 1960s and 1970s.

We thus live in a world with societies with very different demographic profiles. Wealthier countries have mostly completed their demographic transition, while most poorer countries have not. The overall trend, however, is clearly toward completing the transition. Even among poorer countries, in the last 40 years average fertility has fallen from close to 6 children per woman to about 3. In their middle-of-the-road scenario (the medium variant projection), the United Nations Population Division assumes that this trend will continue, making global population growth slow dramatically by 2050. If this scenario comes to pass, world population would reach about 9 billion in 2050, and then approach stabilization at about 10 billion people by 2100 (United Nations Population Division 2011).

The Demography of Subgroups

A wonderful feature of these demographic concepts—cohorts, fertility, migration, and so forth—is that they can all be applied to subgroups of any population, not just to a complete society. Thus, we can speak of the fertility of a particular ethnic or religious group by looking at the age-specific birth rates of women in that group, and compare that fertility to the average in society, or to other groups. We can examine the size of youth cohorts in cities, rather than in the total society—for the migration of young men to cities looking for work often results in cities having age structures that are very different, and far more "youth bulgy," than that of society as a whole.

We can also combine a number of demographic characteristics to understand complex changes and their effects. For example, there is great anxiety among some in Europe about large numbers of Muslim immigrants "taking over" European societies. In fact, the total numbers make this preposterous; Muslims in almost all European countries (excepting only countries that were formerly part of the Ottoman Empire) remain a small percentage, roughly 3 to 6 percent, of the total population (PEW Forum on Religion and Public Life 2009, p. 22). However, most of the Muslims who migrate to Europe settle in or near cities, and concentrate in certain neighborhoods. In certain neighborhoods, they may thus be as much as 25 percent or more of the local population. Moreover, the fertility of Muslim immigrants is usually fairly high, while that of native Europeans is very low. If Muslim immigrants have, on average, twice as many children per household as native Europeans, then looking at elementary school enrollments we may find that even in neighborhoods where 25 percent of the total population is foreign-born Muslims, as many as half of the elementary school children may be from Muslim immigrant families.

The combination of group differences in fertility and selective migration to certain urban neighborhoods can thus give the appearance of a sudden "taking over" of local institutions, creating political anxieties and tensions, even if the overall fraction of Muslim immigrants in the total population remains small. In fact, however, we find that the fertility of Muslim immigrants typically falls after moving to Europe, and falls dramatically in the second generation, creating a rapid demographic transition among the immigrant community, so there is no threat of explosive growth of the kind that we see within Ethiopia as compared to that within France. But without understanding the basic demography behind the phenomenon, we could not understand how the apparent changes could be so large in certain settings, nor grasp the likely trajectory in actual population numbers and behavior.

A Theory of Political Demography: Human and Institutional Reproduction

We now are equipped with the concepts we need to develop a general theory of how population changes can affect political systems and to follow the various chapters in this volume regarding such effects.

Refer back to Figure 2.1. Imagine each "box" or segment of each ring to be peopled with a population of a given size, age distribution, and location. These people develop expectations regarding the exchanges—the flows of goods, services, taxes, work, patronage, benefits, opportunities—among various groups with whom they interact. Many of these exchanges may be extremely one-sided: Peasants may expect few services or opportunities but heavy taxes and work requirements. State rulers may expect to extract large amounts of resources to expend on patronage, consumption, war, and administration. Certain elites—for example church leaders or landlords—have their own expectations regarding relations with the state, other elites, and the populace.

As long as these various exchanges conform to expectations over time, we may expect to see a certain rough stability across generations. Children of elites move into elite positions; children of peasants continue to work the land; states and elites continue to collect the revenues to support their lifestyles; workers continue to earn at least a living that will allow them to survive and reproduce. If these exchanges represent the working of social institutions, then the reproduction of those institutions over time requires that the human elements—the people in the various "boxes" or segments or stations of society—also continue to reproduce in roughly the same proportion to those exchanges as was the case before.

As long as the proportions remain roughly the same, growth (or even decline) can be accommodated. That is, if there are twice as many peasants, but the environment provides twice as much output as before (either due to cultivating more land or cultivating existing land more intensively), then twice as much surplus can support twice as large an elite and twice as powerful a state. However, problems can quickly arise if the numbers of people in various segments do not grow in proportion, causing shifts in the resources available to circulate within the system and creating disruptions or changes in their flow.

To give just one example, let us say that a traditional society allocates land to families by redistribution when couples marry. As long as the number of surviving children per couple is roughly around 2.1, all will be well; on average a couple in one generation will vacate a holding by retirement or death for every couple that marries and seeks a new landholding. But if the number of surviving children per couple should creep up to 2.5, problems will arise. Either some couples will go without land, or parcels will have to be reduced by about 20 percent in size to distribute a parcel to all couples who seek one. Landless couples may converge on cities, creating sudden growth and demand for housing, sanitation, and jobs, or drive down the urban wages for existing workers. If land holdings are reduced by 20 percent, but the productivity of farming remains the same, a problem arises for the state and elites. Typically, in preindustrial societies peasants could survive on half the output of a typical family holding, while the other half was paid in taxes and rents and fees to elites and the state. If the typical family holding is reduced by 20 percent, then the "surplus" produced by each family holding above the peasant's normal expected retained amount will decline by 40 percent. That means the elites and state are left to fight over a greatly reduced available surplus, or forced to squeeze the peasantry to unaccustomed levels. Either increased intra-elite conflict and competition or increased peasant rebellions, or both, become likely.

In fact, for most of history, the number of surviving children per couple was very nearly 2.1. We can be certain of this simply from the arithmetic of population growth. The population of France today is 63 million. If France's population had been growing at a steady rate of 1 percent per year for the last 500 years, then its population in 1500, during the Renaissance and just after the birth of Francois I, would have been only 435,000. In fact, we know from other historical evidence that the population of France in 1500 was closer to 15 million! And in fact, most of France's population growth has taken place recently; as late as 1800, France's population was only about 29 million. Net growth from 1500 to 1800 was thus a barely noticeable two-tenths of a percent per year (Livi-Bacci 2007).

However, while net growth was small, the historical pattern was one of long periods of population stagnation or regression punctuated by other periods of population disruption. In some periods, such as that of the Black Death, population suddenly plunged, leaving lords and peasants and states to scramble to adapt to a changed world, where land was suddenly plentiful and labor scarce. In other periods, such as that of the sixteenth century in Europe, population grew steadily, often at 1 percent per year or more, disrupting landholdings, taxation, elite mobility, and international relations.

Throughout history, the ebb and flow of population—through natural growth, epidemic diseases, and migration—has been linked to the rise and fall of empires, to conquests and revolutions. Periods during which populations were stable in size also tended to be politically quiet. By contrast, periods in which societies showed sustained growth, such as the century from 1550 to 1650, or from 1730 to 1850, were marked by severe political disruptions. Real wages fell and peasants faced shortages of land; social mobility and competition for elite positions increased as more surviving sons and daughters meant that simple inheritance no longer provided for stable succession; and state and urban administrations were stressed by the need to keep food supplies flowing and to enforce order among rapidly growing populations. As these trends persisted over several decades, the result was often rebellions, revolutions, and civil wars (Goldstone 1991).

Given these complex, multiple competitions for resources among popular groups, elites, and the state, a modern theory of political demography would not simply rest, as with Malthus's approach, on assessing the overall balance of population and resources in a society. Rather a theory of political demography would have us approach social analysis through a series of queries aimed at identifying disruptions or holes in the nested hierarchies of peoples and resource flows. Thus we would ask:

1. For the major elite and popular groups in society, what are the recent and expected rates of population increase, age distribution, and geographic distribution? Do these pose any threats to the continuing balanced flow of resources—land, incomes, elite positions—to each group as per their expectations?
2. How will the flow of revenues to the state, and the demands upon the state administration, be affected by the changes in the situation of various population groups? Will there be any shortfalls in revenue or administrative capacity, or problems responding to conflicting demands from different groups?
3. How will the expected changes in population and flows of resources affect the relative power position of different groups, and the relative power of the state and its ability to balance among them?
4. In democracies, we would also ask about the voting behavior of various groups, and whether changes in the size and distribution of those groups across various localities would affect patterns of voting, and the formation of majorities in favor of particular parties.

Using the concepts of demography to pose these questions regarding the dynamics of political systems offers a fresh and powerful approach to identifying major drivers of political conflict and change.

Let us therefore now consider three major population trends that will shape political developments in the coming century.

Three Demographic Trends That Will Shape the Global Future

The world has reached an unusual point. Most of the world's richer countries—in Europe, East Asia (Japan, South Korea, Taiwan, Singapore), and North America—have completed their demographic transition and have stable or very slow-growing populations. Several of them, including Germany and many in Eastern Europe, have seen fertility fall well below 2.0, so that they are forecast to decline in population in the near future unless they have considerable in-migration. By contrast, most of the world's poorer countries—mainly in Africa, the Middle East, and southern and Southeast Asia—have only begun their demographic transition, and so are continuing their rapid population growth. This contrast will govern global demography for the next few decades, giving rise to three important trends:

1. The relative decline of Europe and the Americas compared to Asia and Africa.

The demographic transition began in Europe with the onset of industrialization in 1800, leading to dramatic population growth. However, in the twentieth century the demographic transition ended in richer countries, while it began to spread to Asia and Africa, touching off rapid population growth in those regions that has only begun to slow down. Most of the world's population growth for the next four decades will thus occur outside of the rich countries of today. Between 2010 and 2050 the United Nations projects that the combined population of Europe, the United States, Canada, and Japan will increase by only 105 million, while the population of the rest of the world will increase by 2.3 *billion*. Most striking, in 1950 Europe alone had almost two and a half times the population of Africa; by 2050 this will be completely reversed, and Africa's population will be more than three times as large as that of Europe (United Nations Population Division 2011).

Even though the rich countries of today will remain much wealthier per person than the poorer countries, the combined effect of tremendous population growth in the poorer countries, along with faster per capita income growth in most of them, means that by far the great majority of all the world's economic growth in the next half-century will occur in Asia, Africa, and Latin America. Probably 75 percent of all global income growth to 2050 will come from these regions.

Today's poorer regions will also account for most of the growth in middle-class spending. The World Bank (2007a) projects that the number of "middle-class" consumers in the developing world—those who can buy appliances, homes, and aspire to an automobile—will rise from 400 million today to 1.2 billion by 2030; that will be more than the entire combined populations of Europe, the United States, and Japan in 2030.

Thus, the pattern of the last two centuries, with Europe and other richer areas leading the world in population growth, income growth, and consumption is about to change completely. In the next four decades, population in Europe and other richer areas will remain virtually stable while population, income growth, and middle-class consumption shifts dramatically to the developing world.

2. A fun house mirror of aging: older rich countries and very young poor ones.

In a fun house, there are mirrors that distort the normal proportions of a person's image. If a normal age distribution is one in which most cohorts under age 60 are roughly the same size, and smoothly succeed each other in jobs and spending as they move through their life course, we will see few countries in the world with such age distributions until we reach the mid-21st century. Instead, we shall see mostly severely distorted images, with either excessively old or extremely young populations being more common.

In the richer countries, the elderly will soon outnumber the young. In the United States today, the number of people age 60 or older is about 10 percent less than the number of children under age 15. But by 2030, the U.N. projects that those 60 or older will be a third more numerous than children under 15. In France by 2030, the number of those aged 60 and above will be two-thirds larger than the number of children under 15. In Germany, if projections hold, by 2030 those over 60 will outnumber children under 15 by more than 2 to 1, and by 2050 there will be as many people aged 80 and over as children under age 15 (United Nations Population Division 2011). These are astonishing numbers, never before seen in human history. Unless there is a huge surge of fertility, or rapid migration from abroad, today's richer countries will face incredible burdens finding entry-level workers for demanding jobs in construction, cleaning, transportation, repair work, landscaping, and agriculture, while facing skyrocketing costs for medical and pension support for their aged populations.

By contrast, many poor countries will remain very young. Virtually all of the expected population growth in the next four decades—roughly 2.2 billion more people than today—will occur in the developing world. Two-thirds of that growth will arise in just 15 large, low-income countries (LLICs)—India, Pakistan, Nigeria, Indonesia, Bangladesh, Ethiopia, the Democratic Republic of the Congo, the Philippines, Tanzania, Uganda, Kenya, Sudan, Afghanistan, and Iraq. In many of these countries, one-third to one-half the population today is under 15.

Over the next four decades, even with falling fertility in the developing world, 90 percent of all children born in the world will most likely be born in today's developing countries. By the end of the twenty-first century, the fate of the world will be in the hands of these cohorts.

With rich countries becoming quite elderly, it will be imperative that they integrate their economies, and perhaps even their societies, as much as possible with the younger countries of the world. Only the younger countries will have the manpower to meet the labor needs of companies in the future, to respond to humanitarian disasters and violent conflicts around the world, and to care for the large numbers of elderly in the rich world. Only the developing countries will have the overall economic growth and new markets to drive the world's economy forward. If the rich countries should choose to try to isolate themselves by excluding migrants and discouraging investment abroad, they will find themselves stranded without the economic growth or labor they will need.

Fortunately, a number of the large developing countries in the world—Mexico, Brazil, Turkey, Iran, Viet Nam, China, Indonesia—are entering a "sweet spot" in their demographic transition. They have already reduced their fertility substantially, so that fewer children are being born. Most of their population for the next few decades will be concentrated in their prime working years, from age 15 to 59. These countries are likely to be the chief motors of the world economy for the next 30 to 40 years.

However, the LLICs mentioned above are almost all still in the early stages of their demographic transition, and hence have considerably younger populations, with a third to half of their populations under age 15. They also are poorer than the large developing countries mentioned in the preceding paragraph. Thus, it will be a huge challenge for them to provide education and meaningful job opportunities for their young people. Unless they are able to do so, they face problems ranging from continued poverty and weak government to ideological radicalism, rebellion, and violence.

3. Migration, migration, everywhere.

The world of today, and even more the world of tomorrow, will be a world of people on the move. The proximity of very young populations in Central and northern Latin America, North Africa and the Middle East, and South Asia to richer but rapidly aging populations in North America, Europe, and far eastern Asia, will create enormous forces pulling labor migrants from developing countries into the rich world. If such migrants bring needed labor to developing countries and are able to integrate, learn valuable skills, and either return or send their children to their home societies with those new skills to build new industries and jobs, this will be a win-win situation. However, if migrants run into discrimination and migration barriers, both sending countries and rich potential host countries will lose out.

Migration streams within the developing world will also likely increase. Economic growth in the "sweet spot" countries will act as a magnet to the populations of younger, poorer countries seeking opportunities. And even within developing countries, the flow of migrants from the countryside to the city will dwarf anything yet seen in history. The world's urban population is expected to double in the next 50 years, as developing countries reach levels of urban population—from 60 to 70 percent—that until recently were only seen in the rich world. Already, many of the world's largest cities—Mumbai, Cairo, Calcutta, Jakarta, Lagos, Manila—are found in the world's poorest countries. Around the globe, the number of cities with a million or more population in Asia and Africa will come to outnumber those in Europe, Japan, and North America.

Unfortunately, migration due to hardships and humanitarian disasters is also likely to increase. With poorer countries growing rapidly in population, one can expect shortages of land or the impacts of natural disasters to hit more and more population groups. The violent conflicts that are likely to arise in very poor, weakly governed, but youthful and rapidly growing countries are also likely to drive people out of their homes and countries. The world of the future thus will have to somehow cope with more people moving to cities, across borders in search of work, and in search of assistance or refuge, than ever before.

In short, the world of the future will not simply be the world of today, but with slightly more people. It will be a very different world, given that the distribution of population size, age, and growth rates is shifting markedly from today's richer countries to today's poorer ones. How the world handles this transition will be the key political challenge of the coming decades.

Notes

1. These population data are from United Nations Population Division 2011.
2. These birth rate data are from Index Mundi (2009).

Part II

Population and International Security

3

Demography and Geopolitics

Understanding Today's Debate in Its Historical and Intellectual Context

Neil Howe and Richard Jackson

THE DEVELOPED WORLD IS ON THE CUSP OF A NEW ERA of hyperaging and population decline. By 2030, the elderly are projected to comprise 23 percent of the developed world's population, up from 16 percent today.[1] By 2050, the share will rise to 27 percent—and in Japan and some fast-aging countries of Western Europe it will be passing 35 percent. By midcentury, at least half of Americans will be over age 40 and at least half of Europeans will be over age 50. Meanwhile, working-age populations in almost every developed country will cease growing and in many cases begin to contract, the only major exception being the United States. By the mid-2020s, total populations will also peak and plateau or begin to decline in most countries. Japan and some European nations are on track to lose nearly one-half of their total current populations by the end of the century.

Although the developing world as a whole is still much younger, much of it is also in the midst of the "demographic transition"—the shift from high mortality and high fertility to low mortality and low fertility that inevitably accompanies development and modernization. Because mortality falls first, the transition initially accelerates population growth. But as the transition progresses, fertility falls as well. Since 1970, the average fertility rate in the developing world has dropped from 5.2 to 2.7, the rate of population growth has decelerated from 2.4 to 1.4 percent per year, and the median age has risen from 19 to 27. The demographic outlook in the developing world, however, is shaping up to be one of extraordinary diversity. In many of the poorest and least stable countries (especially in sub–Saharan Africa) the demographic transition has stalled, while in many of the most rapidly modernizing countries (especially in East Asia) the entire population shift from young and growing to old and stagnant or declining is occurring at a breathtaking pace—far more rapidly than it did in any of today's developed countries.

The purpose of this chapter is not to explore the many substantive security issues raised by global aging—as the worldwide demographic transformation is commonly known—but rather to understand the historical and intellectual context within which the debate over these issues will take place. We begin by surveying the recent explosion of worldwide interest in (and worries about) the impact of demography on geopolitics—and the simultaneous growth in research and writing about global aging and its consequences. We then step back and survey what policy leaders and thought leaders have been saying about population and power since the dawn of civilization, as well as how population actually has influenced power over the broad sweep of time.

We conclude that navigating the coming demographic transformation will require creative contributions from both the realist and "idealist" schools of geopolitical affairs. Although the linkage between population and power has long been considered to be solely a concern of the "realist" school, facing up to the challenge of global aging does not simply mean settling for the world as it is. It also means becoming a lot smarter about how to build the world as we would like it to be.

A Dawning Era of Demographic Anxiety

According to the Google news timeline (which catalogues news stories since the mid-1800s), there have been far more mentions of the phrase "population decline" linked with "nation" or "power" during the 2000–2010 decade than in any earlier decade on record. The topic is now hot: Both academics and the general public are starting to pay more attention to the long-term implications of demographic change than they ever have before.

Ten years ago, global aging was hardly on the radar screen of most developed-world policymakers. Today, it dominates almost any discussion of long-term fiscal, economic, or foreign-policy direction. Global demographic trends are monitored and studied at the highest leadership levels—at G-7 economic conferences, at NATO summits, and in U.S. Department of Defense strategy documents. On the domestic front, leaders and legislators debate the impact of demographic aging on everything from unemployment and infrastructure to pensions and health care spending. On the international front, they are learning to use a whole new vocabulary: birth wars, pronatalism, demographic engineering, ethnic competition, diaspora networks, youth bulges, youth deficits, population implosion, aging recessions, and budgetary graying.

Meanwhile, as ordinary citizens learn more about global aging, they are expressing concern over the future of their country, their ethnicity, or their way of life. Questions that were never asked when the prevailing worry was overpopulation—will "we" prevail in the long run? or even survive?—acquire new saliency. As Michael Teitelbaum and Jay Winter put it in *The Fear of Population Decline,* their prescient 1985 book examining the first signs of disquiet over falling fertility in Europe, such worries have "almost always conjured up a multitude of alarming images. Many of them have revealed fears not only about numbers but also about the quality, vitality, or optimistic outlook of a nation's inhabitants" (1985, p. 2).

When expert opinion pushes in the same direction as popular worries, the result is often political action—for example, to enact pronatal incentives. Over the last decade, countries around the world have enacted or begun to consider social policy reforms that would give women an additional inducement to have more children, including Australia, France, Germany, Italy, Japan, Poland, Russia, Singapore, South Korea, Spain, and the United Kingdom. Vladimir Špidla, the European Union's commissioner for employment and social affairs, has asked that all new EU policies be evaluated for their effect on birthrates and family formation (Rosenthal 2006, p. A3).

Throughout the developed world, public opinion has been galvanized by memorable media episodes in each country. Early in 2004, the cover of *Der Spiegel* showed a baby hoisting 16 old Germans on a barbell with the caption: "The Last German—On the Way to an Old People's Republic" (Wattenberg 2004, p. 103). The Japanese government, while passing one of its many fertility initiatives (including a "Fundamental Law Against a Decline in the Fertility Rate"), stirred public controversy by the release of a projection showing the date at which Japan's population would eventually decline to zero (National Institute of Population and Social Security Research 2003). In France, Prime Minister Jean-Pierre Raffarin faced down unions dominated by older workers by announcing that reform of the nation's unsustainable pension plan was necessary for "the survival of the republic" (Lander 2003, p. A9). In Italy, Pope John Paul II characterized "the crisis of births" as a "serious threat" in a nation described by *La Stampa* as "the oldest country in the world, a country of great-grandparents" (Krause 2006, p. 1).

In nearly all of the developed countries, local authorities in rural regions worry about the decline in the number of young native residents, while in urban areas they worry about the growth in the number of young immigrant residents. Television and magazine features about rural towns often focus on the closure of schools and the emigration of youth. Features about urban centers often focus on the difficulties of assimilating foreigners.

When news about aging and fertility decline is covered in the media, the tone is overwhelmingly one of worry—with negative interpretations outnumbering positive interpretations (according to one count) by 13 to 1 (Stark and Kohler 2002). Highest on the list of negative consequences are damage to the economy and loss of national power and influence. The environmental impact, though usually billed as positive, is mentioned much less often. Not surprisingly, the journalistic alarm appears least frequently in countries with relatively high fertility rates (for example, the United States) and most frequently in countries with relatively low fertility rates (for example, Japan).

Over the last few years, many writers and pop-culture creators in the developed world have taken the public's demographic worries and leveraged them into a message of pessimistic declinism. "Why is Europe committing demographic suicide, systematically depopulating itself?" asks George Weigel in *The Cube and the Cathedral* (2005, p. 21). "Japan offers the chance to observe the demographic death spiral in its purest form," notes Mark Steyn in *America Alone* (2006, p. 24). In some cases, the book titles say it all: *La France qui tombe* [*France Is Falling*] (Baverez 2003), *Can Germany Be Saved?* (Sinn 2007), and *The Last Days of Europe* (Laqueur 2007). Notable dystopian visions of an aging and childless social future include the British film hit *Children of Men* (2006); the documentary *Demographic Winter: The Decline of the Human Family* (2008); and the best-selling book, *Minimum,* by novelist Frank Schirrmacher (2006).

In the developing world, demographic projections are triggering a wider range of responses. In higher-fertility regions, many governments are still working to overcome traditional pronatal customs in order to reduce population growth and thereby alleviate poverty and spur development. In regions hit hard by falling fertility and imminent population decline, however, leaders are expressing desperate urgency about turning these trends around. Vladimir Putin, citing his nation's future economic and security needs, has flatly declared Russia's birth dearth to be "the most acute problem facing our country today" ("Vladimir Putin on Raising Russia's Birth Rate" 2006, p. 386). To raise the birthrate, the state is trying to motivate parents through monetary incentives, patriotic clubs, and emotional propaganda. Many nations in Eastern Europe, as well as East Asian nations like South Korea and Singapore (whose fertility rates have plunged to among the world's lowest), likewise feel a sense of demographic vulnerability and have enacted or are considering policy changes. In Singapore, the family-planning slogan used to be "Two Is Enough." Now it is "Three Children or More If You Can Afford It" (Daugherty and Kammeyer 1995, p. 255). Meanwhile, President Mahmoud Ahmadinejad of Iran would like to reverse his nation's recent fertility decline and claims that Iran has the "capacity" to handle 50 million more citizens (Reuters 2006).

For most people living in the developing world, however, demographic fears do not play out at the global or national level with anywhere near the intensity that they do at the subnational level—that is, the level of tribal, racial, and ethnic competition. What economist Milica Bookman calls an "inter-ethnic war of numbers" (1997, p. 1) is now unfolding inside a remarkable number—probably a majority—of developing countries in the Eastern Hemisphere. We merely mention here some of the conflicts that have recently been in the headlines: in Lebanon (between three religious groups); in India (two religious groups); in Pakistan (two religious groups); in the former Yugoslavia (six ethnic groups and three religious groups); in Iraq (two ethnic groups and two religious groups); in Malaysia (two ethnic groups); and in the states of sub–Saharan Africa (where the ethnic, religious, and language divisions are beyond counting). Rising disparities between the growth rates of different groups, with some shrinking while others are still doubling every two or three decades, further intensify the perception of competition.

Whether these conflicts are waged with armed militias or at the ballot box, they are often regarded by participants as explicit struggles for domination in which numbers play a critical role and population growth wins the long-term prize. They, too, constitute a demographic dynamic that will help shape the geopolitics of the next half-century, even if they do mostly unfold beneath the level of international relations.

Demography as a New Focus of Research

Not surprisingly, given the recent attention to population and power in so many countries, there has been a surge of academic and policy research on how demographic change is likely to shape the world's long-term future.

The issue that has received the most attention has been the impact of global aging on government budgets—and, in particular, on the sustainability of public pension and health care systems. This has become the subject of many research institute monographs and several popular books. Among the most notable are the World Bank's (1994) *Averting the Old-Age Crisis*; Barry Bosworth's and Gary Burtless's (1998) *Aging Societies: The Global Dimension*; Peter Heller's (2003) *Who Will Pay?*; and Larry Kotlikoff's and Scott Burns's (2005) *The Coming Generational Storm*. Other topics receiving broad coverage include the impact of global aging on savings and investment, workforce productivity, and international migration.

There is also a growing literature on a variety of specific demographic topics with a more direct connection to geopolitics. The empirical and analytical research on youth bulges and their correlation with outbreaks of civil disorder and regional conflict is impressive. Among the most important works are Esty et al. (1998), Goldstone (1999), Cincotta et al. (2003), Urdal (2004, 2006), Heinsohn (2006), and Leahy et al. (2007). Other topics with potential security implications that are attracting special scholarly interest include changes in family structure in high-income societies (Luttwak 1994; Kurth 2007); the impact of population-related environmental damage on intrastate conflict (Goldstone 2001a); the widening gender imbalance in several East and South Asian societies (Hudson and den Boer 2004); and the implications of differential growth rates between ethnic majority and minority populations (Bookman 1997; Toft 2002; and Kaufmann 2007).

This literature, however, is narrowly focused, and the gaps between the topics it covers are wide. Studies that focus more broadly on the connection between demography and geopolitics remain, as yet, few in number. These include several long reports by U.S. federal agencies and their contractors, including the Central Intelligence Agency (2001), the National Intelligence Council (2004), and the RAND Corporation (Nichiporuk 2000, 2005), as well as our own book, published by the Center for Strategic and International Studies (Jackson and Howe 2008), and a recent essay by Jack Goldstone in *Foreign Affairs* (Goldstone 2010). Although these studies are useful, they are also introductory. Several eminent scholars, most notably Paul Kennedy (1989) and Samuel Huntington (1996), have written geopolitical treatises that touch on demographic trends, but only indirectly. Peter G. Peterson (1999), Phillip Longman (2004), and Ben Wattenberg (2004) have published book-length interpretations of global aging, but these only indirectly touch on geopolitics.

Despite the gaps, the recent wave of research has greatly deepened our understanding of the coming demographic transformation's security implications. It addresses not just how demographic change will affect what Nichiporuk calls a state's "bucket of capabilities" (2000, p. 5), but also national attitudes and aspirations—which may ultimately prove to be even more important.

One crucial area that has received scant attention, however, is the historical and intellectual context to today's concerns over global aging. Why is demography suddenly the object of so much attention? Has this happened before? What have eminent statesmen and thinkers in other historical eras said about how demography shapes geopolitics? What lessons arise from the historical track record itself?

Population and Power: An Ancient Preoccupation

Demographic change shapes political power like water shapes rock. Up close the force looks trivial, but viewed from a distance of decades or centuries it moves mountains. To illustrate how dramatically populations can displace each other over time, the historian Eugene M. Kulischer once reminded his readers that in 900 AD Berlin had no Germans, Moscow had no Russians, Budapest had no Hungarians, Madrid was a Moorish settlement, and Constantinople had hardly any Turks. He added that the Normans had not yet settled in Britain, and that before the sixteenth century there were no Europeans living in North or South America, Australia, New Zealand, or South Africa (Kulischer 1948). As Mark Steyn pithily remarks, "Demographics is a game of last man standing" (2006, p. 3).

That population change contributes to the rise and fall of nations and empires is a fact of great antiquity. That policy leaders and their advisers often ponder its contribution and strive to influence it is also a fact of great antiquity. We approach these facts in reverse order. We look first at what societies have thought and said about population and power and then at what (if anything) the past actually teaches us about their connection.

Let's start with the obvious: From the beginning of history, and almost continuously until the modern era, most societies (or at least their elites) have been seriously concerned about population. With few exceptions, moreover, their main worry has been how to maintain sufficient population growth. They have sought growth at a minimum in order to withstand the ravages of war, disease, starvation, and other unforeseeable catastrophes, and at a maximum to be able to expand by conquering, absorbing, or displacing neighbors.

By most accounts, this powerful "populationist" impulse has its origin in the prehistoric nature of humankind.[2] Anthropologists and sociobiologists have observed that humans are a species that organizes into coalitions (initially families, clans, and tribes) to further their survival. These coalitions in turn foster cultural values and social rules that preserve their own group's integrity and encourage its safety, prosperity—and multiplication. To support the claim that prehistoric societies vigorously promoted fertility, scholars point to abundant evidence: family-formation strategies that maximized births and equated family size with social status (usually through polygamy); the celebration of fertility and the honoring of mothers; and widespread ancestor worship (which pressures believers to procreate in order that they achieve immortality through the worship of their descendants).

Not surprisingly, most later religions—at least those that endured to play a major role in history—continued to encourage large families. This is true of all of the major monotheisms (Judaism, Christianity, Islam, and Zoroastrianism), as well as of Confucianism. In his classic history of population doctrines, Charles Stangeland explains: "Injunctions similar to Jehovah's command, 'Increase and multiply,' are found in the religions of practically every ancient nation. For this almost universal attitude toward population an explanation must be found in the fact that the early nations were in a state of almost continuous hostility; always menaced and menacing" (1904, p. 40).

When the early leaders of political states began to design or enact explicit population policies, they did not need to invent new directives so much as co-opt directives that were already entrenched in the prevailing culture. The rulers of Sumer and Babylonia gave fertility cults official status and installed them on the ziggurats. The great lawgivers Hammurabi, Lycurgus, and Solon codified family norms in a manner that (in the opinion of some scholars) favored higher birthrates. Ancient writers frequently relate, through anecdote, the brutal pronatalism of ancient leaders. In his account of Pericles' famous oration, Thucydides has him tell Athenian women that the best way they can help in wartime is to bear more children. According to Plutarch, Philip of Macedon passed a law forcing his subjects to marry early to fill the future ranks of his army; his son Alexander the Great likewise ordered thousands of his conquering soldiers to marry Persians. (At nearly the same time, the Confucian forerunner Mo Zi was arguing in China that all men should be compelled to marry at age 20, all women at age 15.) Plutarch also tells the story of another

Macedonian, Pyrrhus of Epirus, whose "Pyrrhic victories" against the Roman republic were to no avail. Due to Rome's prodigious birthrate, its losses could be effortlessly replaced after every battle.

"Presumably," writes demographer Johannes Overbeek of ancient civilizations, "fertility was always or almost always praised and policies were aimed at the maintenance of high birthrates" (1974, p. 1). Paul Demeny agrees: "Measures encouraging marriage and sometimes immigration testify to the prevailing populationist sentiment among rulers throughout history" (2003, p. 3). At no time did ancient writers express this populationism with such vehemence as when their policies were failing and their nation's numbers were falling. Observing the demographic decline of Greece in the third century BC, Polybius specifically noted the absence "of continuous wars or epidemics" and blamed it instead on "the ostentation, avarice, and laziness" of citizens who were "unwilling to marry or, if they did marry, to bring up the children born to them; the majority were only willing to bring up at most one or two" (cited in Toynbee 1924, p. 99). During the late Roman republic, Cicero and other statesmen inveighed against the low birthrate of the Roman elite. During the empire, Tacitus compared the large families of the Germans with the small families of the Romans, which he considered a sign of his countrymen's loss of civic and personal virtue.

During the Middle Ages, as Christian Europe devolved into feudalism, rulers seldom worried about births except within their own families; attention to demography as a policy issue practically vanished. The most interesting writers on population and power were Muslims and Chinese (for example, Ibn Khaldun and Ma Duanlin) who lived in regions where empires still thrived.

Intellectual currents again shifted back toward Europe with the Renaissance and Reformation—and especially with the rise of the modern Western nation-state. As they rediscovered classical texts, humanists like Machiavelli began reviving the image of the powerful state, whose strength rested on both the number and quality of its citizens. As they overhauled religion, reformers like Martin Luther attacked the Catholic Church for encouraging celibacy and monasticism and allied the early Protestants behind universal marriage and many children. Channeling these impulses into a full-fledged populationist doctrine were the state-building monarchs, who sought out every tool at their disposal to expand trade, increase tax revenue, arm troops, acquire new territories, hold gaudy courts, and in general celebrate their own autocratic magnificence. Key among those tools (or so these rulers and their advisers thought) were policies that would increase their nation's population.

The era lasting from roughly 1450 to 1750 in Europe thus showcased an unparalleled obsession with the connection between population and power.

Henry IV of France thought that "the strength and riches of kings consist in the number and opulence of their subjects," while Frederick the Great of Prussia considered it axiomatic that "the number of people makes the wealth of states." "In the multitude of people is the king's glory," observed Jacques Bénigne Bossuet, the renowned French orator and political theorist. Bernard Mandeville, the English philosopher and political economist, called a growing population "the never-failing Nursery of Fleets and Armies."[3] As late as the 1750s, Denis Diderot contributed an entry called "Puissance" to the *Encyclopédie* in which he explained that a nation's strength lies in its numbers.

The next turning point came in the late eighteenth century. Enjoying higher living standards and steeply declining mortality rates (especially among children, which was equivalent to a boost in the birthrate), the population of Western Europe began growing at an accelerating rate. The demographic transition was under way. At the same time, many royal advisers and pamphleteers shifted focus and began pointing out some of the costs of rapid population growth, from crowded cities to high rates of unemployment and large numbers of abandoned children. Then, in 1798, an erudite English parson named Thomas Malthus published *An Essay on the Principle of Population*, which offered a radical reappraisal of the effect of population growth on social welfare and state power. A growing population does not make us better off, Malthus argued. By overwhelming the availability of natural resources (especially land), a growing population must ultimately impoverish society and make us worse off. Standard populationist measures, such as bounties for extra children, are not merely ineffective; they are counterproductive.

It would be difficult to overestimate the influence that Malthus has exercised over the subsequent two centuries. As population growth sped up and the Industrial Revolution took off during the "hungry '40s," Europe's emerging bourgeois elites regularly invoked Malthus to justify their new doctrine of market liberalism and their hostility to social welfare programs. Toward the end of the century, imperialists across Europe regularly invoked him to justify their colony-building projects. From the French Revolution to World War I and beyond, most economic and social policy theorists (especially in England) paid homage to his doctrine—from David Ricardo, Frédéric Bastiat, Jean-Baptiste Say, and John Stuart Mill to Herbert Spencer, Alfred Marshall, Henry George, and Sidney and Beatrice Webb. In his famous book on the prospects of Europe in 1919, John Maynard Keynes, persuaded that overpopulation had spawned the twin evils of militarism and bolshevism, wrote that "Malthus disclosed a devil" (1920, p. 10).

Malthus's overpopulation "devil" continued to exert great sway over the rest of the twentieth century. Indeed, during the early post–World War II era, especially from the mid-1950s to the mid-1980s, antipopulationism (and antinatalism) dominated social and foreign policy thinking in the developed world to an extent having few if any historical parallels. The neo-Malthusian resurgence allied itself with the extreme views on the scarcity of natural resources exemplified by Paul Ehrlich's 1968 bestseller, *The Population Bomb*, and the Club of Rome's 1972 report, *The Limits to Growth* (Meadows et al. 1972). It also drew upon more general critiques of "industrial civilization" and the "bourgeois family." Domestically, the resurgence favored abandoning or at least de-emphasizing public incentives to marry or have children. Abroad, it favored aggressive campaigns to reduce birthrates in developing countries—not to prevent them from becoming powerful (though some foreign leaders begged to differ), but rather to alleviate their demographic burden, promote economic development, and encourage a democratic way of life.

Yet even during these recent Malthusian centuries, there have been important countercurrents. It is no accident that Malthus's popularity has roughly coincided with the demographic transition and what Ehrlich rightly called a worldwide "population explosion" unique in human history (a tenfold growth in global population since 1700). Likewise, it is no accident that Malthus has usually fallen out of favor in countries or decades in which population trends have seemed to be moving the other way.

An interesting example is France, which experienced a rapid birthrate decline after Napoleon and hardly any population growth at all after the midnineteenth century. In 1870, France lost the Franco-Prussian War—a defeat widely blamed on inadequate troop numbers. Thereafter, it is hard to find any French thinker of much influence who still subscribed to Malthus's worldview. Instead, leading French intellectuals engaged in endless soul-searching about why the French had so few children, whether feminism was treasonous, whether their static population was a sign of decadence, what sort of pronatalist policies could turn the birthrate around, and indeed whether France could survive another war against Germany's rapidly expanding population (Spengler 1979; Cole 2000). In 1900, a French senator announced gravely to the media: "If French wives had the fertility of German women, we would gain 500,000 children per year" (cited in Cole 2000, p. 195). The French preoccupation with raising their birthrate ultimately gave rise to generous public maternity benefits that help to explain why France (ironically) today has one of the highest fertility rates in Europe.

Another example is the 1930s. Beset by a plunge in fertility, a severe economic depression, and new fears of war, leaders and writers throughout the world suddenly blamed slow population growth for everything from unemployment, trade wars, and political unrest to a more fundamental cultural decline. Keynes changed his mind and (along with his followers) started to advocate population growth. The demographer Enid Charles wrote *The Twilight of Parenthood* in 1934, in which she announced that "in place of the Malthusian menace of overpopulation there is now a real danger of underpopulation" (cited in Longman 2004, p. 75). Oswald Spengler (1918) and P. A. Sorokin (1937) suggested that demographic decline was a symptom of civilizational exhaustion. Growing fascist parties advocated vigorous pronatalism as a cornerstone of their policy agenda. These alarmist worries and policy prescriptions climaxed with World War II. Yet even after the war ended, they remained strong enough to induce many developed nations to incorporate generous family benefits into their early postwar social welfare programs.

The neo-Malthusian resurgence of the mid-1950s to the mid-1980s coincided with an era that in many respects was the mirror image of the 1930s. Starting in the 1950s, the developed world experienced growing affluence and relative freedom from the threat of war. Domestically, it witnessed a renewal of strong population growth, at least until the 1970s. Abroad, it noticed a spectacular acceleration of global population growth as the developing world entered its own demographic transition. From 1950 to 1973, the world's population grew at an average annual rate of roughly 2 percent. It had never before grown at such a high rate for so long—nor, from today's vantage point, does it ever seem likely to do so again. As population projections have collapsed, and as the generation that recalls fascist pronatalism disappears, yet another shift in prevailing attitudes—this time back to worries about population decline—is well under way.

Lessons of History: The Intellectual Tradition

A number of useful themes emerge from this retrospect that will add some historical depth to today's rising new interest in the impact of demographic aging—and, in some nations, demographic decline—on national power.

First, the issue of population and power has an ancient pedigree. Political leaders have worried about it since the dawn of civilization. Over the centuries, moreover, their concern has almost always been to avoid population decline and to encourage population growth. From time to time, great minds have expressed a dissenting point of view (Aristotle, for example, once famously wrote that "a great state is not the same as a populous state"), but there is little evidence that leaders listened to such advice (Aristotle's illustrious Macedonian patrons clearly did not).

Second, to the extent that populationism has yielded to an antigrowth agenda, it has done so in eras of unusual population growth. This explains the overall ascendency of Malthusianism after the late eighteenth century—not just in Europe but in China as well, which also experienced rapid population growth beginning around 1750 (Wang 1999). This also explains why, even over the last two centuries, the direction of thinking and policy has tended to shift back and forth with the prevailing demographic outlook.

Third, the favorite policy prescriptions for encouraging population growth have actually changed very little over the centuries. The senate and emperors of Rome enacted monetary bounties for families with many children, monetary penalties for bachelors, and status-enhancing inducements (like citizenship) for immigrants. Fifteen hundred years later, Louis XIV's finance minister, Jean-Baptiste Colbert, was recommending the same menu of options. And in the capitals of today's developed countries, one finds plenty of policy working papers still pushing a similar program. Even brutal measures of "demographic engineering," such as deportation, relocation, colonization, and genocide, have not changed much. Germany and the Soviet Union used them in the twentieth century. So did the Assyrians, Romans, Mongols, and Turks in earlier centuries.

Fourth, leaders have been perpetually disappointed by their population policies—by how they fail so much more often than they succeed. This has triggered an endless debate over the centuries about how to influence behavior more effectively. The debate has typically pitted paternalists, who believe that people can be made to do their demographic "duty" mostly by means of commands or bribes, against liberals, who believe that better results will come from giving people more economic opportunity and a broader range of social and lifestyle freedom. To raise birthrates, some today advocate policies that would reinforce an exclusive maternal role for women, while others advocate policies that would give women more choices (such as having a career while also raising children). History's track record shows that, though it is the paternalistic policies that have usually been enacted, it is the liberal policies that have usually been more effective.

Finally, from ancient times to the present day, there has always been uncertainty about the direction of causation. Does population growth cause a state to be successful at home and abroad? Or is it the other way around—that is, does a state that is successful (for whatever deep social or cultural reason) merely experience population growth as a dimension of that success? Leaders have usually leaned toward the first answer, because they like to believe that they are in control of the state's destiny. Yet ancient philosophers often inclined toward the second answer. Many believed in an organic metaphor for the polis: Political societies, like human beings, experience birth, growth, maturity, senescence, and death. Young societies are simple, innocent, virtuous, egalitarian, and tend to have many youths. Old societies are complex, experienced, decadent, stratified, and tend to have many elders. In time, all societies naturally cycle from young to old, and it is not clear whether policymakers can do much to change that.

Among the Greeks, Polybius subscribed to this cyclical view of social and political evolution; among the Romans, Tacitus, Juvenal, and even Petronius; in the Middle Ages, Ibn Khaldun; in the Renaissance, Machiavelli. In the 1920s and 1930s, we associate this view with Oswald Spengler's (1918) *The Decline of the West*. In our own day, we may think of Joseph Tainter's (1988) *The Collapse of Complex Societies* or simply Jared Diamond's (2005) *Collapse*. What all of these interpretations have in common is the idea that social evolution—demography included—is governed by a metahistorical dynamic that may not allow much room for leaders or citizens themselves to intervene. Although this doctrine is not one that policymakers will accept easily, it also offers some humbling insights that they would do well not to ignore entirely.

Lessons of History: The Historical Record

Let us now turn to a very different question: What does the historical record itself actually say about the connection between population and power?

In our view, the historical record is fairly clear: All other things being equal, size is an advantage. With its larger population, the bigger state can mobilize larger forces and occupy more territory. With its larger economy (due to its larger population), the bigger state can arm and supply larger forces, exert more pressure on global trade and finance, and enjoy important efficiencies of scale in its markets and public works. With more people and more production, the bigger state can wield more cultural and policy influence on the world stage (soft power) and, if conflict arises, can more easily compel an adversary to settle on terms of its choosing (hard power). Indeed, if the history of war teaches any obvious lessons, one is that victory usually goes to the larger state or alliance—particularly when victory is of critical importance to both sides.

This argument is stressed in almost all of the classics of modern national security literature, from Hans Morgenthau (1948) to A. F. K. Organski (1958) and Hedley Bull (1987). Moreover, it appears to be as valid for the long term as it is for the near term. Armed with exactly this reasoning, Alexis de Tocqueville was able to make his astonishing prediction (in 1835!) regarding the United States and Russia. He wrote that one would stand for "freedom" and the other for "servitude." He also wrote that "each of them seems marked out by the will of Heaven to sway the destinies of half the globe" (de Tocqueville 1863, p. 559). Tocqueville's method, revealed in a footnote, was simple. He observed that these two societies were filling large empty continents, and then he just did the arithmetic.

Here may be a good place, however, to acknowledge some of the limitations of sheer size. Some have suggested that there are important diseconomies of scale—when a state overwhelms its natural environment, for example, or when it becomes overly complex and bureaucratic. Similarly, one cannot blindly compare the size of states without regard to their political type. To say, for example, that in 1914 the Austro-Hungarian empire was "larger" than Great Britain would not be meaningful, since one was a rambling federation and the other was a modern nation-state. Still, while allowing these exceptions and caveats, our overall conclusion stands. Most of the time, it is the larger states that shape the geopolitical order to their liking—an advantage that grows with the degree of crisis and conflict besetting that order.

A further concession is that superior population size, though helpful, hardly guarantees success. Yes, there are many classic instances of total-war struggles for domination in which the larger side came out on top: World Wars I and II, for example, or the U.S. and English Civil Wars. But there are also many counterexamples, such as Queen Elizabeth I against Ferdinand II or Alexander the Great against Darius III. One wonders: Is there perhaps another demographic indicator that may have better or additional predictive value?

An intriguing possibility, suggested by the ancient organic metaphor for state growth and decline, might be to look not just at population size, but also at the rate of population growth. To be sure, a high rate of population growth is by no means a *sufficient* condition for success. Most states with high growth rates are not particularly successful, and indeed many are especially weak, mired in poverty, and prone to civil strife. Yet a relatively high growth rate may be a *necessary* condition for success. Throughout history, in a remarkable variety of instances, those states or alliances that have ultimately prevailed over their neighbors turn out to be those whose populations were growing faster than their neighbors'. In the ancient world, this was true for the Persians, the

Greeks, the Macedonians, and the Romans. In the Middle Ages, it was true for the Norse and the Mongols. In modern Western history, it has been true for Portugal in the fifteenth century, the Netherlands in the sixteenth, Russia in the seventeenth, Great Britain in the eighteenth, Germany in the nineteenth, and the United States in the twentieth. On the other hand, it is difficult to find any major instance of a state whose regional or global stature has risen while its share of the regional or global population has declined.

Ever since Edward Gibbon's account of the barbarian invasions of the Roman empire, historians have noted the unusual dynamism and confidence that sometimes characterize high-growth populations. The eminent historian William H. McNeill (1982, 1990) believes that demographic pressure pushes the entire society toward new and riskier political goals. Often, perhaps most of the time, the energy dissipates. But occasionally a juggernaut is unleashed. McNeill believes that it was demographic pressure that drove the expansion of China and Great Britain in the eighteenth century, triggered the modernization of Japan after the Meiji Restoration, and pushed Central Europe into both World Wars I and II. He notes that "growing populations do not voluntarily leave their neighbors alone and at ease within existing economic, political, and social frameworks" (McNeill 1990, p. 51). Some academic research confirms that higher-growth societies are more likely to initiate interstate conflict (Choucri 1984; Tir and Diehl 1998).

To the extent that the reckless energy of higher-growth societies is driven by their relatively large numbers of young people, this dynamic is related to the youth-bulge model discussed in the security literature. An extreme version of this model has been advanced by the sociologist Gunnar Heinsohn (2006), who believes that nearly all civic energy and risk taking (and violence) in history is driven by the "excess sons" of large families who must undertake new enterprises in order to win social status. In sixteenth-century Spain, these were the "Secondones," the second sons who became conquistadores because they would inherit no land at home. In the twenty-first-century Middle East, he says, they are the prime recruits for terrorist organizations.

The policy implications of the population growth dynamic are subtle. Fast-growing, youthful societies clearly bear close watching due to their greater overall volatility. These societies are prone to instability and state failure. Yet occasionally, one will emerge as a regional hegemon—and this will almost always be a society that is growing more rapidly than its neighbors. Beyond these useful lessons, however, the dynamic does not offer either fast- or slow-growing societies any easy formula for success. Heinsohn is hesitant to offer concrete recommendations. McNeill merely tantalizes his readers with his own cyclical perspective on the rise and fall of nations.

Realism and Idealism in an Aging World

Many are uncomfortable with the proposition that demography shapes the rise and fall of nations, since it seems to hand much of our fate over to the blind forces of multiplication, acquisition, and absorption. There is no denying that demographic change as a force in history has always been considered a staple of the realist school. It is linked to concerns about group survival having deep roots in our biology. It tends to focus more on the ability to prevail and dominate rather than the ability to influence and cooperate. It is sometimes used to justify traditional family structures (as pronatalist) and criticize new and unconventional social norms (as antinatalist). Realists like to say that we can never escape the limits of what the world is, while idealists might complain that excessive focus on population and power is likely to distract us from what the world could be or ought to be.

Today, however, this contrast can be greatly overdrawn. Contemporary social scientists, unlike classical realists, use a method that is both historical and global. They follow the path of each country's social and economic development and acknowledge that the geopolitical order depends upon a working "world system." They do not just focus on how demographic change determines numbers and wealth, but also on how it affects attitudes and aspirations. If, as many realists believe, demographic trends are likely to push today's developed nations into a position of geopolitical weakness, then it may be even more vital that they begin to pursue such idealist goals as acting in concert with each other and inviting certain rising developing nations into their fold.

Both schools, realist and idealist, have been slow to focus on the massive demographic riptide due to sweep over the world during the next several decades. Both need to get busy—improving the long-term projections, debating their implications, and determining the best strategic responses. Preparing for global aging will call on contributions from all schools of thought. It is a mission that will challenge the planning skills of every policymaker and the leadership skills of every statesperson.

Notes

1. The population projections in this paragraph refer to the U.N.'s "constant fertility" variant (U.N. Population Division 2009).

2. For a primer on the sociobiology of the populationist impulse, see Scheidel (2006). For the history of populationism, see also Stangeland (1904) and Overbeek (1974).

3. For Henry IV, see Stangeland 1904, p. 103; for Frederick the Great, see *Oeuvres de Frédéric le Grand* 1846, p. 4; for Bossuet, see *Oeuvres de Bossuet* 1841, p. 457; and for Mandeville, see Hundert 1997, p. 122.

4

America's Golden Years?

U.S. Security in an Aging World

Mark L. Haas

In 2007 Sergei Morozon, the governor of the Ulyanovsk region of central Russia, offered prizes to couples who agreed to take advantage of a "family contact day" and wound up producing babies nine months later, on June 12, Russia's national day. It was the third year running that Ulyanovsk had declared a "sex day" and offered prizes for babies born. The 2007 grand prize was a sports utility vehicle (Bely 2007).

The Ulyanovsk initiative is one part of a nationwide effort in Russia to fight a looming demographic crisis that hovers over much of the world. Simply put, the world's great powers are growing old. Steep declines in birthrates over the last century and major increases in life expectancies have caused the populations of Britain, China, France, Germany, Japan, Russia, and the United States to age at a substantial rate. Aging in Germany, Japan, and Russia has already progressed to such an extent that their populations are shrinking. If current trends continue, some of the great powers of today—and for most of the last century, if not longer—will not be the great powers of the future.

This phenomenon will have critical effects on America's international security interests in coming decades. Most important, global aging will be a potent force for the continuation of American military and economic dominance. Aging populations are likely to result in the slowdown of states' economic growth at the same time that governments face pressure to pay for massive new expenditures for elder care. This double economic dilemma will create such an austere fiscal environment that the other great powers will lack the resources necessary to overtake the United States' huge power lead. This analysis applies even—perhaps especially—to China, which is the state that most analysts point to as America's most likely future rival. China's aging problem will be particularly dramatic over the next 40 years since it is growing old at a pace and extent scarcely before witnessed in history.

Reinforcing these trends is the fact that although the United States is aging, it is doing so to a lesser extent and less quickly than the other great powers, to the benefit of America's relative power position. Consequently, the costs created by aging will be significantly lower for the United States than for potential competitors. Global aging is therefore not only likely to extend U.S. hegemony, but deepen it as these others states are likely to fall even farther behind the United States.

The international security effects created by an aging world are not all positive for American interests, however. Although the United States is in better demographic shape than the other great powers, it, too, will confront massive new costs created by its own aging population. As a result, it will most likely be unable to maintain its current international position. Thus, while the United States in coming decades will be even more secure from great power rivalry than it is today, it (and its allies) will likely be less able to realize other key international objectives, including preventing the proliferation of weapons of mass destruction (WMD), funding nation building, engaging in military humanitarian interventions, and various other costly strategies of international conflict resolution and prevention.

Something New Under the Sun

Rarely can analysts of international politics claim to be documenting new phenomena. Global population aging, however, is one of these revolutionary

Table 4.1 Fertility Rates by Country

Country	Years 2005–2010	When Went Below Replacement
Japan	1.32	1975–1980
Germany	1.36	1970–1975
Russia	1.44	1965–1970
China	1.64	1990–1995
United Kingdom	1.83	1970–1975
France	1.97	1975–1980
United States	2.07	1970–1975

Source: United Nations Population Division 2011.

variables. Never before has humanity witnessed such dramatic, widespread aging in the world's most powerful actors.

Social aging is a product of two long-term demographic trends: decreasing fertility rates and increasing life expectancies. Fertility rates are the average number of children per woman in a given country. For a state to sustain its current population numbers (assuming zero net immigration), fertility levels must be at 2.1 or higher. Today the United States is the only great power that comes close to meeting this requirement, and most are well below this number and have been for decades (see Table 4.1).

The scope of the aging process in the great powers is remarkable. By 2050, at least 20 percent of the citizens in these states will be over 65 (see Table 4.2).[1] In Japan more than one out of every three people will be over this age. As societal aging progresses over the next half century, the populations in Germany, Japan, and Russia are expected to shrink significantly. Russia's population is already decreasing by nearly 200,000 people per year, and Germany and Japan

Table 4.2 Percentage of Population over 65 by Country

Country	Year 1950	Year 2000	Year 2050
United States	8.3	12.4	21.2
Russia	6.2	12.4	23.1
United Kingdom	10.8	15.8	23.6
France	11.4	16.1	24.9
China	4.5	7.0	25.6
Germany	9.7	16.3	30.9
Japan	4.9	17.2	35.6

Source: United Nations Population Division 2011.

are also currently experiencing absolute population decline (United Nations Population Division 2011).

It is worth stressing that predictions for aging in the great powers are unlikely to be wrong. The reason for this certainty is simple: The elderly of the future are already born. Consequently, absent some global natural disaster, disease pandemic, or other worldwide calamity, the number of people in the world who are over 65 will increase dramatically in coming decades. Only major increases in immigration rates or fertility levels will prevent this inevitable rise in the number of elderly from resulting in significant increases in states' median ages. Either outcome is unlikely, however. Immigration rates in the great powers for the next 50 years would have to be orders of magnitude higher than historical levels to prevent population aging (United Nations Population Division 2000). Significant increases in fertility would represent a reversal of a centuries-long trend in the industrialized world, and one that has existed in many states despite the existence of pronatalist governmental policies (Demeny 1999). Aging in the most powerful actors in the system is, in short, a virtual inevitability.

Although aging in the great powers is virtually inevitable, how states respond to this phenomenon is not. The following analysis of the economic and fiscal costs of global aging and the consequent effects on international power distributions are forecasts, not predictions. This chapter's analysis, in other words, is based on extrapolations of current trends. If governments adopt effective countermeasures, outcomes could change for the better. I mention some of these potential remedies at the chapter's end, and Jennifer Dabbs Sciubba discusses these more thoroughly in her chapter in this volume.

Two points on this subject must be stressed, however. First, the costs created by population aging in the great powers are extremely high, thus the policies necessary to counteract the negative effects of this phenomenon must be equally ambitious. Second, there are powerful incentives that work against adopting "aging reforms," most notably the moral pressure of depriving poor seniors of reasonable standards of welfare and the political pressure against taking resources away from a large constituency. Taken together, these facts make the forces working for the continuation of current trends on the subject of population aging very strong. Although most governments in the industrialized world have made policy changes to increase the viability and reduce the costs of their welfare systems for the elderly, none of the great powers has thus far adopted reforms that eliminate the huge gap between anticipated expenditures for the aged and resources set aside for these costs (Capretta 2007; Haas 2007, pp. 123–124).

The Costs of Population Aging

Population aging in the great powers will create substantial economic and fiscal costs. To begin with, graying populations are likely to slow states' overall economic growth. A state's gross domestic product (GDP), in its most basic formulation, is a product of the number of workers and overall productivity. As a country's workforce shrinks as more people enter retirement than enter the labor market, so, too, will its GDP unless productivity levels rise sufficiently to compensate for this loss. By 2050, Japan's working-age population (ages 15 to 64) is expected to shrink by over 30 percent, Germany's and Russia's by 25 percent, and China's by 20 percent (see Table 4.3). To prevent these workforce reductions from translating into overall GDP decline, states' productivity must increase proportionally.[2] Although this is likely to be the case in most of the industrialized countries, workforce contraction will still act as a substantial brake on economic growth in coming decades (Turner et al. 1998, 47).

We are already witnessing this dynamic. For example, even though China is currently the youngest of the great powers, it is experiencing labor shortages that are threatening economic growth. These shortages are due in large part to the aging of China and reductions in the number of 15 to 35 year olds (Bradsher 2007). Experts predict that shrinkage in China's working-age population will result in a loss of 1 percent per year from this state's GDP growth by the 2020s (Jackson 2005). The economic forecasts are even more dire for Germany and Japan, where massively contracting labor forces could result in

Table 4.3 Working Age Population by Country (Ages 15–64)

Country	Year 2005 (in thousands)	Year 2050 (in thousands)	Percent Change
United States	207,534	241,725	17
United Kingdom	40,973	43,090	5
France	40,713	41,633	2
China	970,532	790,010	−19
Germany	54,435	40,839	−25
Russia	103,161	75,705	−27
Japan	80,926	55,446	−32

Source: United Nations Population Division 2011.

Note: Working-age populations in these tables are based on absolute numbers within this demographic group, not actual retirement ages. Because the average effective retirement age in all the great powers except Japan and the United States is well below 65, changes in working-age populations and support ratios are even worse in most cases than indicated. See OECD 2007.

overall GDP growth of roughly 1 percent in coming decades (*Lombard Street Research Monthly Economic Review* 2003).

Compounding these problems, significant social aging may also limit productivity growth. The elderly are likely to be more conservative with their investments than younger people. The more risk averse a society's investment portfolio is, the less entrepreneurship that will be funded, and thus the lower the gains in productivity that should be expected. National savings rates may also shrink in aging states as large numbers of seniors spend down their savings. The Japanese government, for example, has already reported that national savings rates are down substantially from previous levels due to social aging and seniors' consumption of their savings (*Yomiuri Simbun* 2003). Reduced savings rates may lead to rising interest rates and ultimately to reduced rates of productivity increases (England 2002).

In addition to slowing economic growth, an even more important economic effect of social aging is the strain that it places on governmental resources. All governments in the industrialized world have made commitments to pay for substantial portions of the retirement and health care costs of their elderly citizens. The projected increases in governmental spending for the elderly in coming decades are sobering. Annual public benefits to the elderly (both pension and health care) as a percentage of GDP are forecasted to rise by 2040 by 15 percent in Japan (to an overall percentage of 27); by 13 percent in France (to an overall percentage of 29); by 11 percent in the United States (to an overall percentage of 20); by 10 percent in Germany (to an overall percentage of 26); and by 6 percent in Britain (to an overall percentage of 18) (Jackson and Howe 2003, p. 7).

These costs will be an increase of hundreds of billions of dollars to governments' annual expenditures for many decades. To give some perspective on their magnitude, consider the following. By 2040, the annual amount of money that the great powers will have to spend on elder care is going to increase many times what these states currently spend on their militaries, even after adjusting for inflation. Germany will have to increase its annual spending on elder care more than 7 times what it currently spends on defense. France will have to spend more than 5 times as much, and Japan more than 15 times as much (Haas 2007, pp. 120–121).

Pax Americana Geriatrica

Population aging in the great powers will be a potent force for the prolongation of U.S. power dominance in the twenty-first century for three principal reasons.

First, the massive costs created by aging populations, especially in combination with probable slowdowns in economic growth, will create major barriers in the other great powers to increasing their military expenditures anywhere close to matching U.S. defense spending. These factors are even likely to push many of these states to reduce military expenditures from current levels. Second, with aging populations and shrinking workforces, the other great powers will be forced to spend increasing percentages of their defense budgets on personnel costs and military pensions at the expense of purchasing the most technologically sophisticated weaponry. The more money that states spend on military personnel and pensions as opposed to weapons, the lower the likelihood will be of these countries challenging U.S. military dominance. The third factor reinforces both of the previous points. Although the U.S. population is aging, it is doing so to a lesser extent and less quickly than those of the other great powers. As a result, the pressures pushing for the crowding out of military spending in favor of care for the elderly and the increasing substitution of labor for capital within defense budgets will be considerably smaller for the United States than potential great power competitors.

Guns Versus Canes

Given the magnitude of the costs created by the great powers' aging populations, substantial increases in the future in these states' expenditures for economic development and defense are unlikely. We are, in fact, already witnessing in the oldest of the great powers the crowding out of military spending for elderly care. Despite concerns about growing Chinese power and North Korea's missile and nuclear programs, Japan reduced its defense budget every year from 2003 to 2008. In December 2004, Japan cut military spending by 3.7 percent from the average of the previous five budgets. The cuts were engineered by finance ministry officials "who demanded more social spending for Japan's rapidly aging population" (Brooke 2004). The following December the defense budget was reduced by another 0.9 percent to help pay for the "growing burdens [resulting] from an aging population" (Xinhua General News Service 2005). In fact, the Japanese government has stated that by 2015 general expenditures will have to be cut by 25 to 30 percent "to cope with inevitable increases in social security-related spending given the nation's rapidly aging population" ("30% Cut in Spending Needed to Balance Japan's Finances in 10 Years" 2005).

Similar pressure for cuts in defense spending to finance elder-care costs is building in Germany and France. In February 2006 the EU Commission warned Germany that it had to cut substantially discretionary spending across the board "to cope with the costs of an aging population" (White 2006). Germany's finance minister, Peer Steinbrueck, speaking on behalf of the government, agreed with this analysis and promised to put the commission's recommendations into practice. Also in 2006 the French president requested the creation of a new body, the Public Finance Guidance Council. The council's primary purpose is to reduce France's national debt, which has grown significantly in recent years largely due to increasing costs for elder care. The institution's main policy recommendation is to reduce to a substantial degree expenditures "of all public players," including the military (Office of the Prime Minister, France 2006).

The tendency of cutting military spending to pay for elder-care costs is likely to repeat itself in the state that is aging faster than any of the great powers: China. Rising longevity in China and the "one-child policy," which has helped lower dramatically China's fertility levels, have made it a rapidly aging society. China's median age will climb from just under 30 in 2000 to nearly 49 in 2050, which will make China one of the oldest states in the world (the oldest great power in the world today, Japan, has a median age of nearly 45). China in 2005 had nearly 100 million citizens over the age of 65. By 2025, this number will almost double. By 2040, it is expected to more than triple (United Nations Population Division 2011).

In relation to the other great powers, China possesses some advantages when it comes to dealing with the negative effects of population aging. China's current taxation rates and deficit levels are low compared to those of these other states. China's elderly also likely expect lower levels of welfare provision from their government than do citizens in the other great powers. Adding to the effects of this last tendency is the fact that China's illiberal political system lowers the impact of popular pressure for generous social security spending.

China nevertheless will confront in coming decades monumental challenges created by its rapidly aging population. China's elderly have very little savings. Nearly 80 percent of Chinese urban households with individuals aged 55 and over today have less than 1 year of income saved, and only 5 percent have more than 2 years of income in savings (Jackson and Howe 2004).

China has traditionally relied on the family unit to provide for elder care. Increasing rates of divorce, urbanization, and related migration (French 2006), and female workforce participation will, however, place significant strain on this tradition. Decreasing family size will prove especially problematic for preserving elders' welfare within the context of the family. Demographers refer to a rapidly growing "4-2-1" phenomenon in China, in which one child is responsible for caring for two parents and four grandparents (Leung 2006, pp. 413–415). Familial elder care in these circumstances is quite burdensome.

Given the facts of an exploding elderly population with very little savings and a weakening family structure, "the majority of the people in the People's Republic of China" will, according to one expert on this subject, "be obliged to rely heavily on social security pensions after retirement" (Takayama 2002, p. 16). China's government will face both moral and political pressure to meet these obligations. Its leaders have already recognized as much. In a white paper issued in 2004, the Chinese government asserted that social security "is an important guarantee for the social stability and the long-term political stability of the country" (People's Republic of China 2004a, p. 2). Consistent with this thinking, China in 2000 created the National Social Security Fund. This institution's goal is to set aside hundreds of billions of dollars (largely through levying new taxes and selling state assets) to pay off the unfunded pension liabilities that have been accumulated by state-owned enterprises, many of which have become obsolete due to governmental policies since the 1980s (Social Security Administration 2004).

Not even the illiberalism of China's government has immunized it from the forces pushing for increased public spending on welfare for the elderly. In 2002, for example, China's attempts to renege on promised benefits to retirees led to large-scale protests and riots, including in the major cities of Liaoyang and Daqing. The pressure from these protests was so great that the authoritarian Chinese government promised to extend pension benefits to an additional 50 million people (Haas 2007, p. 124).

Although China's commitments to the elderly are modest compared to other great powers (though they are growing), these obligations already outstrip by a wide margin resources set aside to meet them. Three-quarters of all Chinese workers are without any pension coverage, yet independent estimates have found a potential shortfall between China's governmental obligations to the elderly and saved public assets to be as much as 150 percent of GDP (England 2005, pp. 97, 89, 91; Chang 2002). If the percentage of people covered by China's public welfare net continues to grow, fiscal constraints will only worsen.

Finally, it is important to emphasize that China will not be able to "grow" its way out of its aging dilemma. Despite China's very high levels of economic growth since the 1990s, it will become the first country to grow old before becoming an advanced industrial state. Even if China's economy continues to grow in coming decades at rates similar to those it has experienced in recent years, by 2035 its median age will reach the levels of France, Germany, and Japan today, but at GDP per capita levels significantly lower than these states currently possess. Consequently, when China's aging crisis hits with full force, it will, at best, confront similar economic and fiscal constraints as France, Germany, and Japan do today (Eberstadt 2006).

Given the preceding facts and trends, China's political leaders beginning in roughly 2020 will be faced with a difficult choice: allow growing levels of poverty within an exploding elderly population, or provide the resources necessary to avoid this situation. To the extent that these politicians succumb to the significant moral and political pressure pushing for the latter decision, America's relative power position will be benefited.[3]

Increasing Money for Military Personnel, Not Weapons

The crowding out of military and economic development spending for increased care for the elderly is not the only way in which population aging is likely to affect global power distributions. Social aging is also likely to push militaries to spend more on personnel and less on other areas, including weapons development and procurement. This is important because no nation will be able to challenge U.S. military dominance without the ability to wage highly technologically sophisticated warfare (Posen 2003). When states are forced to spend more of their military budgets on personnel than on research, development, and weapons procurement, the odds of continued U.S. military primacy increase substantially.

The oldest of the great powers are already devoting significantly more resources to military personnel than weapons purchases and research. Since 1995, both France and Germany have dedicated nearly 60 percent of their military budgets to personnel. Germany spends nearly 4 times as much on personnel as weapons procurement; France, Japan, and Russia roughly 2.5 times more. The United States, in contrast, dedicates less than 1.3 times more money to personnel than weapons purchases (Haas 2007, pp. 140–141).

Population aging is a key cause of increasing military personnel costs for two main reasons. First, as societies age, more people exit the workforce than enter it. Increasing numbers of retirees in relation to new workers are likely to create labor shortages relative to previous levels of employment. The result of this trend will be increased competition among businesses and organizations—including the military—to hire workers. Consequently, if states' militaries want to be able to attract and keep the best employees, they are going to have to pay more to do so. A 2006 report endorsed by EU defense ministers made precisely these points, stating that the aging of Europe's populations will "inevitably" lead to rising military personnel per capita costs if European forces are to remain effective (European Defense Agency 2006, p. 6).

A second factor that is increasing states' military personnel costs at the expense of weapons procurement is the aging of the military itself. The great powers' pension obligations to retired military personnel are considerable. Russia, for example, in the 2000s consistently spent significantly more on military retirees than on either weapons procurement or military research and development (Haas 2007, p. 142). Similarly, rising pension costs are the second most important reason for increases in Chinese military spending in the last decade (after pay increases for active personnel), according to China's government (People's Republic of China 2004b).

Growing pension costs for military retirees are important for international power relationships because these expenditures, which are not one-time costs but ones that governments will have to pay every year for many decades, do nothing to increase states' power-projection capabilities. Every dollar spent on retirees is one less dollar that can be spent on weapons, research, or active personnel. Consequently, every dollar spent in this area by the other great powers increases the likelihood of the continuation of U.S. primacy.

Aging in the United States: Bad, But Better Than the Rest

Like the other great powers, the United States is an aging society. The costs created by America's aging population will be staggering. According to a 2007 report issued by the trustees of Social Security and Medicare, over the next 75 years expenditures for these programs are forecasted to be nearly $32 trillion more than revenues. If current trends continue, by 2030 these two programs will require nearly half of all federal income tax dollars. By 2040, they will require nearly two thirds of this revenue (Saving 2007).

Despite these expected cost increases, the United States is in significantly better shape to address the challenges created by its aging population than the other powers. The United States is currently the youngest of all the G8 nations. Because it has the highest fertility and immigration rates of all these countries, it will maintain, even strengthen, this position in coming decades. In 2050 the United States' median age will be the lowest of any of the current great powers, in most cases by a substantial extent (China's median age will surpass the United States' by 2025) (see Table 4.4). Perhaps most important, while the working-age populations in all the other great powers are predicted by 2050 to either decline precipitously (China, Germany, Japan, and Russia) or

Table 4.4 Median Age by Country

Country	Year 1950	Year 2000	Year 2050
United States	30.0	35.3	40.0
France	34.5	37.7	42.7
United Kingdom	34.9	37.7	42.9
Russia	25.0	36.5	43.1
China	23.8	29.7	48.7
Germany	35.4	39.9	49.2
Japan	22.3	41.3	52.3

Source: United Nations Population Division 2011.

increase modestly (Britain and France), this demographic group is expected to increase by 17 percent in the United States (see Table 4.3).

The relatively youthful demographics of the United States will help greatly with the fiscal challenges created by social aging. The United States' growing labor force, which will remain larger than that of other countries relative to its retirees over the next 50 years (see Table 4.5), will contribute to an expanding economy, thereby providing the government with additional revenue without having to increase taxes, borrow more money, or cut other spending. In addition, America's public welfare commitments to the elderly are relatively modest compared with those of other industrialized powers (Peterson 1999, pp. 79–80; Jackson 2003, p. 3); and its tax burden is low compared with those of these other states (OECD 2009).

Again, the preceding facts do not mean that the United States will escape the fiscal burdens created by social aging or that this phenomenon will not create negative ramifications for U.S. security. To the contrary, population aging

Table 4.5 Working Age Adults (Ages 15–64) per Senior Citizen (Ages 65 and Over)

Country	Year 1950	Year 2000	Year 2050
United States	7.83	5.35	2.83
Russia	10.49	5.59	2.60
United Kingdom	6.16	4.12	2.50
China	13.58	9.64	2.39
France	5.79	4.06	2.31
Germany	6.90	4.17	1.77
Japan	12.06	3.97	1.44

Source: United Nations Population Division 2011.

will likely create major costs for America's international interests. In the first place, this phenomenon will reduce the amount of economic or military aid that other states will be able to contribute toward the realization of interests that they share with America. Consequently, instead of increasing "burden sharing" with key allies, the United States will have to pay for even more of the costs to realize its international goals than it does today. Furthermore, at the same time that the United States should expect less international aid from its allies, it, too, is likely to experience the slowing of economic growth and the crowding out of military expenditures for elder care. As a result, America will in all likelihood in coming decades have to scale back the scope of its international policies, to the potential detriment of U.S. security.[4]

Nevertheless, as burdensome as the public costs of aging will be for the United States, the public benefits (pension and health care) owed to U.S. seniors as a percentage of GDP will likely remain substantially lower than in most of the other great powers (Jackson and Howe 2003, p. 7). Moreover, America should be better positioned to pay for these costs than the other major actors in the system. Global aging, despite its costs for American interests, will therefore be a powerful force for the continuation of the relative power dominance of the United States.

America's Golden Years?

The world is currently entering an unprecedented demographic era. Never before has population aging been as pervasive and extensive an issue as it will be in coming decades.

Both the opportunities and challenges for U.S. security in an aging world are substantial. The aging crisis in the United States is less acute than in the other great powers, and its ability to pay the costs associated with this phenomenon is significantly better than these states. These facts, however, should neither disguise the magnitude of these costs for America nor lull U.S. leaders into inaction on this critical issue.

The more the United States maintains its enviable demographic position (compared with the other great powers) and relatively superior ability to pay for the costs associated with its elderly population, the more it will be able both to preserve its own position of international power dominance and to help other states address their aging (and other) problems when it is in U.S. interests to do so. Given these objectives, America should raise the retirement age to reflect increases in life expectancies, reduce Social Security and Medicare payments to wealthier citizens, maintain largely open immigration policies to help keep its median age relatively low, and restrain the rising costs of its health care system.

Although the need for reform on the aging issue is clear and compelling, U.S. politicians have failed to lead on this subject. The immigration reform bill failed to pass Congress in 2007; major Social Security reform has not occurred since the 1980s; and Medicare "reform" has mostly expanded obligations. The 2003 prescription drug benefits legislation, for example, increased the program's unfunded liability by $16.2 trillion.[5]

The longer U.S. leaders delay addressing the growing gap between elder care obligations and resources set aside to pay for them, the more painful these policies will be when they come. Such delay may negate the otherwise substantial demographic advantages America enjoys in relation to the other great powers. However, proactive policies that are designed both to take full advantage of the opportunities created by global aging and to mitigate the costs created by this phenomenon will be a major support to U.S. security throughout the twenty-first century.

Notes

1. Throughout the article, I use the "medium variant" of U.N. (2011) population projections so as to avoid what some might consider overly optimistic or pessimistic assumptions. It should be noted, however, that even the medium variant anticipates a significant increase in fertility rates in states that currently have very low numbers in this area. Population aging thus may very well be even more dramatic than this chapter indicates.

2. An aging population does not necessarily translate into labor force reductions if people continue to work past 65. Most retirement ages in the industrial world, however, remain well below this number, and people have been resistant to changing them (OECD 2007).

3. India—which is another state that analysts point to as a potential power challenger to the United States in the future—is likely to experience many of the same aging challenges as China, though a generation or so later (Haas 2007, pp. 131–133; Eberstadt 2006).

4. In June 2009, President Barack Obama recognized that obligations to the elderly threaten all discretionary spending: "The growing cost of Medicare and Medicaid is the biggest threat to our federal deficit.... So if you're worried about spending and you're worried about deficits, you need to be worried about the cost of [these programs]" (Obama 2009).

5. For an analysis of how the United States is potentially squandering its relative demographic advantages, see Capretta 2007, pp. 48–52.

5

A New Framework for Aging and Security

Lessons from Power Transition Theory

Jennifer Dabbs Sciubba

O F ALL THE HACKNEYED SAYINGS IN OUR LEXICON, one stands out as particularly relevant to population aging: "Necessity is the mother of invention." Nowhere is this more apparent than in Japan, home to the world's oldest population. Long aware that they would face a shortage of care workers for their burgeoning elderly population, Japan's government and industry have teamed to develop a line of robots that provide nursing and other health care services. They have washing machines to bathe the elderly, robotic cats that monitor vital signs as the owner "pets" them, and even robotic nurses with videoconferencing capabilities so that family members can "drop in" on grandma or grandpa for a visit ("Personal Robots to Monitor Elderly Vital Signs" 2009). Not only do these robots potentially ease the care-giving burden, they mean big business. Japanese companies make about 70 percent of the world's industrial robots and the Japanese trade ministry expects Japan's robotics market to grow to $63.5 billion in 2025 ("Japan plans robo-nurses in five years: govt" 2009). Japan has turned a population trend that most term an economic disaster into an economic opportunity, demonstrating that aging brings both challenges and opportunities.

Optimism about aging is rare. Media reports, government intelligence documents, defense assessments, think tank publications, and even leading political science journals warn of an aging crisis where dramatic ratios of old versus young paint visions of doom and gloom. These works are pessimistic because they often use an apolitical explanation of the mechanisms by which aging grows to crisis status. The absence of a theoretical framework within which to structure discussion of population aging has led scholars to underestimate the role of the state in mediating the effects of population. There are plentiful descriptions of fiscal constraints, but little consideration of how policies are made, how states affect the global environment, and how the geopolitical environment affects states. Certainly, political scientists bear only half of the responsibility. Some demographers lack knowledge of political and economic theories and may misinterpret how policies are made.

This book project aims to create synergy between political demography and political science. One of the best ways to do this is to apply political science theory to what we know about demographic trends. In the previous chapter Mark Haas aptly forecasts the implications of current aging trends. He demonstrates that all things being equal, demographic structure can be a force for major changes. With 16 percent of the population of developed countries over age 65 and the rest of the world growing by leaps and bounds, it is not hard to foresee the world he describes: the decline of Europe due to bankrupt social welfare systems, a lack of innovation, political takeover by the aged, and crowding out of defense spending (World Population Data Sheet 2008). But, institutional responses can change these outcomes.

This chapter has the modest aim of adding a more theoretical component to our studies of the political implications of population aging. Power transition theory can help identify several points of leverage states can use to play the demographic cards they've been dealt. Aging, like any demographic force, affects states in myriad ways—their labor forces, militaries, and voting public. But when we privilege the political over the demographic we see that the state can play a role in mediating demographic effects, and though powerful, demography is not destiny. It also becomes clear that strong policies that address aging from multiple angles are extremely important for mediating the effects—no one factor will be a panacea. Though there will always be challenges associated with an aging population, its effects are complex and actions at each leverage point will temper those challenges.

This argument is not meant to dismiss past work on aging in political science. Aging is a new phenomenon and early works could do no more than posit hypotheses and share ideas about ways it could matter for politics, society, and the economy. This chapter draws on early thinking by using power transition theory, first formulated by A. F. K. Organski. As Organski himself argued, "Beginnings must be big and breezy; refinements follow later" (1958, p. 307). But, from our big and breezy beginnings we now need to refine. From a brief description of power transition theory, I will move to examine each of its key variables in the context of aging. Rather than test the theory, I use it as a framework to think systematically and suggest implications about the links between aging and security.

Applying Power Transition Theory

One of the reasons that population aging is relevant to political science is because population is an element of a state's power, and power politics orders the hierarchy of states in the international system. The contributions of a healthy, large population to state power have been discussed for centuries, but A. F. K. Organski was one of the first scholars to systematically incorporate population as a factor in theories of conflict. His power transition theory is still popular for explaining the dynamics of international relations and demonstrating how the process of states vying to become the dominant power in the world system leads to conflict. One reason this is a useful lens for aging is because the theory starts from the premise that power is important in the world system. Organski attempted a dynamic theory that would take into account how changes in multiple variables change state power and, when combined with preferences, affect the hierarchy of states in the international system (DiCicco and Levy 1999). Internal developments are key, especially economic ones. Power transition theory is one of the most enduring research programs in the field of international relations and scholars have continuously returned to it to explain systemic shifts, most recently the rise of China. There have been many criticisms of power transition theory and it has been refined over time but it is still useful to structure our discussion of population aging and security.

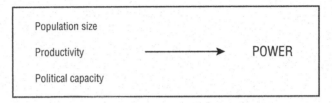

Figure 5.1 Elements of Power Transition Theory

According to the theory, three variables contribute to a state's power: population size, productivity, and political capacity. Power transition theory is a good starting point for thinking systematically about how demography may contribute to security because population size is one of the building blocks of this theory.

The prevailing approach to demography and security leads us to predict that population aging among developed states will reorder the system of great powers and lead to the demise of Russia, Western Europe, and Japan. The tide of population washes up economic turmoil and insecurity as politics and policy disappear—and institutions vanish. When we apply power transition theory, however, we see that states have several points of leverage to prevent complete destruction. As shown in the preceding illustration, a state theoretically has the ability to alter any of the three independent variables—population size, productivity, and political capacity—in their favor and make a positive contribution to their potential power. These, and the factors within each, are the points of leverage for aging states.

Population Size, Reconsidered

Classic power transition theory states the relationship of population to power as the bigger, the better. Size is a key element of power because it provides the potential resource pool that states can mobilize for economic growth, though size alone does not guarantee great power status (Tammen et al. 2000). Organski saw that at its most basic level, population affects a state through providing military manpower and economic production. He argued that supplements, like foreign legions and allies, can help, but a nation needs to have a strong core population of its own (1958).

Though scholars studying population and war have found that states with higher median ages and smaller proportions of youth are the most peaceful states on the planet, there are still security issues (Cincotta et al. 2003). The conventional argument is that with older—and eventually smaller—populations, most European states, Japan, and Russia will be unable to staff and pay for militaries and will likely go broke trying to take care of high proportions of elderly with few workers to support them. The United States and China, with relatively fewer older dependents, are supposedly better positioned to project power in the international system, but even they face challenges associated with aging. The relationship between aging and power is not simple, and I propose that we reconsider the statistics on aging among the great powers and identify points where states have leverage to change trajectory.

An alliance is one of the leverage points underaccounted for in the literature—strength in numbers. What if we stopped thinking about population size just in terms of states, and started thinking about other political units? Even Organski considered population by country *and by political unit.* In his 1958 *World Politics,* this meant looking at China, India, the Soviet Union, the United States and its dependencies, Britain and its dependencies, and so on. Today, we could consider such organizations as the European Union (EU) and the North Atlantic Treaty Organization (NATO). Taken alone, each European state faces a declining population; together, though, they become the third most populous political unit in the world, just behind China and India and ahead of the United States (see Table 5.1).

Contemporary scholarship supports considering political units. Woosang Kim argues that power transition theory is applicable not only to individual powers but also to alliance structures. Challengers will take into account their power plus their supporters' power and also that of the dominant power

Table 5.1 Most Populous States and Political Units in 2010 and 2030, Constant Fertility Variant

2010		2030	
China	1.35 bn	India	1.61 bn
India	1.22 bn	China	1.41 bn
NATO	968 m	NATO	978 m
EU	568 m	EU + Turkey	596 m
US	310 m	EU	506 m
Indonesia	240 m	US	361 m
Brazil	195 m	Indonesia	291 m

Source: United Nations 2011.

Note: NATO and EU 2010 figures are as of June 2011.

and its supporters (Kim 1991). Though progressing with fits and starts, and sometimes facing serious setbacks, over the last several decades member states of the European Union have been growing closer, ceding autonomy in areas traditionally reserved for the state, such as labor policy and control of their borders, and developing common policies. Part of the reason for integration is demography—nearly every EU document mentions Europe's aging trend and low fertility and that joining forces can take greater advantage of comparative strengths. Europe has been growing closer in the area of security policy as well. Most European national leaders support strengthening EU defense; their position can be summed by the minister of defense of the Czech Republic, who holds the 2009 EU presidency:

> By including a defense dimension to the process of Europe's unification … we realized that our efforts might, one day, make the EU a key military as well as political and economic player on the world stage. It is my belief that the EDA has an indispensable role to play in helping Europe to build the defense capabilities necessary to make the EU more independent, more vigilant and better able to address not only "soft" but also "hard" security threats to European interests. (Parkanova 2009, p. 8)

European Union member states have been working to increase military efficiency to reduce reliance on military manpower and relieve pressure on budgets. Whereas most traditional assessments interpret decreased spending on personnel as a sign of weakness, taken in the context of the EU defense goals, spending less on personnel is a necessary step in reducing redundancy and streamlining capabilities. The EU is not the only alliance of aging states, of course. NATO could also be important for helping industrialized Western countries project solidarity and strength. Recently, France recommitted to NATO and the German Federal Ministry of Defense has said, "The North Atlantic Alliance will continue to be the cornerstone of Germany's future security and defense policy" (White Paper on German Security Policy and the Future of the Bundeswehr 2006). Rather than becoming irrelevant in a post–cold war era, NATO could just as likely become more relevant in an era of population aging. Between now and 2050 we could also see the rise (or demise) of other political units, which could become important elements of power in the future. As the Asian Development Bank stated in a 2009 paper, economic integration "can help mitigate many of the negative impacts that aging will have at the domestic level," in part by relying on comparative advantages (Menon and Melendez-Nakamura 2009, p. 5). Alliances can be tenuous and inefficient when compared with the force projection potential of a single state.

The EU is only beginning to combine forces, and often with great resistance. Still, military, economic, and political alliances are increasingly important for aging states in all regions.

There are two other ways to affect population size: immigration and higher fertility. As Haas and others note, the number of immigrants needed to sustain the populations of low-fertility countries like Japan and Germany is immense and prohibitive. Domestic politics demonstrate limited desire to pull the immigration lever. Far-right parties are resurging across Europe, especially in Austria, whose anti-immigrant Austrian Freedom Party (FPÖ) received 18 percent of the vote in the 2008 parliamentary elections (Kraske 2008). Nevertheless, immigration can continue to be manipulated higher and lower as social and economic conditions change.

Higher fertility is a second possibility for changing population size. Much of the pessimism about population size is due to the continuous trend in declining fertility, but new evidence shows that this trend may be slowing down or stopping, though not reversing. Total fertility was "artificially depressed" as a consequence of large proportions of women delaying pregnancy, especially during the 1990s, but the 2010 U.N. population revision reports that industrialized states averaged 1.66 children per woman between 2005 and 2010, up from the 2008 projection of 1.64 and the 2006 projection of 1.35. The 2010 revision projects an even higher fertility for 2010–2015: 1.71 children per woman (United Nations Population Division 2011). Also, the average age of childbearing has stopped rising. Demographer John Bongaarts says that the higher fertility rate will probably continue for some time unless women decide to delay childbirth even further (Block 2009). This addition of 0.3 children can make a big difference in projections for 2030 or 2050.

However, it is not likely that these societies are going to reverse their aging process or that there has been a miraculous turnaround in fertility. Due to demographic momentum these populations will continue to grow older. Also, the 2010 U.N. revisions to data anticipate more favorable fertility in the long run, but we should expect that the global recession may cause couples to delay having children. While I do not want to overstate the contribution that increasing fertility or immigration could make to national power, it is important to at least recognize that we should not take projections for granted as states may have some leverage in this area. For example, making the work environment friendlier for women is one of the most concrete ways Europe and Japan can raise fertility (Europe's Demographic Future: Growing Imbalances 2008).

The composition of the society is also relevant. As Alfred Sauvy once worried, we may end up with a "society of old people, living in old houses, ruminating about old ideas" (quoted in Wattenberg 1987, p. 67). "Old" in an advanced industrial democracy isn't what it was when social security systems were devised. Considering ages 60 or 65 as the point at which people become dependents and stop contributing to society is no longer appropriate. "The population age 65 to 75 is healthier, wealthier, and better educated than this age group in past generations. Future groups of older people are likely to be even better off. They too will redefine 'retirement' and 'old age'" (Friedland and Summer 2005, p. 3). Even with increasing proportions of those over age 65, states can enact policies that allow older persons to help contribute to the state's power. Other aspects of the population's composition are equally important. Literate, healthy, and tolerant citizens are likely to do more to contribute to a state's potential power than those who have not had the opportunity for education and who struggle with basic needs.

Productivity

Applying power transition theory to aging states demonstrates that population is an essential, but not the single, component of power. According to the theory, "[i]n order to be truly powerful the population also must be productive.... But those advantages cannot be realized without political capacity, defined as the ability of governments to extract resources to advance national goals" (Tammen et al. 2000, p. 9). Population supposedly affects power in the long term, but economic growth changes power in the medium term. The power transition argument about economic growth is similar to the general arguments about population aging made in the political science literature: Aging states are economically disadvantaged because of the anticipated future growth in elderly dependents and the accompanying reduction in the proportion of workers. Aging therefore threatens the ability of Europe and Japan to project economic power and fund their militaries because their shrinking labor forces and growing elderly dependents will retard economic growth while the more youthful China and India continue to experience record growth.

Despite these concerns, there are several reasons why the economies of developed aging countries could potentially overcome their demographic structure. First, absolute labor strength is only one driver of economic growth. Technology, efficiency, and capital are also essential. Developed states are attractive for investors because they are stable, have well-educated populations, and have established infrastructures. Less developed states may have higher proportions of working-age citizens but, because they usually lack in the other realms, pose a higher investment risk. Investors looking to diversify and spread risk not only invest in emerging markets where a high return is possible, they also invest capital in states that will bring slow, steady growth, even if at a lower return.

Efficiency is also important. There is no reason that today's workers cannot be more productive than their parents, even if they are part of a smaller cohort. Population aging can be a positive force that drives innovation because societies have to compensate for the changes aging brings. As mentioned at the beginning of this chapter, Japan's technological sector has been growing and adapting to the needs of its burgeoning elderly population.

Finally, aging states can use the global system of trade and finance to their advantage. Ralph C. Bryant of the Brookings Institution is optimistic about aging and "emphasizes that failure to take into account the macroeconomic effects working through exchange rates and cross-border flows could lead to an inaccurate assessment of the net impact of demographic change" (Menon and Melendez-Nakamura 2009, p. 5). Industrialized states continue to enjoy many advantages in the economic realm, despite aging.

Aging states are quite different from aging individuals, whose cognitive capacity may dwindle over time. Japan and Germany are leaders in innovative technology at the same time that they lead the world in aging. Though the median age of these states is rising, there will continue to be a new crop of bright, young minds to complement the experience of older generations. Developed aging states are likely to keep their status as centers of innovation because youthful developing states lack the climate conducive to advancement. Developed states attract the best and brightest from developing countries with superior educational opportunities; developing states have weak institutions, poor governance, and few legal protections for innovation. According to the World Intellectual Property Organization, applicants from Japan, the United States, Germany, and South Korea received 73 percent of total patent grants worldwide in 2006. China's share of filings and patent holdings is growing, but Japanese applicants still owned the majority of patents in force in 2006 (World Patent Report: A Statistical Review 2008). Anne-Marie Slaughter, writing for *Foreign Affairs*, argues that despite China's growth, its gap with the United States is not likely to narrow because of cultural reasons. Educational institutions in the United States emphasize critical thinking and foster a culture of innovation. She argues that:

> A culture that requires a constant willingness to reimagine the world is not one that the Chinese Communist Party is likely to embrace. Indeed, a culture of innovation

requires the encouragement of conflict within a larger culture of transparency and trust, placing a premium on cross-cultural competence. (Slaughter 2009, p. 108)

The same could likely be said of Japan and Germany.

States also have leverage to improve their labor forces, which will be necessary despite other economic levers. Nearly all aging states have large underutilized segments of their working populations. By bringing youth, women, and older workers aged 50 to 64 into the workforce, a state can make short-term strides in the portion of GDP growth attributable to labor.

European and Japanese policymakers are aware of this relationship and have been instituting policies to reconcile work and family life. For example, Germany is notorious for its lack of childcare facilities, which many see as the major obstacle to women rejoining the labor force after having children. In January 2007 the German government instituted a new parental allowance, *Elterngeld,* which entitles every new parent to a state allowance worth 67 percent of their salary, under the condition that they stop working for a year after having a child. The measure has so far been effective in causing a spike in the birthrate in certain communities, like Düsseldorf, though this may be a short-term effect (Benoit 2007). Though studies show that increased female LFP can decrease fertility in the absence of policies that address child care, there is a positive association between child care enrollment and fertility (Hilgeman and Butts 2009).

Demographer David Coleman is similarly optimistic about Europe, given that (prerecession) European economies continued to grow despite declining worker-to-pensioner ratios. He recommends three reforms for European states to combat the ill effects of population aging: Bring more latent laborers into the workforce; alter pay-as-you-go pension systems; and improve worker productivity (Coleman 2005). The Asian Development Bank makes similar recommendations for aging Asia and is also optimistic that this basket of reforms can mitigate the effects of an older age structure (Menon and Melendez-Nakamura 2009). There are many obstacles to these reforms, but trends thus far in aging states towards a more open labor market and stricter benefits suggest that states are making progress.

Are any of these measures actually enough to prevent the decline of military power? They are when we add one more layer: the role of geopolitical concerns. Economic calculations are not the only determinant of defense spending. States that have a strong desire to fund and build their militaries are usually able to find a way to do so. Japan, though it is the most aged state on the planet and has lackluster economic growth, has been moving towards a more independent role with its security forces for at least two reasons: the potentially decreasing role of the United States in Japan's security protection and the development of external threats. For any state, external threats are a powerful driver of defense spending, even when times are tough. During the Great Depression the United States devoted a huge portion of its GDP to national defense to mobilize for World War II, and ran up the federal debt to do so (Historical Tables: Budget of the United States Government 2004). Europe and Japan would likely be willing to do the same, depending on the severity of the threat. Twenty-three of 26 participating member states of the European Defense Agency increased defense expenditure from 2006 to 2007. In total, the EDA increased expenditure by 1.5 percent (Defense Data of European Defense Agency participating Member States in 2007). Especially remarkable are the Eastern European states—with the lowest fertility in Europe—which increased their defense spending by large percentages in order to match Western European states. At the same time, as Haas notes, Japan and many other aging states have been cutting defense expenditures, and relying on debt may not be feasible in the future. We should not place too much emphasis on any statistics without examining how states are spending their money. Are they spending more wisely, focusing on efficiency, for example? Are they putting their money into developing specific capabilities and abandoning platforms that no longer meet their goals? States have many goals—military, social, economic, political—and in their desire to meet these goals states can overcome the limitations of their demography. However, the threat level may need to be higher to incite action in an aging world than a nonaging world, since leaders will be less willing to squander precious resources—lives, expensive equipment, and their reputations.

Political Capacity

Power transition theorists define political capacity as "the ability of governments to extract resources from their populations in order to advance the policy goals of the government" (Tammen et al. 2000, p. 16). The assumption is that as states experience economic growth, the government can get more out of the population in the form of taxes. As was the case with the economic variable, advanced industrialized democracies are thought to have little room to improve in this arena, since taxes are already high, so many assume that there is not much they can do to increase their power. This definition of political capacity should be expanded. To begin, there are other ways for the government to mobilize its people. Historically, youth have been mobilized for military or community service through a draft. Similarly, older persons can be mobilized through senior corps, as we see in many countries, such as the United States. When leaders recognize that older persons have valuable skills to share, they become an asset instead of a burden.

An even broader interpretation of political capacity regards state institutions. Institutions themselves—the political party system, the place of interest groups, the organization of the state—can help states deal with aging because they mediate and articulate the interests of the population, even without leaders taking action in the form of policies to deal with their age structures. Political actions, too, are a key intermediating variable between aging and various political outcomes, like economic growth and military spending. Most assessments of population aging seem to assume that policies offering generous benefits towards the elderly will continue indefinitely. The most common reason given is that growing numbers of elderly voters will ensure that their welfare is protected to the detriment of youth. As one recent book claims, "the political resistance from electorates increasingly dominated by elderly voters is likely to be intense" (Jackson and Howe 2008, p. 66). Evidence from some countries contradicts this assumption. Seniors are often not unified, and there have been cuts to their benefits despite opposition. In Germany, for example, elderly voters are fragmented and spread their support among the main parties (Sciubba 2008). Additionally, Germany, Italy, and Japan are all instituting higher retirement ages, getting rid of early retirement schemes, and working to bring youth and women into the labor market. These measures are being instituted at the same time that their electorates—and often their politicians—are older than ever. Progress is so far uneven; though states are instituting some tough measures, others, like efforts to increase retirement ages, are weak.

Some institutions are better than others for preventing the emergence of age-based interests. The EU mandate that member states institute measures to combat the economic effects of population aging makes a positive contribution to Europe's power. Domestically, the type of party system and role of interest groups in policymaking can make a difference as well. The ability of interest groups to direct policy in the United States may mean that policies that favor the elderly at the expense of other generations—and economic growth in general—are more likely to continue there than in states where interest groups have a more limited role. If that is the case, the United States, though relatively younger than its peers, may actually be at a greater disadvantage as it ages than those peers are. A state with weak institutions may also be disadvantaged.

The type of political system—ranging from authoritarian to fully democratic—may matter as well. Democratic leaders must factor in the demands of various interest groups and the power of voters, whereas less democratic governments can ignore some of these demands. Singapore, with its "managed democracy," illustrates how a system that restricts the role of its citizens can institute the tough measures needed to deal with population aging. The Singaporean government has made taking care of elderly parents the legal responsibility of children (Menon and Melendez-Nakamura 2009). They have also proposed requiring companies to rehire older workers after the age of 62 to raise worker participation and have instituted other measures to make the labor market more flexible, such as wage reforms that will move from seniority-based to job-worth and performance-based compensation (Magnus 2009). China could follow in Singapore's footsteps. Its authoritarian government gives it the ability to be heavy handed with reforms, so they could actually fare well as they rapidly age. Of course, we cannot assume that China won't liberalize. If it does, the power of seniors could go up, but the fact that older Chinese have not been socialized in a democracy means that they might not vote and might support any regime offering cheap benefits. We saw some of this in Russia after the end of the cold war, where those used to living under communist rule preferred the status quo to abrupt change.

Implications

According to power transition theory, war results from a combination of relative power and the goals or preferences of a state. Power parity mixed with dissatisfaction is a recipe for war. By shaping the preferences of competitors to match their own, aging states gain more peace, and secure their position in the international system: "For Power Transition, the important element is similarity of governments' foreign policy goals across time that fosters satisfaction with the status quo.... [S]tates with economic and political institutions similar to those of the dominant power likely will be satisfied with the status quo" (Tammen et al. 2000, p. 23). Despite aging populations—or perhaps because of them—advanced industrial states can have a peaceful security environment if they remain influential on the world stage and retain the ability to shape the preferences of potential challengers. This theory seems to support the thesis that increasing liberalization and globalization will foster peace in an aging world.

Population size and composition are only part of the equation that calculates a state's power, and policies can even affect those variables. States have leverage in their economic productivity and political capacity as well. Furthermore, political science should structure our discussion of the effects of aging. We should not ignore how policies are made, how states affect the global environment, or how the geopolitical environment affects states. Rather, these aspects should be central to our discussions of aging and security. Though the literature underestimates the role of the state in mediating the effects of population aging, by applying power transition theory we can begin to see areas where states have the ability to institute policies that address their demographic structures. As Harold and Margaret Sprout stated in 1945, "Manpower and economic resources are essential, but tools, skills, and organization are required to transmute them into political power and influence" (1945, p. 29). On this point Mark Haas and I agree: Leadership may offset the effects of aging, but that leadership must be strong and competent.

The preceding discussion of population size and age structure makes the argument for increasing European integration and strengthening NATO. According to power transition theory, the future of great power politics depends on Europe's ability to present a united front, which is a major challenge. If NATO grows stronger, so will the power and influence of its members. But there are many obstacles to NATO's development as well. The organization must also take into account the often opposite U.S. position, and U.S. leaders have been in a constant state of marketing and negotiating to strengthen the alliance and find support for U.S. operations in Iraq and Afghanistan. Though Europe and Japan are aging, they can still be beneficial security partners as they fight disease, protect critical infrastructure, or prevent the spread of weapons of mass destruction (Glosserman and Tsunoda 2009).

Also, Russia's recent aggressive behavior with energy, Georgia, and NATO may be part of an emerging pattern. According to power transition theorist Dale Copeland, "the probability of major war increases when decline is seen as both deep and inevitable" (2000, p. 15). Russia's high mortality and aging and dwindling population could thus be a major factor in tense global relations. Copeland says, "A state … that is superior in military power but *inferior* in economic and especially potential power is more likely to believe that, once its military power begins to wane, further decline will be inevitable and deep" (2000, p. 20). Russia's demographic decline may drive the leadership to more aggressive behavior over the coming decade.

Acting on these leverage points does not ensure that states emerge victorious from their battle with aging. Haas and others may be correct that global aging creates pressures that make specific developments more likely than others. But aging is just one pressure among many. Some of these others, such as economic productivity or robust institutions, are likely to contribute to the continuation of the power of aging states, despite their demography. Aging states need bold policies that mediate the effects of their changing demographic structures and should ensure that their goals and preferences mesh so that they can project power collectively. Certainly, no single factor is the panacea for an aging state. While states will certainly face many challenges associated with aging, these states are not destined for decline.

Part III

Demography, Development, and Conflict

6

Age Structure and Development through a Policy Lens

Elizabeth Leahy Madsen

To mark World Population Day in July 2008, President Yoweri Museveni of Uganda released a statement in support of the country's rapidly growing population, a demographic trajectory that leaves the nation with the youngest age structure in the world. "Uganda has got much more natural resources than [developed countries]. How can we fail to cope with a population of 30 million or the subsequent increases?" the president's statement read (quoted in Baguma and Ssengendo 2008). Despite a fertility rate of nearly seven children per woman, a primary school dropout rate of 75 percent, and a recent increase in the poverty rate, Uganda's longtime leader believes that population growth will provide the labor pool and consumer market to spur economic expansion.

Meanwhile, the government of South Korea, a country on a path toward rapid population decline, is expending significant resources trying to turn around its own trajectory, a reverse image of Uganda's. Concerned that the country's population is projected to decline 13 percent by midcentury in its own forecasts, the government has unveiled a suite of incentives to promote higher fertility rates and address population aging (Choi 2009), completing a total turnaround from the intensive family-planning program employed a generation ago.

These two examples illustrate both the diversity of current population trends across the world and the disparities in political engagement and policy response to demographic issues. Although research demonstrates that demography influences countries' security and governance, and demographic trends can respond dramatically to policy decisions, population issues are often treated peripherally or not at all in political discourse. This chapter aims to promote a more comprehensive integration of demography and politics by highlighting the complex relationships between population and development, the ways in which such relationships have been inadequately addressed in countries with very different demographic trajectories, and recommendations for a more inclusive treatment of demography as a political force.

The chapter begins with a review of the research findings related to population and two aspects of development at the global scale, as evaluated through cross-national studies. Next, these relationships are applied to the national setting in two case studies of age structure and development in Uganda and South Korea, whose age structures represent the beginning and end of the demographic transition. The case studies also analyze the interaction between political factors and each country's demographic trends. The chapter concludes by returning to a global perspective to consider how demography fits into the policy dialogue along the age structure spectrum.

Age Structure, Conflict, and Governance

All countries' populations can be classified into one of four major age structure types based on their progression through the demographic transition—the decades-long shift from high to low mortality and fertility rates. The four age structure types relate the share of a population comprised of children and young adults under the age of 30 to the share of older adults above age 60 and are termed *very young, youthful, transitional,* and *mature* (Leahy et al. 2007).

Generally, countries with a "very young" age structure are those in which two-thirds or more of the population is younger than 30. In 2010, there were

49 such countries with a total population of nearly 1 billion, including nearly all of sub–Saharan Africa. Once a country's fertility rate declines below 4 children per woman, it is likely to reach the second category of age structures, those termed "youthful." The 32 countries in this category in 2010, with a combined population of nearly 700,000, included Bangladesh, Pakistan, and the Philippines. Countries in the middle of the demographic transition with a "transitional" age structure have a fertility rate lower than 3 children per woman; between 45 and 60 percent of their population is comprised of young people under age 30. These 56 countries, including China and India, had a combined population of 4 billion in 2010. At the end of the demographic transition, countries with a "mature" age structure have fertility rates at the replacement level of 2.1 children per woman or below; 40 percent or less of their population is under age 30, while up to one-quarter of the population is composed of older adults above 60. In 2010, the 59 countries with this type of age structure totaled 1.4 billion people and included nearly all of Europe.[1]

In an analysis of all new outbreaks of civil conflict with at least 25 battle deaths between 1970 and 2007 (Gleditsch et al. 2002; Uppsala Conflict Data Program and International Peace Research Institute 2008), countries with a very young age structure type were more than three times as likely to have experienced conflict than those with mature age structures that had completed the demographic transition (Leahy Madsen, Daumerie and Hardee 2010). Although there is a decline in risk of conflict with each successive age structure type, the most profound difference in likelihood lies between the first two categories of age structures. Countries with very young age structures are twice as likely to have experienced civil conflict as those with youthful age structures, demonstrating that some degree of fertility decline, even if fertility rates remain well above replacement level, may have broader ramifications.

The associations between age structure and conflict are verified and further quantified by empirical analysis. Urdal (2006) has shown that countries in which the share of young people aged 15 to 24 exceeded 35 percent of the total adult population were 150 percent more likely to experience an outbreak of civil conflict between 1950 and 2000 than those with a more balanced age structure, controlling for level of development and other factors. A youthful age structure is most strongly correlated with outbreaks of conflict in the case of countries with ongoing high fertility rates. Once fertility rates begin to decline and the demographic transition is underway, outbreaks of conflict are less likely, even though a country retains a youthful age structure due to demographic momentum from previous generations of high fertility.

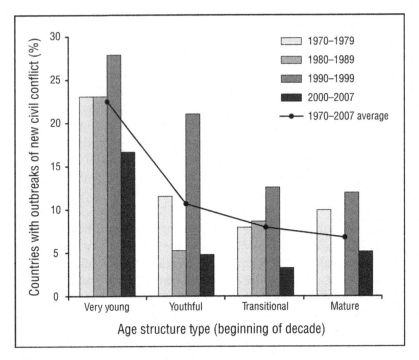

Figure 6.1   Risk of Civil Conflict by Age Structure Type

Research has also examined the relationship between age structure, regime type, and governance. Cincotta (2009) describes a "Hobbesian bargain" in which autocracies and partial democracies are more common in countries with a youthful age structure precisely because such age structures are also prone to instability and conflict. Moreover, if states with a young age structure do attain liberal democracy, they are prone to backsliding or otherwise reverting towards authoritarianism. Once the "youth bulge" ratio of young adults ages 15 to 29 as a share of the working-age adult population falls below 40 percent, countries are more likely to have regimes characterized by liberal democracy.

Other analyses reveal that the probability of a government being rated as a full democracy (Polity IV Project 2008) progressively increases as countries pass through the demographic transition. Between 1970 and 2007, 13 percent of countries with very young age structures and 81 percent of countries with mature age structures were classified as full democracies, on average, at the end of each decade (Leahy Madsen, Daumerie and Hardee 2010). This pat-

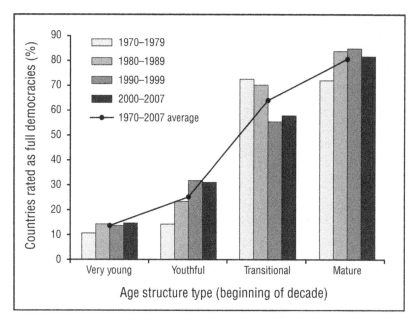

Figure 6.2 Likelihood of Democracy by Age Structure Type

tern continues with other measurements of governance: Countries with very young and youthful age structures are also more likely to be characterized by weak institutional capacity, government corruption, poor regulatory quality, and fewer political freedoms and civil liberties (Freedom House 2008; World Bank 2008).

These research results not only clarify critical relationships between population, conflict, and governance, but also help demographers introduce population issues into the political framework. It is clear that there is no direct causal relationship between population and conflict or population and democracy—no single demographic threshold that, once crossed, leaves a state doomed to upheaval or tyranny. Researchers have widely reiterated that the presence of a young age structure is not sufficient to create conflict, nor does a mature age structure guarantee domestic peace; rather, underlying social conditions that create grievance and make involvement in an insurgency a viable or even appealing option are necessary. In fact, because of the role of factors such as

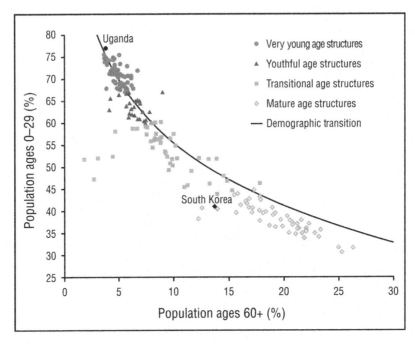

Figure 6.3   Age Structures Along the Demographic Transition, 2005

poverty, inequity, institutional capacity, and social well-being, the relationship is more holistically framed as one between population and development.

A case study approach is helpful in filtering overarching global relationships between demography and development to a smaller scale. Analysis of the connections between age structure, security, governance, and social factors at the country level further illuminates how these macro-level trends unfold among individual states, where most policymakers are focused. For example, in Uganda, which has the youngest age structure in the world, high fertility rates are welcomed by President Museveni, who sees population growth as instrumental to the country's future economic gains. Yet civil conflict is spilling across neighboring borders and growing numbers of young people have few legitimate economic prospects. Meanwhile, the president, nearing 25 years in power, prepares to run for another term. In the case of South Korea, the government has reversed its population policy from actively encouraging smaller family size as recently as the 1980s to rolling out financial incentives in an attempt to turn around a rapidly dropping fertility rate that now approaches one child per woman.

Very Young Age Structures: The Case of Uganda

Despite major strides in increasing agricultural production and improving school enrollment rates, Uganda's very young age structure challenges further development. More than three-quarters of the population is younger than age 30, the highest rate in the world. With a fertility rate averaging nearly 7 children per woman, Uganda remains in the early phase of the demographic transition, and its age structure has been unchanged for decades (Figure 6.4). Even if fertility rates begin to fall at a much faster pace, the country's population would double between 2010 and 2035 (United Nations Population Division 2011).

Despite an annual GDP growth rate ranging between 5 and 11 percent over the last decade (World Bank 2009), Uganda's very young age structure

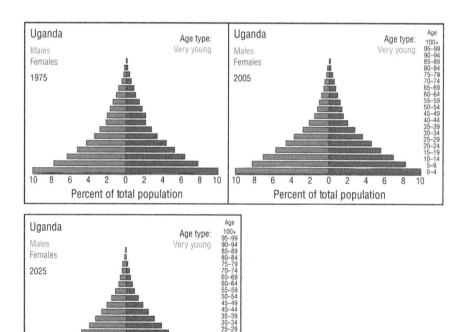

Note: Age structure for 2025 projected based on the medium-fertility variant at United Nations Population Division 2009.

Figure 6.4   Uganda's Age Structure, 1975, 2005, and 2025

is likely to have major impacts on the economy. Eighty percent of the labor force works in agriculture, even as this sector's share of the total economy is falling (Food and Agriculture Organization 2009). However, the availability of cropland is diminishing with each generation as plots are divided among children, creating serious consequences for poverty and food security among much of the population. More than three-quarters of Uganda's people live on less than two dollars per day (World Bank 2009), and the number of people living in poverty has grown rapidly in this decade (Wakabi 2006).

Although policies to eliminate fees for primary and secondary school have met with some success, educational gains have not been matched in employment. Estimates are spotty, but one government official has reported that over 22 percent of Ugandan youth are unemployed, and those with postsecondary education and in urban areas are particularly constrained in finding jobs (World Bank 2007b). The size of Uganda's population ages 15 to 24, those most likely to be entering the labor force, doubled between 1990 and 2010, and this age cohort now represents one-fifth of the country's total population (United Nations Population Division 2011). As the number of students and entrants to the labor market grows, this demographic profile creates dual challenges in maintaining adequate financing for education and generating new jobs.

President Museveni's hold on power has strengthened in recent years. In 2004, he proposed the introduction of a multiparty political system, a move that won praise from international observers. However, in the same reform process, Museveni also rescinded presidential term limits, granted himself authority to dissolve the parliament, and implemented policy changes that restrict the oversight authority of the parliament over cabinet members.

The president's firm approach was perceived as beneficial in the first decades of his presidency, when he was able to achieve economic gains and civil stability following mass murder and economic collapse under two dictators. However, gains toward democracy have been limited; Uganda has been rated as a mixed authority state by the Polity IV Project (2008) since Museveni's ascension to power.

The rapidly growing population compounds concern about the extent to which the lack of democracy, with its attendant deeply enshrined patronage politics and widespread corruption, will inhibit economic development and threaten the interests of the Ugandan people more broadly (Mwenda 2007). Despite declining popularity, Museveni successfully ran for a fourth official term in 2011. Although clashes between protesters and soldiers occurred on the occasion of his visit to a tribal landmark that was destroyed by fire in early 2010 the political transition was free from major violence.

In a 2008 interview, Museveni underplayed the complex interplay between demography and development policies stating, "The population of the whole of Africa is smaller than the population of India. The problem of Africa is not population ... it is underdevelopment, and to some extent, even underdevelopment is caused by underpopulation ... for instance, the phenomenon of exporting raw materials instead of exporting finished products" (International Reporting Project 2008). Such explanations assume that the large potential labor force generated by population growth will inevitably expand beyond agriculture into manufacturing and technical industries. The advancements in human capital required to achieve such an economic transformation are substantial and become more difficult to implement with a growing population. As shown by the experience of the Asian Tigers, fertility decline and associated demographic change together with an educated workforce and capable institutions can motivate rapid economic growth (Bloom et al. 2000). Although these connections are supported in Uganda's official development policies, Museveni's frequent assertions that population growth alone is a sufficient economic force undermine the policies' effectiveness. After a quarter-century in power, the president's politics have become entangled with demographic trends in Uganda, to the detriment of the country's development.

Mature Age Structures: The Case of South Korea

In contrast to Uganda, South Korea's demographic trajectory is generally not received favorably in domestic political discourse. With its exceedingly rapid demographic change, ongoing dialogue about population policies and the complicated security dynamics with an unpredictable northern neighbor, South Korea makes a particularly interesting case study of a country on the forefront of aging.

South Korea's progress through the demographic transition over recent decades has been remarkable. In 1970, the country had a very young age structure with 67 percent of its population under the age of 30, similar in profile to Haiti and Sri Lanka at the time. Although South Korea was still in the middle stages of a mature age structure in 2010, it is projected to have one of the 20 oldest age structures in the world in 2025, even assuming the country's extremely low fertility rate reverses its rapid decline and begins to rise (Figure 6.5).

According to its own estimates, South Korea will achieve an "aged" society, with 14 percent of its population over the age of 65, significantly faster than other developed countries, even Japan (Korea Institute for Health and Social

Affairs 2007). After doubling in less than 45 years at the turn of the century, the country's population is projected to decline 11 percent by 2050 if current fertility rates hold constant (United Nations Population Division 2011). The implications of this rapid decline for the labor market are striking: Under the UN's medium-fertility variant, which assumes an uptick in fertility rates to 1.8 by 2050, South Korea's total population would shrink by 2 percent, but the drop in the potential labor force (as measured by the population ages 15 to 64) would reach nearly 30 percent (United Nations Population Division 2011).

The government's decision to take an active approach to demographic issues in 1961 reflected a very different outlook, given a fertility rate at that time of six children per woman. Developments that year included the formation of a national family-planning program and promotion of a national slogan to "have few children and bring them up well" (Republic of Korea 1994). However, the strong cultural preference for sons emerged as a barrier to fertility decline. By 1971, the government had revised the family-planning slogan to "stop at two regardless of sex" and within the decade had adopted the even stronger word-ing of "a well-bred girl surpasses 10 boys." Through the early 1980s, even as fertility had dropped to replacement level, the government continued to push for even more dramatic demographic change. Its programs did not reflect un-derstanding of the deep-seated factors, particularly related to gender, that were already driving a precipitous decline in fertility. In 1984, the family-planning slogan became "even two are too many." By the late 1980s, the objectives for dramatic fertility decline had certainly been achieved, as the total fertility rate dropped to 1.6 children per woman by 1988.

Demographic and socioeconomic factors explain part, but not all, of South Korea's very low fertility rate. The average age at marriage was already relatively high (21.6 for women and 25.4 for men) when the family-planning program began in the 1960s, and increased further over the ensuing decades (Republic of Korea 1994). By 2005, 16 percent of women remained single at age 50, and births outside of marriage were rare, further motivating low fertility (Suzuki 2008). Abortion is more common than in other developed countries; 26 per-cent of pregnancies are terminated in South Korea (Oum 2003), compared to roughly 20 percent worldwide (Sedgh et al. 2007). The country has also rapidly urbanized, with 80 percent of the population living in urban areas in 2000 compared to 28 percent in 1960 (Kwon 2003).

Other drivers of South Korea's rapid decline in fertility are often described as rooted in culture and different from the motivations behind the more moderate fertility declines in Western Europe (Suzuki 2008). The total fertility rate is much lower than the desired fertility rate, which hovers around 2.2 children

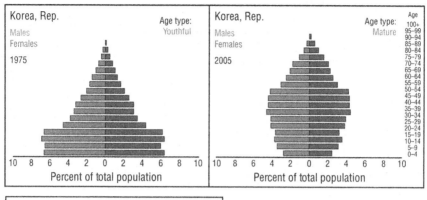

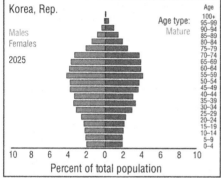

Note: Age structure for 2025 projected based on the medium-fertility variant at United Nations Population Division 2009.

Figure 6.5   South Korea's Age Structure, 1975, 2005, and 2025

per woman, indicating that on average, women are having fewer children than they would like (Suzuki 2008). Because gender roles have remained rigid despite increasing female labor force participation, women find it difficult or unappealing to balance work and family demands (Lee 2009). Economic concerns also play a role, especially after the financial shocks of the 1990s that have recurred a decade later, given the tremendous expenses of private tutoring and college tuition in a society that places a high premium on education. In a 2006 survey, fewer than one-fifth of Korean respondents agreed that their society "is good for raising a child" (Suzuki 2008, p. 34).

In South Korea, as in Japan, fertility rates remain below 1.5 children per woman. Recent research found that a "failure to … facilitate work-life balance and gender equality" may explain these countries' exception from a trend of movement from very low fertility back toward replacement fertility (2.1 children per woman) in the most developed countries (Myrskylä et al. 2009, p. 742).

In 2005, when the national total fertility rate reached 1.08, the country officially shifted to a pronatalist stance with the Basic Law on Low Fertility and Aging Society and a suite of policy proposals announced the following year. Despite the delayed response, the degree of current and projected low fertility and population aging is now viewed as a problem with critical economic and social implications. The government has noted that inflexible gender roles and their impact on employment conditions are also present in the neighboring low-fertility countries, and describes South Korea as part of an "East Asian culture" that includes "Confucian patriarchy." By contrast, Sweden, France, and the United States are identified as relatively high-fertility countries whose policies may serve as a model for South Korea (Korea Institute for Health and Social Affairs 2007). The package of policy incentives announced in 2006 includes child care subsidies, tax breaks, and expanded public education programs, with a total annual budget of 3.8 trillion won[2] (Suzuki 2008).

Various economic consequences of South Korea's changing demography that are likely to be compounded by fluctuating social conditions are generating concern, among them financing care of the elderly. While cultural norms prescribe that older adults are cared for by their offspring, the practice is not universal, and an increasing share of the elderly are living alone (Kim 2000). The government has announced an incremental increase in the official retirement age of 60; yet the effective retirement age for men is 71, second-highest among the OECD countries, and 68 for women (OECD 2006). Raising the labor force participation rate among women is an alternate response to the economic impacts of aging that would carry significant potential benefits. Currently, just over half of working-age women are in the labor force, and the male participation rate is also lower than the average for developed countries. According to analysis by the World Bank, an increase in female labor force participation rates to match those of Japan and in male rates to the OECD average would lift economic growth half a percentage point (Ianchovichina and Leipziger 2008).

South Korea's official transition to democracy occurred in 1987, when the country was in the middle of the demographic transition, but it has only been rated as a "full democracy" by the Polity IV Project (2008) since 1998. Following its recovery from the 1997 financial crisis, the 2004 presidential impeachment, and another changeover of ruling parties in the 2007 election, the country is now described as a consolidated, possibly even a mature, democracy (Chaibong 2008; Kihl 2009). Along with a stronger democracy has come a more active civil society, which is likely to play a stronger role in shaping domestic policies. Although the package of fertility incentives and responses to aging implemented in 2006 was driven from the top, political activists could have more influence in shaping future responses to the consequences of demographic change.

Although much of South Korea's foreign policy engagement focuses on its relationship with China, Japan, and the United States, the national security outlook is dominated by its uneasy relationship with North Korea. Following his inauguration in early 2008, President Lee Myung-bak initially took a cooler stance toward the northern neighbor, designating the relationship as a lower priority than had his predecessors. North Korea's reaction to the new administration has not been favorable, with hostile rhetoric in 2008 followed by a nuclear test and missile launch in 2009. Analysts do not anticipate a thawing in peninsular relations in the near future, and attention has shifted to a potential dynastic succession in the north. Despite a promise for a more active role in international development and other areas of engagement, the country's "national history of security vulnerability induces a natural caution" (Snyder 2009, p. 97). Rapid aging could magnify the existing tendency to take an inward-focused approach, but even with a graying population, the shifting dynamics of the regional balance of power are likely to continue to draw a fair share of political energy in South Korea.

South Korea's political leaders believe that the trend towards ever-lower fertility rates can be reversed, and have identified goals of achieving a total fertility rate of 1.6 by the 2010s and 1.8 the following decade. If the target rates are achieved, the government projects a total population size 14 percent larger by 2050 than if fertility holds constant at the 2005 level. The scale of demographic change being experienced in South Korea will demand a comprehensive set of policies encompassing structural factors, not only relatively easy fixes like increases in the retirement age and more affordable child care. Achieving lasting demographic change will likely require the government to tackle thornier policy dilemmas such as education costs, openness to immigration, and particularly the longstanding barriers to gender equity.

Demographics and the Policy Dialogue

As seen in the opposing trajectories of Uganda and South Korea, the most notable characteristic of current population trends is their disparity, which has created a "demographic divide" unparalleled in history. These differences demand unique policy responses, particularly in regard to projections of the world's demographic future, which are sometimes taken for granted. More than 50 percent of the world's people live in countries with fertility rates higher than replacement level, guaranteeing ongoing population growth for the long term. Within this group, almost 1 billion people live in countries where populations are on pace to double in less than 35 years at current fertility rates. Meanwhile, over 40 percent of the world's population resides in countries at the end of the demographic transition, with fertility rates below replacement level. So far, population decline is underway in 16 countries, concentrated in Eastern Europe, but also including Germany, Japan, and Russia (United Nations Population Division 2011).

While only one region is experiencing population decline—Eastern Europe, which is projected to decline by 3 percent between 2010 and 2025—southern and western Europe and eastern Asia are all projected to have less than 5 percent growth in this period. By contrast, growth continues many times faster in some areas (see Figure 6.6); the populations of eastern, middle, and western Africa are all projected to grow by more than 40 percent in the next 15 years.

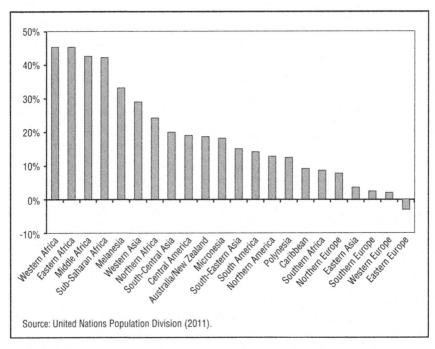

Source: United Nations Population Division (2011).

Figure 6.6   Regional Projected Population Change, 2010 to 2025

Diminished demographic weight among regions such as Europe and East Asia is an unavoidable reality, and there is little doubt that population aging will have significant economic and social consequences. Aging is a new phenomenon in human society—a product of improved public health, in addition to lower fertility rates—and governments' responses are still nascent. With decades of experience, successful policy responses in countries experiencing very young age structures are better understood, yet each country must consider its own underlying conditions.

Because aging is a new threshold, it is difficult to predict how societies will respond and adapt to it. Human ingenuity and adaptability, most clearly represented by technological advancements, diffused the dire predictions of mass starvation predicted by Paul Ehrlich in 1968 even as world population doubled. Today's fast-aging countries are marked not only by their high per capita incomes and advanced industries but also by stable and democratic political frameworks, all of which are likely to serve as protective factors as developed countries continue the aging process.

Numerous policy responses have been proposed, including extending the tenure of working years, importing labor through immigration, addressing the underlying causes of low fertility rates, and modifying health care and social welfare systems. Recent research points to a slight reversal of aging trends in some countries (Myrskylä et al. 2009). However, in cases where fertility reaches rock-bottom rates well below replacement level, demography may be only a symptom of larger social problems related to gender balance and the culture of work (Boling 2008; Morgan 2003). The differentials among developed countries between those where fertility rates hover near replacement level and those where fertility is as low as one child per woman, such as South Korea, are often attributed to the ease with which the policy environment and institutions as well as cultural mores allow women to balance a career and raising a family (Demeny 2003).

Meanwhile, high rates of population growth and youthful age structures are now concentrated in the least developed countries, which are also those most likely to be facing conflict or autocracy and with the lowest capacity to respond to growing demographic pressures. Many of these countries have not replicated the fertility declines experienced elsewhere (Bongaarts 2008). On average, 43 percent of fertility declines achieved through the 1980s can be attributed to family-planning programs (Bongaarts 1997), yet in countries that retain very young age structures, up to half of women of reproductive age have an unmet need for modern contraceptives (United Nations Population Division 2008). Another proven policy intervention for countries at the beginning of the demographic transition is education for girls, which lowers future fertility rates by 0.3 to 0.5 children for each additional year in school (Abu-Ghaida and Klasen 2004). Voluntary family-planning programs and girls' education also result in improved maternal and child health and higher rates of female labor force participation. However, as seen in Uganda, the implications of demographic trends in countries with very young age structures are sometimes misunderstood. For many policymakers, demography receives little more than token attention until its connections to the nexus of security, economics, and development are better understood.

Conclusion

Given the numerous and complex ways in which population trends can affect countries' security, governance, and development, demography certainly deserves a place in political analysis and agenda setting. Countries' relative resilience and ability to adapt shape the global demographic outlook. Although demographic trends have powerful momentum, they are the aggregation of individual choices, or lack thereof, and therefore dependent on policy decisions.

Two sets of challenges exist in promoting a more nuanced approach to demographic policy. First, policymakers' attention to demography is often lacking or bluntly applied, as seen in the simplistic relationship between population and economic growth presented by Uganda's president and in South Korea's delayed response to major cultural and social factors promoting its ultralow fertility. This calls for continued exploration and dissemination of research on the effects of population on development at both the macro and micro levels. Second, policy is typically formulated in an environment of limited budgets and somewhat narrow interests. Demography must be linked to policymakers' sectoral or geographic priority areas to reinforce the strength and impact of existing global-level relationships.

A recent development in Uganda, while potentially promising, shows that longstanding policies are not easily overcome. Some observers suggest that President Museveni's strong rhetoric promoting population growth was calculated to appeal to the social conservatism of certain foreign donors that did not favor family-planning programs. Five months after the change in U.S. administration, President Museveni announced in a statement that "rapid population growth has put a lot of stress on Africa's ecosystems" (Ecological Society for Eastern Africa 2009). This new tack could reflect recognition of shifting political winds in the international donor community or simply represent a speech targeted to its audience. Regardless, with unmet need for family planning measured at 41 percent among women of reproductive age and the country projected to retain one of the world's youngest age structures for decades even if fertility declines, responding to rapid demographic change in Uganda will take more than rhetoric.

Notes

1. Data for age structure are calculated by the author using United Nations Population Division (2011) *World Population Prospects: The 2010 Revision.*
2. $3.7 billion at 2005 exchange rates.

7

The Age-Structural Maturity Thesis

The Impact of the Youth Bulge on the Advent and Stability of Liberal Democracy

Richard P. Cincotta and John Doces

THE UNITED STATES NATIONAL INTELLIGENCE COUNCIL recently speculated that the "easy transitions" from authoritarianism to liberal democracy may have run their course. They warned of a growing tendency for countries to stall along the path toward liberal democracy, to backslide after democratic reforms, or to settle into a regime that guaranteed periodic elections but granted few of the civil liberties and political rights defining liberal democracy (NIC 2006).

The report mirrors a darkening outlook that has been building among analysts for more than a decade (see Carothers 2002; Diamond 1996). This pessimism has spread to diplomats and foreign affairs policymakers, many of whom now conclude that the global trend of political liberalization that began in 1974—what Samuel Huntington (1991) dubbed the "third wave of democratization"—has come to a close, and that the international community should brace itself for a return wave of authoritarian gains.

The results of the following chapter disagree with this assessment. We argue that one of the impediments to liberal regime transition is the political volatility and uncertainty associated with the presence of a large proportion of young adults in the adult population, a so-called *youth bulge* (see Urdal 2006; Mesquida and Weiner 1999; Goldstone 1991; Moller 1968). We argue that the rise in the number of liberal democracies over the past two decades reflects the dissipation of youth bulges in some countries in East Asia and the Americas, and that the leveling off of those numbers reflects a dearth of states currently experiencing this demographic process. Using this model, we predict that another set of demographically maturing states will experience significantly higher probabilities of being assessed as a liberal democracy during the coming decade (2010–2019). Some of these, we predict, will emerge in North Africa and along the northwest rim of South America (Cincotta 2008, 2009); others with potential to rise to high levels of democracy are scattered across western Asia. However, our model, because it is probabilistic, cannot tell us precisely which of these states will first attain a liberal democracy, nor which will fail to follow this path.

Is a mature age structure a fully necessary condition for progress to liberal democracy? The evidence from the following analysis suggests that it is not. Instead, liberal democracy is somewhat easier to achieve, and far easier to maintain, after a youth bulge has dissipated than before. Is there any suggestion that the effects of population age structure are more powerful than the activities of political actors? Not at all; a dissipating youth bulge appears to strengthen the hand of democrats only in states ruled by military "caretaker" regimes, weak personal dictatorships, or partial democracies. The most noncompetitive autocracies—single-party autocracies (for example, China, North Korea, and possibly the future Iran) and strong personal dictatorships (Russia, Singapore, Cuba)—seem, so far, to be virtually impervious to the effect. Because of the mediating power of political actors and the historical and contemporary institutional variation among states, we contend that trends and forecasts using the relationship between age structure and liberal democracy are most appropriately expressed as statistical likelihoods, alerting policymakers to demographic opportunities for political liberalization rather than communicating the certainty of change.

Terms and Definitions

Liberal Democracy

Throughout the following set of analyses, regime type is assessed using Polity IV polity scores. These scores are a composite variable, derived from the subtraction of the autocracy variable from the democracy variable in Polity IV data, published by the Center for Systemic Peace and George Mason University (2008 update; see Marshall and Jaggers 2009). Polity scores range from -10, a value assigned to the most autocratic regimes, to +10, which is assigned to the most democratic. In our analyses, regimes with polity scores ranging from +1 to +10 are considered democracies; those scored from -10 to -1 are considered authoritarian regimes. A liberal democracy is defined by scores ranging from +8 to +10, the same range used by the State Failure Task Force (SAIC 1995) to define its highest democracy category, which it labeled "full democracy."

Ranges of Polity IV scores are also used to define the other regime types mentioned in this chapter. Dictatorships inhabit the opposite extreme of the polity-score spectrum from liberal democracy, ranging from -10 to -8. A regime with any negative score, -10 to -1, is labeled an autocracy. A regime with a positive score, +1 to +10, is considered a democracy.

The range of polity scores that we have used to define liberal democracy (+8 to +10), corresponds roughly to the category "free" used by Freedom House in its annual assessment of regime type and progress (Freedom House 2008). Much of the analysis elaborated in this chapter was also performed and published using Freedom House scores (Cincotta 2008, 2009) with virtually identical results, although Freedom House's assessment criteria and weighting differ somewhat from those used to generate Polity IV data.[1]

The Youth-Bulge Proportion

In this research, the term *youth-bulge proportion* refers to the fraction of young adults aged 15 to 29 years within a country's total working-age population (ages 15 to 64). Thus, for a country with 4 million young people aged 15 to 29 years, and a total working-age population aged 15 to 64 of 10 million, the youth-bulge proportion would be 0.4. In 2009, youth-bulge proportions ranged from 0.50 to above 0.60 in the countries with the most youthful populations, such as Zimbabwe (0.62) and Afghanistan (0.53), and below 0.30 in the most demographically mature countries, such as Japan (0.24) and Italy (0.25).[2]

This and similar proportions and ratios have been used as indicators of a youthful age distribution in the political science and international relations literature. Some define young adults as the population aged 15 to 24 years and the meaningful measure of adults as spanning the ages 15 and older (Urdal 2006). Others have utilized the ratio of young adults (in the numerator) to only the older adults (in the denominator), employing various definitions for those groups (Mesquida and Weiner 1991). Still other studies have used the proportion of children and young people, 0 to 29, in the total population (Leahy et al. 2007).

When plotted as a function of the secular trend of increasing median age, each of these indicators declines monotonically. However, some scholars (Collier and Hoeffler 2004; Fearon and Laitin 2003) have mistakenly employed nonmonotonic youth-bulge functions (young adults divided by the total population) in their analyses of political violence, conflating youthful and more mature age structures, and confounding their results (discussed by Urdal 2006, p. 608).

All of these indicators also differ from the common use of "youth bulge" in the demography literature, where researchers have generally defined a youth bulge as a disproportionately large group of adolescents and young adults in an age structure with smaller childhood and older-adult cohorts. In this case, graphs depicting the population age structure show a bulge in the middle. However, our measure of the youth-bulge proportion as the ratio of young adults to all working-age individuals excludes children aged 0 to 14. Thus a country can have a very large youth-bulge proportion, relative to its working age population, even if it also has an even larger number of children aged 0 to 14. Indeed, in fast-growing countries whose age pyramids typically have a very broad base (large numbers of children) but small tops (few older people), the youth-bulge proportion is quite large. Moreover, the youth-bulge proportion can remain high in such countries for up to two decades even once fertility begins to fall, as it takes that long for the new, smaller birth cohorts to have an impact on the relative size of the young adult population.

Thus, despite significant global declines in the total fertility rate (TFR; the lifetime average number of children a woman is expected to bear) over the past four decades, a large youth-bulge proportion persists in about half of all countries listed by the United Nations for 2010. (For purposes of discussion, a large youth-bulge proportion is >0.42, that is at least 42 15-to-29-year-olds per 100 persons aged 15 to 64). These high youth-bulge proportion states are currently concentrated in sub–Saharan Africa, the Middle East and North Africa, the South American Andes, in the midrib of the Central American isthmus, on the island of Hispaniola, and in the Pacific Islands.

Ché Meets Hobbes: The Age-Structural Maturity Thesis

The thesis underlying our analysis builds on two existing models of political behavior. The first, known as the *authoritarian bargain* (Desai et al. 2009), is a restatement of a basic element of Thomas Hobbes's theory of the social contract; it assumes that citizens prefer to exercise basic freedoms, but asserts that they are willing to relinquish political rights to an authoritarian when they perceive threats to their personal or economic security (Hobbes 1994, originally 1651/1658).

When civil order breaks down, markets are disrupted, property becomes insecure, and investments move elsewhere. Because of the fears of citizens and, more importantly, the sensitivities of the commercial and security-sector elites to disorder, political violence tends to bolster the power of authoritarians in office or, in democracies, signal elected leaders to roll back restraints on executive authority. Because of this relationship, revolutionary violence rarely spawns a sustained high level of democracy. Should violence climax in regime change, other types of less-than-liberal regimes tend ultimately to emerge (Schmitter 1980). However, if society turns politically quiescent and unthreatening, elites as well as common citizens should be expected to grow intolerant of the regime's cronyism and lack of accountability, and its restrictions on commerce, social mobility, and speech.

Thus, where the streets are unthreatening, authoritarians typically find support waning. As both Huntington (1991, pp. 115–116) and Schmitter (1980) noted, under quiescent political conditions and improving economic conditions, authoritarians tend to experiment with gradual liberal reforms, to negotiate their own safe transition from power, and ultimately relinquish the reins of power to more liberal regimes. Such exits have been most common among nonideological autocracies and partial democracies, particularly caretaker military regimes and decaying personal dictatorships.

The second model, the *youth-bulge model,* seeks to explain the relatively high frequency of political violence associated with national and subnational populations in the early phases of the *demographic transition* (the transformation from high to low birth and death rates). Proponents of the youth-bulge model argue that relatively high values of the youth-bulge proportion are indicative of a social environment in which political actors, whether state or nonstate, find it relatively easy to politically mobilize young adults, particularly young men (Urdal 2006). Put another way, youth-bulge conditions—fostering unemployment, depressed wages, high entry-level job competition (Easterlin 1968), a youth-dense street culture, and gang formation—lower the costs of overcoming collective action constraints among young men who, as a group, tend to be highly idealistic, sensitive to peer approval, prone to risk taking, and naïvely accepting of ideological explanations. Researchers have shown that a large proportion of young people in the working-age population are associated with elevated levels of violent crime (Cohen and Land 1987) and political violence.

Hypotheses

The age-structural maturity hypothesis, the most general hypothesis of our analysis (H_{GEN}), is stated as:

> H_{GEN}: *A state whose population age structure is very youthful (characterized, in this research, by a relatively large proportion of young adults in the working-age population) is less likely to be assessed as a liberal democracy than states with a more mature age structure.*

Other researchers have noted a strong and consistent relationship between age structure and liberal democracy for the period from 1970 to 2005 (Cincotta 2008, 2009; Leahy et al. 2007), but have not controlled for contributions of other structural factors. In this chapter we stipulate that the age-structural contribution is separable from the contributions of other underlying variables for which there is prior evidence of an association with democracy.

Having attained statistical support for the age-structural maturity hypothesis from a large-N analysis (for which methods and results are summarized later in this chapter), we test two explanatory effects—an advent effect and a stability effect—expressed in the following two specific hypotheses (H_{ADV}, H_{STAB}), that could contribute to the strength of this general relationship.

> H_{ADV}: *A youthful age structure tends to impede the advent of liberal democracy.* States with populations having a large proportion of young adults in the working-age population are less likely than states with smaller proportions to attain liberal democracy.

> H_{STAB}: *A youthful age structure tends to destabilize liberal democracy.* When liberal democracy is attained by states with a large youth-bulge proportion, that regime type is unlikely to be continuously sustained.

Analytical support for both of these hypotheses would suggest that opportunities to establish and maintain liberal democracy should improve in states as the youth-bulge proportion declines.

In addition, we pose a group hypothesis (H_{GROUP}), to generate expectations of the number of liberal democracies within regional groupings of states.

H_{GROUP}: *A regional group composed of states with mature age structures is likely to exhibit a greater proportion of states that are assessed as liberal democracies than a group composed of states experiencing more youthful age structures.* Therefore, as the mean youth-bulge proportion of a regional grouping of states (each state equally weighted) experiences decline, one can expect a larger proportion of that group to be assessed as liberal democracies.

If valid, a group model derived from this hypothesis could be employed, using demographic projections, as a straightforward means of predicting the proportion of states within a regional group that are likely to be assessed as liberal democracies at a future date (later in this chapter we test the validity of such a model to predict the rise of liberal democracies among states from the former Soviet sphere of influence).

Methods and Data Sources

The following analysis musters evidence from a range of sources: (1) anecdotally, from relevant literature and country trends; (2) statistically, from a multivariate logistic regression analysis of state-level time series data; (3) statistically, from evidence from a single-variable analysis of regional time series data; and (4) graphically, from evidence of verification from a novel test of the regional model (using the countries that have emerged from the former Soviet Union and Eastern European states).

Large-N Global Analysis: Multivariate Logistic Regression

In this element of the analysis, our objective is to test our general hypothesis: to assess the degree to which the probability of a specific regime type is determined by the youth-bulge proportion, while controlling for other independent variables that have been theoretically or empirically associated with regime type. Four regime types were selected: dictatorship (polity score ranging from −10 to −8); autocracy (−10 to −1); democracy (+1 to +10); and liberal democracy (+8 to +10). Each regime type (Y_i) was, in turn, assigned the role of the dichotomous dependent variable[3] in a fixed effects logistic regression model.

The logit model, which follows, includes terms for four continuous independent variables (X_j) and two dummy variables (dichotomous independent variables). The independent variable of primary interest, the youth-bulge proportion, is expressed as a percentage (from U.N. estimates, U.N. Population Division 2007). The Penn World Tables, version 6.2 (Heston et al. 2006), is the common source for values of the following three continuous control variables: real GDP ($PPP) per capita; annual growth rate of real GDP ($PPP) per capita; and trade openness. The model also includes two dummy variables (D_k, where D = 0 or 1): OECD-membership states and OPEC-membership states. The full model can be written as follows:

$$logit(Y_i) = \beta_0 + \beta_1 X_1 + \beta_2 X_2 + \beta_3 X_3 + \beta_4 X_4 + \gamma_2 D_1 + \gamma_2 D_2$$

The panel of data that were applied to this model was drawn from a 154-state annual dataset spanning all world regions from 1970 to 2004, from which the algorithm generated frequencies from 54 multidimensional groups for regression (see Hosmer and Lemeshow 1989). The control variables (X_2, X_3, X_4, D_1, D_2) are discussed below (youth-bulge proportion, X_1, was discussed previously in this chapter).

Real GDP per capita. This control variable indicates the level of domestic product per capita at current prices, adjusted for differences in the price of a standard market basket of goods (purchasing power parity, $PPP), and is introduced to capture the empirically demonstrated contribution of income to regime type (Przeworski et al. 2000). States with a high level of income are likely to exhibit a relatively large middle class, a group typically associated with the consolidation and stability of democracy (Acemoglu and Robinson 2006). We expect real GDP per capita to be positively associated with democracy.

Real GDP per capita growth. Empirical associations between the rate of economic growth and regime type are typically weak (Przeworski et al. 2000). The most commonly held theoretical view—frequently used to explain the stability of regimes in China and Singapore—maintains that states with economies experiencing higher per capita rates of economic growth are more likely than others to sustain their current political regime, regardless of type (Ulfelder and Lustik 2007). Thus, we expect the advent of democracy to be less likely in autocracies and dictatorships that have shown strong economic growth, and we expect democracies that would otherwise be unstable to last longer where they exhibit increasing per capita incomes.

Trade openness. To account for the effect of trade openness, a measure of exports plus imports as a percentage of GDP is included as a control variable. Analysis of similar indicators suggests to several researchers that trade openness has impeded political liberalization in low- and middle-income states (Reuveny and Li 2003), while others reach the opposite conclusion (Balaev 2009). Thus, we hold no expectations for a clear association between this variable and democracy.

OECD Membership. A dummy variable indicating whether or not a state is an OECD member is included to account for unspecified effects on regime type of long-term institutional and economic development, beyond the effects of real GDP per capita. We expect associations between OECD membership and democracy to be positive.

OPEC Membership. A dummy variable indicating whether or not a state is an OPEC member is included to account for effects of oil export profits on regime type. We expect associations between OPEC membership and democracy to be negative (Ross 2001).

Regional Analysis: Setting Up Regression Models to Test the General Hypothesis

The objective of our single-variable regression analysis is to determine if, and how well, the youth-bulge proportion can statistically predict the tendency of states, within a region, to be assessed as liberal democracies. To fulfill this objective, state-level youth-bulge proportions were used to generate nine sets of regional youth-bulge means (Y_r) in five-year intervals, from 1970 to 2005, for five regions: North and South America, Europe, the Middle East and North Africa, and Other Asia and Oceania.[4] The proportion of liberal democracy in those regions, the dependent variable, was calculated from Polity IV data. The regional means (X_r), weighted by the number of countries in each region, were used to generate ordinary least squares linear regressions, for each interval year (t), such that

$$Y_{rt} = \beta_{0t} + \beta_{1t} X_{rt.}$$

We tested the hypothesis that all slopes and elevations of these regression lines were equal, and found the differences to be not significant (0.95-confidence level, 35 degrees of freedom). The 45 regional means, spanning from 1970 to 2005, were then used to generate a regression line predicting the probability of being a liberal democracy, given the youth-bulge proportion.

After generating the regional group model, we undertook an effort to validate it by examining regime patterns that emerged among the former communist states of Eastern Europe, the states that emerged from the dissolution of the Soviet

Union in 1991, and Mongolia. While the 29 states[5] assessed in this regional analysis are, geographically, socioeconomically, and demographically a surprisingly variable array, their shared regime characteristics during the post–World War II period and their abrupt transition at the end of the cold war provide common political and temporal starting points that make them an interesting test case.

We graphically assessed the distribution of the former Soviet-sphere states according to their youth-bulge proportion and compared this distribution to the distributions produced by two alternative indicators: per capita income, using World Bank income classes based on gross national income per capita (World Bank 2009); and educational attainment, using the IIASA/VDI educational attainment data by age and sex (Lutz et al. 2007). In the latter analysis, our indicator is the proportion of secondary and tertiary educated individuals within the population aged 25 to 44 years, the peak productive working years (Skirbekk 2007).

Advent and Stability Analysis: Small-N Comparisons

We also set up small-N preliminary analyses that were designed to test the advent (H_{ADV}) and stability (H_{STAB}) hypotheses. To test the stability hypothesis, we identified instances from 1965 to 1989 in which states attained liberal democracy ($n = 24$), and then determined the proportion of these states that either retained or lost this assessment over the next 20 years. We then graphically analyzed these cases at three levels of the youth-bulge proportion, <0.39, 0.40 to 0.49, >0.50 young adults per individual in the working ages, and three levels of stability, 1 to 10 years, 11 to 20, and >20 years. We then tested the resultant distribution of 9 cells for nonrandomness (X^2, 6 d.f.). We assumed that the lack of a relationship between age-structural maturity and the stability of new liberal democracies would suggest an "advent effect."

Results and Findings

Evidence from the Literature: Przeworski's Puzzle

In research exploring relationships between regime type and development, Przeworski and coauthors (2000, p. 98) concluded that democracies at a moderate level of economic development—with an annual gross domestic product (GDP) of at least $4,000 per capita, adjusted for purchasing power parity (PPP)[6]—were much more likely to sustain that regime type than less developed democracies, but found little evidence to suggest that economic development led to the onset of democracy. The authors also found that, even within income categories, states with rapidly growing populations and elevated death rates tended to be dictatorships. Low-fertility states were most often democracies. And while they admit to being "bewildered by this fact" (p. 218), the authors ignored the possibility that age-structural change, the delayed product of fertility decline, could facilitate or sustain democracy—although they noted a large difference between the age structures of democracies and dictatorships (p. 266).[7] After a detailed analysis and discussion, Przeworski and coauthors concluded that democracies, more than authoritarian regimes, create the perception of stability and support that encourages small families.

Their conclusion is at odds with history. From the 1960s through the 1980s, authoritarian regimes in Asia and Latin America—including those in charge in South Korea, Taiwan, Indonesia, Thailand, Mexico, and Brazil (states that would later join democratization's third-wave)—were the most enthusiastic initiators and supporters of family-planning programs, achieving the lion's share of fertility decline and improvements in maternal and infant health status long before being replaced by democrats (see Tsui 2001). In contrast, programs in democratic regimes—for example, in the Philippines, Pakistan, and India—have often been hampered by a lack of administrative continuity and political commitment (Rosen and Conly 1996). As for authoritarianism's year-to-year association with elevated population growth and death rates, both are characteristics of a youthful age structure, which should—according to the age-structural maturity model—impede high levels of political liberalization.

Evidence from Trends Among Recently Democratized States

Evidence of a maturing age structure effect emerges in observations of trends in selected third-wave countries (see Figure 7.1). As youth-bulge proportions steeply declined into the vicinity of 0.39, liberal democracies evolved in these states with only one example, Thailand, of military preemption and backsliding. And even Thailand's political strife has remained relatively nonviolent, both sides avoiding direct confrontation. The virtual disappearance of violent political confrontation and military coups from the more demographically mature states of Asia and Latin America is a striking reversal.

Many states still bear the political scars of attaining liberal democracy "demographically too soon." Where high levels of democracy emerged long before the youth bulge declined—as in Venezuela, Colombia, Ecuador, India, Pakistan, Malaysia, Fiji, and others—states retreated to less democratic

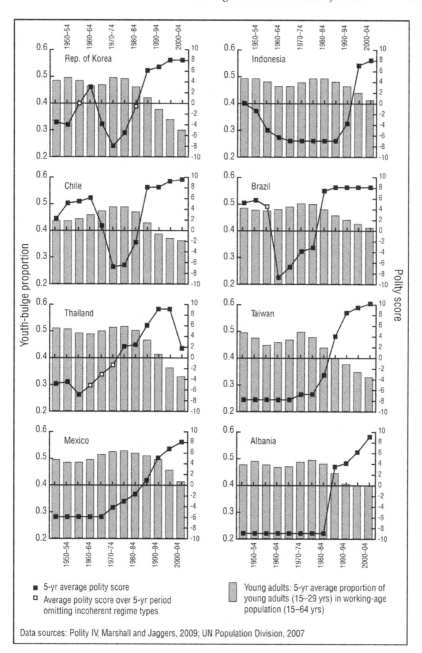

Figure 7.1   Trends in the Polity Scores and Youth Bulge Proportions of Eight States During the 1990s

regimes, sometimes relatively briefly (for example, India's Emergency, 1976 to 1978), in other cases for decades (Malaysia, 1969 to the present). A few liberal democracies have doggedly persisted through their youth bulge, largely due to strong commitments of a broad swath of the political and commercial elite, such as in Costa Rica and Jamaica, or through the power of visionary leaders, for example Nehru in India, and Mandela in South Africa.

Nonetheless, some of these liberalized youth-bulge states have endured high levels of political unrest (particularly India), or criminal violence (particularly South Africa, Jamaica, and Mexico). If youth-bulge theorists are correct, such strife has a high probability of continuing apace in these states until their age structures significantly mature. However, age-structural maturation is occurring rapidly in Jamaica, Mexico, and across Latin America and the Caribbean (with the exception of Haiti). The southern states of India, once wracked by widespread political violence, are passing rapidly through their age-structural transitions, which coincide with rising educational attainment and income growth, and with a virtual absence of political violence. Meanwhile the fertility and age-structural conditions of India's central northern states of Uttar Pradesh and Bihar appear stalled (Haub and Sharma 2007), suggesting that economic and political problems in these states—including an ongoing Maoist insurgency—could feature prominently in India's future.

Evidence from the Large-N and Small-N Analyses

The coefficient estimates that were determined by the fixed effects logistic regression analysis, controlling for per capita income, economic growth, and trade openness, and OECD and OPEC membership from 1970 to 2008, suggest that the size of the youth-bulge proportion has contributed significantly to the probability of regime type, as specified in each of the four models tested: dictatorship, autocracy, democracy, and liberal democracy models (see Table 7.1). A relatively large youth-bulge proportion is associated with a high probability of dictatorship or autocracy, but negatively associated with democracy and liberal democracy. In each model, all control variables, with the exception of real GDP per capita growth, were significant statistical contributors. Growth of real GDP per capita was not significant in any of the models.

Relatively high values of real GDP per capita and trade openness were associated with democracy and liberal democracy, and negatively associated with autocracy and dictatorship. As expected, OECD-member states were statistically associated with democracy and liberal democracy, and OPEC-member states with autocracy and dictatorship.

Our test of the stability hypothesis, though limited to 24 instances between 1965 and 1989, found that maintaining liberal democracy for more than 20 years was significantly less likely ($p<0.10$) among states that were first assessed as a liberal democracy with a youth-bulge proportion above 0.39 young adults per working-age person, than those that became a liberal democracy at proportions below that value.

Evidence and Predictions from the Regional Analysis

Evidence for our hypotheses can also be drawn from regional data. Country-level youth-bulge proportions, averaged regionally, and the proportion of liberal democracy in a region have been consistently negatively correlated, with a statistically similar slope, from 1970 to 2005. This regional age-structural maturity model (see Figure 7.2) predicts that when the average country-level young-bulge proportion reaches 0.39 in a multistate region, then 50 ± 3 percent (the mean and two-tailed 0.95-confidence interval) of all states are likely

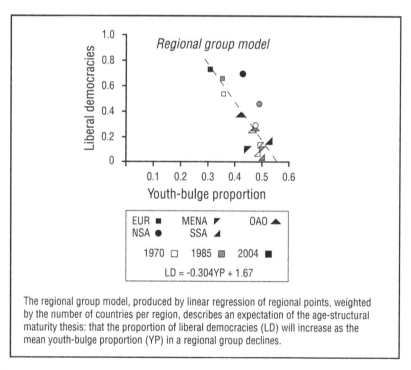

The regional group model, produced by linear regression of regional points, weighted by the number of countries per region, describes an expectation of the age-structural maturity thesis: that the proportion of liberal democracies (LD) will increase as the mean youth-bulge proportion (YP) in a regional group declines.

Figure 7.2   The Regional Group Model

to be assessed as liberal democracies. This regional relationship was virtually stable, from 1970 to 2004, despite the unprecedented degree of age-structural and political changes that occurred throughout the world.[8]

Demographic projections could be used to help differentiate subregional clusters of states and isolated states as either demographically favorable, or unfavorable, for transition to liberal democracy. Among subregional clusters that, on average, were scored below liberal democracy in 2008, two clusters stand out; both experienced continuous fertility decline through the 1990s, and thus are set to experience a dissipating youth bulge. One cluster comprises states along the northern coast of Africa: Morocco, Algeria, Tunisia, Libya, and Egypt. Each has yet to experience liberal democracy. The other cluster stretches along the northwestern rim of South America: Ecuador, Colombia, Venezuela, and Guyana. Each achieved liberal democracy in the past; none was able to sustain it.

According to the U.N. Population Division's medium-fertility variant (2007), by 2015 both clusters will reach an average youth-bulge proportion of 0.39—the 50-percent likelihood level for liberal democracy (see Table 7.1). The South

Table 7.1 Probability of a Specified Regime Type

	Dictatorship	Autocracy	Democracy	Liberal Democracy
Youth-bulge proportion ($ln(100X_1)$)	1.960 (0.394)**	0.729 (0.289)*	−0.775 (0.290)**	−1.710 (0.308)**
Real GDP ($PPP) per capita ($ln(X_2)$)	−0.280 (0.052)**	−0-.546 (0.044)**	0.673 (0.046)**	1.100 (0.063)**
Real GDP ($PPP) per capita growth ($X_3$)	−0.007 (0.005)	0.002 (0.004)	0.004 (0.004)	−0.004 (0.006)
Trade openness (X_4)	0.297 (0.061)**	0.250 (0.047)**	−0.205 (0.048)**	−0.325 (0.058)**
OECD-member state (D_1)	−2.300 (0.301)**	−2.424 (0.193)**	2.379 (0.193)**	1.944 (0.153)**
OPEC-member state (D_2)	1.371 (0.132)**	1.572 (0.152)**	−1.603 (0.155)**	−1.760 (0.197)**
Observations (n)	5306	5306	5306	5306
Number of data groups analyzed	54	54	54	54

Notes: The dependent variables (regime types) are determined as follows: a dictatorship is defined as a regime with a Polity IV polity score from—10 to—8; an autocracy,—10 to—1; a democracy +1 to +10; a liberal democracy, +8 to +10.

*indicates that the coefficient is significant at $p=0.05$

**significant at $p=0.01$.

American cluster is projected to reach 0.40 by 2010. In each cluster, we forecast (conservatively) that there will be at least one liberal democracy by 2015.

A Test: Emergent Regimes in the Former Soviet and Eastern European States

How can the political outcome in these states help test the age-structural maturity thesis? If their regime transitions are consistent with this thesis, a larger proportion of age-structurally mature states should rise to liberal democracy, leaving behind (in less democratic categories) states with a high youth-bulge proportion. In practice, however, one should expect regime transitions to be retarded by the persistence of Soviet-era institutions, entrenched leadership and their political networks, and in the Balkan states, the rearrangement of borders. Yet, if the group model is usefully predictive, the proportion of liberal democracies in this cold-war cluster should ultimately rise to the level expected by the group model.

By 2004, both age structures and regimes were in transition in the states (then 27) of the former Soviet Union, Eastern Europe, and Mongolia. The mean youth-bulge proportion of this group had dropped to 0.37, while its proportion of liberal democracies had plodded upward to 44 percent (12 liberal democracies), still short of the 56 ± 4 percent expected. By 2008, 2 states had been added to the group (Montenegro and Kosovo), the model's expected proportion of liberal democracies had increased to 58 ± 4 percent, and the observed proportion of liberal democracies was 59 percent (17 of 29 states).

As expected by the age-structural maturity model, liberal democracies were distributed nonrandomly (X^2 test for nonrandomness, $p = 0.05$), dominating the more mature categories (<0.39 young adults per working-age adult), while autocracies dominated categories with a larger youth-bulge proportion (Figure 7.3). Similarly, World Bank income-per-capita classes produce a nonrandom distribution (X^2, $p = 0.03$) that was ordered as expected; liberal democracies dominate in the high- and upper-middle-income categories. However, educational attainment data for these states (2000 data) produced a distribution, among the four attainment categories used, that is not statistically different than a random distribution ($p = 0.17$).[9]

Discussion and Conclusions

In this chapter, we employed diverse methodologies, at various levels of analysis, to gauge the strength and extent of recent interactions between a state's population age structure and its chances of attaining and maintaining liberal

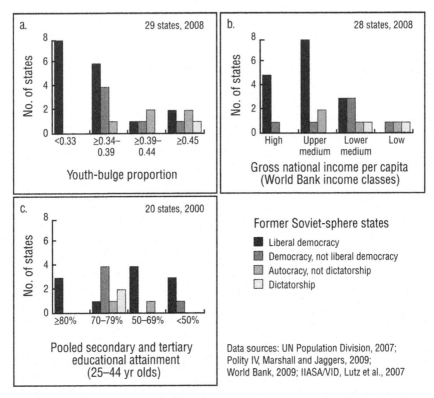

These histograms demonstrate the ability of the youth-bulge proportion (a) to predict the frequency of liberal democracy in the former Soviet-sphere states, and compares it to two alternative indicators: World Bank gross national income per capita (Atlas Method) classes (b), and the pooled proportion of secondary and tertiary educational attainment in the peak years of productivity, from 25 to 44 years of age (c). The youth-bulge proportion and income classes produced distributions of these regimes that were ordered in a manner consistent with expectations, while educational attainment did not.

Figure 7.3   Youth Bulge and Liberal Democracy

democracy. Even when other known correlates of democracy were controlled, our analysis supports the hypothesis that states with a relatively large youth-bulge proportion experience substantially lower probabilities of being assessed as liberal democracies than those that have experienced a greater degree of age-structural maturation.

Policy Relevance and Pertinent Caveats

Can the age-structural maturity model be used by diplomats and policymakers to better understand global trends in political liberalization? It can. The model could have alerted policymakers to the otherwise unexpected ascent to liberal democracy of Taiwan, Indonesia, Thailand, and South Korea (see Figure 7.1), and Malaysia's early decline from high polity scores. Moreover, the model makes sense of the prior tendency of numerous Latin American states, which embraced liberal democracy "demographically early," to retreat to less democratic regimes thereafter—Venezuela being the most recent example. It also sheds light on the tenuousness of Indian and the Philippine democracies, which have suffered sporadically through insurgencies and entrenched forms of political violence (note that Freedom House's assessments of both the Philippines and India have been less favorable than Polity IV's over the past two decades).

Despite the age-structural maturity model's capacity to resolve many of democratization's mysteries, users should beware: Strong political actors and institutions are quite capable of thwarting the model's predictions. Age-structural effects do not seem strong enough to undermine steadfast, charismatic leaders, like Russia's Vladimir Putin, Cuba's Fidel Castro, or Singapore's Lee Kuan Yew. Similarly, a declining youth bulge has hardly perturbed the most intensely ideological one-party regimes, China and North Korea—states that have dismantled the commercial, intellectual, and media elites, and reconstructed their own version. Iran's regime could similarly purge these actors as its age structure matures.

A second caution: Migration and ethnoreligious compositional shifts challenge aspects of the age-structural maturity model. For example, where a decline in the youth-bulge proportion reflects a large influx of temporary labor migrants relative to the size of the indigenous population, as in the oil-producing Arab Gulf States, labor relations and ethnic tensions may force policy changes, but wholesale political liberalization seems unlikely.[10] Neither does it seem that state-level age-structural trends provide much insight into the political future of states in which a youthful ethnoreligious group is gradually displacing an older group that is holding the political reins of state power.

The forecasts that emerge from age-structural maturity theory are not deterministic; they are statistical. To use them, researchers and policymakers must learn to accept their probabilistic nature, and combine them with (or juxtapose them to) the country-specific qualitative analyses that are commonly used. If they do, age-structural maturity theory offers much more than ever they had before—a simple and reasonable means to gauge the likelihood that states will function as liberal democracies.

Notes

1. Freedom House scores, which are the average of political rights and civil liberty scores, range from 7, the most autocratic regimes, to 1, the most democratic. The category "free" (as

opposed to "partly free," and "not free") is assigned to regimes with scores ranging from 2.5 to 1. Analysts typically identify a liberal democracy as a regime assessed as "free."

2. In this chapter, youth-bulge proportions were calculated from U.N. Population Division (2007) estimates and medium-fertility variant projections elaborating population (both sexes) by age.

3. A dichotomous variable has two possible values, 1 (true, it fits within this class) or 0 (false, it does not fit).

4. Countries with fewer than 1.0 million residents in 2004 were excluded by the Polity IV database and are therefore excluded from regional calculations in this paper. The five regions used in calculations and shown in Figures 1 and 2 are: *North and South America* (NSA), which aggregates the U.N. regions of North America, South America, and the Caribbean; *Europe* (EUR) which comprises all states in the U.N. designation (including Russia); *Middle East and North Africa* (MENA) which includes Algeria, Cyprus, Egypt, Iran, Iraq, Israel, Lebanon, Libya, Jordan, Morocco, Tunisia, Turkey, Syria, and Yemen, omitting the Gulf States (Saudi Arabia, Oman, United Arab Emirates, Bahrain, Qatar, Kuwait) where age structure is heavily influenced by the presence of temporary labor migrants; and *Other Asia and Oceania* (OAO) which includes all Asian states east of Iran, plus Australia, New Zealand, Papua New Guinea, and Fiji.

5. The 29 states in the region are Albania, Armenia, Azerbaijan, Belarus, Bulgaria, Croatia, Czech Republic, Estonia, Georgia, Hungary, Kazakhstan, Kosovo, Kyrgyzstan, Latvia, Lithuania, Macedonia, Moldova, Mongolia, Montenegro, Poland, Serbia, Slovak Republic, Slovenia, Romania, Russia, Tajikistan, Turkmenistan, Ukraine, and Uzbekistan. It omits Bosnia and Herzegovina, which Polity IV database classifies as incoherent (interrupted, without a clear central authority) and Germany, which includes the territory governed by the former East German state.

6. This value is in 1985 U.S. dollars adjusted for purchasing power parity.

7. The authors discuss the effects of age-structure (characterized using proportions in three age groups: <15, 15 to 65, >65 years of age) on democracy in their discussion of differences in birth rates between democracies and dictatorships (p. 266). Although schemes for characterizing age structures are very basic, they nonetheless find statistical differences between democracies and dictatorships, largely based on the proportion of children (<15), but attribute no significance to it. They attribute age-structural differences to differences in fertility.

8. Eight OLS linear regressions were generated from regional data, weighted by the number of countries in each region, for data at five-year intervals from 1970 to 2005. Statistical differences between regression coefficients and intercepts were not significant (0.95-confidence level).

9. In the educational attainment data set generated by IIASA and the Vienna Demographic Institute, data are missing for Albania, Azerbaijan, Belarus, Georgia, Moldova, Tajikistan, and Serbia-Montenegro. At the time of our analysis, the final year of these data was 2000.

10. Since the early-1960s, petroleum producing states in the Arab Gulf Region (Saudi Arabia, Oman, United Arab Emirates, Kuwait, Qatar, and Bahrain) have encouraged temporary migration to provide labor and technical expertise to support their petroleum and construction industries. These workers typically leave before retirement age. Because of the large proportion of experienced labor migrants between 30 and 40 years of age in the Arab Gulf States, state-level age structures tend to be considerably more mature than that of the indigenous subpopulation.

8

Youth Bulges and Violence

Henrik Urdal

YOUTH OFTEN PLAY A PROMINENT ROLE IN POLITICAL violence, and the existence of a "youth bulge" has historically been associated with times of political crisis (Goldstone 1991, 2001b). Generally, it has been observed that young males are the main protagonists of criminal as well as political violence.

But are countries and areas with youthful age structures, or "youth bulges," more likely to experience political violence? The issue has received increasing attention over the past decade following the more general debate over the security implications of population pressure and resource scarcity. In "The Coming Anarchy," Robert Kaplan (1994) argued that anarchy and the crumbling of nation states will be attributed to demographic and environmental factors in the future. More recently, youth bulges have become a popular explanation for the current political upheavals in the Arab world and for recruitment to international terrorist networks. In a background article surveying the root causes of the September 11, 2001, terrorist attacks on the United States, *Newsweek* editor Fareed Zakaria (2001) argued that youth bulges combined with slow economic and social change have provided a foundation for an Islamic resurgence in the Arab world.

Samuel Huntington qualified the "Clash of Civilization" by adding the dimension of age structure:

> I don't think Islam is any more violent than any other religions [...]. But the key factor is the demographic factor. Generally speaking, the people who go out and kill other people are males between the ages of 16 and 30. During the 1960s, 70s and 80s there were high birth rates in the Muslim world, and this has given rise to a huge youth bulge. But the bulge will fade. Muslim birth rates are going down; in fact, they have dropped dramatically in some countries. (2001)

This chapter presents and discusses the results from an empirical study of youth bulges and political violence identifying a general statistical relationship between age structure and political violence.[1] It is important to note, however, that this finding represents a probabilistic relationship. A young age structure does not make countries destined for violence; in fact, most countries with large youth bulges avoid armed conflict most of the time. But youth bulges represent a challenge that governments have to address by providing opportunities for youth to participate in education, in the labor market, and in governance. Where such opportunities exist, large youth bulges can be a blessing rather than a curse. Recent research suggests that in the context of declining fertility and thus lower dependency ratios large youth cohorts can be a vehicle for economic development, a so-called demographic dividend, rather than conflict (e.g., Kelley and Schmidt 2001).

Youth Bulges: Providing Opportunity and Motive for Conflict

The literature on youth bulges has focused in particular on spontaneous and low-intensity unrest like nonviolent protest and rioting. However, youth bulges may also increase the risk of more organized forms of political violence, like internal armed conflict. This chapter first traces the youth bulge argument back to some early "generational" contributions, and then draws on two dominant and competing, albeit not mutually exclusive, theoretical traditions in the study of civil war; one focusing on opportunities and the other on motives for conflict.

Some theorists have proposed that youth cohorts may develop a generational consciousness, and especially so out of awareness of belonging to a generation of an extraordinary size and strength, enabling them to act collectively (Braungart 1984; Feuer 1969; Goldstone 1991). However, violent conflict between groups only divided by age is rare. The generational approach has some serious shortcomings with regard to the explanatory power of the relationship between youth bulges and violence. The development of generational consciousness may explain the formation of youth movements that can function as identity groups. Identity groups are necessary for collective violent action to take place. But it is not necessary that identity groups be generation-based for youth bulges to increase the likelihood of armed conflict. Furthermore, the generational approach does not offer explanations for the motives of youth rebellion nor does it provide a sufficient explanation for the opportunities of conflict. It is clear that if large youth bulges that hold a common generational consciousness would always produce conflict, we would have seen many more instances of violent youth revolts. Conditions that provide youth bulges with the necessary motives and opportunities for armed conflict are discussed below.

Both the opportunity and the motive perspectives are macro-level frameworks that attempt to explain events essentially consisting of a series of individual-level decisions associated with joining a rebel or terrorist organization or not, by focusing on economic, political, and social structural features. The opportunity literature, often coined the *greed perspective,* has its roots in economic theory and focuses on structural conditions that provide opportunities for a rebel group to wage war against a government (Collier 2000; Collier and Hoeffler 2004). These are conditions that provide the rebel group with the financial means to fight, or factors that reduce the cost of rebellion, such as unusually low recruitment costs for rebel soldiers. Former World Bank research director Paul Collier has suggested that relatively large youth cohorts may be a factor that reduces recruitment costs through the abundant supply of rebel labor with low opportunity cost, increasing the risk of armed conflict (Collier 2000, p. 94). According to the opportunity perspective, rebellion is feasible only when the potential gain from joining is so high and the expected costs so low that rebel recruits will favor joining over alternative income-earning opportunities.

The motive-oriented tradition, or *grievance perspective,* has its origins in relative deprivation theory and tends to see the eruption of political violence as a rational means to redress economic or political grievances (Gurr 1970; Sambanis 2002, p. 223).

Motives for committing political violence can be economic (like poverty, economic recession, or inequality), or political (like a lack of democracy, or the absence of minority representation or self-governance). Most of the literature on youth bulges and political violence arguably falls into this tradition. It focuses on how large youth cohorts facing institutional crowding in the labor market or educational system, lack of political openness, and crowding in urban centers may be aggrieved, paving the way for political violence (e.g., Choucri 1974; Braungart 1984; Goldstone 1991, 2001b).

While useful as ideal models, the distinction between the motive and opportunity perspectives is sometimes overstated. First, in its simplest form, the motive perspective overpredicts political violence; the existence of serious grievances is not sufficient for collective violent action to erupt (Kahl 1998). The likelihood that motives are redressed through political violence increases when opportunity arises from the availability of financial means, low costs, or a weak state. Second, while opportunity factors may better explain why civil wars break out, this does not necessarily mean that actors cannot also have strong motives (Sambanis 2002, p. 224). Third, many factors may equally well be described as representing both opportunity and motive. A young impoverished person may be considered both a potential low-cost recruit, and at the same time an aggrieved individual motivated by economic and political exclusion. Below, the most relevant contextual factors suggested to affect the relationship between large youth cohorts and conflict are discussed.

The Cohort Size Effect

The mere existence of an extraordinarily large pool of young people is a factor that lowers the cost of recruitment, since the opportunity cost for a young person generally is low (Collier 2000, p. 94). This is an assumption that hinges on the extent of alternative income-earning opportunities. If young people are left with no alternative but unemployment and poverty, they are increasingly likely to join a rebellion as an alternative way of generating an income.

New research in economic demography even suggests that the alternative costs of individuals belonging to larger youth cohorts are generally lower compared to members of smaller cohorts. According to the "cohort size" hypothesis, "other things being constant, the economic and social fortunes of a cohort (those born in a given year) tend to vary inversely with its relative size" (Easterlin 2000, p. 1). So not only do youth bulges provide an unusually high supply of individuals with low opportunity cost, but an individual belonging to a relatively large youth cohort generally also has a lower opportunity cost relative to a young person born into a smaller cohort.

The influence of the size of youth cohorts on unemployment is also emphasized in the motive-oriented literature on civil violence (e.g., Moller 1968; Choucri 1974; Goldstone 1991, 2001b; Cincotta et al 2003). If the labor market cannot absorb a sudden surplus of young job seekers, a large pool of unemployed youths will generate strong frustration. In extreme cases, the challenge to employ large youth cohorts can appear overwhelming. In Saudi Arabia, approximately 4 million people will be added to the labor force over the current decade, equaling two-thirds of the current Saudi national workforce (Winckler 2002, p. 621). The socioeconomic problems associated with "youth bulges" have been argued to potentially provide fertile ground for recruitment to terrorist organizations (Lia 2005, p. 141).

Demographic Dividend

Results from recent studies on population and economic growth suggest that the relationship between large youth cohorts and political violence could be muted if youth bulges precede significantly smaller cohorts. Generally, high growth rates in the nonworking, or dependent, age groups are associated with lower economic growth, while increases in the working-age population are positively associated with economic growth (Kelley and Schmidt 2001; Williamson 2001). Such a "demographic dividend," flowing from increased savings as the relative number of dependents decreases, could have a generally pacifying effect. The rapid growth of East Asian economies since 1975 has been partially explained by a dividend from a lowered dependency burden. While the realization of the dividend largely depends on the social, economic, and political environment, we may expect that when countries experience declining dependency ratios that increase the potential for economic growth, the relationship between youth bulges and political violence will generally weaken.

Economic Growth

The overall economic performance of a society is an important factor determining the income forgone by joining a rebel movement, and thus the opportunity for rebellion. Economic growth over a longer period may act as a proxy for new income opportunities (Collier and Hoeffler 2004, p. 569). For large youth cohorts, the economic climate at the time they enter into the labor market is particularly crucial. To the degree that income opportunities are determined by general economic performance, large youth cohorts are likely be rendered particularly susceptible to lower income opportunities when economic conditions generally deteriorate, reducing the income they forgo by signing up as rebels. The motive-oriented literature also shares the concern over economic decline. Youth belonging to large cohorts will be especially vulnerable to unemployment if their entry into the labor force coincides with periods of serious economic decline. Such coincidences may generate despair among young people that moves them towards the use of violence (Choucri 1974, p. 73).

Education

A tool that countries can exploit to respond to youth bulges is the expansion of higher education. Can this serve as a strategy to reduce the risk of political violence? Higher levels of education among men may act to reduce the risk of political violence. Since educated men have better income-earning opportunities than the uneducated, they would have more to lose and hence be less likely to join a rebellion (Collier 2000). A recent study based on interviews with young soldiers presents strong micro-level support for the expectation that poverty, lack of schooling, and low alternative income opportunities are important reasons for joining a rebel group (Brett and Specht 2004).

Rebel recruitment is thus more costly and rebellion less likely the higher the level of education in a society (Collier and Hoeffler 2004). This is not inconsistent with the motive-oriented literature. However, it has been suggested that when countries respond to large youth cohorts by expanding opportunities for higher education, this may produce a much larger group of highly educated youths than can be accommodated in the normal economy. Unless the government is able and willing to absorb a surplus of university graduates into the public sector, prevailing unemployment among highly educated youth segments may cause frustration and grievances that could motivate political violence. It has been argued that high unemployment among educated youth is one of the most destabilizing and potentially violent sociopolitical phenomena in any regime (Choucri 1974, p. 73), and that a rapid increase in the number of educated youths has preceded historical episodes of political upheaval (Goldstone 2001b, p. 95). It has been argued that the expansion of higher education in many countries in the Middle East, producing large classes of educated youth that the labor market cannot absorb, has had a radicalizing effect and provided new recruits to militant organizations in the area (Lia 2005, pp. 145–146).

Lack of Democracy

When being used to assess the role of democracy, the opportunity and motive perspectives yield opposite predictions. The opportunity literature suggests that the opportunity for political violence is greater the less autocratic a state is, while the motive-oriented literature argues that the greater the political oppression and the lack of political rights, the greater the motive for political violence. Several empirical studies of regime type and civil conflict have found a curvilinear "inverted U" relationship between democracy and conflict, suggesting that starkly autocratic regimes and highly democratic societies are the most peaceful (Hegre et al. 2001). This relationship is assumed to arise as a result of both opportunity and motive, as semidemocratic regimes may have greater openings for conflict compared to autocratic states. At the same time, lack of political rights may also constitute a motive for conflict. It has been suggested by proponents of the motive perspective that when large youth groups aspiring to political positions are excluded from participation in the political process, they may engage in violent conflict behavior in an attempt to force democratic reform (Goldstone 2001b). The potential for radical mobilization for terrorist organizations is argued to be greater when large educated youth cohorts are barred from social mobility by autocratic and patriarchic forms of governance (Lia 2005, p. 147).

Urbanization

While institutional crowding has been the major focus, geographic crowding has also been argued to generate motives for political violence (Brennan-Galvin 2002). Since terrorism is essentially an urban phenomenon, states undergoing rapid urbanization may be particularly likely to experience increased risks of terrorism (Lia 2005, p. 141). If youth are abundant in a relatively small geographical area, this may increase the likelihood that grievances caused by crowding in the labor market or educational institutions arise. Historically, the coincidence of youth bulges with rapid urbanization, especially in the context of unemployment and poverty, has been an important contributor to political violence (Goldstone 1991, 2001b). Youth often constitute a disproportionately large part of rural-to-urban migrants; hence, in the face of large youth cohorts, strong urbanization may be expected to lead to an extraordinary crowding of youth in urban centers, potentially increasing the risk of political violence.

A Global Study of Youth Bulges and Internal Armed Conflict

The Importance of Measurement

Acknowledging that the understanding of youth differs vastly between societies, here youth refers to those aged 15 to 24, which is also the definition employed

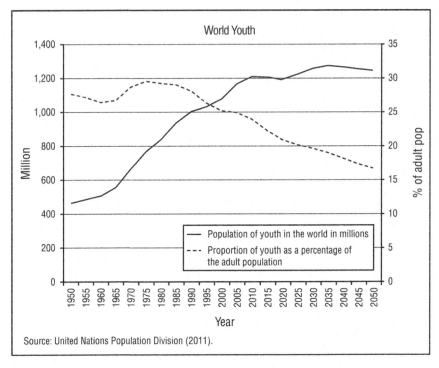

Source: United Nations Population Division (2011).

Figure 8.1   World Youth Population, 1950–2050

by the United Nations. While there is significant regional as well as local variation, the total number of youth in the world is now growing at a much lower
rate than in the previous five decades, and is expected to remain relatively
constant between 2010 and 2050 (See Figure 8.1, solid trend line measuring
millions of youth globally). The dotted line in Figure 8.1 shows the size of the
youth population aged 15 to 24 as a percentage of the total adult population
of 15 and above, excluding those younger than 15 years.

Two recent authoritative studies of civil war, by Paul Collier and Anke
Hoeffler (2004), and James Fearon and David Laitin (2003), found no effect
of youth bulges on the risk of war outbreak. However, both studies used a
flawed measure of youth bulges, dividing those aged 15 to 24 years by the total
population, including all cohorts under the age of 15 years in the denominator. Such a definition is highly problematic both theoretically and empirically. First, most theories about youth revolt assume that violence arises from
competition between younger and older cohorts, or because youth cohorts

experience institutional "bottlenecks" due to their larger size compared to previous cohorts. Second, when using the total population in the denominator, youth bulges in countries with continued high fertility will be underestimated because the large under-15 populations deflate the youth bulge measure. At the same time, countries with declining fertility and relatively smaller under-15 populations—which are in a position to experience economic growth driven by age structural change—score relatively higher.

The implications of measuring youth bulges in different ways are illustrated in the scatterplot in Figure 8.2. Here, all countries are plotted according to their values on the two different youth bulge measures in year 2000. The horizontal *x*-axis shows the value on the recommended measure, where youth bulges are defined relative to the total adult population (YBAP), while the vertical *y*-axis represents the flawed measure of youth relative to the total population (YBTP). The deviations from a linear trend line increase as the relative size of youth cohorts grow. The observations marked by the larger, lower circle are countries that have large youth cohorts, but also very large populations under the age of 15. Many countries in sub–Saharan Africa belong in this category, as do countries like Guatemala, Nicaragua, Afghanistan, Laos, Iraq, Yemen,

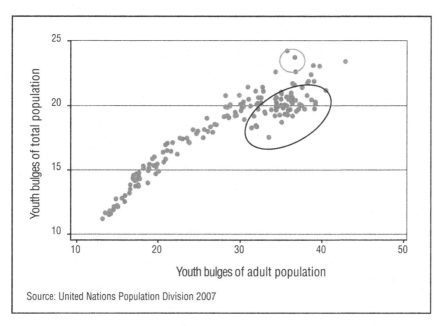

Source: United Nations Population Division 2007

Figure 8.2   Age Structure by Different Definitions

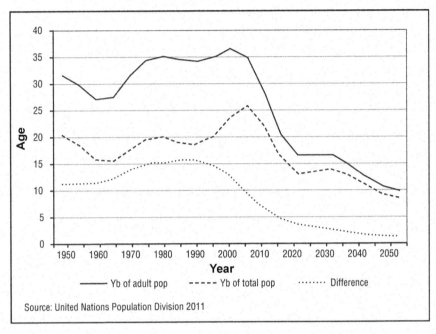

Figure 8.3   Age Structural Changes in Iran, 1950–2050

Maldives, and Papua New Guinea. In statistical models that assess the impact of youth bulges on conflict, this latter group of countries will have considerably less impact on the results when using the YBTP measure rather than the YBAP measure. The two outliers in the smaller circle are Libya and Iran, both of which experienced very steep declines in fertility in the 1990s and are now just starting to see an opportunity for a "demographic dividend."

The difference between the measures is further illustrated in Figure 8.3, showing the age structural transition in Iran. The difference between the two measures is greatest in the initial phase of the youth-bulge peak, and declines rapidly along with reduced fertility levels. Again, this underscores the importance of using a measure that is not deflated by large under-15 populations.

A Cross-National Study of Youth Bulges and Violence

In a recent cross-national time-series study of the 1950–2000 period, I found that the presence of youth bulges increases the risk of conflict outbreak significantly.[2] The statistical relationship holds even when controlling for a number of other factors, such as level of development, democracy, size of the country, and conflict history, and the results are also robust to a variety of technical specifications.[3] For each percentage point increase that youth make up of the adult population, the risk of conflict increases by more than 4 percent. When youth make up more than 35 percent of the adult population, as they do in many developing countries, the risk of armed conflict is 150 percent higher than in countries with an age structure similar to most developed countries. In 2000, 15- to 24-year-olds made up 17 percent or less of the total adult population in almost all developed countries, the median being 15 percent. The same year, 44 developing countries experienced youth bulges of 35 percent or above.[4] A claim that youth bulges are particularly volatile when they pass certain thresholds does not seem to be supported (Huntington 1996). There is evidence, on the other side, that youth bulges seem to be associated with a higher risk of conflict in countries with high dependency ratios, while countries that are well underway in their demographic transitions are likely to experience a "peace dividend."

If youth bulges increase the likelihood of armed conflict, how and why do they matter? While the conflict risk does not seem to increase when youth bulges coincide with long-term per capita economic decline, high dependency ratios, expansions in higher education, or strong urban growth, the results suggest that the effect of youth bulges is greater in the most autocratic regimes as well as in the most democratic states. It could indicate that youth bulges provide greater opportunities in autocracies and greater motives in democracies. Beyond the youth-bulge measures, low development (measured as high infant mortality rates), semidemocracy (neither full democracies, nor stark autocracies), larger country size (measured as total population), and recent conflict history are all associated with a higher conflict risk. In Figure 8.4, the combined effects of youth bulges and regime type are shown in a three-dimensional graph. It shows that democracy is associated with conflict onset in an inverse U-shaped relationship, meaning that intermediary regimes are more conflict prone than both democracies and dictatorships. The curve is not perfectly symmetrical around the mean value 0; full-fledged democracies do have a slightly higher risk of conflict than stark autocracies. Countries with the value of +1 on the regime scale are most conflict prone. Compared to the most conflict-exposed regimes, fully developed democracies (+10) are almost 40 percent less likely to experience a conflict, while consistent autocracies (-10) are 60 percent less exposed, all other variables at their mean values.

Finally, there is support for the suspicion that a flawed measure is the reason why previous studies by Collier and Hoeffler and Fearon and Laitin have failed

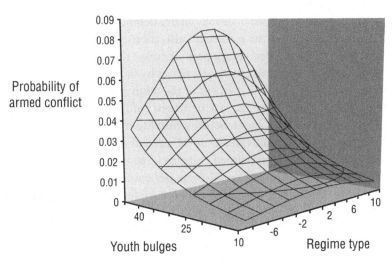

Figure 8.4   Youth Bulges, Regime Type and Armed Conflict

to detect significant effects of youth bulges. If the measurement they suggest, the YBTP,[5] is applied to the conflict onset model, youth bulges are no longer statistically significantly associated with conflict. The measurement conceals the opposite effects that age structure may have under the different conditions of low and high fertility levels. Another reason why these studies do not find any effect of youth bulges is that they exclusively look at high-intensity wars and do not include minor conflicts. When the empirical study presented in this chapter is restricted to only onsets of civil wars with at least 1,000 battle-related deaths per year, the youth-bulge measure loses statistical significance in the basic model.[6] Thus, youth bulges appear to increase the risk of onset of minor conflict, but not of major wars.

A Geriatric Peace?

By 2050, the world will have undergone a dramatic shift in the age structure of the adult population compared to 1950. During the 1950–1990 period, youth between 15 and 24 years made up more than 25 percent of the adult population in Asia, Africa, and America. By 2050, however, the United Nations Population Division (2011) predicts that only sub–Saharan Africa will still have young adult shares above 25 percent, while most other world regions will have young adult shares below 15 percent. The main reason for this shift is the global decline in fertility that began in the 1960s and that has gained increasing momentum over the last decades. Will this aging world also become a more peaceful world, creating a "geriatric peace"?

What is clear from the demographic projections is that most developing countries will over the next decades experience age-structural transitions that represent a considerable potential for a demographic dividend. If governments are able to take advantage of this situation, by providing schooling and employment opportunities for young people, we might expect to see this turn into a "peace dividend." Looking ahead using the U.N. population projections, it can be noted that the three world regions with the highest current risks—sub–Saharan Africa, Asia, and the Middle East and North Africa—can expect relatively rapid declines in the demographically determined risk levels after 2010. While the most rapid decline in risk levels will take place in sub–Saharan Africa, large parts of the Middle East and North Africa could, based on the demographic factors, face risk levels almost as low as in present-day Europe.

It is important to stress, however, that age-structural transitions only represent an opportunity for economic growth and a "peace dividend." Where governments fail to provide opportunities for young people to participate in economic, social, and political life, instability may result even under more favorable demographic conditions. Both among countries that have entered the demographic "window of opportunity" and among countries that will experience high youth bulges for decades to come, is it necessary to monitor the situation of young people and implement appropriate policies. It has also been suggested that a particular focus should be on cases of "echo-booms," that is, rapid increases in the youth population after periods of gradual decline (Jackson and Howe 2008).

It is interesting to note that two prominent international rogue states, Iran and Libya,[7] are both moving rapidly toward a demographic window of opportunity and a more mature population structure. It is, however, unclear whether the governments of the two countries might be able to seize this opportunity to achieve economic and social progress, not to say whether demographic maturing could contribute to moderate these states' behavior in international politics. A recent review of youth exclusion in Iran suggests that overcrowding in educational institutions and a rigid labor market prohibit the full realization of the demographic dividend (Salehi-Isfahani and Egel 2008; Salehi-Isfahani and Dhillon 2008). Furthermore, due to past high fertility, Iran will experience an "echo-boom" amounting to a 30 percent increase in the population aged 15 to 24 years over the next decade (Jackson and Howe 2008). This will add considerable strain on Iranian educational institutions and labor markets.

In many countries with recent conflicts, large youth bulges combined with high levels of youth exclusion could fuel renewed conflicts and jeopardize fragile peace settlements. Providing opportunities for large youth cohorts in postconflict settings, not limited to former combatants, could significantly increase the likelihood of stability and sustainable peace. In some of the most severe conflicts in the world, large and growing youth populations and high levels of youth exclusion represent major challenges to conflict termination and settlement.[8] In Palestine and Afghanistan, the youth populations between the ages of 15 and 24 will increase by approximately 45 percent between 2005 and 2015 (United Nations Population Division 2011). If opportunities for young people are not improved in these countries, we could easily see increased recruitment to extremist movements like Hamas and the Taliban. Similarly, in many poor countries in sub–Saharan Africa the lack of opportunities for young people could fuel conflicts, in particular those involving resource rents. In the Democratic Republic of Congo the youth population 15 to 24 years old will increase by 38 percent from 2005 to 2015.

Conclusion

Population growth and a young age structure can be both a blessing and a curse. From a more optimistic perspective, youth bulges can be regarded as an increased supply of labor that can boost an economy. This could further be expected to reduce conflict propensity—a "peace dividend." While such development is certainly possible, structural aspects of the economy will probably determine the significance of this positive effect of age structural transitions. While the youth-bulge hypothesis in general is supported by empirical evidence, the ways that youth bulges influence conflict propensity still remain largely unexplored empirically. However, this study provides evidence that youth bulges, poor governance, and failing economic growth can be explosive. This represents a considerable security challenge to many developing countries, particularly in sub–Saharan Africa, Asia, and parts of the Arab world. However, states are to some extent able to reduce the risk through the provision of opportunities for young people, primarily by providing education and employment opportunities.

Generally, the importance of youth bulges in causing political violence is expected to fade in most parts of the world over the next few decades because of declining fertility. The general relationship between age structure and conflict is weakened as countries experience declining fertility rates and become positioned to take advantage of their young age structures to achieve demographic dividends. Many countries are currently moving into this category. However, for states that will experience high fertility levels and great youth shares for years to come, especially in some countries in the Middle East, Africa, and parts of Asia, age composition still warrants some caution.

In order to avoid instability and violence in particular, states should focus on monitoring economic opportunities for young people, and particularly on providing both employment or educational opportunities for youth. While expanding opportunities for education generally pacify youth cohorts, it has also been suggested that as opportunities for higher education are expanded, lack of employment opportunities for highly educated youth may contribute to instability.

Limiting migration opportunities may increase the risk of violence in some countries with large youth bulges if not compensated for by increased domestic employment opportunities. Emigration may work as a safety valve in countries with large youth cohorts. In a recent survey, almost half of all Arab youth expressed a desire to emigrate resulting from concerns over job opportunities and education (United Nations Development Program 2002). If migration opportunities are increasingly restricted without domestic initiatives in place to provide opportunities for youth, developing countries that previously relied on exporting surplus youth may experience increased pressures from youth bulges accompanied by a higher risk of political violence.

Some areas stand out as particularly promising for further study of youth bulges and political violence. Additional disaggregated, subnational studies can provide better tests of some of the relationships concerning youth opportunities and violence. Disaggregated studies could also address the claim that differential age structures between identity groups contribute to explaining interethnic conflict dynamics. However, structural models are limited in the sense that they purportedly explain individual-level behavior while in reality we have very limited micro-level evidence explaining what motivates youth who engage in political violence. Hence, a promising next step in the study of youth and violence would be surveys of youth in both conflict and nonconflict settings aimed at explaining variations in perceptions and perpetration of violence.

Notes

1. Two other studies reporting similar findings are Daniel C. Esty, Jack A. Goldstone, Ted Robert Gurr, Barbara Harff, Marc Levy, Geoffrey D. Dabelko, Pamela Surko, and Alan N. Unger (1998), and Richard P. Cincotta, Robert Engelman, and Daniele Anastasion (2003).

2. For conflict data, see the PRIO/Uppsala dataset: Nils Petter Gleditsch, Petter Wallensteen, Mikael Eriksson, Margareta Sollenberg, and Håvard Strand (2002). Conflicts are defined according to a set of specific criteria, of which at least 25 battle deaths per year is one.

3. For a full report of the results, see Urdal (2006).

4. The results were corroborated by similar effects of youth bulges on measures of terrorism and riots/demonstrations.

5. Fearon and Laitin (2003) and Collier and Hoeffler (2004) measure the male youth population over total population. Including both sexes, as applied here, produces only a marginally different measure.

6. However, this nonresult is sensitive to the model setup. When applying a slightly different way of modeling peace history, the term remains statistically significant.

7. Iran was among the three states named the "axis of evil" by former U.S. president George W. Bush, while Libya was included in the extended list by former U.S. ambassador to the U.N., John R. Bolton.

8. There are, however, no systematic large-N studies of youth bulges, conflict duration, and termination.

9

Demography, Climate Change, and Conflict

Richard Matthew

GOVERNING A PARCHED AND PACKED PLANET MAY PROVE to be the overarching political challenge of the twenty-first century. This challenge will not be easily met. As global issues, demographic change and climate change have much in common that militates against quick and simple policy solutions.

First, the stakes are very high—each variable has the potential to adversely and dramatically affect virtually all human values, practices, and institutions. The effects of poor decisions could be catastrophic, which may make policy-makers far more comfortable with taking small and cautious steps.

Second, both variables have considerable momentum, and because of this they are best depicted as long-term (over 30 years) challenges. Responding to long-term challenges is not a very attractive proposition for political or business leaders who worry that the return on substantial investments made today could take decades to materialize—if at all. Moreover, long-term challenges, because they are inevitably characterized by disagreement and uncertainty about how things will unfold in the years ahead, are relatively easy to set aside for further study.

Third, both are highly controversial topics, in that they are flashpoints for many global asymmetries and inequities that have long and complex histories. What obligations or constraints should developing countries accept on their behavior when the principal anthropogenic causes of climate change have been clearly linked to the activities of developed countries? Why should poorer countries of the South reduce population growth, and diminish the political leverage that comes with numbers, when the ecological footprints of Northern families and communities are so much greater? But, on the other hand, how much responsibility should those in developed countries bear for the unforeseen consequences of decisions made decades and even centuries ago? And now that we know the likely environmental consequences of deforestation and fossil fuel use, don't developing states have a responsibility to change course instead of making things worse?

Fourth, both demographic change and climate change result from many variables and have diverse and dynamic effects. These are not issues that lend themselves to straightforward cost-benefit analysis or simple formulas for defining stakeholder roles and responsibilities. Indeed, they force policymakers and others to work with complicated and evolving scenarios rather than simple, tried-and-true cause-and-effect models.

Fifth, and finally, both challenges are global in scale and demonstrate two of the key features of contemporary forms of global change: They are fast moving and highly connected to, and interactive with, other trends and variables (see Held et al. 1999). With so many actors, values, and institutions in play, coordinating fair and effective responses in a timely fashion is extremely difficult. For these five reasons—and perhaps others as well—it is not surprising that much frustration has been expressed by both governments and citizens about the slow pace of change. In short, fertility rates remain high in much of the world, and carbon dioxide and other greenhouse gas emissions continue to build in the atmosphere. The world seems destined to become hotter and more crowded—an outcome almost no one wants to witness or cause—and this in spite of almost four decades of consensus-based scientific reports, high-level international meetings, and increasingly dire warnings (IPCC 2007a and b; Reiss 2001; Stern 2006).

These global challenges share traits that make them difficult to address. They also interact in ways that add further complexity to each—but that may provide some opportunities for the sort of win-win policies around which it may be easier to mobilize support. The purpose of this chapter is to consider the broad trends in demographic change and climate change; examine the interactions between them and identify the key political implications of these interactions; and suggest some directions that state and nonstate actors should pursue.

Characteristics, Trends, and Their Interactions

Demographic Change: Characteristics and Trends

Demography is a complex field that generates a wide range of findings and predictions. Since this volume is about demographic change, I limit my focus here to only those features of world demography that appear to be directly relevant to the issue of climate change, a selection based on broad consultation of the recent, but rather sparse, literature on the subject (especially Dyson July 2005; Goldstone 2008/2009; McNeill 2007; O'Neill, MacKellar, and Lutz 2001; Population Action International May 2009; Raleigh and Urdal 2007; Smith 2008; and Urdal 2008). In simple terms, these features include the number of people on the planet; the key attributes of the world's population such as age and geographic distribution; consumption patterns around the world; and, of course, the trends in each of these areas.

Since the beginning of the twentieth century, world population has grown from 1.6 billion to about 7 billion today (2011). The current rate of growth is about 1.1 percent, and the medium prediction of demographers at the United Nations is that population will reach 9.2 billion by 2050 (United Nations Population Division 2007). As Jack Goldstone notes, "Countries are growing today for two major reasons: high population growth rates and demographic momentum." (2008/2009, p. 2) The former is evident in South Asia (Nepal and Pakistan), the Middle East (Afghanistan, Iraq, Jordan, Saudi Arabia, and Yemen), and parts of Africa such as the Democratic Republic of the Congo. The latter is evident in countries with vast populations of fertile women, such as China and India, where the absolute number of people is increasing significantly even though growth rates are low—0.5 and 1.1 percent per year, respectively. One consequence of this is that South Asia and sub–Saharan Africa are growing dramatically as a portion of world population—from 649 million and 26 percent in 1950 to 2.3 billion and 35 percent in 2008, and on to an estimated 4 billion and 44 percent by 2050 (Urdal 2008). These parts of the world are becoming more and more crowded—in sharp contrast to the North where, "[d]uring the next several decades, the population of most European countries ... will shrink substantially, due mainly to a sharp decline in the number of children per couple (Goldstone 2008/2009, p. 5).

South Asia and sub–Saharan Africa are becoming crowded—and remaining poor. According to the World Bank, from 1981 to 2001 the percentage of desperately poor people in the world (that is, people who are living on less than one dollar per day) declined from 40 percent to 21 percent, but the number of people lifted from extreme poverty declined by far less—from 1.5 billion to 1.1 billion. Indeed, some regions of the world, such as sub–Saharan Africa, witnessed substantial increases in the numbers (from 164 million to 314 million) and percentage (from 41 percent to 46 percent) of desperately poor (PovertyNet 2004). Because of high population growth rates and population momentum, there continues to be a steady flow of children into dire poverty, a flow that offsets the gains made in global poverty reduction.

In geographic terms, people are relocating from rural to urban areas, or finding their rural areas rapidly transformed into urban areas, as globally urbanization is taking place at a rate of 2.2 percent per year. A 2006 special feature in the journal *Foreign Policy* noted that by 2015 there will be 21 megacities in the world, almost all located in developing countries. The editors examined the biggest challenges in six of these: earthquakes in Tokyo, flooding in Mumbai, pollution in Mexico City, crime in Sao Paulo, overcrowding in Seoul, and sanitation in Lagos, Nigeria. These sorts of urban challenges are extremely difficult to resolve; in fact, the editors suggest that only Tokyo and Seoul are likely to address these problems effectively.

Also of interest from a demographic perspective, the age gap between North and South is changing, as many OECD countries move towards average ages in the mid- to late 40s, with large parts of the population over 65 and retired, and substantial portions in their 80s and 90s. This creates new demands for services such as social security and healthcare, while shrinking the labor force. In the South, however, average population age is as low as 15 in some countries, and in the mid-20s overall. In these areas, yet another notable demographic trend has to do with the growth of Islam. Many developed countries are worried about the volatility of large numbers of undereducated, underemployed, and youthful fundamentalists in countries such as Bangladesh and Pakistan (Goldstone 2011). Social unrest can compel a government to invest heavily in security and also encourage it to use its position to provide benefits to certain social groups in an effort to consolidate and strengthen its support base, and to neglect some public goods as well as the development of new policies (see Kahl 2006).

Finally, patterns of consumption are changing as the global middle class, concentrated in the so-called BRIC nations (Brazil, Russia, India, and China) expands dramatically and with it the desire for motorcycles and cars, larger houses, meat, and other commodities that require large amounts of energy to produce, distribute, and operate (Conca 2002; Dauvergne 2008).

Climate Change: Characteristics and Trends

The science behind climate change is well-known (IPCC 2007a and b). Scientists estimate that absent any mediation, the sun would heat the earth to an average of about -18 degrees centigrade. This does not happen because greenhouse gases in the atmosphere trap heat from the sun, resulting in an average world temperature of about 15 degrees centigrade, a temperature that many believe is critical insofar as providing a congenial environment for diverse life forms is concerned. The principal greenhouse gas is water vapor, but there are many others, several of which have increased in concentration due to human activity, including carbon dioxide, methane, and halocarbons. Scientists have identified a clear trend of global warming and through extensive research spanning some 50 years have determined that this is the result of anthropogenic greenhouse gas emissions from industry, transportation, the heating and cooling of residential and commercial buildings, and energy production, as well as from other human activities that have affected carbon cycles such as deforestation and agriculture. In simple terms, less carbon is being stored in forests and underground as coal or oil, and more is being added to the atmosphere where it acts to trap heat from the sun. Since 1850, average global temperature has increased by one degree centigrade. Today very few skeptics exist who contend that global warming is not taking place or that there is another, natural explanation for the increase that has been observed.

There remain areas of great uncertainty. Scientists are unsure about whether global warming will lead to more or less cloud cover, and how this will affect weather. They are not at all certain about what will happen to the vast reservoirs of methane trapped in the earth's permafrost, they are still learning about the implications of massive glacial melt, and they have yet to develop tools for predicting how weather will change at a local scale. But scientists do know a great deal about what has transpired in the last 150 years, and they are not at all sanguine about what this means for the world. The pervasive sentiment is that research may shed light on some of these areas of uncertainty but it is not likely to generate much optimism about the rate and implications of climate change.

To help guide policy, scientists in 11 countries have developed 23 models for predicting what could happen over the next century. If the world continues to rely on carbon-based energy, population growth continues at its current rate of about 1.1 percent, and "dirty" technologies continue to be used, these models predict an average increase of as much as 6.4 degrees centigrade by 2100 (IPCC 2007a and b). Even in the best-case scenarios, with clean technologies, renewable energy, extensive mitigation, and a stable world population, scientists believe the planet cannot avoid warming by at least one more degree—this already has occurred in the oceans and will gradually be transferred to the land. The big question, then, is what will a 1 to 6.4 degree centigrade increase in global temperature mean for humankind?

Scientists worry about two general categories of effect. The first has to do with what we are already experiencing—such as changes in the distribution of water that affect agriculture and other human activities, increases in the number and intensity of severe weather events, longer heat waves and droughts, continuing desertification, biodiversity loss wherever species are unable to adapt to an altered environment, and more flooding. They worry that as temperatures rise, things will become worse on all these fronts. The second category has to do with effects that are unknown. Here the concern is that global warming may push ecosystems across critical thresholds, causing dramatic and unforeseen knock-on effects such as sudden gas releases, rapid glaciation, or unprecedented microbial explosions. In both cases, scientists are worried that any benefits that accrue from global warming—such as longer growing seasons in some regions or easier access to natural resources previously trapped under ice—will be dwarfed by the costs—such as widespread famines, global pandemics, and mass migration into marginal or hostile lands.

Climate-Population Interactions

There are two fundamental linkages between the forms of demographic change and the type of climate change described above. First, most of the demographic trends are likely to increase the anthropogenic causes of global warming. For example, Kerri Smith argues that on "a global scale, per capita carbon dioxide emissions from fossil fuels have hardly changed since 1970, hovering around the 1.2-tonne mark .... This average varies hugely from nation to nation, but the general trend is that as the population has grown, emissions have increased in proportion" (2008, p. 1). Urbanization aggravates matters further, as there is considerable evidence that the energy needs of cities are much greater than those of rural communities (e.g., Homer-Dixon 2006). The burgeoning, consumption-oriented middle classes of the BRIC nations add yet another source of climate stress. Perhaps the only variable running counter to all this is the shrinking and aging of many OECD countries, which suggests the potential for a parallel reduction in energy demand.

The second important linkage is the mirror image of the first. Ironically, while the young and expanding populations of Asia and Africa are likely to increase their contribution to global warming, their actions may also be increasing their vulnerability to climate change effects. In other words, the sort of demographic changes predicted for the next few decades will not only intensify the carbonization of the atmosphere, they will also increase the number of people with heightened vulnerability to adverse climate change effects. There are several reasons for this. First, much of the population growth is occurring in places that are already vulnerable to water scarcity—namely sub–Saharan Africa, South Asia, and the Middle East. Climate change is expected to aggravate the problem of water scarcity in these same areas (Brown et al. 2007). For example, "more than 1.6 billion people in South Asia could face acute water and food shortages from the melting of the Himalayan glaciers as a result of climate change, warns Asia Development Bank" ("Glacier Melt a Looming Threat" 2009, p. 1).

Second, many of the activities that will be accelerated by population growth also increase vulnerability to climate effects, such as the annual clearing of over 15 million hectares of tropical forest, which is the principal source of food, fuel, and livelihoods for some 2 billion people in the developing world. Deforestation reduces the natural buffer to flooding and soil erosion, and thus intensifies the impact of climate change-related stressors such as severe weather events and drought.

Hot Spots

Following the publication of the 2007 IPCC reports, a number of analyses appeared suggesting ways in which climate change could adversely affect international security and the condition of the poor (see Barnett and Adger 2007; Brown et al. 2007; Campbell 2008; CNA 2007; German Advisory Council on Global Change 2008; Giddens 2009; IPCC 2007a and 2007b; Maas and Tanzler 2009; McNeil 2008; OXFAM 2008; and Smith and Vivekananda 2007). According to the German Advisory Council on Global Change's report, *World in Transition: Climate Change as a Security Risk*, "Climate change will overstretch many societies' adaptive capacities within the coming decades. (2007, p. 1) The report highlights a set of "conflict constellations" (p. 2) related to climate change centered around degradation of fresh water; decline in food production; increase in storm and flood disasters; and environmentally induced migration—all in climate-sensitive areas that lack the capacity to manage these challenges. The areas deemed to be at greatest risk are North Africa, the Sahel, Southern Africa, Central Asia, South Asia, China, the Caribbean and Gulf of Mexico, and the Andean region and Amazonia (pp. 2–4). These are the hot spots of the twenty-first century.

Similar concerns have been expressed in the CNA Corporation's report, prepared by a group of retired generals and admirals known as the Military Advisory Board, on *National Security and the Threat of Climate Change* (2007). This report concludes that "Climate change acts as a threat multiplier for instability in some of the most volatile regions of the world" (p. 6). Further, "Projected climate change will add to tensions even in stable regions of the world" (p. 7).

The general sentiment of much recent writing is that climate change will weaken states that are already not able to provide a minimal set of public goods, with its most immediate adverse effects on agricultural economies, which are overrepresented in the poor and conflict-prone regions of the world. Therefore it will amplify conflict and insecurity, increase migration, deepen sensitivity to disasters, and disrupt sustainable development and poverty alleviation efforts—especially in South Asia, the Middle East, and sub–Saharan Africa.

Political Implications

What, then, are the main implications of the interaction between climate change and demographic change in those areas of the world where the effects are likely to be most severe and the capacity to manage them most limited? There are at least four areas of concern. It is important to note that while this typology may suggest that these are fairly discrete issues, there is considerable overlap across and dynamism among the four.

State Failure and Violent Conflict

A substantial body of work has emerged since the 1992 U.N. Earth Summit in Rio de Janeiro seeking to link the scarcity or degradation of natural resource to state failure and violent conflict (e.g., Bannon and Collier 2003; Deudney and Matthew 1999; Gleick 1989, 1993; Hauge and Ellingsen 1998; Homer-Dixon 1999, 2000; Kahl 2006; and Myers 1993). Typical of this literature, the work of Thomas Homer-Dixon (1999, 2000) focuses on the adverse social effects of scarcity of water, cropland, and pasture—areas of scarcity that current climate change research suggests will intensify throughout much of Africa and Asia. For Homer-Dixon, scarcity results from one or more of three causes: a real decrease in the supply of a resource (for example, the depletion of a fishery due to overfishing or global warming); an increase in demand due to population growth or changes in production or consumption practices; or institutional factors (for example, the privatization of resources in a manner that benefits a few at the expense of the many). Faced with one or more form of resource scarcity, Homer-Dixon argues that developing societies often respond through resource capture (one group seizes control of the resource) or ecological marginalization (people are forced to move into resource-poor lands). Either of these processes can lead to or amplify violent civil conflict. Homer-Dixon concludes that the explanatory weight of resource scarcity in violent civil conflict will likely increase over time.

Working within this framework, Colin Kahl (2006) has sought to clarify the link between natural resource scarcity and violent conflict by arguing that the former can lead to state failure or state exploitation. State failure occurs when demographic and environmental stress undermine the functional capacity and social cohesion of the state; state exploitation happens when the weakened state acts to preserve itself by aligning with some social groups and allowing them greater access to or full control over the scarce resource.

Although familiar scholarly arguments exist that challenge the empirical support for these theses and offer alternative explanations of violent conflict and state failure, many academics, policymakers, and nonstate actors have found these "environmental change, state failure, violent conflict" arguments compelling. Moreover, while the historical record reveals few unambiguous cases where conflict can be traced to resource scarcities, the future impacts of climate change could well produce scarcities of water and arable land far greater than any seen in recent history. Thus, unprecedented, climate-induced resource scarcities could become far more important drivers of conflicts in the future. Insofar as this perspective holds some explanatory value, we can anticipate increases in state failure and violent conflict in areas where climate change reduces the availability of water, arable land, and other vital natural resources.

Migration and Climate Refugees

Climate change-related food insecurity, flooding, and drought are widely expected to add to other migration pressures such as the "push factor" of poverty and violence and the "pull factor" of urban and Western labor markets. According to the influential review led by Sir Nicholas Stern (2006), "200 million more people may become permanently displaced due to rising sea levels, heavier floods, and more intense droughts" by midcentury (p. 56). However, there are few—if any—places on the planet that are willing to welcome millions of poor immigrants fleeing degraded environments. As with other population flows, climate change is expected to amplify movement within countries, especially from rural to urban environments, as well as movement across borders. In either case, so-called climate refugees may become implicated in violent conflict, or simply confront global civil society with a chronic humanitarian crisis.

Henrik Urdal argues that the

> potential for and challenges related to migration spurred by climate change should be acknowledged, but not overemphasized. Some forms of environmental change associated with climate change like extreme weather and flooding may cause substantial and acute, but mostly temporal, displacement of people. However, the most dramatic form of change expected to affect human settlements, sea-level rise, is likely to happen gradually, as are processes of soil and freshwater degradation.

He adds that "individuals respond differently to changes in their environment, and coping and adaptation mechanisms involve a range of options short of permanent migration" (2008, p. 5).

Urdal's measured assessment needs to be considered alongside the more pessimistic perspectives that foresee hundreds of millions of people displaced by drought and famine in their homelands into the attractive economies and safe havens of industrial countries in Europe and North America. In either case, however, there are solid reasons for predicting that climate change will affect population flows on a scale that demands careful policy consideration and probably new institutions and budget lines.

The Disaster Trap

According to the 2009 report of the International Federation of the Red Cross and Red Crescent Societies (IFRC), "In terms of natural disasters and their impacts, 2008 was one of the most devastating years. While hazards are largely unavoidable, especially with the growing threat of climate change, they only become disasters when communities' coping mechanisms are exceeded and they are unable to manage their impacts. The world's poorest and most vulnerable people are those most at risk" (p. 7). Chapter 4 of the IFRC report focuses in on the problem of climate change with the following argument:

> The threat of disaster resulting from climate change is twofold. First, individual extreme events will devastate vulnerable communities in their path. If population

growth is factored in, many more people may be at significant risk. Together, these events add up to potentially the most significant threat to human progress that the world has seen. Second, climate change will compound the already complex problems of poor countries, and could contribute to a downward development spiral for millions of people, even greater than has already been experienced. (p. 95)

As the Red Cross report makes clear, disaster response is enormously costly—which is why the theme of the 2009 report is on the importance of early warning and early action systems. Disasters divert funds that might otherwise be used for infrastructure, skills development, and livelihood creation into emergency relief, which can place downward pressure on a government's functional capacity. At the same time as the government's poverty reduction and other programs may be losing funds, profiteers can emerge who benefit from the chaos that often surrounds the distribution of disaster response funds, and communities may begin to grow dependent on this costly form of assistance. These pieces can become reinforcing, creating a disaster trap in which the incapacity to invest in development amplifies vulnerability to disasters that require more and more costly responses and that create groups within a society that accept and benefit from this situation (Klein 2007). The contributions of climate change and demographic change to this bleak scenario are becoming increasingly evident.

Maldevelopment and Setbacks to Poverty Reduction[1]

In spite of many successes in reducing poverty and encouraging development, a sizable portion of the world's population remains desperately poor. As Paul Collier argues, "The real challenge of development is that there is a group of countries at the bottom that are falling behind, and often falling apart." He adds, "The countries at the bottom coexist with the twenty-first century, but their reality is the fourteenth century: civil war, plague, ignorance" (2007, p. 3). In short, national and international development strategies have succeeded for a portion of the world, but have failed miserably for the bottom 20 percent. Collier identifies a series of reasons for this: These states are often trapped into violent conflict, victims of an abundance of lootable natural resources such as oil or diamonds, surrounded by other unstable and violent countries, and governed by corrupt and incompetent officials. These, for Collier, are the challenges that must be addressed if this group is to be lifted from poverty.

Climate change adds yet another challenge to this already daunting list for all of the reasons noted above. State failure, violent conflict, population displacement, and disasters make poverty reduction and sustainable development difficult in obvious ways. Climate change also complicates sustainable development and poverty reduction because the vast network of state and nonstate actors pursuing these goals, for the most part, have not yet assessed how their activities affect climate change and vice versa, and are far from determining what new approaches need therefore to be developed, tested, and implemented.

Policy Recommendations

Given the scale and variety of problems likely to develop in those places where demographic change and climate change intersect, the sooner steps are taken to modify the trends, build adaptive capacity, and reduce vulnerability, the better.

Mitigation

The most obvious solution to the problems described above is to reduce greenhouse gas emissions. This could be done in four general ways: (1) by improving the efficiency of energy use in transportation, buildings, and other areas where there is considerable waste; (2) by moving towards alternative sources of energy that do not emit greenhouse gases such as nuclear power and renewable forms such as wind and geothermal; (3) by protecting natural carbon storage systems such as forest cover, and developing new ways of capturing and storing carbon; and (4) by reducing consumption by changing behavior and reducing or reversing population growth.

In his 2006 report, Stern recommended that the world invest 1 percent of GDP into mitigation activities; following the evidence provided by the 2007 IPCC reports, he revised this upwards to 2 percent (Stern 2006; Burtraw and Sterner 2009). The mitigation challenge is indeed enormous. The 2009 U.N. report *Promoting Development, Saving the Planet,*

> recognizes a maximum temperature increase of 2°C above preindustrial levels as the target for stabilizing carbon concentrations at a level that prevents dangerous anthropogenic interference in the climate system. This corresponds to a target greenhouse gas concentration (in terms of carbon dioxide equivalents (CO_2e)) of between 350 and 450 parts per million (ppm) and to global emission reductions of the order of 50–80 per cent over 1990 levels, by 2050. In terms of actual emissions, this would be equivalent to a reduction from roughly 40 gigatons of carbon dioxide ($GtCO_2$) at present to between 8 and 20 $GtCO_2$ by 2050. (p. vi)

While the authors of this report argue that development and mitigation can be reconciled for the developing world, there are many observers alarmed by how little has been achieved to date and by the slow pace of change. Homer-Dixon, for example, suggests that the global dependence on fossil fuel is too deeply entrenched to modify to the extent called for by the IPCC and others, and predicts a series of large-scale breakdowns for the years ahead (2006).

As noted above, reducing or reversing population growth is often regarded as an integral part of mitigation and the techniques for doing so—such as family planning and better education, especially for women—are well-known and will not be reviewed here.

Geoengineering

If mitigation is not successful in stabilizing the global climate system, some scientists suggest that governments may need to explore geoengineering on a planetary scale. Proposals include taking steps to alter the reflectivity—or albedo—of the earth's surface such as scattering dust particles in the atmosphere, developing artificial carbon storage systems, and introducing iron into the oceans to absorb atmospheric carbon dioxide by encouraging phytoplankton blooms. The obvious questions regarding geoengineering are: Can we design and implement such enormous projects? Are they economically viable? And what negative externalities could we be setting up?

Adaptation Through Innovation and Cooperation

The alternative to mitigation that does have widespread support is adaptation. Given that climate effects are already being experienced, and that global warming is going to continue under every conceivable scenario, some degree of adaptation will be required regardless of any mitigation and geoengineering strategies adopted.

> Adaptation is a socioecological process of change or adjustment to new or modified circumstances. Within the context of climate change, it is understood as actions that people take in response to, or in anticipation of changing climate conditions to reduce adverse impacts or take advantage of any opportunities that may arise (Adger, Arnel, and Tompkins 2005). The need for, type, and scale of adaptation depends on the kind of change taking place, as well as the vulnerability of people and natural systems to this change. (Hammill and Matthew 2009, p. 14)

Elsewhere Anne Hammill and I have argued, following McGray et al. (2007), that we can "imagine an adaptation spectrum, where the activities at one end are basically development activities that reduce multiple forms of vulnerability, while those at the other end are designed specifically in response to reducing vulnerability to the real or anticipated impacts of climate change per se" (2009, pp. 15–16). The key message here is that development in ways sensitive to climate change is a form of adaptation that reduces vulnerability, alleviates poverty, and empowers communities and households with the knowledge and capacity required to manage adverse climate change effects. Cooperation between developed and developing countries in seeking innovations to respond to climate vulnerability, and to take advantage of any promising climate-related opportunities for new livelihoods, will have to be part of the adaptations needed to cope with a planet that will have several billion more people while facing a more severe and more variable climate than any in recent history.

Note

1. This section is adapted from a longer discussion in a draft paper by Anne Hammill and Richard Matthew entitled "Sustainable Development and Global Change," September 2009.

Part IV

Demography and National Politics

10

Racial Demographics and the 2008 Presidential Election in the United States

William H. Frey

T HE PREVIOUS CHAPTERS HAVE SHOWN HOW LONG-TERM national and global population trends can shape international security issues, and influence political development and risks of violent conflict. But even in the most advanced industrial nations, population changes can also have a major impact on politics. In particular, in democracies shifts in the proportions of various groups in the voting population—the young and old, religious and ethnic groups—and in their locations can have a highly significant and disproportionate impact on the outcomes of elections. This is particularly true if certain groups congregate in crucial areas such as major cities or states or regions with nearly evenly-divided political allegiances, or voting participation rates start to alter for specific groups.

The election of Barack Obama as the first African American, multiethnic president has been touted as a transformative event in a country that is experiencing dramatic demographic change. Obama's strong support among blacks, Hispanics, and other fast-growing minorities suggests that future national candidates need to pay great attention to the issues embraced by minorities as they become major players in the electorate.

Nonetheless, as in the two previous elections, whites voted for the Republican candidate (John McCain), though in lesser numbers; and they still comprise the vast majority of voters. This is especially the case in some large slow-growing battleground states, which might have swung for a stronger Republican candidate if not for this white retreat. The voter populations in faster-growing parts of the country are more in flux, and it is in these areas where the recent election represents more of a transformation.

What do the hard data on racial and ethnic shifts and voting imply about this so-called transformative election? I will explore a few topics that shed some light on this question.

National Minority Voting and Turnout

From a national perspective, there is no doubt that minorities played an important role in Obama's victory. With respect to voting margins (the percent voting for Obama minus the percent voting for McCain), he won blacks, Hispanics, and Asians (see Figure 10.1). In each case, he did better in 2008 than John Kerry did in 2004. Moreover, whites voted Republican less than was the case in 2004.

These voting margins become magnified when we consider that minorities composed a larger part of the voter base in 2008. Two million more blacks voted in 2008 than in 2004, as well as almost 2 million more Hispanics and close to a million more Asians. About half a million fewer whites voted in 2008 than in 2004. So the composition of the voting population shifted more to minorities.

Nonetheless, there still is a population-to-eligible voter "translation gap" among minorities (see Figure 10.2). Among every 100 whites in the population, 77 of them were eligible voters, as the rest were either too young to vote or noncitizens. However, among every 100 Hispanics in the population only 42 of them were eligible voters because a much higher share of Hispanics are under 18 and a significant share are noncitizens. This is also the case for Asians, and somewhat less so the case for blacks. Thus, when one translates the racial

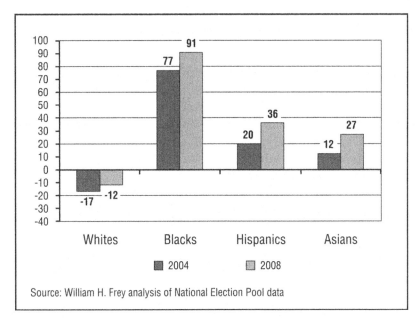

Figure 10.1   Democratic Margins by Race

composition of the population into the racial composition of the eligible voters, the latter has a larger share of whites (73 percent of eligible voters versus 65 percent of the population) and a smaller share of minorities.

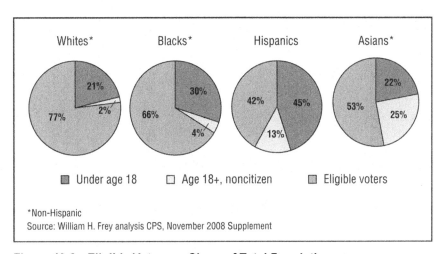

Figure 10.2   Eligible Voters as Share of Total Population

Still, minority voter representation has increased since 2004 because of an increase in the turnout rates (voters per eligible voters) for Hispanics, blacks, and Asians with the 2008 election. Twenty-six states had a higher Hispanic turnout in 2008 than in 2004, with notable increases for Georgia, North Carolina, and Florida. Thirty states had a higher black turnout in 2008 than 2004, with big gains for Nevada and Georgia. In contrast, there was actually a slight decline in the national turnout rate for whites in 2008 compared to 2004.

What is the overall impact of these changes? In brief: a more diverse national voting population. In 2008 almost one in four voters were minorities, up from just over one in five in 2004 (see Figure 10.3). And Hispanics accounted for 7.4 percent of all voters, compared with 6 percent in 2004. There are nine states where Hispanics exceeded the national share of voters—these are led by New Mexico, where Hispanics composed one out of three voters, and California and Texas where they composed one out of five. The remaining six states with above average shares of Hispanic voters are Florida, Arizona, Nevada, New York, Colorado, and New Jersey.

If the United States had a simple majority selection process for presidential voting, these minority shifts would be of minor importance except in very

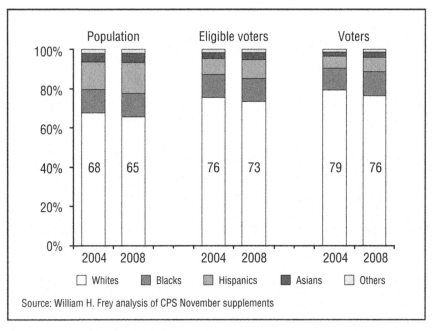

Figure 10.3   2004 vs. 2008 Comparisons

close races, as whites' share of total voters remains over 75 percent. Yet in the electoral college system of the United States, the outcome of presidential elections depends on victories in specific states, and at the state level minority votes—especially in the future, given differential rates of local minority growth—can play a crucial role in determining outcomes.

Minorities and Battleground States

Local demographic trends are particularly important in battleground states, where Republicans and Democrats are very close in numbers and either party can potentially win. The victors in these states are usually the winners in national elections. To investigate these trends, I defined battleground states as those 17 states where either Obama or McCain won by a 10-point margin or less. I also defined as battleground states Nevada, New Mexico, and Wisconsin—states that Obama won by more than 10 percent in 2008 but that have seen much closer races in recent elections.

Since I postulated that it would be the demographically dynamic states that would provide minority-driven wins for Obama, I classed these 20 states as either "fast growing" or "slow growing" based on their 2004–2008 population growth (see Figures 10.4 and 10.5). The 10 fast-growing battleground states are located in the Mountain West and in the Southeast, whereas the slow-growing ones are in the Northeast and Midwest.

The racial profile of voters in each group of states is distinct. More than a quarter of voters (27.5 percent) in fast-growing battleground states are minorities, compared with only 11.5 percent in the slow-growing states. Moreover, the minority population is growing much more rapidly in the fast-growing battleground states. For example, between 2004 and 2008 the number of Hispanic voters grew by 28 percent in these states, compared with only 8.3 percent in the slow-growing battleground states.

As it turned out, Obama took the majority of states of each group: six of the ten fast-growing battleground states (each of which shifted from Republican to Democratic since 2004), and seven of the ten slow-growing ones—including previous Republican-leaning Ohio, Indiana, and Iowa. Somewhat unexpectedly, minorities played an important role in *both* groups of states.

This is illustrated by looking at what happened in Florida and Ohio, two states that voted for Bush in 2004 but for Obama in 2008.

Florida is a fast-growing battleground state that epitomizes others. Here, minorities both increased their share of voters (to 29 percent from 24 percent

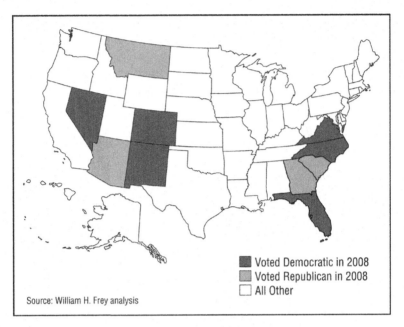

Figure 10.4 Fast-Growing Battleground States

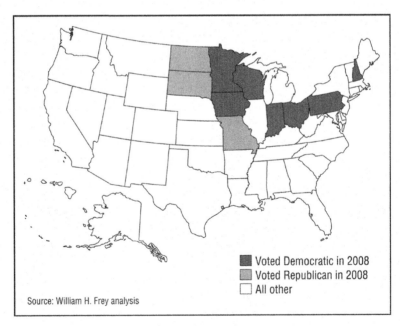

Figure 10.5 Slow-Growing Battleground States

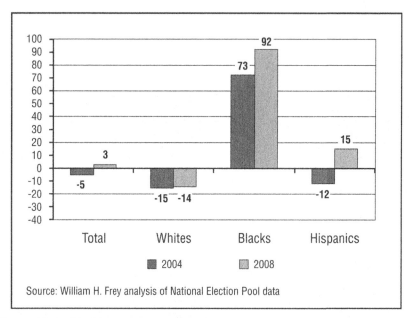

Figure 10.6   Florida—Democratic Margins

in 2004), and increased their margins for the Democrats (see Figure 10.6). Indeed the black Democratic margin increased from 73 to 92, and the Hispanic margin flipped from a Republican to Democratic advantage.

In Ohio, minorities also mattered, but in a different way. This slow-growing battleground state has had a largely unchanging white voter base (85 percent white), which drove a Bush victory in 2004. This time, Ohio's white Republican margin shrank—thus enabling its small black-dominated minority to have a greater impact (see Figure 10.7). Blacks responded by increasing their Democratic margin from 68 to 95, pushing the state into Obama's column.

How and Where Did Minorities Elect Obama?

How and where did minorities affect Obama's victory? The answer lies in Figure 10.8, which shows that Obama carried 29 states. Among these, whites voted Democratic in 19 states, accounting for 223 electoral votes—below the 270 needed to win the election. But in the remaining 10 of these states,

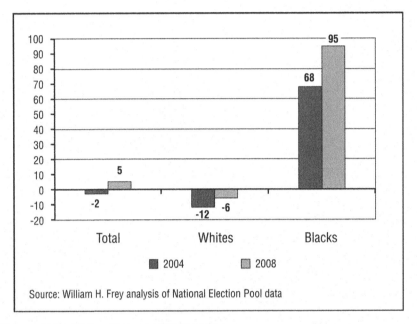

Figure 10.7 Ohio—Democratic Margins

accounting for another 142 electoral votes, minorities were responsible for Obama's victories—and the presidency.

Seven of the ten states where minorities made the difference for Obama had voted Republican in 2004. These included the fast-growing battleground states of Nevada, New Mexico, Virginia, North Carolina, and Florida, as well as the slow-growing battleground states of Indiana and Ohio. The three remaining states, Pennsylvania, Maryland, and New Jersey, also in the slow-growing Northeast region, voted Democratic in both 2004 and 2008.

Thus, minority support for Obama was instrumental toward his success, but not just because it occurred in fast-growing states with rising Hispanic populations. Obama's victory also depended on shrinking white Republican margins along with larger minority Democratic margins in states with smaller minority (largely black) populations. The latter was not widely predicted in advance of the election, but came about because of low white turnout and enthusiasm for the Republican candidate, John McCain. These particular circumstances in both fast-growing and slow-growing battleground states set the stage for minorities to make a critical contribution toward the election of Barack Obama.

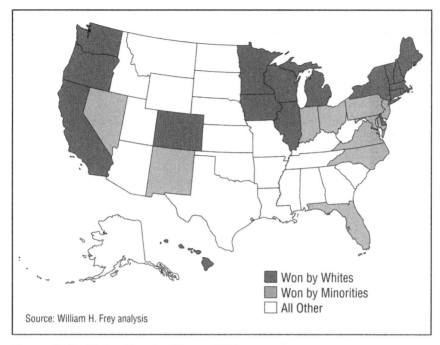

Source: William H. Frey analysis

Figure 10.8 States Won by Obama 2008

Minorities and Future Elections

What does this imply for the future? Certainly the upcoming younger generation of voters (those under 25 years old) will be more racially diverse than in
the past. Much attention was given to these voters in 2008 by virtue of their
strong support for the multiracial Democratic candidate, Obama. By 2020
this age group will be nearly half minority and is moving in that direction for
the elections of 2012 and 2016. Thus, one might expect that especially in the
more youthful, fast-growing parts of the country, the momentum may swing
toward the Democrats or at least toward candidates who appeal to a broad
spectrum of racial groups.

Yet a contrasting voter bloc is the "65-plus" population, an age group that the
bulging baby boom voters will begin inhabiting over the next several elections.
Not only will the voters in this age group increase dramatically in numbers and
show characteristically high turnout rates, but they will also remain predominantly white through at least 2020. Moreover, they will continue to compose
disproportionately large shares of voters in slow-growing parts of the country.

With issues like the viability of Social Security and medical care (of interest to seniors) on the horizon, as well as the need to provide quality educations for future generations of workers (important to young adults), there are almost certain to be region- and generation-specific fissures between the young and the older voting blocs, which will differ from each other along racial and cultural fault lines. The challenge for both parties will be to select national candidates who can successfully appeal to these distinct generations and the regions they reside in.

11

Demography and Immigration Restriction in American History

Brian Gratton

The United States entered the twenty-first century as it had the mid-nineteenth and the twentieth, contending with immigration. In each period, a powerful nativist movement sought restriction of immigrants' entry or of their rights. Immigration historians stress irrationality and prejudice in explaining these movements. But they are first and foremost products of two necessary and near sufficient demographic forces: very high volume of arrivals and sharp changes in immigrant origins. When confronted by large numbers of immigrants of new ethnic origins, most Americans see restriction as a solution to the threats the new arrivals pose. These threats are not merely irrational, and their economic and political dimensions imperil most the fortunes of the immigrant groups that came before. Change in ethnic origins undermines the support previous immigrant groups give to open-door policies for their kin. From the late nineteenth century forward, "nativism" found considerable support from persons who were themselves of immigrant origin. Indeed, in the early twentieth century, the only broad restrictionist policy in our history succeeded because of the rise to political power of persons of previous immigrant origin, who had good reason to oppose new foreigners.

Nativist Periods

Major nativist movements have occurred at four times in American history: in the 1850s, in the 1870s, in the early twentieth century, and in the early twenty-first. Sharp increases in the proportion of immigrants in the population and changes in their ethnic origins mark each of these xenophobic periods. These essential demographic factors appear as well in the early eighteenth century, but, instructively, did not provoke nativism. Involuntary immigrants from Africa represented as much as 40 percent of the colonial population, and, as Figure 11.1 reveals, much greater shares in the South (Fogleman 1992, 1998,

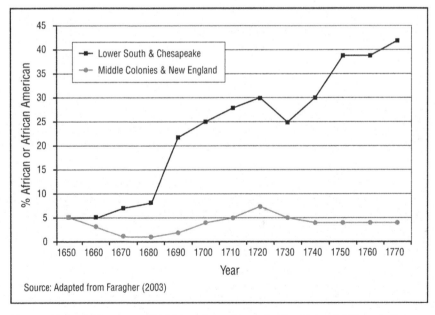

Figure 11.1 Africans and African Americans in the Colonial Population

p. 44; Faragher et al. 2003). The African-origin population constituted the fundamental immigration issue, both in terms of numbers and cultural challenge. But this problem had a solution that fit the basic restrictionist impulse: the near-complete separation of African-origin persons from the majority community. Exclusion from citizenship, indeed from most social rights, undermined opposition to their arrival.

Aside from Africans, immigration before the 1840s was almost entirely British in origin. In the eighteenth century, only Germans constituted a substantial and distinct linguistic and cultural group. Persons of British origins—that is, English, Irish (largely Protestant), Welsh, and Scots—constituted more than 70 percent of white immigrants. The result was ethnic homogeneity. Surname analysis suggests that about 60 percent of the white population in 1790 were of English origin. Other British groups accounted for another 20 percent, and only persons of German origin, at about 9 percent, constituted a non-British group of any size (Purvis 1984). The domination of British-origin Protestants became still more complete in the initial decades of the nineteenth century, when immigration was modest. After 1820, Irish and other immigrants provoked intermittent conflict, especially in anti-Catholic episodes such as the burning of the Charlestown Convent in 1834. But, as Oscar Handlin argues, no sustained nativist movement arose (1991).

The 1840s presented the first substantial demographic pressure since the African slave trade, in the form of German and especially Irish Catholic immigration, in the latter case driven by the potato blight that threatened their livelihoods in Europe. The volume of immigration was unprecedented, with rates exceeding 14 immigrants per 1,000 residents (substantially higher among working-age males). Sharply distinct in ethnocultural terms, this flood provoked an intense xenophobia. Figure 11.2, "Immigrants by Period," illustrates the demographic factors in this and other eras. Using individuals' records from the Integrated Public Use Samples (IPUMS; Ruggles 2009) of the United States decennial censuses from 1850 to 2000, it displays three aggregate immigrant categories, assigning immigrants to the primary period of arrival of their national group: (a) Mid-nineteenth, constituting those from nations that dominated the streams before 1895, primarily German, Irish, English, and Scandinavian arrivals; (b) Early twentieth, those who prevailed between 1895 to 1921, primarily Italians, Jews, Slavs, and others from southern and eastern Europe; (c) Late twentieth, arriving after World War II, the largest contingent from Mexico, but including other Latin Americans and Asians. The share each category makes up of the American population as a whole greatly underestimates proportions in certain sex and age groups. As an example, in 1880, while immigrants were about 14 percent of all persons, they were 28 percent of males aged 30 to 49. Where they concentrated, immigrants could constitute substantially more than half of labor and marriage markets.

There are four basic features in the display, starting from the initial context of low immigration, ethnic homogeneity, and restriction of social rights for African Americans:

1. The sudden arrival of an immigrant-based demographic regime just before the Civil War
2. The equally abrupt arrival of a second immigrant-driven demography in the late nineteenth and early twentieth centuries
3. The sharp decline in all immigrant-based effects after 1920
4. The resumption of immigrant-driven demography after 1970

Sheer demographic pressure corresponds well with periods of nativist reaction in the mid-nineteenth century, the beginning of the twentieth, and the end of that century and beginning of the twenty-first. Anti-Chinese agitation in California in the 1870s does not have a national profile, but we witness the same demographic impact there. Mass immigration should be the first step toward explaining restrictionist movements (Tichenor 2002, pp. 87-113; Coolidge 1909, p. 358).

The second step should be shifting origins of the immigrants. New origins provide rich fields for cultural aversion and, in fact, prejudices change to fit new immigrants while avoiding maligning those who came before. As Figure 11.2 attests, the question in 1860 was the capacity of an intensely Protestant Anglo-American population to accept Catholic immigrants. The fear voiced in the nativist movement emerged not from race, as is often claimed, but from religion. By the early twentieth century, different sources began to crowd out Irish and German arrivals. That many were Catholic did not inspire sustained objection, since Catholic mid-nineteenth-century immigrants and their descendants made up a large share of the American population (O'Gorman 1895). Early twentieth-century restrictionism divided the good from the bad using a new science of racial classification. After 1970, when Latino and Asian sources overshadowed European immigrants of any kind, nativism could rely neither on religion nor on a racism rejected in American law and culture. But a new characteristic, illegality, provided considerable ideological purchase. While the rhetoric and ideology changed, the stimulus remained constant: a change in ethnic origins.

Two periods are notable for ethnic harmony rather than conflict, and for the absence of the two essential factors: Before 1850, an ethnically homogenous

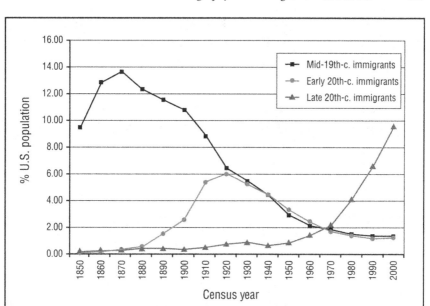

Figure 11.2 Immigrants by Period

white population excluded from the polity the only large and culturally challenging immigrant group. The other era began in the 1920s and lasted through
the 1970s. Due in part to the restrictionist acts of the 1920s, the proportion of
immigrants in the American population fell drastically, reaching its nadir in
1970, when only about 5 percent of the American population was foreign born.

Popular Opinion, Political Parties, and Immigration Policy to 1965

When restrictionist movements arose, they built themselves upon broad antipathy to immigrants. Yet, the American people rarely had their wishes expressed
in immigration policy (for the classic theoretical treatment, see Freeman 1995;
Tichenor 2002). American political parties manage to serve employers, ethnic
groups, and themselves without suffering too greatly at the polls. Politicians
usually face an electorate that opposes high levels of immigration, but for
whom that issue is rarely paramount in their voting. In contrast, for certain

lobbyists, immigration is paramount. Two stand out: employers seeking cheap labor and ethnic groups hoping to keep the gates open for their co-ethnics.

Employers, ethnic groups, and parties faced their first stiff challenge to this mutually beneficial arrangement in the Know Nothing revolt against Irish immigrants in the 1850s—many a politician lost his seat for refusing to take the movement seriously. The 1840s famine in Ireland provoked a flood of destitute Catholic arrivals. They crowded into slums in the northeastern coastal cities and then ventured into the interior, carrying with them the liabilities that the devastation of Irish society had engendered and building a religious infrastructure as they settled (Miller 1985). The men in this Irish population, hostile to the antislavery movement, antagonistic to temperance, and enthusiastic about local governments being generous to the poor, soon found a political home in the Democratic Party. That affiliation provoked anti-Papist anxieties about the threat of the Catholic Church to the new republic and became central to the tense theater of politics in the 1850s. The Know Nothings saw the Irish Catholic arrivals not as a racial problem but as a political one. They proposed a political solution: longer naturalization terms. The chief goal of this restriction of rights—a milder version of the exclusion of African Americans—was to thwart the political power already exercised by the Irish and the Catholic Church in the Democratic Party. Economic grievances also drove the Know Nothing movement, and these have been a consistent and rational source for working-class opposition to immigrants. Skilled workers lost the most from the competition of unskilled Irishmen, in the deskilling process that American manufacturers used to lower labor costs (Anbinder 1994; Voss-Hubbard 2002; Ferrie 1999).

The Civil War inflicted a deep wound on nativism, bringing legitimacy and political power to immigrants. The service of immigrant soldiers, the dispersion and economic success of Germans, and the rapid assimilation of the children of immigrants entrenched the first great wave politically and socially. After Reconstruction, the Democratic Party in the North depended fundamentally on the allegiance largely of Irish voters. Having initially flirted with Know Nothings to secure their support, Republicans by 1864 expressed the belief that "foreign immigration ... should be fostered and encouraged" (Woolley and Peters 2011). Republican immigration policy came from the labor demands of influential capitalists in the party.

In only one case were such employers defeated, and the politics of that defeat are instructive. Chinese immigration into mid-nineteenth-century California, encouraged by employers seeking cheap labor in a tight market, was demographically imposing, and culturally still more so. Anti-Chinese agitation emerged in mass resistance among white workers who competed directly with the Chinese. The startling feature in the anti-immigrant movement was the fervor of immigrants within it. Hubert Bancroft described Denis Kearney, the leader of the Workingmen's Party, as a man whose thick Irish brogue entranced an "ignorant Irish rabble" (Nunis 1967, p. 277; Bancroft 1887, p. 738; Hart 2009). Ignorant they may have been, but their agitation led to the Chinese Exclusion Act of 1882, the first crack in national Republican and Democratic support for immigration. In this case, federal law could accommodate intense local opposition to immigration without undermining the national open door policy (Tichenor 2002). The Republican Party only capitulated when it became clear that it could not win elections in California if it defended Chinese immigration. Restriction could single out a group by racial means, without offending other immigrant-origin groups upon whom both parties depended for votes, and without affecting employers elsewhere in the nation. The Democrats jettisoned their "open gates" planks in 1876 and demanded the exclusion "of a race not sprung from the same great parent stock," and Republican platforms soon echoed this sentiment. The embedded lesson was that immigrants could be divided one against the other.

Race had emerged as the useful rationale, but the economic competition behind anti-Chinese campaigns reflected a clear understanding by workers of the risks of high immigration. Samuel Gompers, himself an immigrant, worked hand-in-glove with the anti-Chinese movement in California, and the American Federation of Labor's strong stand against Chinese immigrants forecast the hostility unions would eventually show to European immigrants (Mink 1990, pp. 76-97). As A. T. Lane's close examination shows, union leaders' emerging hostility to southern and eastern European immigrants on the East Coast was not racial but economic (1987). Direct evidence from surveys taken in the late nineteenth century makes it clear that the mass of workers had a strong anti-immigrant stand. In the mid-1880s, the Wisconsin Bureau of Labor and Industrial Statistics (1888) interviewed workers and asked whether immigration injured their trade—of the 869 responses in a state with a very large immigrant-origin population, 428 reported that it had, 291 that it did not, and 150 did not respond. Those reporting less effect came from rural areas in which there were few foreign nonagricultural workers. Some workers were reluctant to deny co-ethnics an opportunity they had themselves enjoyed—a Milwaukee courier stated, "I am a foreigner and as such am satisfied with the laws as they are," but most linked immigration restriction to other devices for reducing competition. As a carriage painter stated, "Stop immigration. Enforce the school laws; stop child labor in shops and factories" (p. 52).

By 1895, the impetus behind a new restrictionist movement had strength-ened: First, immigration from the traditional northwestern sources fell, while that from southern and eastern Europe rose dramatically; and second, a severe depression sharply raised unemployment. Gary Richardson has analyzed three surveys by the Kansas Bureau of Labor and Industry in the mid-1890s. Each asked male wage earners whether they favored the restriction or absolute sup-pression of immigration (Richardson 2005). In a broad range of wage-earning occupations, from petty clerks to railroad and factory workers, Richardson finds strident opposition to open borders. Over 90 percent of the wage earn-ers supported reduction or an outright end of immigration, a percentage that barely changed even if the respondents were themselves immigrants.

A closer examination of these and other surveys reveals an ethnic dimen-sion that explains these odd results (University of California 2009). In an 1895 Michigan poll of female domestics in agriculture, about 40 percent of the women reported that they thought that immigration injured their present occupation—in the same year, a survey of 1,250 teamsters found that 62 per-cent thought their occupation directly injured. Again, over 90 percent called for restriction of "foreign immigration." The ethnic composition of these samples bears attention: The workers are often, if not mid-nineteenth-century immigrants, then the children of that wave. In the near 30 percent foreign-born among Michigan teamsters, Canada, Germany, Ireland, and England dominated. In the Kansas samples less than 20 percent were foreign born, but nearly half had a foreign-born parent, with the principal countries of origin Ireland, Germany, and Scotland. The immigration these workers opposed was no longer from their countries of origin.

The economic effects of immigration in the *fin de siècle* labor market again drove the growing opposition. Skilled trade union leaders feared the deskilling that undermined their trades. But unskilled labor also lost out. In contrast to the antebellum period, the early twentieth century saw direct, negative wage effects for the masses of unskilled and semiskilled workers in the United States (Hatton and Williamson 2008; Goldin 1994). Such workers were largely im-migrants or the children of immigrants, but from an earlier era. However much an elite racialized ideology appears in nativist rhetoric from the period, the political force on the ground was from an economically endangered working class, largely of ethnic origin.

This new constituency for restrictionist policy subverted political parties' heretofore successful policy of open gates. The Democrats held firm as the ground shifted beneath them, sating themselves with repeated attacks on Asians and contract labor, planks seen in Republican platforms as well. As late as 1892, the Democrats saw fit to "condemn and denounce any and all attempts to restrict the immigration of the industrious and worthy of foreign lands" (Woolley and Peters 2011). The first crack in the two-party wall appears in the September 11, 1888, letter of acceptance by Benjamin Harrison of the Republican Party's nomination for president. Harrison called for "proper immigration" with "inspection and limitation." By 1892, when the inability of the Republican Party to win a majority of American voters had become painfully apparent, Harrison linked immigrants to disease, criticized the effects of labor competition on working people, and advised not just the exclusion of "the vicious, the ignorant, the civil disturber, the pauper, and the contract laborer," but emphasized the need to "check the too great flow" (Woolley and Peters 2011).

The 1896 Republican platform called for a literacy requirement, a position their victorious presidential candidate, William McKinley, endorsed in his state of the union address. During his earlier career, McKinley had regularly called for restriction on new immigration, finding it an effective means for getting votes from constituents with older immigrant roots. Other Republicans surmised that voters were moving toward restriction (Vought 2004; Zeidel 1986; Phillips 2003). In his first annual message to Congress, on December 3, 1901, Theodore Roosevelt called for a system of inspection that would keep out the "influx of cheap labor." Roosevelt did not characterize the new southern and eastern European immigrants as racially inferior, but agreed that they threatened American workers and society (Lane 1987, p. 158; Gerstle 2001). The ascendancy of a more critical view became fully apparent in the 1912 Republican platform, which protested "the constantly growing evil of induced or undesirable immigration."

The literacy test provided restrictionists a perfect political vehicle, since it differentiated among national groups. Literacy rates were high in the old northwestern European sources, and low in the regions from which new immigrants came. The discriminatory capacity of the test was well-known by the 1890s; indeed, leading spokespersons of earlier ethnic groups endorsed it. In 1890, Emil Praetorius, editor of the St. Louis *Westliche Post,* observed in Congressional testimony that "The only thing that we, in the German-American Press, are looking favorably upon is this test of intelligence (*sic*)," noting that it would not affect Germans but would bar Hungarians and Italians (U.S. Congress. House. *Report of the Select Committee on Immigration and Naturalization 1891*; Zeidel 1986, p. 42). Its discriminatory characteristics largely explain its 1897 endorsement by the American Federation of Labor, the strong support given it by unions in the early twentieth century, and the appeal it had to politicians

(Lane 1987). Large majorities in favor of the literacy test carried the Senate and the House from the late nineteenth century on. In 1913, the lame duck President Taft vetoed a literacy test; the Senate overrode his veto, but the House failed to override by five votes. From this point forward, through the 1917 Literacy Act and the 1920s laws that simply stipulated which national groups would get access, the Republican Party sought restriction, but of a particular kind. The core strategy was a differential prohibition, one that separated old immigrants from new ones. Instead of appealing solely to persons of long native origin, as usually portrayed, nativism raised the appeal of politicians among persons from previous immigrant waves.

This broader constituency explains a noted paradox in American political history: a business-friendly party with remarkable attractiveness to working-class voters. Shortly after Harrison's address in 1892 and before the critical election of 1896, the Republican Party's dire fortunes underwent "a complete reversal" (Degler 1964, p. 42). Republicans maintained a majority status for nearly 40 years, and it was based upon new success among urban, working-class voters. As Carl Degler has famously observed, the shift of voters in the 1890s occurred in cities in which immigrant voters were at least 30 percent of the population. Degler wonders at the "the paradox of urban support for a Republican party in the 1920s that ... pushed for restrictions on immigration" (Degler 1964, pp. 49, 56). The paradox resolves when one realizes that "immigrants," and especially their children, do not constitute a single entity, and their interests are not identical. Older immigrant groups were much more likely than natives to compete with new immigrants for economic and political resources.

Change in the origin of arrivals undermines the conventional support ethnic groups give to their own kin's right of access. It also provides fertile field for cultural antipathy, but the prejudices arrived at are designed to fit the moment. What is consistent is that the older groups bore the brunt of the economic and political competition brought by large numbers of new immigrants. A strategy to differentiate among ethnic groups depends upon the political demography of immigrant-origin voters. The unique success of restrictionist policy in the early twentieth century came about because that demography was highly propitious. First, the new immigrants had almost no political power; only after 1920 did they equal in number those from the mid-nineteenth century. Many intended to return to their home counties, evincing little interest in becoming American citizens and voting (Wyman 1993). Even among those with civic aspirations, the path to the ballot box was rocky. Rising hostility to them had led to the stiffening of suffrage requirements: citizenship, residency, literacy, and English-language rules expanded in state suffrage law in the late nineteenth and early twentieth centuries (Keyssar 2001). Naturalization rates were correspondingly low. In 1910, 18 percent of foreign-born Italian men and 26 percent of Russian-born men (most of Jewish descent) had voting rights. In contrast, among immigrants who had lived in the United States for 30 years or more, the rate was 91 percent (Ueda 1982; Bloemraad 2006; Gamm 1989).

Even this approach distorts "immigrant" influence in politics. What counted far more were the electoral opinions of the second generation, all citizens by birth. Figure 11.3 uses the same three period categorizations to capture the power of the children of immigrants. Until 1930, those from the mid-nineteenth-century group were overwhelmingly dominant. In 1910, there were 4,433,870 native-born males 21 years and over with a parent from the mid-nineteenth-century group. In contrast, only 169,075 male children of the new immigrants were 21 and over. These demographic characteristics set the terms for the debate over restriction and reveal the essential role played by persons of immigrant origin. In the 1908 presidential election, about 23 million persons voted. In 1910, males 21 and over from the first and second generations of the

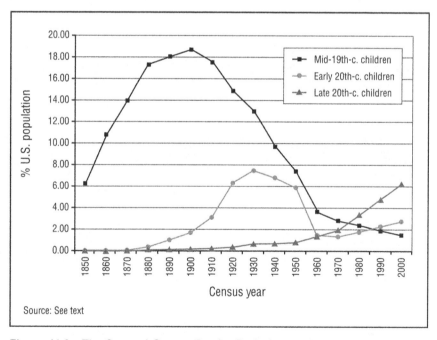

Figure 11.3   The Second Generation by Period

mid-nineteenth-century wave comprised 8.5 million persons. Assuming a naturalization rate of 80 percent for the first generation, this group constituted one-third of the American electorate. The recent-immigrant origin group, assuming a naturalization rate of 25 percent in the first generation, comprised less than 4 percent of the electorate. Except in electoral districts where they had concentrated, they had no influence on outcomes. Immigration control aimed at the mid-nineteenth-century groups would have been difficult to enact. Laws against the new arrivals, however, would provoke little defense and might tap a deep reservoir of resentment.

Testing the Role of Immigrant-Origin Voting

The best single analysis of the success of early twentieth-century restrictionism suffers from the confounding of "immigrant" voting with this broader view of immigrant-origin constituencies. Claudia Goldin (1994) confirms the negative impact of immigrants on the wages of American workers, grounding the rational, economic basis for restrictionism in the early twentieth century. But, in her political analysis, Goldin folds all immigrants into one bloc. Examining congressional votes on the basis of states, and, on a smaller scale, cities, leads her to the conclusion that many have taken, that immigrant populations opposed restrictionist legislation.

As Goldin admits, states are excessively aggregate units. The best measure is the district itself. What was the role of immigrant-origin constituencies at the district level? The tests provided here use two legislative roll calls, the first the House vote to overturn Wilson's veto of the Literacy Act in 1917, and, the second, the House vote to confirm the initial immigration restriction act in 1921 (U.S. Congress 1917, 1921). Both passed by large margins, with considerable support from both parties. In each case a "yes" vote was a vote for restriction. Martis (1982, 1989) allows linkage of districts with counties for each Congress, so that the demographic characteristics of districts may be measured. Where two or more districts shared counties or parts of counties, we linked each district to all counties in which it had some stake. We recorded the "yes" and "no" votes for each district on the two roll calls, and also registered whether the representative was Republican, Democrat, or Other (the very few Progressives, Socialists, etc.).

Using the 1920 PUMS, we calculated proportions of the population of males 21 and over (the potential electorate until 1920, when women first voted) coming from the mid-nineteenth-century immigrants (imm1), their native-born children (2g1), the early twentieth-century immigrants (imm2) and their native-born children (2g2). Table 11.1 presents logistic regressions for the probability of a "yes" vote on each roll call. The excluded category is the male population without direct immigrant origin (neither of the first nor the second generation). The literature often leaves out the monolithic South (purely Democratic and purely restrictionist); regressions without the five Deep South states had almost no effect on the results, none on its substance, and are not reported. We do not control for other potential causal effects, and ecological regressions cannot disentangle the separate effects of immigrant groups who live in the same districts. These groups were highly likely to live near one another—the Pearson Correlation Coefficient in districts is 0.458. Given these cautions, what can these regressions, as well as undisplayed results from other tests tell us?

First, as Table 11.1 indicates, the population without direct immigrant origin, which has an odds ratio of 1.000, was more strongly associated with "yes" votes than any immigrant-origin population. A higher percentage of the native-born of the native born (native) in a district increased the probability of a "yes" vote by the representative. Second, compared to this population, only recent immigrants were significantly linked to a "no" vote. For example, in the 1921 vote, their odds ratio was significantly less than 1 at 0.842. That impact is robust, maintained in all regressions attempted. Third, immigrants from the mid-nineteenth-century group and their children have coefficients reduced from that of nonethnic populations, but these are not significantly different. In 1917 the coefficient for immigrants themselves was 0.985 and insignificant. Given the high level of coresidence, even these differences may be due to more recent immigrant groups. In regressions not shown that combined fathers and sons, the mid-nineteenth-century group

Table 11.1 Logistic Regression of Vote on Percentage in Each Group of Males 21 and Over

All States—1917 yes vote			All States—1921 yes vote		
Group	Odds Ratio	p-value	Group	Odds Ratio	p-value
imm1	0.985	0.535	imm1	0.953	0.2117
imm2	0.920	<.0001	imm2	0.842	<.0001
2g1	0.978	0.3417	2g1	0.969	0.5056
2g2	0.931	0.4409	2g2	0.911	0.5278

Source: See text. Men without direct immigrant origin constitute the excluded category.

at times had a significant effect, but none on the order of the newer group. For the 1921 vote, the coefficient for mid-nineteenth-century immigrants and their children was marginally significant at 0.970, compared to the strongly significant coefficient of 0.860 for the recent immigrants and their children.

Fourth, these results and the distribution of population groups by districts expose a grand opportunity for Republicans and an imposing problem for Democrats. The Republican Party was associated with a "yes" vote, reflecting its restrictionist policy, yet Republican representatives were *more* common in immigration-origin districts—on average Republican districts had a constituency that was about half of immigrant origin, while Democratic district populations were only one-quarter immigrant origin. Republicans could and did vote for a differential restriction policy without facing full-scale rebuke unless the district had a large proportion of recent immigrants. This was, in fact, a small share of the districts. About a fifth had at least 20 percent of the potential voting population in this group, whereas two-fifths had at least 20 percent from the children alone of the mid-nineteenth-century wave. In Senate races, the state is the district: Only 5 states (all in the Northeast) had more than 20 percent of their potential voting population from recent immigration-origin sources. In contrast, 8 states had more than 20 percent of the electorate from mid-nineteenth-century immigrants, 17 states had more than 20 percent of the electorate from the children of mid-nineteenth-century immigrants, and 29 states had over 20 percent of their electorate tied to mid-nineteenth-century immigrants if we include both immigrant fathers and their sons. The Republican Party could advance restrictionism—so long as it distinguished among immigrants—with considerable expectation of success in almost all districts.

The Democratic Party, in contrast, confronted a dilemma. Its proimmigrant policy was already bankrupt in the South and it only provoked enthusiastic support in the few districts with large recent immigrant populations. But the party more often held seats in districts with native populations or large mid-nineteenth-century origin populations hostile to new immigrants. This is true even excluding the Deep South. The result was that in traditionally Democratic districts, the Republican Party competed well arguing for restriction or forced local Democrats into restrictionist votes. In those with large mid-nineteenth-century origin electorates, the Democrats' open door policy had no particular appeal. And only in the few with recent immigrant populations did Democrats have an advantage over their Republican opponents.

A Coda: Demography, Restrictionist Policy, and Politics, 1965 to the Present

The nativists' unusual success in the 1920s came from the breakdown of the two-party system that traditionally subverted popular demands for restriction. Theirs was a sustained victory, lasting until 1965, and it rested on a persistent antagonism toward immigrants among Americans. The earliest polls of popular opinion repeat the findings from workers' surveys in the late nineteenth century. In 1946, 51 percent of Americans wanted fewer or no immigrants at all from Europe ("The Quarterly Poll" 1947, p. 476; Simon and Alexander 1993, pp. 31-32). Since 1965, as Figure 11.4 reveals, a near-consistent question reveals the American public's animosity to high levels of legal immigration. Illegal immigration raises substantially larger majorities in opposition.

In accordance with public opinion, the 1952 McCarran-Walter Act confirmed the 1920s quota systems. But, by the early 1960s, those ethnic groups

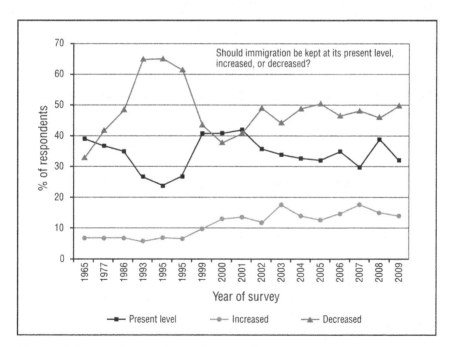

Figure 11.4   Popular Opinion on Immigration Levels, 1965–2009

that had been powerless in the 1920s had become politically potent. The descendants of southern and eastern European immigrants represented critical constituencies for politicians like John F. Kennedy. As presidential archives reveal, demands from Italian, Polish, and Greek organizations came out of a frank desire to increase the number of persons of their ethnicity allowed to enter, although the petitioners cast their appeal, as proimmigration lobbies have since the 1850s, in universalist tones, pointing to the openly racist nature of quota legislation (Wong 2006). The approach fit the times, one in which civil rights had a special significance. The result, the highly tolerant 1965 Hart-Celler Act, also fit the demographic moment: The proportion of immigrants in the population was the lowest it had been in over 100 years (Figure 11.2).

The bill's proponents, such as Senator Edward Kennedy, assured the public that there would be no increase in the number or change in the type of immigrants. In these assurances, Kennedy erred. Flows shifted abruptly from small numbers of Europeans to large numbers of Asians and Latinos, particularly Mexicans, who comprised almost 40 percent of legal and still higher percentages of illegal arrivals. Change in volume and ethnic origin had the standard effect in the nativism witnessed today. Restriction proposals—deprived of religion or race as devices—rely on a new dividing line, illegality. Such differentiation provides a powerful ideological justification, since it casts those in favor of open gates as supporters of illegal activity. It also has great appeal among those who arrived legally in earlier periods. The new restrictionism has considerable force at the state and local level, exhibited in a host of laws that restrict immigrant rights. Still, the major parties, along with their traditional allies among employers and persons of recent immigrant origin, have continued to seek a proimmigration policy.

As an instance, the 1986 Immigration Reform and Control Act, promoted and signed by Ronald Reagan, pushed through an amnesty for illegal immigrants, generating further legal and illegal immigration. Memories of this act reverberated in the intensely negative public reaction to bipartisan, highly tolerant bills in Congress in 2006 and 2007. These failed, but restrictionist policy conforming with popular opinion remains unlikely. The early twentieth-century demographic conditions that allowed one party to succeed through a differential restriction policy no longer exist. A century of Mexican immigration, interrupted only briefly in the 1930s, has made Mexican Americans much more deeply embedded in the political and social structure than were Italians and Poles in 1910. Other Latin American and Asian groups are now in their fourth decade; the second generation among them is of voting age. As a result,

Latino and Asian-origin voters make up a larger share of the electorate than Italians and Poles and Jews did in the early twentieth century.

Whether these demographic conditions will lead to a still more tolerant policy revolves around two poles, the first the victory of the Democratic Party in 2008, and the second, the deep recession emerging in the same year. In 1933, when Franklin Delano Roosevelt moved into the White House, the scenario was strikingly similar to that Barack Obama observes today. The coalition that elected Roosevelt included ethnic groups disparaged in previous anti-immigrant rhetoric. In the coalition that elected Obama, Latinos played a similar role and they demand from the new administration immigration reform, by which they mean regularization of the status of the millions of undocumented workers in the United States. This goal meets the conventional intent of ethnic groups to facilitate access to the United States by their kin and links Democratic ethnic lobbies to the employer wing of the Republican Party. But, perhaps most important, it could richly reward the Democratic Party. In the short run, meeting this demand would be politically costly, perhaps disastrous. As unemployment deepens, a proposal to grant legal status to millions more workers, and to give them welfare and social services, will be a hard sell. It could cost the Democrats dearly in the 2012 elections.

In the long run, however, regularization is a demographic treasure box, the political opportunity of a lifetime for a party that has, since the 1840s, depended on immigrant-origin voting blocs. Amnesties not only provide access to citizenship for the undocumented but set in motion the right of legal immigration by their relatives; they also invariably prompt more illegal immigration. All these encourage the growth of populations friendly to the party. The result, leaders might well hope, will be generation after generation of Democratic voters. The calculus, then, requires weighing the short-term electoral costs of appearing proimmigration in a recession against the long-term electoral benefits of policies that could make the party dominant in the twenty-first century.

12

The Changing Face of Europe

David Coleman

Powerful demographic forces are transforming the populations and societies of European countries. Some arise from endogenous changes in European populations themselves; the uncertain direction of developed populations as they enter, without maps or compasses, the unknown region of long lives and low fertility that lies beyond the demographic transition. Population aging is certain for all, population decline already a reality for some and a prospect for many others. For reasons internal and external to Europe, other immigrant populations are coming to shape its future. If that migration continues, its scale and its geographical origins will reshape European populations, probably irrevocably. On recent trends the end of the twenty-first century would witness a marked discontinuity with the past in the ethnic and religious composition, and eventually the physical appearance, of the people. Depending on the pattern of integration, social and political change could also be profound. This would be a globalization more complete, although asymmetrical, than any analogous process affecting, for example, the economy or communications.

Problems with Data

Data on migration are unsatisfactory in most European countries, and mostly absent on ethnic origin and religion. Few countries actually measure migration flow across their borders. Most rely on annual changes in registers of population, or the residue between successive population estimates and natural change. However, efforts to improve data on flows within the European Union have had some success (Poulain, Perrin, et al. 2006). Data on foreign, immigrant, or foreign-origin population "stocks" are little better (Salt, Singleton, et al. 1994). Estimates of the numbers of invisible illegal immigrants—the dark matter of migration statistics—are inevitably very approximate (Salt 2000). Until recently, most routinely published statistics for European countries referred to foreign citizens, not immigrants. That has seriously underestimated the magnitude of immigrant or foreign-origin populations, by up to one-half in some European countries (Dumont and Lemaitre 2005).

The Demographic Eclipse of Europe

Europe's demographic transition is now nearly over. With natural increase finished or at a low level, in relatively aged populations whose demographic momentum has mostly run out, Europe as a whole cannot avoid being numerically marginalized by developing countries that are only part way through their own transitions. Their much higher rates of natural increase, and the more enduring momentum of their growth, guarantee about 3 billion more people globally. Like Europe a century ago, they now have population to spare, and it is coming north at a rapid pace: 60 million from the third world resided in the developed world by 2007. Net immigration into both the European Union's core 15 countries[1] and the United States is over 1 million immigrants per year (Figure 12.1), assuming return migration from the latter of about one in three. In 2006, the gross inflow into all 27 countries of the European Union was 3 million, of which 60 percent was from non-E.U. countries, with the rest of Europe, the Americas, Asia, and Africa each contributing about one-quarter of the non-EU immigrants (Eurostat 2008).

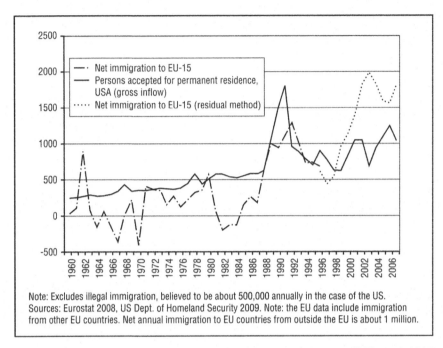

Note: Excludes illegal immigration, believed to be about 500,000 annually in the case of the US.
Sources: Eurostat 2008, US Dept. of Homeland Security 2009. Note: the EU data include immigration
from other EU countries. Net annual immigration to EU countries from outside the EU is about 1 million.

Figure 12.1 Immigration to the EU-15 Countries (Net) and to the US (Gross), 2007

European countries have very different levels of fertility and net immigration. In the United Kingdom and most of Scandinavia, fertility is now close
to replacement level and immigration, on top of natural increase, is driving
population growth to levels not seen for decades (Figure 3; Sobotka 2009).
Where natural increase has ceased (e.g., Germany, Greece, Italy, Russian Federation), net immigration has prevented, or slowed, population decline (Salt
2005). The effect of migration upon the diverse population futures of selected
European countries is shown in Figure 12.2.

Migration is volatile. None of these projections will come to pass in detail.
They show the consequences if recent trends continue.

Effects Upon the Ethnic Composition of the Population

As a consequence of these migration flows, especially since the 1960s, populations of foreign origin, both European and non-European, have risen to
proportions seldom if ever seen before in recent historical times. Differences

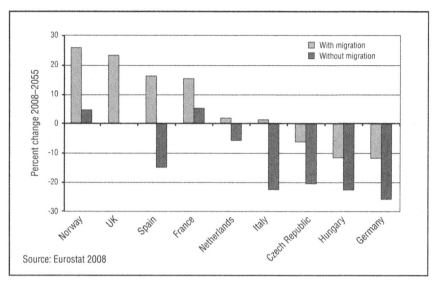

Figure 12.2 Projected Percent Growth With and Without Migration

in expectations and values have challenged the receiving societies' politics, constitutions, schools, and community relations, especially when the robust traditional values of the newcomers encounter a weakened sense of identity on the part of Europeans. In some groups, perceptions of separate identity have persisted, or even strengthened, among the native-born generation, along with difficulties in education and integration into the workforce.

Because of the obvious policy importance of these developments, some European and other national statistical offices have made formal projections of the future sizes and composition of the new populations (discussed in detail in Coleman 2006). Most European countries do not have the long experience of significant racial diversity of the United States, and some, like France, have constitutions that forbid any categorization of the population that might compromise the equality of citizenship.

These projections do not employ the self-ascribed ethnic or racial categories familiar in the English-speaking world. Such data are not collected in continental European countries. Instead, projections are based upon the analogous concept of "foreign origin" or "foreign background" constructed from register data on citizenship and birthplace, which are themselves lacking in the countries of the English-speaking world. Those populations are defined on a two-generation basis (foreign immigrants, plus persons born locally but with one, or both, parents foreign immigrants). After the second generation, all persons of immigrant descent are assumed to become part of the indigenous population, and to be henceforth Dutch, Danish, etc., and thus statistically invisible. Between one-third and one-half of the foreign-origin populations in European countries around 2000 were themselves of "Western," origin, mostly European. But the projected increases are mostly in the "non-Western" groups. So far we know little about the third generation of postwar immigrants in Europe. But given the size, stability, segregation, and self-sufficiency of some of those populations, reinforced by the immigration of new spouses and dependents, the assumption of identity with the indigenous population after two generations may be optimistic.

In recent years continued growth of those populations has diminished the share of the indigenous population in the national total, bringing with it the long-term prospect of its displacement as the majority. Any population with subreplacement fertility, with a regular net inflow of population of foreign origin, must diminish as a proportion of the total, and eventually be replaced by that immigrant-origin population, except for persons of mixed ancestry, who are likely to become numerous (Steinmann and Jaeger 2000). Almost all Western countries have subreplacement total fertility and positive immigration and therefore face that outcome unless birth or migration rates change. With replacement fertility, the indigenous population would persist, but continued migration will diminish its share of the total.

Around the year 2000 in Western Europe foreign-origin populations composed between 8 and 19 percent of the total and were projected to reach 20 to 30 percent in 2050. No comparable data exist for Central and Eastern European counties. There, international migration has been more modest, and was negligible before the fall of the communist regimes except with fraternal socialist countries. Although immigrant minorities are growing, future diversity there lies more in the growth of indigenous minorities through differential fertility and the selective emigration of the majority population. The most rapidly growing indigenous minority is the statistically and socially ill-defined gypsy (Roma) population of between 6 and 8 million people in the Central and Eastern European countries. Their fertility rate, little touched by the post-1990 downturn, can be double that of the population average, as in Hungary in the 1990s (Meszaros 1999).

In the projections of the foreign-background population in Sweden (Statistics Sweden 2004), fertility of the non-Western immigrants was assumed to remain higher than that of Swedes, and migration was kept constant. These projections extended only to 2020, but the provision of a zero migration projection to 2050 permits an extension to 2050 on the simple assumption that the additional population, over and above that arising from natural growth,

will be of immigrant origin. On that basis, the foreign-background population would increase to about 30 percent of the national total by midcentury.
Norway's high immigration is expected to promote correspondingly high
proportions of foreign-origin population, from small beginnings as late as
the 1980s (Statistics Norway 2008). In the equivalent Dutch projections (e.g.,
Alders 2006), successive revisions have reduced the projected population of
foreign origin to below 30 percent by midcentury, following some tightening
of immigration and asylum rules. Some downward revisions are also apparent
in the projections for Denmark, for similar reasons.

The projections for the United Kingdom described here from 2001–2051, are
based on the ethnic population distributions in the 2001 census. They assume
constant migration, near-convergent fertility, and uniform mortality across
all groups, improving over time as in the Government Actuary's Department
(GAD 2006) 2004-based projections. The 12 standard official categories are
projected separately, grouped here into 3 major divisions: British, Scottish, and
Irish; the non-British white population; and the nonwhite ethnic minorities
(Figure 12.3). On these assumptions, nonwhite minorities would compose

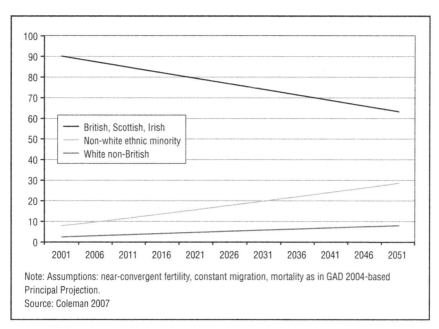

Note: Assumptions: near-convergent fertility, constant migration, mortality as in GAD 2004-based
Principal Projection.
Source: Coleman 2007

**Figure 12.3 Projection of UK Population, 2001–2051, Combined into Three
Major Groups**

29 percent of the U.K. population and the white non-British 8 percent by 2051 (corresponding roughly to the "non-Western" and "Western" foreign-origin populations used in the projections described above; Coleman 2007). Although not constrained to any total, the projected overall population in 2051 is just half a million more (69.7 million to 69.3 million) than the official 2004-based projection, which incorporates no ethnic subdivisions. The most recent (2008-based) official projections put the 2051 U.K. population at a much higher level—77 million—primarily as a result of a more realistic higher net migration assumption of 180,000 per year, and higher fertility (ONS 2009).[2]

All the projections of foreign-origin population that have been published for European countries deliver a similar message (Figure 12.4). Their growth rates are roughly linear, with a similar slope in different countries, despite varied source countries of origin. Even on the assumption of the assimilation of the foreign-origin population after two generations, the projected linear growth continues unchanged up to the end of the projection periods.

We lack equivalent projections for other European populations. But other evidence shows that similar processes are in train throughout Western Europe (Ediev et al. 2007). Recent official estimates put the proportion of foreign-origin population in Germany at 19 percent of the total, and one in three of those

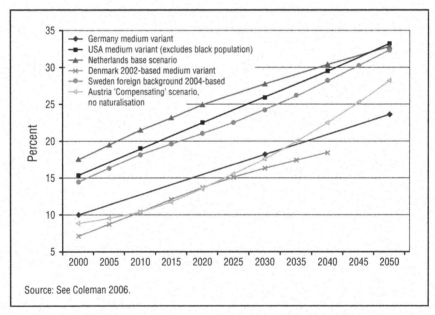

Source: See Coleman 2006.

Figure 12.4   Comparison of Results of European Foreign-Origin Projections

aged under five. In France, for example, 23 percent of births are to immigrant women, similar to the 24 percent of births to immigrant women in England and Wales in 2007, and 25 percent to foreign women in Germany. Annual contributions to the population from foreign immigration often approach or exceed that from overall births. Some of the latter will be, in any case, births to immigrants. In 2007, annual net immigration to Spain (702,000) exceeded total live births by 44 percent, and in eight other European countries, net immigration was at least half the number of annual live births (from 50 percent in Sweden to 93 percent in Switzerland). In Western Europe, among larger countries only France, (9 percent), Germany (7 percent) and the Netherlands (-1 percent) had notably lower proportions.

The countries of original European settlement overseas are in the vanguard of these changes, most dramatically in the case of the United States. The United States is the first major population in the modern world to have forecast officially and in peaceful circumstances a transfer in the dominant population group, from one that has been a majority since the creation of the country to others primarily of recent immigrant origin.

The 2008 projections, though restricted to midcentury, expect that the formerly numerically dominant white non-Hispanic population—the face of America portrayed almost exclusively in history, literature, politics, and media—is projected to become a numerical minority in 2046 (U.S. Census Bureau 2008). As in the European cases, much of the growth comes from immigration. Between 1990 and 2000, the Hispanic population alone increased by 13.3 million, 47 percent from immigration. From 2000 to 2007, Hispanics accounted for 50.5 percent of U.S. population growth, compared with under 40 percent in the 1990s (Fry 2008).

Can the American experience of ethnic change, so far in advance of what is happening on the other side of the Atlantic, offer any lessons for what may come to pass in Europe?

"White flight" in relation to black inflow is well-known at the neighborhood level in the United States, and at the metropolitan and even state level as regards Hispanic immigration (Frey 1996). Academic studies in Europe, while documenting inflows and outflows by ethnic or immigrant groups, seldom discus internal migration in those terms, and some are at pains to deny it (Finney and Simpson 2009). Media and public opinion treat it as established fact, both from major cities and from the United Kingdom itself and from other European countries (e.g., the Netherlands).

The 50 percent benchmark has no special demographic significance, but it does have considerable psychological and political impact and attracts media attention. If total population is on the cusp of being majority ethnic, then a substantial majority will already be so among school children and urbanites. At the local level throughout Europe, transitions in the balance between indigenous and immigrant populations are becoming more common. Among the 32 London boroughs (average population 230,000) 2 were already majority nonwhite at the 2001 census, and according to a report by Data Management and Analysis Group (DMAG 2008) report, a further 6 are projected to join them by 2031. At the smaller scale of wards—a local government area of about 10,000 people—only 17 were majority nonwhite in 1991, 9 of them in London. By 2001 that had increased to 45, 22 of them in London. However at the bottom of the age pyramid, the position looks quite different. In London (population 7 million) in 2007, 60 percent of all births were to foreign-born mothers (not the same as nonwhite ethnic minority), and in 24 out of 32 boroughs such births composed more than half the total, in some cases over 70 percent (ONS 2008, Table 9.2). In Europe, major cities are on the edge of this transition. In 2006 the population of immigrant origin in the four major Dutch cities of Rotterdam, Amsterdam, The Hague, and Utrecht was increasing annually and had reached 46 percent, 49 percent, 46 percent, and 31 percent respectively (COS [Rotterdam Center for Research and Statistics] 2006, p. 10), and according to press reports of COS statements, expected in the case of Rotterdam to be majority non-Dutch by 2012 (NIS News Bulletin 2009). Major urban subdivisions have already passed that milestone.

The Faces of the Future?

So far ethnic groups have been discussed as though membership in them was unambiguous; whether defined bureaucratically by the register statistics of continental European countries or by the individually self-ascribed racial or ethnic descriptions of the United States and United Kingdom. Natural human inclinations are beginning to erode that neat picture. They may end up, in the very long run, destroying it altogether. That is because, if minority populations become more integrated into the educational system and the labor market and more dispersed geographically, the opportunities for sexual unions across ethnic or racial lines become more numerous. When minority groups are numerically very small, and especially if they are predominantly male, a high proportion of their unions may be outside the group, even if socially marginalized. Larger populations tend to have a more balanced sex ratio and to be more self-sufficient in services and facilities that reaffirm ethnic identity and help to confine social interactions to the group. Adherence to patterns of arranged marriage and strong preferences for marriages within closely defined religious, ethnic clan, or kin lines keep interethnic unions at a low level, for example, among Asians and Turks in Europe, especially Muslims, and some North African populations (Coleman 2004). But in general, more and more children are born with mixed parentage as time goes on. They may identify, or be identified, as members of either parental group. But many are content, or even anxious, to describe themselves as of mixed or multiple ancestry.

The ethnic categories used in the English-speaking world can easily include a category of "mixed ancestry": But European registers have no category for mixed citizenship or partial immigrant origin or background. Persons with one locally born parent are usually considered to be "native" or "indigenous." Furthermore the expansion of "diversity" arising from "mixed" categories fits the "multicultural" policies prevalent in the English-speaking world; continental European insistence on the primacy of "citizenship" encourages more binary assumptions. Statistics on marriages of local citizens with foreign citizens, readily found in official continental European publications, may, in fact, mean little. Many of the partners of apparently mixed origin are likely to belong to the same group, except that one is naturalized, the other not.

In the past, mixed unions usually incurred social obloquy or even legal sanction. They tended to be private affairs, conducted secretly both by the good and great and by the humble, from Jefferson downwards, and the children marginalized (with some pleasing exceptions, notably the poet Alexander Pushkin in nineteenth-century Russia). People of mixed origin have now emerged from social obscurity into global prominence. The eminent geneticist Steve Jones has described the face of the future, claiming that the future is brown (*The Times* 7 October 2008). If so, it is a long way off and some groups will quickly become browner (or paler) than others. For example, the 2001 Census of England and Wales revealed that a high proportion of the population claiming at least some black Caribbean origin were in fact of mixed origin and the proportion increased progressively in the younger cohorts.

Formally speaking, when people identified themselves by ticking the official box marked "Mixed White–Black Caribbean" they were lost statistically to the "Black-Caribbean" population, which was to that extent diminished in number (Figure 12.5). The self-ascribed white population may even eventually gain by this process, because through self-ascription a number of the offspring of mixed groups may be labeled (by their parents) as being "white." For example, in the 2001 census of England and Wales, 55 percent of the children of Chinese mothers were identified as Chinese, 29 percent as mixed, and 12 percent as white. Of the births to Caribbean mothers, 71 percent were described as Caribbean,

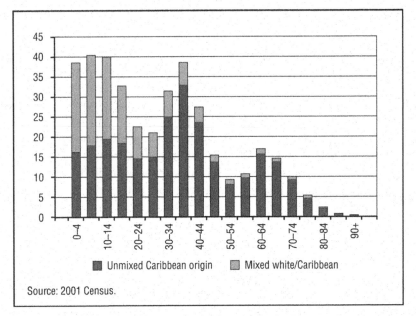

Figure 12.5   Population of Mixed Black Caribbean Origin Compared with All Black Caribbean Origin, England and Wales 2001

18 percent as mixed, and 5 percent as white. The "mixed" population created in this way is not a "sinking" category. Only 55 percent of the children of mothers who were themselves of mixed origin were described as "mixed," 33 percent were described as "white." There is movement of identity onwards to other groups, backwards to parental groups, and sideways to apparently unconnected groups, between generations and even within individuals (Platt et al. 2005; Doyle and Kao 2004).

This proceeds at different levels and speeds in different populations. In England and Wales, high levels of interethnic unions, marital and informal, have been noted for a long time between the black Caribbean, African, Arab, and Chinese populations and whites, generally increasing over time (Figure 12.6; see also Platt 2009). Among South Asian populations, however, and especially among the mostly Muslim Pakistanis and Bangladeshis, they are much less prevalent and did not increase over the 1990s at least (Berrington 1996; Coleman 2004). All these groups favor arranged marriages on strict religious and caste lines, and in the case of Pakistanis, to close relatives. That preference sustains the importation of spouses from the region of origin at a

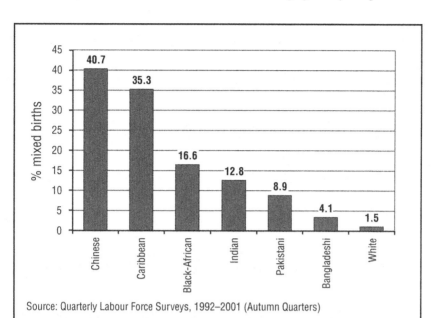

Figure 12.6 'Mixed' Births as a Percent of Total Births by Ethnic Group of Mother, UK, 1992–2001

high level, as in many continental European countries among Turks and others. Additionally, among Muslims, out-marriage of girls is forbidden under harsh sanction (in theory and sometimes in practice, sentence of death), and children of non-Muslim brides are expected to be brought up as Muslims.

Even if preferences in partner choice remain at their present level, the numbers of people of mixed origin, and their proportion in the population, can be expected to increase. Continued immigration of people of mixed origin, the natural increase of the existing mixed population, and the new additions from mixed unions all contribute. The only data on hand for Europe come from the United Kingdom. This projection, part of that described earlier, assumes that fertility, immigration, and the distributions of parentage by mixed origin remain as they were in 2001. On those assumptions the mixed population without the contributions from new mixed unions would grow to just over 2 million and to 3.6 million when they are taken into account. The latter figure would make the mixed populations the largest minority "group," albeit a highly heterogeneous one. Those conclusions, however, assume no "ethnic migration" of identity into the majority "white" category. We know that this does occur at quite a high level in terms of self-ascription, as noted above, although in terms of actual biological ancestry it reinforces Jones's point. These complexities are already becoming difficult (see Hollman and Kingcade 2005). After a time, the complex ancestries of mixed populations would defy categorization and ethnic categories would begin to lose meaning.

Probabilistic projections of U.K. population by Sergei Scherbov (Coleman and Scherbov 2005) tell a similar story using a different model based on four groups only: white, black, Asian, and mixed. White and "mixed" total fertility rate (TFR) was assumed to converge to 1.85, non-European to 2.0. White net immigration was assumed to cease, nonwhite net immigration to continue at the then-current rate of 147,000 per year. The median of the 1,000 runs makes the mixed-origin population the biggest "minority" at the end of the twenty-first century, heading exponentially towards being the biggest group of all (Figure 12.7). That is apparent from the age-structure profile even at midcentury. Mixed unions and their offspring are expected to increase: from 20 percent of births to the black population up to 35 percent, and from 13 percent of Asian births to 25 percent. While groups differ in the probability of interethnic marriage, within each group all individuals are assumed to have the same probability of marrying outside the group. Here, "mixed" is an "absorbing" category; no "mixed" children are reclassified as "white," "black," etc.

A different kind of statistical treatment provides more detailed insights and a much longer timescale. Here, the matrix of the ethnic origins of children compared with the origins of their mothers used in the projections above has been incorporated into an iterative stochastic migration matrix by A. J. Boyce of St John's College, Oxford (Figure 8). It models the cumulative "migration" of members of one group into another group (in both directions) from one generation to the next. It shows the number of generations that must elapse before each group shares 95 percent common ancestry with any other group, starting from an assumed level of zero relatedness (i.e., no common ancestry). The probabilities of exchange between groups are kept the same throughout, and no demographic growth is assumed.

When incorporated into a cluster analysis (Figure 12.8), those results correctly reflect the relative distance between groups as revealed by the incidence of offspring of mixed unions between each pair of groups. That technique has long been used to indicate the biological or social distance between groups as reflected by the prevalence of mixed unions or of (fruitful) sexual contact (Coleman 1980). Thus the white and the mixed and Chinese populations are shown to be relatively close, as are all the South Asian groups. Because it reflects an iterative process, the diagram can also show the number of generations that must elapse before each set of groups becomes almost indistinguishable by

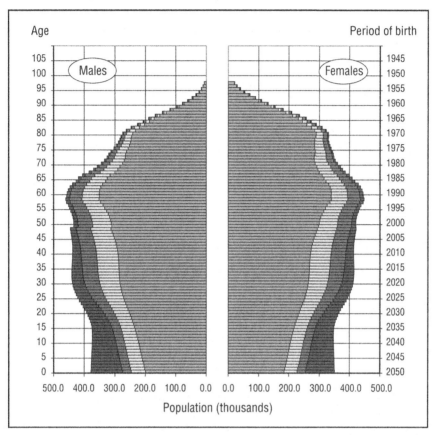

Figure 12.7 Probabilistic Projection of the UK Population Distribution by Sex, Age, and Major Groups at 2050 ("mixed" is shaded black)

ancestry, on the simple assumptions of the model. Those are very long times indeed. Thus the fusion of all the white groups takes 15 generations or about 420 years, and the group of the mixed, Chinese, and other, 35 generations, or 980 years. The combined black and Asian groups (the latter divided sharply by religion) each take about 45 generations to unite, and the whole set of populations become one after 75 generations or 2,100 years.

These outcomes seem to be incompatible with the results of the earlier deterministic and probabilistic projections. But the methods are measuring different things, and both models are somewhat experimental. Initially, groups are assumed to have no common ancestry. The requirement of 95 percent common ancestry is a very exacting one, while just one generation of interethnic union

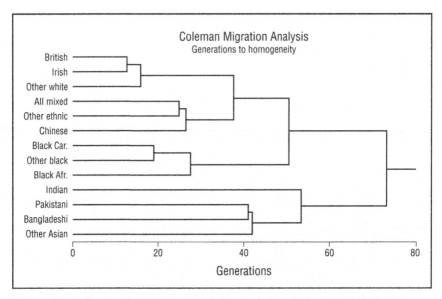

Figure 12.8 Number of Generations Required to Elapse Before 95% Common Ancestry Achieved, Based on Matrix of Mother/Child Ethnic Origins in 2001 Census of England and Wales

is all that is needed to produce a "mixed" offspring. Furthermore, it assumes the continuation of the relative proportions of ancestry in the population that were current in 2001, so that the eventual future "homogeneous" population would have about 80 percent white ancestry. The "mixed" population projected in the more conventional projections remains highly heterogeneous, it is not one "unified" population at all. Nonetheless, the results suggest that, except in the very long run, we should not get too excited about the prospect of the entire Western world losing any of its identities, native or immigrant.

A Third Demographic Transition?

These developments have provoked the suggestion that a "third demographic transition" is in progress; namely the permanent ethnic transformation of developed societies (Coleman 2006). The first demographic transition—the radical reduction of vital rates and the concomitant aging of the population—is now expected to become universal and irreversible. The second—the erosion of traditional values in sexual relations and living arrangements in enlightened societies protected by welfare—is as yet incomplete. Its completion, its permanence, and its universal acceptance in demography, hang in the balance. The third demographic transition would be a change in the composition of the population itself, the universalization of new ethnic diversity, leading possibly to the replacement of the original population by new ones through immigration and differential fertility. Such a transformation may be inevitable in countries with persistent low fertility. Without migration, these nations would in the long run cease to exist; with it, their territory would increasingly become populated by others. The consequences would be irreversible. The major query is how inevitable is it?

The answer to that rests primarily upon international migration, directly, and indirectly through births to immigrants, that is the main engine of ethnic change. It is widely assumed that immigration into Western Europe, the United States, and elsewhere will continue at a high level, despite the current recession (Dobson, Latham, and Salt 2009). Employers favor labor migration. Pressure groups are generally supportive, even when electorates are not. As immigrant-origin populations grow, chain migration through arranged marriages and the inflow of dependents from Asia and North Africa has grown with them in the absence of any marked changes in preferences (Lievens 1999; Lesthaeghe 2000). Population aging and the end of population growth in some countries is claimed to underwrite a growing future demand for labor. On that view, the recent inflow is a natural and necessary consequence of Europe's low growth; a component of the second demographic transition, sucking in population from a world reservoir of more abundant external sources of people. However, these hydraulic analogies, which liken the population of Europe to the operation of a lavatory cistern, should be rejected. Fertility rates in European countries are all increasing (Myrskylä, Kohler, and Billari 2009) while most third world emigration rates have been falling (Hatton and Williamson 2009).

Of course immigration can still go down as well as up, often directly or indirectly in response to measures to restrict it (Germany, Denmark, Netherlands; Figure 4). The effect of policies has been underestimated (Hollifield 2000) in analyses dominated by economic modeling. Asylum seeking in Europe has declined since the early 2000s. Policy changes in the Netherlands and in Denmark accelerated the removal of failed asylum seekers and substantially restricted migration for purposes of marriage.

But it is very difficult to restrict immigration in liberal democracies (Freeman 1994). Furthermore, the political importance of growing migrant populations may make restrictive immigration policies even more difficult to introduce. It has been claimed that no U.S. presidential candidate can now support major restrictions on immigration, whatever Congress may propose, because of the electoral influence of the Hispanic vote (Pew Hispanic Center 2008). Others put the spotlight on the paralysis that usually affects the U.S. political system in attempting to move away from any status quo.[3] Those forces are also making themselves felt in Europe, notably in the United Kingdom where citizens of Commonwealth countries may vote in national elections without being U.K. citizens and where the minority ethnic vote exceeds the electoral majority in a number of constituencies held by government ministers. Immigrant pressure groups have emphasized for many years (e.g., Anwar 1979) their potentially important effect upon electoral outcomes.

Immigration and intermarriage will diversify the gene pool, detaching national citizenship from ethnicity and ethnicity from ancestry. At this point, those of mixed background have a number of "ethnic options" (Waters 1990): They can become members of the majority ethnic group, emphasize their minority heritage, or opt for a "mixed" identity. Much depends on the extent to which immigrants and their descendants regard themselves as having acquired a new identity along with their new citizenship, and the extent to which they are accepted as insiders by the original inhabitants. The larger immigrant-origin communities become, the less the need to adapt to local norms, except insofar as it is required to participate in the economic realm. Instead, local norms may have to adapt to them, and local schools, facilities, and labor markets acquire and preserve an ethnic character. Foreign policy, too, is affected as immigrant lobbies press for favorable attitudes to causes of concern to their regions of origin, not otherwise the business of the country of settlement. Local politicians' chances of being reelected may depend on their attitude towards controversies that strictly belong overseas: the status of Kashmir, of Punjab, Israel versus Palestine, Kurdistan, and others. Again, whether all this is a just and reasonable response, reflecting a new diversity of rights, or an unreasonable challenge and complication to the national interest, is a matter of argument.

Coping with Increased Diversity

The developments described above may be regarded as the biggest set of unintended consequences of government action, or inaction, affecting European society in peacetime. No European government intended to set in motion policies with the intention of leading to foreign-origin populations of up to one-fifth of the total, with the prospect of that proportion increasing to up to one-third of the total population by midcentury. It is a safe bet that no electorate would have voted for it.

Two great imponderables at least hang over these demographic trends. First, even without further increase, how will European societies manage even the diversity that has already been created, as well as that which is probably to come? No consensus set of policies or principles has yet emerged. Different countries appear to be taking different tracks: the United Kingdom drifting into multiculturalism; the Netherlands government adopting a firm multicultural policy in 1980 and then reversing that policy with equal deliberation at the end of the 1990s; France attempting, with slightly less assurance than hitherto, to maintain a firm republican principle of the indivisibility of citizenship. None has yet been obviously very successful. Yet the process of diversification and minority growth has primarily been peaceful, if not entirely happy, with people of different origins often taken for granted as colleagues at work, and as neighbors, although less often as friends. The progress of interethnic unions is one indicator of close encounters, although very unequal between different groups. If inflow and diversification progress faster than integration, then one section of the population will advance while another will have to retreat.

The face of Europe has already been changed. How far that change progresses to something closer to a transformation depends partly on who accepts whose cultures and norms, or invents new ones, but above all on the future pace of immigration. A number of reasons have been put forward to support the widespread assumption that it will and must continue at a high level. But none of that is inevitable. Unforeseen events may severely depress—or increase—inflows. The supply of natives may increase with higher fertility, the supply of third world emigrants falter; in which case the "third demographic transition" may never truly arrive.

Notes

1. That is the members of the European Union prior to the May 2004 expansion—Austria, Belgium, Denmark, Finland, France, Germany, Greece, Ireland, Italy, Luxembourg, Netherlands, Portugal, Spain, Sweden, and the United Kingdom.

2. Revised, detailed projections of the ethnic minority populations of the United Kingdom will be published in Coleman (2010).

3. Personal communication from Professor Philip Martin, University of California, Davis, Chair, U.C. Comparative Immigration & Integration Program.

13

"Go Forth and Multiply"

The Politics of Religious Demography

Eric P. Kaufmann and Vegard Skirbekk

> Probably the most subversive and effective strategy we might undertake
> would be one of militant fecundity: abundant, relentless, exuberant,
> and defiant childbearing. Given the reluctance of modern men and
> women to be fruitful and multiply, it would not be difficult, surely, for
> the devout to accomplish—in no more than a generation or two—a
> demographic revolution.
>
> —*David Bentley Hart, conservative American*
> *theologian (cited in Joyce 2009, p. 179)*

POLITICAL DEMOGRAPHY ASKS HOW SHIFTS IN THE BALANCE of population among
groups affect power. Elsewhere in this volume, we have seen how differential

growth between nation-states, often linked to age structure, impacts upon international politics. The same is true of the population balance between civilizations like the West and the Islamic World (as popularized by Huntington 1996). Within nation-states, groups based on age, ethnicity, and other social criteria grow or decline at different rates, reshaping power and culture. Religion slots into this domestic matrix, but, unlike ethnicity, operates strongly at both the national and global levels. Religions can change their relative strength within countries and across the globe as a whole. Islam, for instance, can simultaneously grow in Europe and the world. These two-level trends may even flow from one another.

Religion often tracks ethnic change because it can serve as the boundary marker distinguishing ethnic groups from each other—even if few are believers. But while ethnic conflicts rarely mobilize kin beyond neighboring states or specific diasporas, religions like Islam or Orthodox Christianity may command wide international allegiance, raising the possibility of civilizational bloc dynamics (Huntington 1996).

What, then, is religion? Rather than enter onto this fiercely contested terrain, we opt to follow the definition of religion as actions, beliefs, and institutions that invoke the supernatural (Taylor 2007, p. 429). We are interested in the relative power of the major civilizational religions. Which are rising or falling? How does this affect domestic and international power relations? In many settings, switching between religions is prohibited by law or social norms. But even in restricted environments, religious preferences can be expressed in the form of differences in how intensely people follow their religion: how strictly they adhere to doctrine and how often they attend worship. Are conservative, moderate, or secular groups growing? Is attendance at services increasing?

Certain demographic properties of conservative, moderate, and nonreligious populations may be highly consequential since they can alter the balance between religious fundamentalism and secularism over time. Relevant demographic properties include fertility rates, the degree of intergenerational transmission of faith, and the age structure and net migration rates of different intensity groups. In much of the world, people are born into their religion and maintain their affiliation across the life cycle because religious markets are regulated by legal or social norms. Even in the West, the demography of religion often matters more than groups' relative success in winning converts and retaining members. In this chapter, we consider how demographic forces affect religions—whether defined in terms of faith traditions or intensity groups. We examine both the domestic and global contexts, and present cohort component-based population projections that enable us to peer, with a degree of accuracy, into the religious future.

Religion and Politics

The realms of God and Caesar are never completely separated. In some cases, the link between religion and politics is official; in others, it operates tacitly (Philpott 2007, p. 507). Even if there is a constitutional separation of religion from state, as in the United States, religions may still influence politics and the national security calculus. Electoral cleavages and party systems, foreign and domestic policies, mass culture and national symbolism—all may be affected by the plate tectonics of religion, even in secular democracies. So much so that religion remains one of the strongest electoral cleavages even in ostensibly "secular" Europe.

Nearly all of today's wars are civil wars, that is, they take place within states rather than between them. During the period between 1945 and 1999, 40 percent of civil wars claiming at least 1,000 battle deaths involved religion, with the proportion rising sharply in more recent decades. Most of these involved clashes among groups that differed in regard to both ethnic and religious identities, but in 10 cases, major civil wars took place entirely within one religious tradition. Nearly all of the latter—90 percent—were struggles within Islamic countries between Islamists and their rivals in government and civil society (Toft 2007a). Terrorism, too, increasingly draws on religious passions: Whereas just 2 of 64 terrorist movements were religious in the 1980s, this jumped to 46 percent by 1995 (Philpott 2007, p. 520).

Broadly speaking, shifts in religious traditions mimic ethnic shifts in their effects. For example, the growth of European Islam has sparked both ethnic and religious disquiet among the secular and Christian majority, with ethnic and religious anxieties reinforcing each other (see Coleman 2006, and this volume). Religion and ethnicity do not always overlap, however. The rise of Pentecostalism in Brazil, Korea, and China has led to hand-wringing among Catholics, communists, and Confucians, but does not affect the ethnic balance in these countries (Martin 2001). So, too, with secularization in Christian countries.

Ethos or Ethnos?

The American literature on religion and politics draws an important distinction between the *ethnoreligious* and *religious restructuring* paradigms (Guth, Kellstedt, et al. 2006). The ethnoreligious perspective places the accent on religious denominations, the quasi-ethnic identities bequeathed by history into which individuals are often born, and which structure the concrete congregations to which individuals belong. The ascriptive aspect to many religious denominations means that they are often linked to ethnic groups. This is true not only of archetypal "ethnic religions" like Judaism, or Druze or Armenian and Amharic Christianity, but also of Catholicism (linked to the Irish, Polish, many Southern Europeans, and Latin Americans), Lutheranism (German, Baltic, or Scandinavian) and black Protestantism. Even Mormonism and Mennonite Christianity partake of this ethnic character.

By contrast, the religious restructuring or "culture wars" perspective avows that belief dynamics cutting *across* religions are more important than the affiliation divisions *between* ethnic or religious groups when it comes to attitudes and voting behavior (Guth, Kellstedt, et al. 2006). You can be a traditionalist Catholic or a lapsed Catholic. Biblical literalists can be found within "moderate" denominations like the Northern Baptists or Episcopalians while theological modernists exist even within "fundamentalist" denominations like the Southern Baptists. Thus, theological intensity crosscuts boundaries of affiliation. Though religious affiliation and religious intensity are related, the fit is imperfect. The only category that neatly fits both the ethnoreligious and religious restructuring paradigms are the nonreligious, who are unambiguously modernist and nonaffiliated.

Overall, in the United States and the world as a whole, the most religiously fundamentalist (regardless of denomination) tend to vote for conservative parties, while religious moderates and seculars lean to the left. In Catholic Europe, church attendance is one of the strongest predictors of vote choice, with nonattenders backing the Social Democrats and attenders opting for the more conservative Christian Democrats (Guth, Kellstedt, et al. 2006; Norris and Inglehart 2004, pp. 206-207; Girvin 2000). The great exceptions are immigrant groups, who tend at once to be more religious and left-leaning than their host populations (Dancygier and Saunders 2006). This reflects the lower socioeconomic status of most immigrants. However, as with Muslims in Europe or Hispanics in America, immigrants' social preferences are frequently conservative, as reflected in Hispanic opposition to abortion and gay marriage (Swift and Webby 2008).

In the often undemocratic context of the Muslim world, a more violent version of the "culture wars" pits Islamists against theologically more moderate state governments, nearly all of which style themselves Islamic but insist on the right of the state to supersede religious authority. Earlier, we noted that civil wars have broken out in nine Muslim countries in recent decades. Political Islam prioritizes the implementation of *shari'a* law and questions the legitimacy of the Muslim state. The entire apparatus of state-appointed imams and state mosques is pilloried for rendering Islam subservient to an idolatrous nation-state. Many political Islamists, like Egypt's Muslim Brotherhood, Algeria's FIS, or Pakistan's Jamaat-e-Islami favor the ultimate restoration of an Islamic caliphate, which would entwine religion and politics.

Others trace this lineage all the way back to 1924, when the Ottomans abolished the Caliphate. Even those political Islamists who are reconciled to the state, and seek to reform it, deem current governments to be *takfir* (apostate), and place their loyalty to the Islamic *umma* (community of believers) above that to their nation-state. Islamists seek to return to a judicial system based on *shari'a,* with a strongly patriarchal division of labor and restrictive social mores regarding music, television, alcohol, and dress. The "excarnation" of folk displays of religious practice (i.e., religious music, carnival, dancing, drama) by puritans was a central aim of the Protestant reformation and is also an important theme within contemporary Salafi Islam (Munson 2001; Taylor 2007, p. 614).

Similar conflicts have riven the Judaic world. The fast-growing ultra-Orthodox, or Haredi, Jewish community entered into conflict with non-Orthodox Jews in Israel soon after the birth of the state. The Haredi world is a largely self-contained one with rules governing all aspects of daily life. Like Hutterites or the Amish in America, they live in separate communities or districts with little contact with the secular Jewish world. These practices, along with the use of Yiddish in some cases, help to sharpen the boundary between insiders and outsiders as both sides label each other (Davidman and Greil 2007).

The Haredim, in common with conservative American Christians and Islamists, have entered the public sphere and begun to influence politics. Orthodox rabbis view themselves as the guardians of the religious purity of the state and steadfastly seek to exercise this prerogative. Haredi parties have refused to relax proscriptions on civil marriages; only religious marriages presided over by Orthodox rabbis are recognized by the state. They have fought to narrow the definition of who qualifies as a Jew (and hence can be an Israeli citizen or immigrate) to the exclusion of converts and those without a Jewish mother. They also campaign against Sabbath desecration and the violation of kosher norms such as the selling of leavened bread during Passover (Efron 2003).

Conservative religious movements have been matched in vigor by their secular opponents. The story begins in the 1960s West, where higher education and a new centralized television media achieved mass penetration, acting as a conveyor belt for secular liberal values (Taylor 2007, pp. 492-495; Inglehart 1990, pp. 74-75, 252, 262). The secular liberalism of the 1960s therefore polarized the population in many parts of the world: The moderately religious majority either gravitated to outright secular liberalism or retrenched into conservative religion. In fact, conservative movements can be seen in part as a response to secular individualism and the breaching of traditional mores. This is especially true of the Christian Right in the United States, but, in a more indirect way, is also relevant for fundamentalist Jewish and Islamic movements.

The Demography of Religion

In their comprehensive work on global religion and politics, Norris and Ingle-hart remark that "rich nations are becoming more secular, *but the world as a whole is becoming more religious*" (2004, pp. 22-23, emphasis added). They trace this to the pronatalist thrust of major world religions, as well as the fact that many more children are born in the religious developing world than in the more secular rich world. Even if every country became less religious, the higher population growth of the more religious countries would render the median global citizen more religious. This is confirmed by data from the World Religion Database (WRD), shown in Figure 13.1 (Johnson and Grim 2009). These data only measure affiliation, and thus tell us little about the intensity of

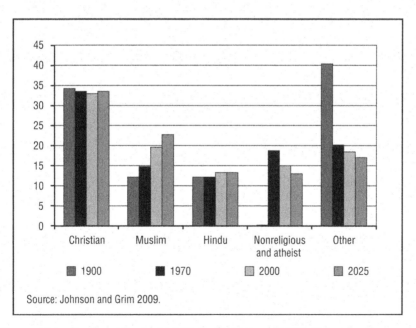

Source: Johnson and Grim 2009.

Figure 13.1   Past and Projected Global Religious Affiliation

belief within these religions. Still, they are instructive. First, note the rapid past and projected expansion of Islam, almost entirely through rapid population growth. Christianity, which is three times more successful at conversion than Islam, is nevertheless attached to slower-growing societies or ethnic groups, thus has barely maintained its global presence.

Shifts in the strength of other faiths reflect social or political changes rather than demographic change. Atheism/nonreligiosity has won converts from Christianity in Europe and most of its settler societies, but lost substantial ground back to Christianity since 1970 with the demise of world communism. Other (principally animistic) faiths have declined sharply due to conversion to Christianity and Islam, principally in Africa.

The Demography of Conservative Religion

Recall that differential ethnic population growth has been implicated in a number of ethnic conflicts. This raises the possibility that the same may hold for uneven religious population growth between fundamentalists and others. We are used to thinking about the high fertility of particular religious traditions, such as Catholicism or Islam. However, demographers have increasingly found that as societies modernize, differences *between* religions become less important than differences *within* religions in determining fertility (Westoff and Jones 1979). Strict Muslims become more like strict Catholics than lapsed Muslims.

Religious demography pulsates with increasing velocity in the current period. Why? In earlier eras, high fertility and mortality were characteristic of all populations. Today, by contrast, high fertility is more a matter of choice, and mortality is generally low, so members of groups that opt for higher fertility manifest rapid rates of increase across a few generations. Today, conservative religious values tend to be associated with higher fertility, while liberal or secular values predict lower birthrates. This is a feature of what demographers call second demographic transition theory (Surkyn and Lesthaeghe 2004; Lesthaeghe 2007). Here we briefly consider the cases of Judaism, Christianity, and Islam in their respective heartlands.

Israel and the Jewish Diaspora

Nowhere is the religiosity–fertility nexus as stark as in Israel and the Jewish diaspora. A recent Israeli government report shows that a third of Jewish primary schoolchildren are ultra-Orthodox (in 2010), rising to half if we add the modern Orthodox. Within Israel as a whole, just 41 percent of primary schoolchildren study in the secular state system, with the balance comprised of modern Orthodox, ultra-Orthodox, and Arab children (Wise 2007). These largely religious Jews (along with Arabs) will form the majority of adult Israelis in the not-too-distant future. These trends have radical implications in a society founded by secular Zionists.[1] Even with their small numbers, the ultra-Orthodox already have held the balance of power in the Knesset and are courted by the major parties.

The Israeli case simply illustrates, *in extremis,* a dynamic whose effect moves from the demographic to the social and then to the political sphere. Among ultra-Orthodox Jews (Haredim), for instance, fertility rates *rose* from 6.49 children per woman in 1980–1982 to 7.61 during 1990–1996; among other Israeli Jews over the same period, fertility declined from 2.61 to 2.27 (Fargues 2000). Haredi fertility remains self-consciously high, backed by social networks and taboos that also prevent defection to secular Jewish society. On current trends, Haredi and modern Orthodox Jews will form a majority of Israeli Jews soon after 2050. The same trends can be observed in the Jewish diaspora, adding further weight to the political rise of the Haredim (Wise 2007). Once a minor player, fundamentalist Jews will emerge as a major political bloc. Israeli domestic policy will be most affected, but Haredi influence may also hamper Israel's capacity to achieve peace with the Palestinians. This is because the ultra-Orthodox have expanded into new settlements in the Occupied Territories and across the Green Line in greater Jerusalem. They now oppose ceding post-1967 land for peace and seek unbridled access to the holy sites of the city.

United States

In the United States, white Catholics no longer have higher fertility than white Protestants (Westoff and Jones 1979), but women with conservative beliefs on abortion (whether Catholic, Protestant, or Jewish) bear on average nearly two-thirds of a child more than those with pro-choice views. Conservative denominations have higher fertility than more liberal ones, not to mention seculars (Hout, Greeley, et al. 2001; Skirbekk, Kaufmann, and Goujon 2010). American research also suggests a significant link between various measures of religiosity—congregational participation, denominational conservatism, attendance—and fertility (Hackett 2008). Individual-level relationships are reproduced through compositional effects at the state level, hence there is much higher white fertility in states with large Mormon or evangelical Protestant populations. Indeed, there was a correlation of .78 between white fertility rates and the 2004 vote for George W. Bush, an effect strongly mediated by religious traditionalism (Lesthaeghe and Neidert 2006).

During much of the twentieth century, women in conservative Protestant denominations bore on average almost a child more than their counterparts in more liberal Protestant denominations. This was the main reason why conservative Protestants increased their share of the white Protestant population from roughly a third among those born in 1900 to nearly two-thirds of those born in 1975 (Hout, Greeley, et al. 2001). This led to a "tipping point" in the late 1970s, when evangelicals were first mobilized as a political force for the Republican Party (Bruce 1998). This change has biblical parallels. Rodney Stark suggests that Christians' rapid expansion between 30 and 300 AD may have been caused by its relatively low mortality and high fertility rates. This set the stage for the rise of Christianity as the official religion of Rome after 312 (Stark 1996).

Secular Americans are much younger than average but their TFR is just 1.66, among the lowest of any American religious group. This will cause American seculars to age rapidly even if they maintain their current flow of young defectors: By 2040, the average nonreligious American will be 41, older than the typical American Protestant fundamentalist. This aging, combined with low fertility, will cause the currently fast-growing seculars to peak around 2030 at around 18 percent of the population and begin a slow decline thereafter. Hispanic Catholics will increase through immigration and high fertility from 10 percent today to 18 percent in 2040. The demographically vibrant Muslims and Mormons will both overtake the Jews by 2030, possibly altering the domestic constraints on American Middle East policy. In all these cases, demography is the main driver of change (Skirbekk, Kaufmann, and Goujon 2010).

The fertility gap between Americans with conservative and liberal attitudes on abortion and homosexuality has been widening in recent decades. Building in assumptions about the age structure, fertility, immigration, and switching behavior of these populations over the life cycle, we find that American religious conservatism will most likely strengthen in the years to come unless liberals close the fertility gap (see Figure 13.2).

The paradox is that the American population will grow more diverse, limiting the power of white evangelical Protestants and the Republican Party, but will simultaneously empower a multifaith coalition of moral conservatives. In this sense, California's majority vote for Proposition 8 opposing gay marriage may be a sign of things to come. It passed with a combination of white evangelical, Mormon, black Protestant, and Hispanic Catholic support in a state that also voted overwhelmingly—61 percent—for Barack Obama's Democrats.

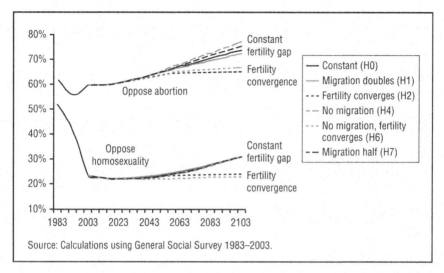

Figure 13.2   Projected Trends in Religious Opinion Under Various Scenarios

Europe

What of European Christianity? The conventional wisdom holds it to be in free fall (Bruce 2002). This is undoubtedly correct for Catholic Europe, while Protestant Europe already has low levels of religious practice, with as few as 5 percent of younger cohorts attending church weekly. Yet closer scrutiny reveals an increasingly lively and demographically growing Christian remnant. More importantly, a major source of religious growth in Europe is immigration. Western Europe's population of non-European extraction is projected to triple between now and 2050, from roughly 4–5 percent to 12–15 percent, possibly reaching as high as 25 percent in more diverse nations like Holland, France, and Britain (Coleman 2006 and this volume). These minorities are the product of demographically buoyant source regions, but it is important to stress that their population growth is a product of agrarian poverty rather than the traditional—not fundamentalist—religion that many bring with them.

Perhaps 60 percent will be Muslims, who show few signs of secularization except in France (Jackson, Howe, et al. 2008, p. 123). In England, more Muslims attend services each week than the established Anglicans, and a majority of London's Christians are nonwhite. Muslims in Europe generally have a younger age structure and higher fertility than native Christians, which further drives religious growth. Against this background, the low fertility of

Table 13.1 Total Fertility Rates by Religion, Europe and the USA, 2001–2003

	Spain	Austria	Switzerland	United States
Catholic	–	1.32	1.41	2.3
Active Catholic	1.77	–	–	–
Nominal Catholic	1.41	–	–	–
Protestant	1.45*	1.21	1.35	2.21
No Religion	1.00	0.86	1.11	1.66
Muslim	1.57*	2.34	2.44	2.84
Average	1.37	1.33	1.50	2.08

Source: Goujon, Skirbekk et al. 2007; Skirbekk, Goujon et al. Forthcoming.
*Few observations.

the religiously unaffiliated—whether European or American—is notable, as we can see in Table 13.1.

Several studies have examined the connection between European religiosity—whether defined as attendance, belief, or affiliation—and fertility. Nearly all find a strong, statistically significant effect even when controlling for age, education, income, marital status, and other factors (Adsera 2004, p. 23; Frejka and Westoff 2008; Berghammer, Philipov, et al. 2006). Traditionally, education was seen as the key determinant of a woman's fertility rates. Yet in many of these European studies, a woman's religiosity is as or more important than her level of education in determining the number of children she will bear over a lifetime.

We can observe the working out of these demographic patterns in projections of two fast-growing Western European populations, the nonreligious and Muslims. Here we use data from Austria and Switzerland, the only Western European countries that have consistently collected census data on religion, enabling us to construct estimates of switching behavior as well as religious demography. Figure 13.3 shows two estimates of the nonreligious ("none") population of these countries, which has expanded extremely rapidly through secularization in recent decades. The first, labeled "current" shows the growth trajectory of the nonreligious on current trends. The second set of lines, labeled "low" asks what would happen if religious defection dropped to zero by the end of the projection period. Notice that the growth curve of the "nones" is convex in all cases, a reflection of weak secular fertility and immigration. This leads to largely flat growth curves by the end of the projection period. A slower pace of secularization—perhaps caused by fewer secularism-prone moderate Christians and more secularism-resistant Muslims—could spell the end of secularization by 2020 in Austria and 2025 in Switzerland.

The convex growth curves of the nonreligious contrast with the concave shape of predicted Muslim growth, which will carry Islam to 11 percent of the

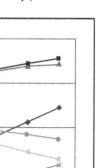

Figure 13.3 Trends in Nonreligious and Muslim Populations, Austria and Switzerland

total population in Switzerland and 17 percent in Austria by 2050. Moreover, Austria's Muslim proportion in 2000 (3.7 percent) and Switzerland's (4.2 percent) are broadly representative of Western Europe as a whole (Pew 2011). The general prognosis, then, is for a more secular Europe for several decades, but with a return to increased religiosity beyond 2050, with a substantial and growing Muslim component.

Immigrants and young people tend to participate less in the political process, but are overrepresented in expressions of political violence. This augurs toward a new dispensation in which European leaders can get elected without Muslim votes but must mind their "Muslim street" when crafting foreign policy. By the 2020s, we should expect to see a rapid rise in the Muslim electorate, which may shift the electoral calculus toward immigrant votes and away from anti-immigrant votes. This can already be seen in municipal elections in Brussels and Antwerp, with their large Muslim populations, where both socialist and Christian Democratic parties have courted the Muslim vote by fielding Islamic candidates rather than trying to compete for white nationalist votes with the far-right Vlaams Belang (Jacobs, Martiniello, et al. 2002).

The Muslim World

In most Muslim countries, the demographic transition is still in its middle-to-early stages, so we do not expect as dramatic a religious fertility effect as in Israel, Europe, or America. Still, we might ask: Do conservative Islamists have higher fertility than moderate Muslims, and what might we see in terms of Islamist population growth? We can begin at the country level, since governments tend to be authoritarian—though the Arab Spring may ultimately change this—in many Muslim countries, and hence wield greater influence over religiosity and fertility than in the West. In most Sunni societies, conservative Islam has clearly delayed the onset of secular demographic processes, raising fertility. Pakistan is an interesting case, because it contrasts markedly with poorer Bangladesh next door. In Pakistan, religious authorities resisted birth control more strenuously than Bangladesh, where Deobandi fundamentalism and the influence of anti-birth-control preacher Abu Ala Mawdudi is weaker than in Pakistan (see Figure 13.4).

The result is that Pakistan's population may reach 400 million by 2050, over 150 million more than if it had adopted a Bangladeshi-style program from the 1970s (Karim 2005, pp. 50-51; Cleland and Lush 1997). In Pakistan, 40 percent

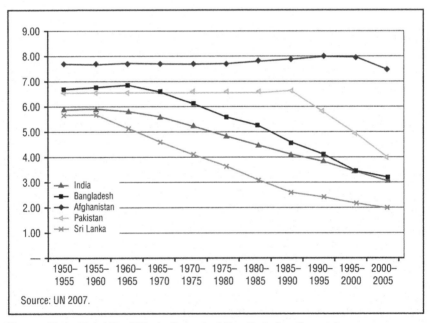

Source: UN 2007.

Figure 13.4   Total Fertility in Selected South Asian Countries

of the population is under 14. Total fertility rates in Somalia, Afghanistan, Yemen, and the Palestinian Territories are also exceptionally high, still exceeding five children per woman. In the Arab Middle East, Islamist pressure delayed the implementation of family planning in most countries by two decades compared to other developing countries. Today, Islamist pressure is partially responsible for slow or stalled transitions to replacement level fertility in many countries (Jenkins 2007, pp. 8, 21; Fargues 2000; Winckler 2005, pp. 212-220).

Yet the imperatives of state—notably reducing the fiscal drain and social demands of a large youth cohort—has nudged even the most reluctant of hands. Among the many Muslim societies that have embraced family planning, few are more striking than Iran. In the 1960s and 1970s, the Shah pursued a westernization policy focused on getting women outside the home into education and work and making contraception widely available. The TFR declined from 7.3 to 6.3 between 1966 and 1976. Then came the Iranian revolution in 1979, prompting a return to traditional gender roles and an abrupt end to family planning, raising fertility back up to 7.0 by 1986. But Khomeini's regime moderated its views as policymakers and intellectuals lobbied clerics, who eventually sanctioned family planning as a policy in keeping with the precepts of Islam (Abbasi-Shavazi, Hossein-Chavoshi, et al. 2007). The result was one of the most dramatic declines in fertility seen anywhere in the world. Still, state policy could reverse itself if determined conservative factions gain power. The Taliban have assassinated workers at birth control clinics, and pronatalist statements have been uttered by Iran's hardline Mahmoud Ahmedinedjad and Palestinian leaders. Even Turkey's moderate Islamist prime minister, Recep Tayyip Erdogan, played the pronatalist card in 2002. "Have babies," he told the crowd. "Allah wants it" (Caldwell 2005).

Do Islamist women have more children than other Muslims? Fundamentalist Islam is still a modernizing movement compared to the more heterodox folk Islam of the Muslim countryside (Gellner 1981). In Iran, Islamist Persian districts are no more fertile than average (Abbasi-Shavazi, Hossein-Chavoshi, et al. 2007). In Turkey, at the province level, the Islamist (AKP) vote and mosque density are unrelated to fertility rates. Instead, higher fertility seems to be related to traditionalism, as measured by arranged marriage, payment of a dowry, membership in a patrilocal family, rural residence, and illiteracy. Kurdish ethnicity is also associated with higher birth rates.[2] Muslim religiosity and fundamentalism *per se* count for little (Yavuz 2005).

Yet other evidence points to an emerging gap. One study found a modest fertility premium for Islamist women in parts of South Asia, Indonesia, and Africa (Berman and Stepanyan 2003, p. 30). This was confirmed in the cross-national World Values Survey of 1999–2000. Muslim respondents in Algeria, Bangladesh, Indonesia, Jordan, Pakistan, Nigeria, and Egypt, who agreed that *shari'a* should be the law of the land, enjoyed a considerable fertility advantage over women who opposed *shari'a*. Among urban women, fertility is almost twice as high (3.2 versus 1.8) amongst the most pro-*shari'a* sector of opinion than amongst women least in favor, whereas in rural areas, the ratio is less than 3:2. In line with second demographic transition theory (SDT), we might hypothesize that in rural, underdeveloped areas, religious beliefs take a backseat to material realities, such as access to family planning or the economic benefits of larger agricultural families, in discriminating between the more and less fertile. In urban areas, where economic incentives for children are lower and costs higher while birth control technology is more widely available, values may be a better predictor of reproductive behavior. This is borne out in surveys of European Muslims, a fully urbanized population with no material incentives to have children and unfettered access to birth control. In this population, the most religious Muslims are over 40 percent more likely—even with many control variables—to have more than two children than the least pious Muslims (Westoff and Frejka 2007).

The arrival of large rural populations in the teeming slums of Muslim cities created the popular base for Islamist revival after 1970 (Kepel 2002). The urban populations of developing regions are expected to increase further, from 43 percent of the total today to 67 percent in 2050 (Goldstone 2009). This also means that religious intensity will become increasingly important for fertility, leading to fundamentalist growth in Islamic societies. The principal casualty of a more self-conscious fundamentalist Islam experiencing a growing fertility premium will be moderate, "taken-for-granted" Islam, which will begin to lose religious market share to fundamentalists, much as liberal Protestants or reform Jews have lost in the West. Conservative Islam increases fertility, but not yet to such an extent as to suggest an imminent surge in the Islamist population on the scale of the Haredim of Israel. We therefore expect to see a significant fertility-driven Islamist revival only over several generations, that is, beyond 2050.

Da'wa, the "Call to God," has already enjoyed a powerful resurgence in the Islamic world due to Saudi funds and the failure of the secular postcolonial state in the Middle East and South Asia (Wickham 2002, pp. 119–149). This has reshaped politics in the region, strengthening political Islam. Conservative Muslim demography could reinforce these trends, with Islamism using its demographic momentum from the present era to delay or reverse the onset of secularism.

The New Religious Landscape

Changes in the religious composition of a country, and of the world, can have far-reaching political consequences. Shifts in the balance between religious traditions can alter the relative power of nations and civilizations. Within nations, shifts in the religious makeup of the population often follow ethnic changes and result in similar anxieties, political realignments, and conflicts. The religious restructuring perspective opens up a further aspect of religious demography that may well prove the most enduring: namely, the differential growth rates between fertile conservatives and low-reproducing liberals. During periods of "culture war" polarization—as is the case today between seculars and fundamentalists—migration and fertility may be the deciding factors.

In the context of the second demographic transition, religious women tend to have more children than nonreligious women. Conservative religious families are larger than theologically liberal families. Conservatives also are better at retaining their children within the fold than liberals. Seculars are growing through religious decline in much of the West but will be constrained by exceptionally weak demography. The net result is growing fundamentalism, an implosion of moderate religion, and a short-run rise in secularism that will ultimately give way to decline over several generations. Immigration also matters. In Europe, immigrants tend to be more religious than natives and their arrival in an alien context activates religious identity. Over several generations, this process will lead to significant religious population growth—especially among Muslims, introducing value-based tensions. Secularization may therefore stall or go into reverse sooner than expected: We predict this will occur in Europe and the United States around 2050. Examining the major Abrahamic faiths in their respective heartlands, we find that demographic fundamentalist revival is most advanced in Israel and the Jewish diaspora, where ultra-Orthodox Jews are poised to become a majority of the Jewish population after 2050.

The shift to more religiously fundamentalist populations will render societies more puritanical and ultimately less secular and may sacralize existing civil conflicts, making them more protracted and harder to resolve. Important changes will occur within a decade or two in Israel, where the projections are already causing political ructions. In the United States, Europe, and the Muslim world, fundamentalists have markedly higher fertility than others, but this advantage is typically in the quarter- to half-child range (roughly a 10–25 percent advantage) rather than the 100–200 percent fertility advantage enjoyed by the Haredim within global Jewry. Thus, significant change will only occur over several generations—boosting the long-term fortunes of the

Christian Right in the United States and Salafist Islam in the Muslim world. Immigration is more significant than fertility in causing short-run change, and will power both Muslim and fundamentalist Christian growth in Europe, with Muslims accounting for 10–15 percent of the West European total by 2050. This will raise a formidable challenge to the integrating mechanisms of European societies. It may also import the culture wars between fundamentalists and secularists—a staple of Islamic, Jewish, and American Christian politics—into Europe, reorienting electoral cleavages and challenging domestic security.

Notes

1. By secular (and secularization), we mean those who (a) seek to separate the political sphere from the influence of religious authority, and (b) in their private life, do not regularly attend places of religious worship or believe in the sacredness of a particular religious belief system. See Bruce 2002 for the distinction between public and private secularism.

2. Of course, Kurds and tend to be more religious than average, so a religious effect may operate indirectly.

Part V

Demography in Ethnic and Religious Conflicts

14

Wombfare

The Religious and Political Dimensions of Fertility and Demographic Change

Monica Duffy Toft

In 1993, Yasser Arafat, leader of the Palestinian Liberation Organization (PLO), predicted that the "ultimate victory" over Israel was inevitable and easily within reach. He described a powerful weapon that threatened to "blow up Israel from within." Yet he did not foresee Palestinians accomplishing this task with traditional weapons of war; rather, the ultimate Palestinian weapon was a "biological time-bomb": fertility (Ben-Meir 1993).

Whether high Palestinian fertility is a consequence of theology, culture, or other factors is subject to debate. However, it has been evidenced widely that there is a positive correlation between religiosity and fertility (Lehrer 2004,

p. 707). Traditional religions advocate almost universally for distinct gender roles and large families, condemning practices—such as abortion, divorce, and homosexuality—that impede fertility (Norris and Inglehart 2004, p. 23). The high fertility rates of religious people, particularly in less developed countries where religion is more deeply engrained in the culture, entail that the world as a whole is becoming more religious. Yet in many cases, religious groups consciously and actively pursue high fertility rates as part of a strategy for growth.

Secular nationalists can be just as pronatalist. Arafat's secular PLO provides a good example. Hitler, Stalin, and Ceaucescu in Romania offer other examples. And in some cases, religion and nationalism are combined, as in Israel where Jewish identity and faith are intimately connected. The establishment of the state of Israel came about in large part to unite and protect the people of the Jewish nation and faith.

This practice of "wombfare" is the tactic of using fertility as a political weapon against competing ethnic or religious groups; it is viewed as a long-term strategy for defeating a rival. What follows are four cases of wombfare that highlight different aspects of differential demographic growth: Christians and Muslims in Lebanon; Zionist Israeli Jews, ultra-Orthodox Israeli Jews, Israeli Arabs, and Palestinians in Israel/Palestine; the fundamentalist Christian Quiverfull movement in the United States; and Mormons in the United States. In some instances, high fertility is seen as a mandate from God, with little consideration of what it means for politics, while in others it is part of a strategy to strengthen a group's numbers to advance a broader political agenda.

Lebanon: Christians versus Muslims

Christians once constituted a clear majority of the Lebanese population, with a decidedly pro-Western political stance that welcomed the French mandate following World War I. In the 1920s, however, as the country expanded into areas with larger Muslim populations and a stronger Arab identity, Christians and Muslims in Greater Lebanon envisioned two very different trajectories for their country: one aligned with Europe, the other unified with Syria. The Constitution of 1926 thus required equal representation of Christians and Muslims in public offices. The 1932 census, conducted under French mandate, solidified the Christian grip on the country's power structure, enabling Christians to fix representation in Parliament at a ratio of six Christians to five Muslims. In 1943, the French established Lebanon as a state, with the goal of creating a Western ally in an overwhelmingly Muslim region.

In 1948, the mass exodus of Palestinians from the newly created Israel and into bordering states threatened to upset the precarious Christian majority; however, the Lebanese government sought to derail this problem by granting Lebanese citizenship to all Palestinian Christians while denying it to most Palestinian Muslims (Fargues 2001). After the 1960s, substantial numbers of (predominately Christian) foreigners living in Lebanon emigrated, as did many Lebanese citizens (Soffer 1986).

Although industrialization and urbanization of the 1970s revitalized the Lebanese economy, these same trends exacerbated underlying sectarian tensions. Mass-based social movements formed around these sectarian divisions, which then competed for power. This competition led to a dramatic increase in Christian-Muslim conflict and violence. Between 1975 and 1990, Lebanon dissolved into a brutal civil war waged by an ever-increasing number of sectarian militias, complicated further by Israeli and Syrian invasions. The war ended with the negotiation of the Ta'if Accord, a constitutional reform package that curbed presidential power, augmented the standing of the prime minister and Speaker of Parliament, and required equal representation of Christians and Muslims in Parliament and other high-level government positions. The war had virtually eliminated integrated neighborhoods, such that Christians, Muslims, and their representatives in Parliament became increasingly separated and entrenched (Chamie 1977, p. 367).

In the context of sectarian divisions, unofficial censuses since 1932 have shown that the Christian population has continued to shrink, while the Muslim population has grown significantly. In 1956, Christians were estimated to constitute 54.7 percent of the population; by 1998, this proportion had fallen to 42.6 (Fargues 2001, p. 116). Supporting these surveys, a 1971 study found that fertility rates for Lebanese women varied substantially depending on their religious sect: the average number of births for Shi'a women was seven; for Sunnis, slightly under six; and for Druze, five. Among Christians, the average fertility rate for Catholic women was slightly less than five, and for non-Christians, slightly over four (Chamie 1977, p. 367; Faour 1989).

Based on unofficial census data, it is clear that Muslims now constitute a majority of the Lebanese population, though their representation in government does not reflect this. In the long term, the once dominant Maronite Christians are left with three unpalatable options. First, Christians could attempt to retain the status quo, maintaining their strong political standing as an ever-shrinking minority in an increasingly undemocratic system. However, confronted with a growing Muslim majority with allies throughout the Middle East, maintaining Christian dominance would be impossible without the support of Lebanese

Christians living abroad, as well as foreign allies (Soffer 1986). This option led to the first war and would likely lead to a continuation violence. Second, the Christians could return to the original "small Lebanon" consisting of Mount Lebanon and Junieh (in which Christians constitute 90 percent of the population) and retain their political power there. Such as option would require surrendering the majority of Greater Lebanon to Muslim control, an outcome that is unlikely to be acceptable to either side. Third, Christians could do away with equal Christian-Muslim representation and their monopoly on the presidency, accept democratic Muslim dominance, and reenter national politics as a minority. This option could offer the most promising prospects for enduring peace; however, convincing Christians to surrender their political dominance voluntarily would be exceedingly difficult, particularly in a region where Christians are a marginalized minority. Additionally, overhauling the political system would reshape Lebanese identity significantly.

Israel/Palestine

A multidimensional example of wombfare can be observed in the case of Israel/Palestine, where Israel's secular Jews find themselves facing differential fertility rates from Palestinians, Israeli Arabs, and ultra-Orthodox Jews. The situation is compounded by the widely held perception that demography is an "existential question" for Israel (Zureik 2003, p. 621), in that Israel's fundamental identity as a Jewish, democratic state would be impossible to maintain unless the majority of its citizens were Zionist Jews.

The establishment of the state of Israel represented the fulfillment of the Zionist strategy of creating demographic "facts on the ground" through high Jewish birthrates and immigration. Arabs were perceived as a demographic threat to this project from the beginning (Portugese 1998, pp. 27–28). Concern for Jewish fertility grew as the Holocaust threatened both the existence of a worldwide Jewish population and future immigration to Palestine (Portugese 1998, p. 73; Fargues 2000, p. 455).

From 1948 to 1967, Israeli government leaders actively promoted immigration and fertility policies, successfully establishing a Jewish majority in the nation for the first time in the history of the Zionist settlement project (Davidson 1978, pp. 42–43). Yet by the mid-1950s, Jewish immigration had fallen, and government support for demographic research and fertility policies grew. In 1962, Prime Minister David Ben-Gurion established a Committee for Natality Problems tasked with developing policy recommendations regarding fertility (Portugese 1998, p. 76).

After 1967, Israel's demographic concerns compounded with its acquisition of the West Bank, East Jerusalem, the Gaza Strip, the Golan Heights, and the Sinai Peninsula during the Six-Day War. In each of these areas, Arabs dwarfed the Jewish population, reaffirming the importance of immigration and fertility to maintaining the Jewish majority in Israel. To that end, in 1968 the government established a Demographic Center in the prime minister's office, which promoted larger Jewish families through media campaigns and low-interest housing loans (Portugese 1998, p. 77). Individuals from various political camps sought to retain the occupied territories in different configurations for reasons of physical security and ideology (Abu-Ayyash 1976, p. 83). Yet the marginalization of Arabs in the Occupied Territories and pronatalist government incentives did little to resolve the disparity in fertility between Jews and Arabs. Coupled with rising nationalism among Palestinians, the high Arab birthrate posed a serious long-term threat to Israeli security.

By 1985, Arab children under the age of four in Israel, the West Bank, and the Gaza Strip outnumbered Jewish children under four for the first time (Friedman 1987). Jewish women had on average 2.85 children in 1985 with a steady decline into the 1990s, though this number was skewed upward by ultra-Orthodox Jewish women, who had an average of 8.0 children per woman. By comparison, Palestinian Arabs in the West Bank had an average of 6.3 children, and 6.8 in Gaza (Fargues 2001, pp. 472-473).[1] Jewish immigration from the former Soviet Union (Zureik 2003 and *Jerusalem Post* 2002) and Ethiopia (Ben-David 2008)[2] provided some respite from dire demographic predictions in the late 1980s and early 1990s.[3] Yet by 2007, non-Arab immigrants accounted for just 15 percent of population growth (Israeli Statistical Abstract 2008, Table 2.3).

Today, fertility patterns in Israel and Palestine underscore the rising importance of demography to security: The total population of Israel and the Palestinian territories in 2000 stood at around 9.7 million, including 5.4 million Jews (56 percent of the population) and 4.3 million Arabs (44 percent) (Statistical Abstract of Israel, various years; Zertal and Eldar 2005/2007).[4] Noting current birthrates, population expert Arnon Sofer estimates that by 2020, there will be 6.4 million Jews and 8.8 million Arabs in Israel, Gaza, and the West Bank (Foa 2002).

Significantly, by 2025, approximately 12 percent of Israelis will be ultra-Orthodox Jews. The high birth rate of this group has already begun to exercise an impact on national and international politics. Though they populate many of the Jewish settlements in the Palestinian territories, ultra-Orthodox Jews are traditionally anti-Zionist and are exempt from serving in the Israeli Defense

Forces (Bronner and Kershner 2009). Additionally, they are increasingly aligned with the political right, such that the rising popularity of the right-wing Yisrael Beiteinu party can be attributed in part to ultra-Orthodox support. Their political power is closely linked to their influence on religious life, in that they seek to toughen conversion laws to exclude Reform and Conservative converts to Judaism and oppose granting citizenship to non-Jewish Soviet immigrants (Freedman 2000, pp. 78-79). Finally, the ultra-Orthodox have the potential to exercise an economic strain on Israel, since the vast majority of ultra-Orthodox men attend *yeshiva* full-time rather than work (Bronner and Kershner 2009). The international consequences of the rise of the ultra-Orthodox will be far-reaching as well in that they will alienate Israel even further from its Muslim and Arab neighbors and will complicate its partnership with the United States.

The government of Israel seems to have finally acknowledged the consequences of the differential growth rates of populations, especially the Arabs, and what it means for Israel as a Jewish and democratic state. In December 2000, the Institute for Policy and Strategy at the Interdisciplinary Center in Herzliya hosted its first annual conference on national security for senior government and defense officials. Noting birthrate trends, the conference summary stated: "[T]he threat is developing rapidly, while the pace of developing a national policy dealing with the threat is slow" (Arad et al. 2001, p. 52). The summary argued for, among other initiatives, a birthrate and development policy that would guarantee a Jewish majority in the various regions of the country (pp. 53–54).

In the spirit of the Herzliya Conference, and feeling increasingly threatened by an Arab population growing both in size and in nationalist aspirations, in 2002 Israel began construction on a "security fence" with the stated goal of preventing terrorism at the height of the Second Intifada. Yet the location of the fence, which juts into Palestinian territory in several places to encircle Israeli settlements, supports the idea that demography is of greater concern to Israel than short-term physical security (Settlements in Focus 2005). Since its inception and continuing today, Israel seems to accept that it is indeed facing a situation of wombfare from the Arab/Muslim population.

Israel has few appealing policy options for addressing the demographic trends of Palestinian and Israeli Arabs. One option, a population transfer of Palestinians out of Israel, has found widespread public appeal: Sixty percent of Israeli Jews support this option (Zureik 2003, pp. 619-620). Second, Israel could offer abridged citizenship to Arabs; this resembles Israel's current policy most closely (BBC News 2007). Third, Israel could offer full citizenship to Arabs; however, this would invariably require Israeli Jews to surrender great political power (Rouhana and Sultany 2003, p. 10). Finally, Israel could accept the two-state solution advocated by the international community. This option is the only possibility that would not violate the Zionist logic of a Jewish, democratic state; yet it would require abandoning the hope of a "Greater Israel" encompassing much of the land many Jews believe was given to them by God. Even then, if current birthrates were maintained, one-fourth of Israel's population would be Arab within a generation. This last option, while likely an imperfect resolution to Israel's uncertain future, remains the most workable alternative at this junction, taking into account both the dim hopes of future Jewish immigration to Israel and the domestic and international pressure on Israel to treat all of its citizens justly.

Quiverfull: Christians versus Muslims, Christians versus Secularists

A third group with a strong pronatalist culture is the Quiverfull movement,[5] a transnational and interdenominational grassroots movement of fundamentalist Christians. Distinguished by their embrace of large families and rejection of all forms of natural and artificial birth control, adherents of the movement organize informally through Internet forums, literature, and conferences. They aim to reverse the declining birthrates of Protestant Christians in Western countries since the early twentieth century (Joyce 2006).[6]

The Quiverfull movement began to take root in the 1980s, following the publication of its foundational text, Mary Pride's *The Way Home.* According to Pride, the use of birth control within marriage creates a "contraceptive mentality," which leads women to view everything related to reproduction as their choice alone and invariably spirals into acceptance of abortion. As an antidote to such a perspective, which Pride argues contradicts biblical teaching about the family, women should embrace submission to their husbands and motherhood as a full-time, stay-at-home occupation. A core principle underpinning this status is accepting that women's bodies do not belong to them, but to God. To that end, women's lives should be a sacrifice to God, a role Pride glorifies with the title "maternal missionaries" (Pride 1985).

The Quiverfull movement prescribes strict gender roles, in which men are designated as leaders and providers for the family, and women are submissive partners whose primary occupation is to care for their children. Stephanie Coontz of the Council on Contemporary Families points to the rising popularity of the Quiverfull movement in the conservative Christian press as evidence of a reaction against feminism and an attempt to reclaim traditional gender roles (Finan 2006).

In addition to fulfilling the perceived biblical mandate to have large families, Quiverfull adherents view themselves as the champions of Christian culture against the threat of Islam. As Quiverfull author Nancy Campbell states, "We look across the Islamic world and we see that they are outnumbering us in their family size, and they are in many places and many countries taking over those nations, without a *jihad,* just by multiplication" (Hagerty 2009). Adherents point to declining birthrates in Europe and rising rates in the Islamic world to support their claims about the urgency of the threat and the need to save Christian culture. This point, too, is linked to September 11, 2001, since Quiverfull adherents point to the terrorist acts committed on that day as a harbinger of the rise of Islamic extremism (Joyce 2006).

Alongside the threat of Islam lies the specter of "race suicide," which, while rarely stated explicitly, infuses the rhetoric of the movement. Leaders speak frequently of falling European birthrates, ethnic conflicts, and Latino immigration to the United States to support their view that the decline of Western society is imminent, and that multicultural society breeds anarchy (Joyce 2006). Allan Carlson and Paul Mero, coauthors of *A Natural Family: A Manifesto,* echo this vision of the world, lamenting that Americans import their babies rather than give birth naturally (Carlson and Mero 2007). In essence, it is about maintaining and expanding Christendom.

Such thinking is consistent with the wider neo-Calvinist Dominion theology of which it forms a subset. Dominion theology is increasingly influential on the Religious Right. Rather than wait passively to be rescued during the Rapture, a premillennial dispensationalist position held earlier by most U.S. fundamentalists, today's revitalized Christian Right believes that building a righteous society on earth is their duty now; that they need to be active participants in restoring God's kingdom; and that Christ will not return until the kingdom is established. Moreover, this task can and should be accomplished through politics (Harding 1994).

For Quiverfull adherents, an existential threat to Christian culture is a grave issue that elicits an active response. Thus, it is unsurprising that militaristic language infuses the movement's rhetoric. As Rachel Scott writes in *Birthing God's Mighty Warriors,* Christian mothers are charged with building an army for God to fight a culture war (Scott 2004). Husbands and wives, too, are implicated in this war. According to Mary Pride: "Submission has a military air.... When the private is committed to winning the war, and is willing to subject his personal desires to the goal of winning, and is willing to follow the leader his Commander has put over him, that army stands a good chance of winning" (Joyce 2006, p. 16). The roles of "private" (wife), "leader" (husband), and "Commander" (God) demand acceptance and leave no room for questioning, since wives' failure to obey the better judgment of their husbands could result in the demise of the movement.

New York Times columnist David Brooks downplayed the militaristic aspect of the movement in a 2004 article, in which he claimed that Quiverfull mothers were too busy taking care of their children to wage a culture war (Brooks 2004). His remarks were criticized strongly, however, by one parent on the Quiverfull online forum, who claimed that raising children was in itself her "battle station" in the long-term plan to win the culture war demographically (Joyce 2006). Indeed, the ultimate goal of the Quiverfull movement transcends raising children: Through their numbers, they seek to reclaim Western society for conservative Christianity.

Mormonism: Mormons versus Non-Mormons

In the United States, members of the Church of Jesus Christ of Latter-Day Saints (LDS) are widely noted for their high fertility rate: A 1983 study found that the average American Mormon woman has 3.3 children, compared to 2.4 for Catholics, 2.3 for conservative Protestants, and 2.0 for liberal Protestants (Heaton and Calkins 1983). Yet Mormon women do not eschew birth control, nor do they seek to achieve explicitly political goals through demography (Heaton and Calkins 1983). Rather, a strongly pronatalist theology, history, and subculture contribute to the high fertility rates among Mormon women (Heaton and Goodman 1985).

Mormon theology places a great deal of emphasis on the centrality of the family to the afterlife. Before birth, human souls are in a state of "preexistence," during which the spirit awaits an opportunity for entrance into the world through a body. These human spirits themselves were created by a divine mother and father; thus, they are inherently holy, and their opportunity to enter the world should not be denied. Early church leader Brigham Young strongly advocated high fertility rates in order to allow these spirits to experience life: "It is the duty of every righteous man and woman to prepare tabernacles for all the spirits they can" (Young 1856, p. 56). The LDS Church teaches that human spirits are born into a "temporal existence" on Earth, during which they can be perfected. A perfectible life is incomplete until temple marriage, which is eternal and indispensable for salvation, or "exaltation" (Heaton and Goodman 1985, p. 346). Marriage is characterized by male headship (virtually all

Mormon adult men are holders of the priesthood) (McQuillan 2004, p. 45) and female submission, and husband and wife attain their full purpose when they give birth to children. After death, the couple enters a "postmortal existence" together. In their exalted state, they create new worlds and give birth to new human spirits, which remain in a state of preexistence until they, too, receive temporal bodies (Hastings, Reynolds, and Canning 1972).

Coupled with the LDS Church's decidedly pronatalist theology is its early history, which was very conducive to high birthrates and continues to influence the contemporary church. In the nineteenth century, Mormons immigrated to rural Utah in order to escape persecution and establish a holy "city on a hill," where religion and public affairs were closely intertwined, and involvement in the church extended beyond weekly services to social organizations, charity work, tithing, and proselytizing (McQuillan 2004, p. 46). Thus, church teachings pervaded every sphere of life, increasing the likelihood that believers would be diligent in their faith. In this context, a high birthrate was likely and necessary for the nascent church's survival, as it helped the early Mormons "to secure the land, found experimental mission settlements, establish a viable market economy, and proselytize, thereby 'increasing the glory of Zion'" (Hastings, Reynolds, and Canning 1972, p. 19).

Pronatalist writings from the late nineteenth century are linked closely to propolygamist writings. Thus, the LDS Church found itself on the defensive against external attacks on institutions it viewed as fundamental to Mormonism (Hastings, Reynolds, and Canning 1972, p. 20). Because of the centrality of the family to the faith, pronatalist writings often employed dramatic, confrontational language: Fertility was linked to the "fate of the nation," and attempts to curb it were evidence of the "moral depravity of women," which risked "race suicide" if it remained unchecked (Musser 1904). In essence, the family was indispensible to the survival of the church, culture, and civilization itself. In addition to its strongly pronatalist theology and history is an equally pervasive pronatalist Mormon subculture. Large families are regarded as indicative of faithfulness (McQullan 2004, p. 29). Young married couples are urged by their local churches to begin having children early and are discouraged from deliberately delaying or spacing births (Hastings, Reynolds, and Canning 1972, p. 22). Often, they are reminded that procreation is the sole purpose of sexual intercourse, and that using it exclusively as a means to satisfy lust prevents spirit children from entering the world. Likewise, unmarried people are strictly prohibited from engaging in sex: The LDS Church historically has been opposed to comprehensive sex education in public schools, and in the past it frowned upon welfare programs for unwed mothers (Hastings, Reynolds, and Canning 1972, p. 23).

While Mormon women do have significantly larger families than their Catholic and Protestant counterparts, it is important to note that higher fertility is by no means universal. First, birth control is widely accepted and used by Mormons, and has been for decades (Christensen 1945–1946). Second, Mormon women exhibit different fertility rates that reflect social factors: Those who are born into large families themselves, who live in areas with high concentrations of Mormons, and who attend church frequently have more children than their counterparts who are born into smaller families, who live where Mormons are a minority, and who are less observant (Heaton and Calkins 1983, p. 110). However, LDS theology and culture continue to exercise a very significant positive impact on Mormon birthrates.

There is little doubt the American government wanted Utah to become less of a bastion of Mormonism through immigration and assimilation. However, even at its height in 1920, the non-Mormon population never topped 40 percent and by the late 1990s, they constituted only a quarter of the population. Such dominance of Mormons in Utah has resulted in considerable local and national political clout: In 2000 Republicans received 94 percent of the Mormon vote and in 2004, 97 percent—the most partisan voting record of any ethnic or religious group in the United States.

The Varieties of Wombfare

As evidenced by the four case studies, wombfare takes varying pathways depending on the circumstances of the ethnic or religious groups involved. The table below lists the commonalities and distinctions of the four case studies of wombfare discussed above.

Some groups—most notably Israeli Jews and Quiverfull Christians—encourage high birthrates in order to attain greater influence within their society and pursue explicitly political goals. Others—Mormons, and arguably Lebanese Muslims—achieve high fertility rates for economic, cultural, or religious reasons. Yet even in the latter two cases, politics has become intertwined closely with fertility and religion: Nineteenth-century Mormons fled west to escape religious persecution by forming their own communities, but external political pressure ultimately persuaded the church to change its stances on polygamy (abandoning this doctrine in order to fulfill a condition of statehood for Utah) and race (granting the priesthood to black men in 1978, after the civil rights

Table 14.1 Comparing Cases of Wombfare

Cases	Political Theology	Pronatalism	Advanced Violence?	Impact on Politics
Lebanon		Ethnic	Yes	Reconfigured representation of Christians and Muslims in government
Christians	Quietist			
Muslims	Quietist			
	Few, if any, overt appeals for higher Christian/ Muslim fertility; birthrates reflect worldwide trends			
Israel				Shaped debate on settlement of land, statehood, and most recently the security fence
Ultra-orthodox	Quietist	Religious	Mixed	
Palestinian Muslims	Activist	Ethnic and Religious	Yes	
Zionists	Activist	Ethnic	Yes	
	Religious appeal for higher ultra-Orthodox Jewish fertility; political appeals for Jewish and Muslim fertility			
Quiverfull	Activist	Religious	No	Influenced by worldwide Christian and Muslim demography trends; seeks to advance social conservatism in American politics
	Religious appeal for high fertility; political gain considered a benefit			
Mormonism	Quietist	Religious	Yes	Allowed Mormons to resist assimilation and keep political control of Utah
	Religious appeal for high fertility in order to build a new society			

movement heralded changing mainstream views on race). Likewise, Lebanese Muslim birthrates reflected transnational determinants of fertility including religion, education, and socioeconomic status; however, the realization that their numbers should accord them more political representation than their Christian compatriots contributed to interreligious violence, a brutal civil war, and ultimately a significant shift in Muslim political representation.

The connection between fertility and religion is evident. However, how it plays out in politics often is not. Phillip Longman warns about the inevitable political strength that conservative religious voters will hold if they continue to maintain high birthrates, and argues that progressives are left with only one option: They must emulate the traditional family structure and high birthrates of the Quiverfull and similar movements (Longman 2004). In essence, what Longman is advocating is that secularists engage in their own form of wombfare. The problem is that without a religious mandate, increasing fertility rates, or even just maintaining current rates, will be difficult. More than theology is involved. Culture, development, and the distribution of political and economic resources all play an equally important role. Nevertheless, it is clear that ethnic and religious groups often consider fertility and children as part of a longer-term political strategy; therefore understanding these demographic dynamics is critical to understanding whether and under what conditions these dynamics will lead to harmony or discord.

Notes

1. The latest figure reported by Fargues is for 1995, with Arab Palestinian women in Gaza having an average of 7.4 children.

2. Most Ethiopian Jews arrived in the 1980s and 1990s, although the last official airlift occurred in August 2008. There are an estimated 9,000 Jews still living in Ethiopia.

3. Most immigrants from the Soviet Union to Israel, however, were not Jewish. According to one count, "of the 246,037 non-Jews who received Israeli citizenship, 221,428 have been from the former Soviet Union"(Mualem 2002).

4. As of 2009, the total population of Israel proper had grown to 7.4 million. Although the number of Jews had risen to 5.6 million, the Arab population had grown significantly faster, to 1.5 million (Bassock 2009).

5. The group takes its name and religious foundation from Psalm 127: 3-5: "Like arrows in the hands of a warrior are sons born in one's youth. Blessed is the man whose quiver is full of them. They will not be put to shame when they contend with their enemies in the gate."

6. The year 1930 marked the beginning of the biblically prophesied "70 years in Babylon," because thereafter, children were considered a choice. This period ended on September 11, 2001, after which a renewed emphasis was placed on the family (Scott 2004).

15

Deter or Engage?

The Demographic Structure of Ethno-Nationalist Mobilization

Christian Leuprecht

Wombfare is often a tactic deployed by fundamentalists who foment intra-ethnic conflict, but as the case of Israel demonstrates, can also be seized upon by rival ethnic groups contending for power, land, or symbolic primacy. Demography need not be actively wielded to result in conflict, however. In fact, unintended differences in the timing of fertility transition between ethnic groups can also set the stage for violence.

We have a pretty good understanding of the conditions affecting fertility, of the groups that are prone to conflict, and where discord is likely to arise. By contrast, the microcausal mechanisms that drive the probability of violence, the onset of violence, and its intensity remain elusive, especially insofar as demography is concerned. This chapter posits demography as an intervening variable that affects the propensity of groups to resort to violence over choosing alternative strategies. Whereas most variables in the social sciences principally lend themselves to *ex post facto* analysis, the ability to project fertility and mortality trends into the future with a remarkably high degree of certainty distinguishes demographic factors as independent variables in their own right that stand to be harnessed to project risk and guide efforts at mitigating and preventing conflict.

Provided that Fearon (2006) is correct in asserting that the mere desire to resolve conflict is insufficient, what conditions affect the decision of ethnic groups to enter into violent conflict or engage in peace negotiations? Starting from the proposition that "the simple phenomenon of differential population growth rates is translated into changing political potentials" (Wriggins and Guyot 1973, p. 16), this chapter offers a theoretical exploration supported by indicative empirical evidence of the logic(s) by which demographic structure is thought to affect conflict.

A controlled comparison accounting for alternative explanations such as the relationship between a group's size and access to political power (Posner 2004; Cederman, Wimmer, and Min 2010) is beyond the methodological scope of this chapter. Instead, it confines itself to two natural experiments to generate hypotheses. Relative group size, shifts in group size, and their trajectory towards transition (groups becoming close in size) have already been posited as independent demographic variables (Toft 2007a), as have youth bulges (e.g., Urdal 2006, 2007). Size and youth, however, are merely symptomatic of population structure. The comparative study of population age structures allows us to control for both size and youthfulness. Demographic projections have the added advantage of factoring in migration. Although complementing other work on population size and youth, relative age structure provides a more comprehensive and reliable independent variable.

Israel/Palestine

In an apocalyptic article entitled "The Demographic Jinni: The End of Zionist Dream?" geographer Arnon Soffer presents projections by Israel's Central Bureau of Statistics to draw attention to the changing demographic balance between "Jews and Arabs in the Land of Israel." "The Jews in the Land of Israel want clear and concise answers" to what Soffer refers to as "the demographic problem." That article was published in *Ha'aretz* in March 1988. The answer came in December in the form of the first Intifada. Of course, the Intifada was not an "answer" to counterassertions by an Israeli geographer. But Yasser Arafat, an architect of the Intifada, is on record as having said that the Palestinian woman's womb is his best weapon, a reference to God's promise in Genesis 18-21 that Sarah's dead womb would bring forth life. Similarly, future Israeli Prime Minister David Ben-Gurion testified to the Central Committee of the Histadrut on December 30, 1947 that:

> In the area allocated to the Jewish State (by the United Nations) there are not more than 520,000 Jews and about 350,000 non-Jews, mostly Arabs. Together with the Jews of Jerusalem, the total population of the Jewish State at the time of its establishment, will be about one million, including almost 40 percent non-Jews. Such a [population] composition does not provide a stable basis for a Jewish State. This [demographic] fact must be viewed in all its clarity and acuteness. With such a [population] composition, there cannot even be absolute certainty that control will remain in the hands of the Jewish majority.... There can be no stable and strong Jewish state so long as it has a Jewish majority of only 60 percent. (Masalha 1992, p. 176)

Indeed, demography has long been identified as a key fault line between Israeli Jews and Palestinians (e.g., Fargues 2000; Soffer 2000).

The proportion of Arabs in historic Palestine has been growing apace.[1] A recent census counted about 5.4 million Israeli Jews. That contrasts with 1.4 million Israeli Arabs (not all naturalized) and 4 million more Arabs in the West Bank and Gaza. By 2025, the populations of the West Bank and Gaza are projected to burgeon to 4.4 and 2.9 million, respectively. Parity between Jews and Arabs currently residing in historic Palestine had been forecast to be reached between 2007 and 2013 (Courbage and Fargues 1997, p. 157). It has already been reached, with population growth among Israeli Arabs outpacing the Israeli average by 15 percent and growth among Arabs in the Gaza Strip and West Bank outpacing the Israeli average by 50 percent.

The relative number and rate of growth of Israeli Jewish and Arab populations is controversial. In absolute terms, Arab increase has been formidable: From 156,000 who remained after the dispersion of 1948—all of whom were granted Israeli citizenship—to 1.4 million today. In the last two decades alone, Israel's Arab population has doubled. Similarly, the population in the Occupied Territories has more than doubled, to 4 million, in 30 years—and it is expected to double again in the next quarter-century. Growth of this magnitude is indicative of a youthful population structure. Indeed, almost half the population is under 15. On average, a third of the Palestinian population is 15 or younger, but in Gaza this rises to well over half the population.

Although the proportion of youth has now peaked, it is only projected to decline marginally over the coming years. Concomitantly, the total fertility rate (TFR) is still about 5.6 children per woman. While a handful of countries have a greater proportion of youth and/or higher TFRs, Gaza actually has among the highest TFR of any jurisdiction in the world. These figures are well above the average for Arab states. As a result, the United Nations projects the annual rate of natural increase in the Occupied Territories between 2001 and 2015 at 3.3 percent, well above the Arab-state average of 2.1 percent. The discrepancy is even more impressive when one considers that the arc of Muslim countries stretching from Egypt to Pakistan have the second-highest rates of natural increase in the world (behind sub–Saharan Africa).

Compared to other Islamic societies and the Middle East, natural increase among Palestinian Arabs constitutes an aberration. The Palestinian population in smaller Israel entered its demographic transition two generations earlier than the Palestinian population in the Occupied Territories. The former peaked at an average annual rate of natural increase of 43.5 per 1,000 during the period 1961–1965. Trends in the Occupied Territories are reversed: Natural increase has been on the rise since the early 1970s—largely due to improvements in health care and sanitation, decelerated emigration, and a burgeoning population pyramid (Gilbar 1997, pp. 12, 19-20, 23-24, 53-56). The current rate of natural increase in Gaza is estimated at 3.95 percent, in the West Bank it is 3.32 percent—compared with 1.48 percent for the Jewish population.

By contrast, the proportion of Arabs among the population of smaller Israel appears to have remained constant at 19 percent since the inception of the state in 1948. In 1948, 872,700 people lived in Israel, four-fifths of whom identified as Jewish. Of the 6.5 million people who lived in smaller Israel in 2001, a historic nadir of 77 percent identified as Jewish.[2] Those figures include Israeli settlers in the Occupied Territories and an undisclosed proportion of the 700,000 Israeli citizens estimated to reside in the United States. If these two groups are factored out, the proportion of the Jewish population of smaller Israel is closer to 70 percent. By 2020, that proportion is projected to contract by another 5 percent. Notwithstanding apparent continuity, the ratio between Jewish and Arab residents has been shifting (even once the negligible 4 percent of Israel's population that identifies as neither Arab nor Jewish is factored in).[3]

The two populations' age structures are also shifting. In 1982, the median age of Israeli Jews was 25.1, while that for Israeli Arabs was 16.9. By 2001, the gap had widened. The median age of Israel's Jewish population was now 30, while the average age of the Arab population was only 19.6. Half of Israel's Arab population is under 20 years of age and 40 percent is under 15. The corresponding proportion for Jews is only a third (Census of Israel 2001). By contrast, the proportion of youth among the Israeli population is 28.1 percent, its TFR is 2.7, and the United Nations projects Israel's annual rate of natural increase at 1.6 percent.

In addition, the balance of net Jewish migration in recent years has been negative. This calls into question Israeli's nation-building strategy of demographic dominance of the Jewish population (Lustick 1999; Yonah 2004).[4] It is no accident that Israel's main airport is named after the strategy's architect and country's first prime minister. David Ben-Gurion noted:

> Without high, constantly growing, Jewish immigration to Israel, without a significant increase in the rate of Jewish births in the country, we are condemned to become a minority, even if the threats of the Arab dictators to exterminate Israel are thwarted by our national army. To ignore this danger is tantamount to the attitude of *après moi le déluge.* (cited in Courbage and Fargues 1997, p. 153).

Migration is causing the gap between Jewish and Arab populations in greater Israel to close more rapidly. During the late 1960s, high mortality and emigration among Palestinians compounded to cancel out any demographic gains from natural increase. Twenty years hence, the available avenues of emigration had been closed and fertility cut in half. For all intents and purposes, total growth now equaled natural increase (see Figure 15.1).

Arabs have grown exclusively through natural increase. Hampered by a comparative disadvantage in TFR, the primary source of Jewish population growth in Israel has been immigration, not natural increase (CBS 2001, Table 2.2; Courbage and Fargues 1997, p. 156; Goldscheider 2002, p. 25). Notwithstanding a spike in immigration over the past twenty years, Figure 15.2 shows that the requisite immigration underpinning Israel's nation-building strategy has proved elusive, especially in light of strong population growth among Palestinians in the Occupied Territories.

In recent years, Jews have been leaving Israel at an annual average rate of about 3.3 per 1,000 residents.[5] By contrast, the rate of *aliyah*—the "ingathering of exiles" of an estimated world Jewry of 12.9 million of whom only about one-third actually lives in Israel—is only about 1.1 per 1,000 residents (CBS 2001, Table 2.2 in loc. cit.). These observations are confirmed by Israel's Central Bureau of Statistics registering an annual excess of departures over arriving passengers at Ben Gurion airport.

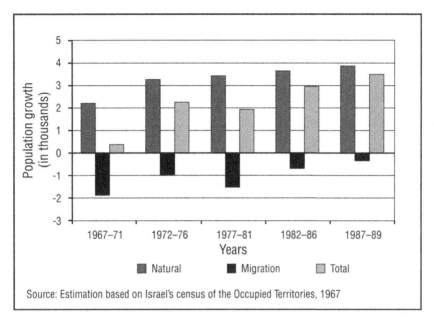

Figure 15.1   Components of Population Growth Among the Arab Population in the West Bank and Gaza Strip, 1967–1989

Counterfactually, had there been no immigration in the 1970s, the proportion of the Jewish population in Israel would have been only 65 percent instead of 85 percent (Friedlander and Goldscheider 1979, Table 7.6). In the 1990s, Israel welcomed 200,000 to 300,000 non-Jewish, non-Arab immigrants, mostly from the former Soviet Union (Dellapergola 1998). This is confirmed by the 2001 census, where an unprecedented 4 percent of those surveyed identified neither as Jewish nor Arab. While the practice of non-Jewish immigration may keep Palestinians at bay, it also accelerates the growth in the proportion of Israel's non-Jewish population.

Jewish numbers also mask severe intra-Jewish divergence between the disproportionately high (and rising) fertility of ultra-Orthodox (Haredim) and other more conservative religious Jewish groups (e.g., Fargues 2000; Toft 2002; Kaufmann 2007). Haredim, who do not serve in the military, oppose the Zionist idea, and largely do not pay taxes, are considered by many Israeli Jews to be a security liability. When they are factored out, the Zionist majority in Israel shrinks significantly. The fact that the Haredim and Arabs now account for half of Israeli primary schoolchildren is a matter of great concern to Israeli policymakers (Cincotta and Kaufmann 2009).

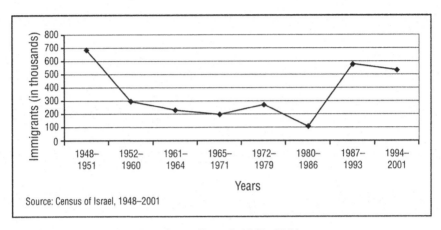

Source: Census of Israel, 1948–2001

Figure 15.2 Total Immigration to Israel, 1948–2001

Curiously, one outcome of soaring ultra-Orthodox fertility has been a shift in the balance of Israel's population back toward Jews (Morland 2009). Meanwhile, Israeli Arab fertility is falling, and while Israeli Arab women still bear, on average, in excess of four children, this represents a decline of 33 percent from an average of six children per woman only two decades earlier. The convergence of Arab and Jewish Israeli fertility suggests that ethnic change will slow down, limiting the long-term threat to smaller Israel's Jewish majority. Indeed, projections suggest that by 2020, the Arab proportion of Israel's population will rise only marginally, to 23 percent.

Northern Ireland

"The basic fear of Protestants in Northern Ireland is that they will be outbred by the Roman Catholics. It is as simple as that," surmised Terence O'Neill, Unionist Prime Minister of Northern Ireland, in the wake of his resignation in 1969.[6] As in the Israeli-Palestinian conflict, demographics have long been identified as a putative driver of conflict in Northern Ireland (Doherty 1996; Poole 1983; Boal 1995; Compton 1991).

When the province of Northern Ireland was created in 1921, Protestants outnumbered Catholics 65:35. But, owing to a higher TFR, natural increase among Catholics has long had the intrinsic potential to undermine the Protestants' majority (Hepburn 1994, p. 116). Northern Ireland's Protestant majority entered the demographic transition—from high to low birth and death rates—60 to 80 years earlier than the Catholic minority (Jones 1960, p. 155; Compton 1976, p. 441). However, Catholics' disproportionate emigration rates offset their fertility advantage until the 1950s. The Catholic minority supplied 60 percent of the province's emigrants prior to this period (Lyons 1971, p. 745; Compton 1982, p. 91). Emigration thereby acted as a "pressure valve" that "released" part of the Catholic population. For a variety of reasons, including the structure of relative opportunity and transaction costs associated with migration, emigrants have empirically been shown to fall primarily between the ages of 15 and 40. By altering the age structure among Catholics artificially, emigration further undermined their population growth until emigration slowed in the 1950s.

However, in the 1950s, due in part to the spread of the British welfare state, Catholic emigration slowed, permitting population growth to drive ethnic change. The compound effect of age-structure differences and higher fertility (Figure 15.3) in the Catholic population has been to increase the Catholic proportion of the population since the end of World War II. Today's ratio is about 53:47, a significant development given, as Figure 15.3 shows, that this is the largest share Catholics have enjoyed since 1861. Demographic developments over the past 150 years are thus an inextricable part of the conflict—and the peace—in Northern Ireland. Indeed, the proverbial writing had been on the wall for Protestants since Catholic demographics rebounded in the 1930s.

The upswing is a function of age structure. In 1971, between 38 percent and 47 percent of the Catholic population was under the age of 16, whereas

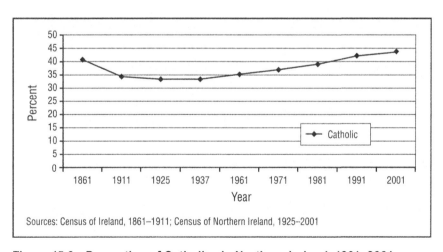

Sources: Census of Ireland, 1861–1911; Census of Northern Ireland, 1925–2001

Figure 15.3 Proportion of Catholics in Northern Ireland, 1861–2001

Table 15.1 Catholic and Protestant Age Structures in Northern Ireland, 2001

	Catholic	Protestant
Under 18	53.8%	46.2%
18–65	48.9%	51.1%
65+	37.7%	62.3%

Source: Census of Northern Ireland 1926–2001. Data aggregated by author based on disaggregated information in table CAS306: Age By Community Background [Religion or Religion Brought Up In].

Note: The term *Catholic* includes those respondents who gave their religion as Catholic or Roman Catholic. Protestants include "other Christians." These data exclude those who state "none" or "other" as their faith. Some thus claim that the dyadic coding Protestant/Catholic is increasingly unsuitable (Doherty & Poole 2002).

only 28 percent of Protestants fell into that category.[7] In other words, the reproducing cohort of the Catholic population was about 50 percent larger than that of the Protestant population. Crude Protestant birthrates were healthy compared to the European standard: 19.3 per 1,000 in 1961 and 18.0 per 1,000 in 1971. Despite waning fertility, Catholics continued to enjoy a comparative advantage over Protestants: Their rates stood at 28.1 in 1961 and 25.4 in 1971 (Compton 1982, p. 86-89). The peace process in Northern Ireland coincides with two demographic phenomena. First, the Unionist majority has been steadily diminishing, and a majority of school-age children in the province are now Catholic (see Table 15.1).

Second, fertility rates have been declining recently, especially among Catholics. As the Catholic population entered the demographic transition in the 1960s, it started to age. Yet Catholics maintained significantly higher fertility (3.2 to 2.3) and larger families (3.1 to 2.4 children) as late as 1991 (Compton 1991). Although natural increase decelerated as a result, in the initial stage of the demographic transition, the large base of the Catholic population pyramid still produced a high number of crude births, hence the Catholic advantage we see in 2001 (Table 15.1). However, in the long term, although the Catholic population remains younger than the Protestant population, the probability of violence is likely to be tempered by slower Catholic growth in the future.

Population Trends and Ethnonationalist Conflict

Intuitively, immigration by the majority might be thought to stoke conflict by bolstering the majority's demographic dominance. Yet, neither immigration by

Protestant Unionists to Northern Ireland post-1922 nor by Jews to Israel during the second half of the twentieth century confirms that proposition. Demographic consolidation among the majority does not appear to affect the demographic equilibrium with respect to conflict. By contrast, as a minority's demographic advantage founders, the cost of conflict rises, which precipitates a strategic shift toward nonviolent engagement. The Irish Republican Sinn Fein party warming up to the peace process as the Catholic fertility advantage over Protestants began to wane is a case in point.

In Northern Ireland, we find (1) a compound effect of population aging among groups in conflict, and (2) a diminished fertility premium of the minority over the majority as a result of converging population age structures among populations going through the demographic transition. The slowing Catholic demographic advantage helped Protestants overcome commitment problems and enabled a shift from violence to successful bargaining and, eventually, a mutual commitment to a sustainable bargain. By contrast, in the Israeli-Palestinian conflict, we observe just the opposite: The age structures of the groups in conflict differ substantially and fertility convergence is a long way off. The result is both a proportionally larger youth cohort and a relative advantage in size for the minority. Examining age structure in addition to crude population size and fertility differences allows us to analyze—and project—population trajectories more accurately.

Perhaps an even more significant finding is that emigration serves as an independent variable in explaining within-case variation in violence: In both Northern Ireland and Israel-Palestine, emigration appears to have tempered violence by manipulating population structure and, in the process, mitigating both the size and youthfulness of minority populations. Conversely, as this exit option ceased, the propensity for violence rose in both cases.

In Northern Ireland, emigration—an intentional strategy of the Protestant-dominated Stormont regime (Patterson and Kaufmann 2007)—had artificially distorted the age structure of the Catholic population. Without emigration, the proportion of the 15–40 cohort would have been larger and, by virtue of the reproductive cohort being larger, the base of the Catholic population pyramid would have been broader because the children of emigrants would not have been born abroad. This would have generated a larger youth cohort and accelerated asymmetric population growth. Emigration delayed that development, but a decline in emigration after World War II exacerbated the cleavage of ethnic fertility differences to power differential population increase.

Similarly, in Israel age structures had stabilized artificially. On the one hand, Palestinians were either dispersed or emigrated. On the other hand, diaspora

Jews immigrated to Israel. By the mid-1990's, however, the sources of Jewish immigration had largely been exhausted and, in recent years, Jews have increasingly resorted to *yerida*—commonly defined as the emigration of Jews from Israel—to the point where Israel's net migratory balance is now negative. At the same time, migration has become increasingly difficult for Palestinians. The impact of the younger Palestinian population structure on differential growth was amplified as a result. Palestinians now brought to bear the brunt of their younger population structure unmediated by either Jewish or Palestinian migration.

Conversely, population aging among Catholics coincided with violence gradually subsiding. Aging among both the Protestant and Catholic populations preceded the peace process. Still, differential growth proceeds apace. Time is on the Nationalists' side, just as—as Arafat's remark about the weapon of the womb exemplifies—it is on the side of Palestinians in the Occupied Territories. In Muslim legend, a *jinni* is a spirit associated with demonic forces and powers. Demography appears to have that Janus-faced potential: Demographic change can be as much a source for deterrence as for engagement. The evidence marshaled from the conflicts in Israel-Palestine and Northern Ireland generates the following hypotheses. The propensity for violence decreases:

H1: as the population structures of groups in conflict enter the demographic transition and age; and;

H2: the further their population structures converge.

Furthermore,

H3: migration is an intervening variable insofar as it moderates or aggravates both population structure and the pace of convergence.

For the purposes of early intervention and preventative diplomacy, then, these findings suggest we should be concentrating our efforts on conflicts where at least one of the two parties has a young age structure, with particular emphasis on cases where the age structures of groups in conflict differ significantly. In such conflicts, we must be alert to the potentially destabilizing effects that can issue from a failure to resolve the conflict: Demographic pressure will continue to mount as long as minority grievances linger.

Notes

1. References to territory in the Israeli-Palestinian conflict are inexorably political and wrought with controversy. None of the territorial references in this article should be mis-

construed as implicitly biased. To this end, references to the "West Bank" and "Gaza" are to population developments in one or both of these territories respectively as delineated today. Historic Palestine refers to the territory covered before the creation of the state of Israel, that is, current-day Israel, the West Bank, the Gaza Strip, but also territory stretching into what is today the Golan Heights. Greater Israel refers to the Land of Israel as laid out in God's covenant with Abraham in Genesis 15:18-21. It is commonly taken to include Israel, the Palestinian territories, Lebanon, parts of Syria, Jordan, Egypt, and possibly portions of Iraq, Saudi Arabia, and Egypt. In the Israeli vernacular, however, it is almost interchangeable with Historic Palestine, that is, it refers to the state of Israel, the Palestinian territories, and the Golan Heights. Finally there is smaller Israel, which refers to the state of Israel as delineated prior to 1967.

2. Using the same data, CBS 2001 Table 2.27, Toft (2002) pegs the Jewish proportion of the State of Israel at 82 percent. The arithmetic by which the proportion of Jews among the Israeli population is arrived at by subtracting the proportion of the Arab population from the whole is based on the spurious assumption that any non-Arab Israeli must be a Jew.

3. Effectively, this ratio refers to residents, not citizens: About 20 percent of Arabs on Israeli territory, including Arabs in East Jerusalem and the Golan Heights, have been denied Israeli citizenship.

4. One Israeli diplomat observes: "The Palestinians have never made a secret of their intention to try to bring down the Jewish state by flooding it with hundreds of thousands of Arabs from abroad" (Shoval quoted in *New York Times* [1994, p. 3]). The actual size of the Palestinian diaspora may be controversial. Uncontroversial, by contrast, is that the Palestinian diaspora bordering the State of Israel is larger than the state's total Jewish population. Of 1.5 million Palestinians in Jordan—half of Jordan's population—1 million, that is, one-third of Jordan's population, are refugees. The proportion of refugees among the Palestinian population in Lebanon is 85–90 percent (332,000), 90 percent in Syria (302,000), 40 percent in the West Bank, and two-thirds in Gaza. Ergo, any right of return would inexorably have detrimental consequences for the numerical balance of power between Jews and Palestinians in Israel and the areas west of the Jordan river. See also Curtiss (1997).

5. The Central Bureau of Statistics records only "Departures and Returns of Israeli residents remaining abroad continuously for one year or more." No inference can be drawn from these figures about the demographic impact of emigration on the Jewish character of the Israeli state. In fact, Jewish immigrants continue to be counted as de jure "residents" of Israel, providing they visit Israel at least once every four years (Curtiss 1997). That means many of the (estimated) 700,000 Israeli citizens residing in the United States, with the exception of their children providing they have never been "residents" of Israel, would continue to count as residents of Israel. If that is indeed the case, then there may already be fewer than 4 million Jews permanently residing in Israel.

6. From a speech shortly after he resigned as Prime Minister of Northern Ireland, cited in Gillespie and Jones (1995, p. 105).

7. Due to an estimated 9 percent of (probably mainly Catholic respondents) who failed to identify their religious identification (which is different from identifying with no religion at all), estimates of the Catholic cohort for the 1971 census vary (Compton 1982, 98-100).

16

Demographic Change and Conflict in Contemporary Africa

Elliott D. Green

> Perhaps the most important thing to understand when comparing African societies to those of other regions of the world is that historically speaking, the continent has the lowest population density of any of the major continents. This crucial fact has shaped all aspects of African life.
> —R. O. Collins and J. M. Burns (2007, p. 40)

THE POLITICS OF POPULATION GROWTH IN CONTEMPORARY Africa has largely been a neglected topic. While there is growing interest in the long-term causes and consequences of Africa's historically low population density (Austin 2008; Herbst 2000; Nunn 2008), there remains relatively little interest in assessing the political consequences of demographic change in contemporary Africa. My goal here is thus to assess these consequences, especially in relation to issues of conflict and violence.

The literature on conflict and demography has long moved away from a simple Malthusian model whereby high population density leads directly to violence. Rather, as suggested variously by such authors as Goldstone (1991), Homer-Dixon (1999), and Kahl (2006), high population growth can lead to violence only indirectly, through such mechanisms as rigid political institutions, the high salience of group cleavages, unequal access to resources, and the lack of institutional inclusivity, among other factors. However, the analysis of these mechanisms has largely remained at the nongeographical level, with little attention to why or how population growth might affect some parts of the world more than others.

In this chapter I focus on the link between conflict and demographic change in sub–Saharan Africa. I argue that historically low population densities in Africa have indirectly provided the opportunities, motives, and collective action necessary for conflict via poverty, inefficient land-holding structures, and ethnic diversity, respectively. More specifically, I claim that recent population growth has combined with these three variables to produce a specific type of conflict, namely "sons of the soil" conflict over land. The preponderance of this type of conflict across Africa can thus can be traced to a large and, by world historical standards, very quick shift from low population densities to high population growth over the past century and a half.

The chapter is structured as follows. First, I explain how Africa's historically low population densities have resulted in poverty, communal and unequal land-holding structures, and ethnic diversity. Second, I detail how modern high population growth has impacted African states negatively through these three processes, giving examples from Sudan and the Democratic Republic of Congo. Finally, I conclude with some wider thoughts on political demography in Africa.

The Consequences of Low Population Density in Modern Africa

Debates have raged among historians as to the causes of Africa's low population density: While some have suggested that Africa was sparsely populated due to "ancient rocks, poor soils, fickle rainfall, abundant insects and unique prevalence of disease" (Iliffe 2007, p. 1), others have placed more emphasis on the role of the intercontinental slave trade in extracting people from the continent (Nunn 2008; Zuberi, Sibanda, Bawah, and Noumbissi 2003). Regardless of the causes, there is almost universal agreement that precolonial Africa's population density was low and, due to large population growth elsewhere, sharply decreasing relative to other regions by the beginning of the colonial period in the late nineteenth century. The political and economic consequences of low population density have not, however, drawn as much attention. Here I focus on three major consequences for precolonial and colonial Africa, namely poverty, a communal and unequal property rights system, and ethnic diversity, each of which I examine in order.

Poverty

There is good evidence that Africa's low population density has posed an impediment to economic development in at least three ways. First, economists and historians have long emphasized how Africa's high land-to-labor ratio has led to high labor costs and a subsequent reliance upon labor-saving, land-extensive agriculture (Austin 2008). As a result, there were few incentives to increase agricultural productivity, while widely dispersed farms were difficult to link together with transport infrastructure (Herbst 2000).

Second, a scarcity of labor also meant that slave raiding arose before the arrival of the Europeans, thus aiding the development of the intercontinental slave trade (Iliffe 2007). The effects of the slave trade were economically pernicious in many ways. Not only did it "remove labor from a labor-scarce continent, the opposite of what the economies required for long-term growth" (Austin 2008, p. 613), but it also weakened state development, with an increasing effect after independence (Nunn 2008). Moreover, ethnic fractionalization, whose negative effects on economic development have been widely discussed (Easterly and Levine 1997), has a positive relationship with historic slave exports, suggesting that the slave trade "impeded the formation of broader ethnic identities" (Nunn 2008, p. 164).

Third, a low population density put Africans at a severe disadvantage in resisting the onslaught of European imperialism, whose links with economic underdevelopment in Africa are now well established in the literature (Acemoglu, Johnson, and Robinson 2001). Many scholars have noted the remarkable speed with which Europeans conquered the continent, which was in part due to the continent's low population density. Thus, given a choice between resisting colonization and escaping to open land away from colonial domination, most Africans naturally chose the latter option (Herbst 2000). Indeed, the most prominent example of African resistance to imperialism, namely the Ethiopian defeat of the Italians at Adowa in 1896, was in large part a consequence of

Emperor Menelik's ability to draw upon an army of 100,000 soldiers compared to less than 20,000 for the Italians (Iliffe 2007, p. 171). What made Ethiopia different in this regard was her highlands, which across Africa account for 4 percent of total land mass but almost 20 percent of its population, and which allowed for a great abundance of population in central and northern Ethiopia (McCann 1995, pp. 23, 89).

Communal and Unequal Land Rights

As already noted, low population density meant that labor was much scarcer a commodity than land in precolonial Africa, which explains why the concept of private property was often absent, while laws regulating labor, marriage, and cattle ownership were regularly highly detailed and intricate. Far from being inefficient at the time, economists like Binswanger and Deininger (1997) have suggested that this lack of land ownership rights was not problematic in that the benefits of private property were outweighed by their enforcement costs. However, in their subsequent attempts at codifying customary laws according to individual "tribes," European colonizers created systems of land tenure that were dually problematic. First, the creation of customary law by tribe rather than by country meant that each colonial state had multiple and overlapping systems of land tenure. Precisely because land rights were largely uncodified in precolonial times, these property laws were contradictory and ever-changing according to new interpretations of what constituted African custom.

The second problem caused by the codification of customary land law was the way colonialists vested these customary land rights in tribal chiefs and thereby created local "decentralized despots" across rural Africa (Mamdani 1996). These chiefs, whose power over their subjects was enhanced by colonial restrictions on labor movement outside Africans' designated tribal territories, suddenly found themselves in charge of vast amounts of land and were thus able to gradually acquire control over large tracts of land. Moreover, colonial rulers allowed non-Africans to take up ownership of supposedly "ownerless" land, both as settlers and investors. The consequence of allocating land to both tribal chiefs and non-Africans, while beneficial to colonialists, was to create a highly unequal system of property rights ownership.

Ethnic Diversity

Africa is widely known for its high levels of ethnic diversity (Easterly and Levine 1997), and there is a good deal of evidence that low population density has been a significant cause of this diversity, either indirectly or directly. As regards the former, we have already seen that low population density led to an inability to resist colonialism, and there is evidence that colonialism itself contributed to higher levels of ethnic diversity. For instance, in colonial Ghana "missionary and colonial policies, by providing educational and administrative benefits based on tribal boundaries, gave incentives for local chiefs to emphasize linguistic differences from their neighbors" (Laitin 1994, p. 623). It is thus not surprising that Michalopoulos (2008) finds a positive and significant relationship between British, French, German, and Portuguese colonization and ethnolinguistic fractionalization for a worldwide sample of countries.

There is also evidence for a direct link between low population density and ethnic diversity. Africa's ethnic diversity may have even been greater in the precolonial period, inasmuch as many missionaries "reduced Africa's innumerable dialects to fewer written languages" due to budgetary constraints (Iliffe 2007, p. 239). Moore and colleagues (2002) have suggested that cultural and biological diversity are correlated, inasmuch as areas that support highly diverse ecological environments do not create the incentives for local inhabitants to establish the large trading networks that can lead to the creation of larger ethnolinguistic groups. In other words, biological diversity could be responsible for both cultural diversity but also the aforementioned abundance of disease that contributed to low population densities in most of Africa. This proposition has also found empirical validation by Michalopoulos (2008), who shows that precolonial population density is inversely and significantly related to ethnic fractionalization, even with continental dummies and other controls.

Africa Under High Population Growth

The low population density that did so much to contribute to poverty, inefficient land rights, and ethnic diversity has not, however, been a constant factor throughout African history. As noted in Tables 16.1 and 16.2, sub–Saharan Africa had a larger population than Europe between the fourteenth and eighteenth centuries. After experiencing negative population growth between 1600 and 1900—the only region in the world to do so over this period—since 1900 Africa has suddenly experienced one of the largest growth spurts ever recorded in human history.

The causes for this shift are simple: Africa is the last region of the world to enter the demographic transition, whereby societies move from a high birth/high death equilibrium to a low birth/low death equilibrium via a high

Table 16.1 Sub-Saharan African Population and Ratios, 1300–2050

	Sub-Saharan African Population	Africa/Europe*	Africa/World
1300	60 million	85.7%	13.9%
1400	60 million	115.4%	16.0%
1500	78 million	116.4%	16.9%
1600	104 million	116.9%	18.0%
1700	97 million	102.1%	14.3%
1800	92 million	63.0%	9.6%
1850	90 million	43.1%	7.3%
1900	95 million	32.2%	5.8%
1950	186 million	47.3%	7.3%
2000	669 million	130.2%	10.9%
2050**	1,960 million	361.0%	21.1%

Sources: (Biraben, 1979, p. 16; United Nations Population Division 2011)

*Excluding ex-USSR

**UN Projection (Medium Variant)

birth/low death transition phase. It is this intermediate period that produces high population growth, via both high fertility and low mortality. What is remarkable about the transition in Africa is that the continent is experiencing large increases in population despite the fact that, thanks to war, HIV/AIDS, malaria, and other diseases, mortality still remains relatively high compared to other parts of world.

The evidence suggests that, in part due to the political stability and Western medicine introduced by colonialism after World War I (Clapham 2006), African fertility and population growth rates rose for decades to peak in 1983 and 1990, respectively (Iliffe 2007). Yet, at 41.7 births per annum per 1,000 people, African birth rates remain at almost twice that of the next highest

Table 16.2 Average Annual Population Growth Rates, AD 0–2050

	SS Africa	Asia	Europe*	World
0–1600	0.14%	0.04%	0.07%	0.05%
1600–1900	–0.03%	0.33%	0.40%	0.35%
1900–2050**	2.02%	1.16%	0.41%	1.16%

Sources: (Biraben, 1979, p. 16; United Nations Population Division 2011)

*Excluding ex-USSR

**UN Projection (Medium Variant)

region (Latin America, 23.1 births), and its average fertility rate, while in decline, is not converging with the rest of the world (Zuberi et al. 2003). This extraordinarily quick shift from negative population growth in the early nineteenth century to a peak of positive growth of around 3 percent a year in the late twentieth century has given Africans very little time to adjust to the very different political, economic, and social conditions brought by rapid population growth.

One result of this sudden change has been a high level of civil strife, specifically "sons of the soil" conflict over land between migrants and natives. While this type of conflict has received a growing amount of attention from scholars (Bates 2008; Boone 2007; Dunn 2009; Geschiere and Jackson 2006; Jackson 2006), with the exception of Green (2007) no one has attempted to explain its origins through a political demography framework. Thus, I now return to the three outcomes of low population density outlined above and how they have interacted with high population growth in the postcolonial era.

Poverty

Not surprisingly, political economists have long suggested that poverty and economic decline can lead to conflict, especially in Africa. More specifically, Fearon and Laitin (2003) argue that poverty inhibits governments from developing their militaries and suppressing insurgencies, while Collier (2006) suggests that poverty decreases the opportunity costs for rebellion compared with nonviolent activities. The relationship between poverty, population growth, and conflict is also well established. Goldstone (2002) shows that the combination of rising urbanization, a good proxy for rural population pressure, and low levels of GDP/capita lead to an increased propensity for conflict. More specifically, high-fertility countries in the initial phase of the demographic transition often see a "youth bulge" of 15- to 24-year-olds, who are already easier to mobilize politically due to fewer responsibilities and openness to new ideas. When youth bulges coincide with low economic growth, thereby leading to under- and unemployment, this combination can have a strong link with civil wars (Keen 2005; Urdal 2006).

Land Rights

As noted above, upon independence, African states had land tenure systems that were largely communal, with very unequal distribution of what small amount of private property did exist. As regards communal land, most postindependence regimes nationalized communal land ownership, with some states like Ethiopia, Nigeria, Tanzania, and Zambia going so far as to nationalize private land as well. Moreover, the nationalization of public land only exacerbated inequalities in private land ownership inasmuch as it allowed politically powerful Africans to acquire and expand their land holdings. Yet at the same time that states were nationalizing land ownership, population density in some regions had grown to the point where many rural Africans could no longer access enough land in their "tribal" areas. Efforts that had previously focused on expanding the amount of land under cultivation, which was easy with low population densities, had thus run their course by the 1980s in such places as Niger (Raynaut 1988). As a result, rural-rural migration became an increasingly viable option, especially to other regions which had lower population densities and good quality farmland. Thus labor migrants who had the ear of the government could access nationalized land in new areas, and, as these labor migrants generally came from areas that were more developed than those to which they migrated, resentment and "sons of the soil" rebellion developed amongst the many indigenous populations.

Ethnic Diversity

There has been a vast literature on the relationship between ethnic diversity and conflict, especially since the 1990s. Easterly and Levine (1997), for instance, argue that ethnic diversity, as measured by the ethnolinguistic fractionalization index, "is a meaningful predictor of the potential for ethnic conflict as measured by its worst possible manifestations" (p. 1223), namely civil war and genocide. Moreover, the evidence from literature on "sons of the soil" conflict shows a greater propensity for violence when "natives" and "settlers" are from different ethnic groups. Thus, what dampens this type of conflict in more homogenous countries elsewhere is what also exacerbates it in ethnically diverse regions like Africa (Kahl 2006). Moreover, the absence of cross-cutting cleavage groups, as exist in India, has helped to accentuate ethnic differences in Africa. Indeed, not only do ethnic differences make the demarcation between settlers and natives easy, but they also allow for easier collective action among the natives, who are usually the instigators of "sons of the soil" conflict (Fearon and Laitin 2010). A growing literature thus suggests that ethnicity can provide the resources for collective action, specifically through the existence of ethnic norms and institutions that enforce cooperative behavior (Habyarimana, Humphreys, Posner, and Weinstein 2007).

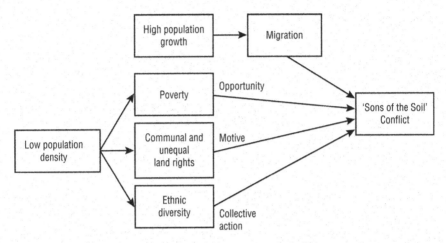

Figure 16.1 Demographic and Institutional Contributions to "Sons of the Soil" Conflict

Empirical Analysis

The above analysis shows how low population density can indirectly provide the opportunities, motives, and collective action necessary for rural conflict over land. First, poverty lowers the opportunity cost to engage in violence, while also raising the value of land relative to other resources. Second, the unequal distribution of private land and the nationalization of public land creates a motive to gain control over land for the purposes of redistribution. Third and finally, ethnic diversity helps to provide for collective action among groups who are already primed for violence. Figure 16.1 summarizes this causal story.

In order to test this theory empirically I focus here on two prominent contemporary case studies, namely the Sudanese civil war in Darfur since 2002 and the civil war in the eastern Democratic Republic of Congo (DRC) since 1996. Both wars are obviously very complex in origin and I make no pretense here to examine all explanations for their outbreaks, which in both cases had much to do with external factors, individual agency, and a variety of other causes. Rather, my goal here is merely to demonstrate that both conflicts can be explained by my political demography theory.

Civil War in Darfur, Sudan

In the precolonial era, Sudan had very low population densities. Thus, with large amounts of available land, farmers such as the Masalit of Darfur in western Sudan "would farm an area of land until productivity declined and then move on to establish a new community" (Bilsborrow and DeLargy 1990, p. 140). This low population density also contributed to the use of slavery in precolonial Sudan, whereby northern Sudanese would raid the south for slaves whom they would bring north to work as agricultural laborers or soldiers. In particular, Darfur lay at the heart of one of the major trans-Saharan slave routes, whereby African slaves were exported to Egypt and beyond. Moreover, as elsewhere, low population densities contributed to Sudan's "enormous ethnic and linguistic diversity" (Collins 2008, p. 8), whose complexity has been the subject for numerous studies.

In the colonial period, the British colonialists instituted an indirect tribal administration in Darfur, where each *dar* (province) was "an ethnic territory in which the dominant group had legal jurisdiction" (De Waal 2005, p. 193). More specifically, this system meant that land was communally administered by local paramount chiefs, who would allocate land rights to their ethnic brethren. Low population densities for most of the twentieth century meant that in Darfur "there was sufficient free land" such that a "very substantial settler population" from northern Sudan could move into the area through the 1970s without any problems (De Waal 2005, p. 193).

At the same time, a variety of economic and political factors encouraged more migration into the area and hardened differences between natives and migrants. First, President Gaafar Nimeiry's government nationalized 99 percent of land in Sudan in 1970, thereby leading to growing inequalities in land ownership as politicians, soldiers, and bureaucrats acquired land at the expense of the politically powerless. Second, Nimeiry attempted to build Sudan into the "breadbasket of the Middle East" by acquiring large tracts of land for mechanized agriculture in the 1970s. While successful in the short term, this policy had the more serious longer-term consequences of promoting even more land infertility, displacing farmers and pastoralists from their land, and adding to the country's growing problems with external debt and inflation. The resultant economic collapse of the late 1970s was only exacerbated by structural adjustment policies imposed by the World Bank and several years of drought, leading to chronic food shortages and the outbreak of famine in Darfur in the early 1980s (Bilsborrow and DeLargy 1990; Collins 2008). Third, Nimeiry's government centralized local government power in its Regional Government Act of 1980, thereby taking away power from the former tribal chiefs who had previously prevented internal migration and giving it to increasingly Islamist cadres allied with Khartoum (Manger 2006). For these multiple reasons nomadic migrants from northern Sudan and Chad flowed into parts of Darfur previously dominated by farmers, leading Darfur's population to increase from 1.1 million in 1956 to 6.5 million in 2003, or an annual growth rate of 4 percent. Moreover, increasing desertification pushed up population densities on arable land even higher, with farmers responding by expanding the size of their plots to compensate for the decreased rainfall and an increased population (Fadul 2006). These patterns thus led to the closure of many nomadic migratory routes and increasing conflict between pastoralists and farmers.

Simultaneously, an increase in Arab supremacism in Sudan and the region led to an increased emphasis on "Africanism" by the Sudanese People's Liberation Movement (SPLM) rebel leader John Garang and other supporters of a "new Sudan" not dominated by Arabs. This increasing polarization thus helped to promote ethnic and racial differences between "Arabs" and "Africans" in Darfur, despite the fact that these differences had little to no historic basis in Darfur. As such many *Fur* "started to talk about Darfur 'being for the *Fur*,' and that the Arabs were foreigners who should leave" (Manger 2006, p. 19).

The various clashes between different migrant and native groups that had started in the 1970s continued through the famine and beyond a brief Arab-Fur conflict in the late 1980s. Increasing efforts at Arabization in the region inevitably led to the formation of the Sudanese Liberation Movement among the *Fur* and other non-Arab Darfuris, whose leaders deliberately copied their name from the SPLM of southern Sudan. In response, in 2003 the Khartoum government armed local and Chaddian immigrant Arab militias, the *janjawiid*, who themselves were largely unemployed youth (Mamdani 2009). Thereafter the conflict quickly spiraled out of control, with internal ethnic divisions within the SLM only further halting cease-fire efforts.

Civil War in the Eastern Democratic Republic of the Congo (DRC)

In the eastern DRC, as elsewhere in Africa, precolonial population densities were low enough that the private alienation of land was largely nonexistent, and migration could take place without any serious land pressures. Moreover, the region was a site for slave traders from both Zanzibar (to the east) and the Kingdom of Kongo (to the west). As a result, the region became ethnically diverse due to various waves of migration and different understandings of ethnicity; indicative in this regard were confused understandings over whether President Mobutu was ethnically Ngbandi, Mongo, Ngala, or even "Sudanic" or "Bantu" (Young 1976, pp. 194-195).

In the colonial period, the Belgian government codified customary land laws but only for land "already under the practical control of traditional authorities," with all other land henceforth declared property of the colonial state, with the goal of using these vast amounts of virgin land for plantations and wildlife parks (Vlassenroot and Huggins 2005, p. 126). Due in part to the mass deaths of Congolese under early Belgian colonial rule and decreasing fertility levels, the Belgians encouraged Rwandan migration to the DRC after acquiring Rwanda from the Germans after World War I. While the Rwandans were welcomed by plantation owners, they were viewed as foreigners by local Congolese, despite the fact that many Kinyarwanda speakers had lived in the DRC before colonialism. Thus Belgian attempts at creating a Banyarwanda (ethnic Rwandan) chiefdom in the North Kivu province failed due to local opposition, leading Rwandan migrants to purchase local land instead.

The eastern provinces were already a site of high population density relative to other parts of the DRC due to high fertility rates and high quality soil that drew migrants. By the 1950s, fertility rates had stopped increasing in the Kivus but started to sharply rise elsewhere; as a result, after 1950 population growth across the DRC took off at over 3 percent per year and was accompanied by increasing urbanization and the clearing of new lands in rural areas (Romaniuk 1980; Shapiro 1995). In particular, the "unrelenting population growth" in eastern DRC led to the usual consequences of a growing group of migrant and landless laborers (Vlassenroot and Huggins 2005, p. 138).

After independence, President Mobutu echoed other African rulers with his 1973 land law, which abolished customary land and declared all land the property of the state. Henceforth, those Congolese who had been able to access education during the colonial period and thereafter gain favor in Kinshasa, which included the Banyarwanda in North and South Kivu provinces and the Hema in Ituri province, were able to take advantage of these land laws to allocate themselves land (Pottier 2006; Vlassenroot and Huggins 2005). Thus, already by the early 1980s there was evidence of "resentment against 'intruders'" in the Kivus, where a local judge claimed "he [would] do everything to ensure that ancestral land does not pass into 'foreign' hands" (MacGaffey 1982, pp. 102-103). Yet simultaneously the Congolese economy started to collapse, with an increased acceleration after 1990 as the end of the cold war led to both a drop in U.S. aid to Mobutu's government and to the abandonment of the International Coffee Agreement that had previously helped to secure good prices for local coffee growers. In 1996, Laurent Kabila thus launched his rebellion that overthrew Mobutu's regime in 1997 and led to "sons of the soil" conflict in both the Kivus and Ituri province, which we examine briefly in turn.

Previously, the Kivus were the site of the colonial plantations and Rwandan immigration discussed above. Due in part to ongoing postcolonial migration from Rwanda and Burundi, population growth in the Kivus was thus even higher than other parts of the DRC at more than 4 percent annually between 1948 and 1970, compared to a Congolese-wide growth rate of 2.6 percent over the same time period (Vlassenroot and Huggins 2005, p. 140). Combined with increasing Banyarwanda purchases of the former colonial plantations after 1973 and the DRC's economic collapse, this growth meant increasing inequalities in land ownership. As a result, local politicians from non-Banyarwanda ethnic groups initiated violence against the Banyarwanda in 1993; a subsequent ceasefire was forged, only to be broken by the influx of more than 1 million Rwandan refugees the next year as a result of the Rwandan genocide. The genocide thus heightened ethnic differences between non-Banyarwanda on the one hand and Banyarwanda and their ethnic Banyamulenge brethren in South Kivu on the other, leading the former to accuse the latter of being "foreign" or *allochtone*. This split manifested itself violently between different rebel factions, with the Banyarwanda and Banyamulenge initially represented by the Rally for Congolese Democracy, while the non-Banyarwanda were supported by the Congolese government and Mai Mai rebels; all groups contributed greatly to the civil war and postwar violence in the eastern DRC.

Ituri province, located north of the Kivus on the Ugandan/Congolese border, is split demographically between Hema pastoralists and Lendu farmers, with the latter claiming to be more indigenous to the region than the former. As noted above, due to political connections with Kinshasa, many local Hema had acquired land after 1973, and continued to do so through the 1990s when Hema landowners started expelling Lendu squatters, leading prominent Lendu to organize into self-defense groups. The resulting violence was only exacerbated by the Hema-dominated rebel movement *Union des Patriotes Congolais* (UPC), whose leaders talked of Hema *originaires* and Lendu *nonoriginaires* or "visitors" on local radio stations in tones worryingly reminiscent of the Rwandan genocide (Pottier 2006). The conflict quickly spiraled out of control, with Ugandan and Rwandan intervention contributing to the conflict before UPC leader Thomas Lubanga was arrested by the International Criminal Court in 2006.

Demography and Politics in Africa

In this chapter I have argued that Africa's historically low population density left it with a legacy of poverty, communal and unequal property rights, and an ethnically diverse population upon independence. High population growth since the mid-twentieth century has interacted with these three legacies and produced large amounts of rural "sons of the soil" conflict over land. The examples of civil wars in contemporary Sudan and the DRC gave empirical evidence for this argument.

As with other recent scholarship, the chapter thus suggests that a neo-Malthusian direct relationship between demography and conflict is implausible. However, it also suggests that the general neglect of demographic factors by many scholars has not been helpful in furthering our understanding of African conflict. As such, four obvious policy suggestions present themselves. First, fertility decline should be an obvious target, inasmuch as high fertility has encouraged rural-rural migration. Second, a focus on rural economic growth would help to alleviate rural poverty and address Africa's ongoing rural-urban gap. Third, the redistribution of land rights towards cultivators and away from landlords and the state could alleviate much rural conflict as well as spur economic growth, although good land reform is obviously much easier said than done. Fourth and finally, it may be possible for politicians to make ethnic diversity less politically salient through various nation-building policies, as perhaps took place in Nyerere's Tanzania (Miguel 2004).

Further research into this area is obviously important to refine the conclusions presented here. Certainly more analysis of the causes and consequences of internal, rural-rural migration is badly needed, especially considering its general neglect in the social sciences relative to urbanization and international migration (Skeldon 2008, pp. 6-7). The relationship between population density, population growth, and economic growth could be more refined. Finally, more historical analysis of the long-term relationships between demographic change and different types of conflict would be helpful in understanding better the phenomena discussed here.

17

The Devil in the Demography?

Religion, Identity, and War in Côte d'Ivoire

Ragnhild Nordås

"**E**very time I went to ask for [my identity card], they shook their heads," Yaya Kone, an officer in the Ivoirian rebel group MPCI explained.[1] His name may have given him away. To the authorities, his status as "true" Ivoirian could be questioned. "If I'm not Ivoirian, where am I supposed to be from?" Kone added. To them, he was a "foreigner," a Dioula, part of the influx of Muslims who had created a rupture in the religious balance that "threatened the social peace" of the country.[2]

According to Huntington (1996) and a variety of other scholars (e.g., Barber 1996; Lewis 1990, 2003; McTernan 2003), the main conflicts in this century will take place along the fault lines between civilizations (i.e., world religions)—

particularly in the encounters between two rapidly growing world religions, Islam and Christianity. Huntington argues that religious groups clash because of changes in the demographic balance between them. Demographically expanding groups put pressure on slower-growing groups, which can lead the latter to turn to violence (Huntington 1996, 259). Despite the regularity with which this argument is made, the religious demography–conflict link has not been rigorously tested.

The current study seeks to shed light on the role of demography on conflict, focusing particularly on cultural demography and civil war. This is achieved by examining the role of religious demography in the prelude to the outbreak of war in Côte d'Ivoire that had been commonly referred to as a conflict between Muslims and Christians. The country is situated on one of the fault lines that cuts across Africa from west to east, where Huntington observes a series of disputes "between the Arab and Muslim peoples of the north and animist-Christian black people of the south" (Huntington 1996, p. 256). In this case, as Huntington argues, demography threatened to shift the balance of political power and provided incentives for the elite to pursue policies that subsequently made the country fertile soil for violent mobilization. However, although demography is an important backdrop, the real "devil" rests not in demographics (or religion) *per se*, but mainly in elites' repressive strategies in response to the changing demographic landscape.

Demography and the Diversity–Conflict Nexus

There are various explanations for civil war. The most prominent are economic: seeing conflict as being driven by either greed or grievances (Collier and Hoeffler 2004). Some theories focus on political factors, typically regime characteristics (Hegre et al. 2001). Others emphasize the role of geography—such as terrain and natural resources (Buhaug and Gates 2002). A further category of theses concern demographic factors such as population size and cultural diversity (e.g., Fearon and Laitin 2003; Huntington 1996).

Scholars of demography find that the demographic factor has played a critical role in many intrastate conflicts. Notable instances of demographically driven conflicts include clashes in Assam, Nagaland, and Tripura in northeast India, as well as the conflicts involving Tamils in Sri Lanka, groups such as the Karen and Kachin in Burma, Mindanao Muslims in the southern Philippines, Acehnese in Indonesia; and the Tuaregs in Mali (Fearon 2004; Weiner 1978).[3] Demographic explanations for wars take a variety of forms. For instance, Goldstone (1991) explains civil wars in the early modern world as a consequence of population growth which generates revolutionary pressure on states. Another example that has received considerable attention is Weiner's (1978) argument that indigenous groups facing demographic pressure from internal migrants become likely candidates for so-called "sons of the soil" conflicts against newcomers or the state. Similarly, Toft (2007b) argues that differential growth rates of culturally defined groups can lead to conflict. For instance, declining majorities may launch preventive wars in response to rising minorities. Huntington (1996) proposes that countries are particularly vulnerable to conflict when there are fertility-driven changes in the demographic balance between religious groups.

The importance of cultural demography turns on two fundamental sets of factors. One concerns the assumed nature of cultural identities, and the other the concrete attributes in time and space. In terms of the nature of cultural identities, a primordial view of conflict sees it as a function of the differences in identities themselves. Such identities are taken as given, salient, and unchanging. The instrumentalist approach, by contrast, interprets identities as shaped or created by political entrepreneurs through discourses and/or behavior. In this interpretation, identities can be created, maintained, and changed to serve the interests of political entrepreneurs. These interests are therefore the real factor driving conflict.

With respect to attributes, three different elements of cultural demography can be important: (1) group size, (2) geographical settlement patterns, and (3) changes in these over time. Each represents a potential security challenge. For example, a group's population size could be a proxy for its power, as it can translate into soldiers, resources, or votes. Size can matter because it affords different opportunities to challenge the state. The geographical distribution of groups can also be an attribute of interest. For instance, a group's demographic dominance within a particular locale can increase its mobilization potential and heighten the legitimacy of its claims to self-determination. In a democratic setting, the geographical distribution of groups can also help determine how votes are translated into power. Changing ethnic geography can therefore prompt a violent instrumentalist response, because threatened groups may opt for potentially countervailing measures.

Changes in group size and/or geographical settlement patterns over time (nationally or locally) are important as well. They have the potential to escalate tensions between groups: (a) directly, through affecting power balances; or (b) indirectly, by initiating behavior that increases such tensions. Specifically, a growing minority could signal a future threat to the majority in terms of increased political, economic, and social pressures and competition for jobs, land, and other resources. Accordingly, the declining majority may engage in countermeasures to reduce the power of the growing minority, and/or the growing challenger might decide to challenge the state due to its strengthened position.

Only a subset of the aspects and approaches to cultural demographic conflict considered above have been rigorously examined in the existing literature. Moreover, these works suffer from numerous problems. First, there is a primordialist bias because the overwhelming majority of studies only study the direct effects of diversity on conflict.[4] This inherently assumes ethnic and/or religious differences are the source of conflict and division (e.g., Huntington 1996). It therefore overlooks other possibilities, such as the political manipulation of identities and shifts in their salience over time. To properly examine the nature of identities, we should allow for the possibility that they are dynamic in their content, with implications that vary from one context to another. Few studies—and certainly no large-N comparative analyses—treat identity as instrumental or dynamic.

Second, religious demography is most often measured through a snapshot of the numerical strength of different groups at the aggregate national level (e.g., Reynal-Querol 2002). There are several problems with this approach. For one, such macro-level studies risk overlooking important causal relationships as the empirical measures are overaggregated and the models not properly specified to capture change over time. In addition, most demography measures in conflict studies neglect patterns of religious and ethnic settlement. They also fail to capture variation over time in group size and geography. In addition, the measures only allow for a primordial logic, since cultural identities are taken as *a priori* given and unchanging.[5]

To properly study the relationship between cultural demography and conflict, we need to allow for variability in both the nature of identity and the attributes that are measured. In other words, an identity may be either primordial or instrumentally created; its boundaries and content may change or persist; and different identity markers may be salient in some contexts but inconsequential in others. Moreover, different demographic attributes of countries matter for conflicts in different times and places. We therefore need to unpack the measures of demography and disaggregate them across time and space as well as account for the actors involved. In sum, this calls for a more micro-level approach than that used in much existing literature.

Indeed, many of the limitations of the current literature revolve around methodology. Most work on the demography–conflict nexus has been of the large-N, quantitative variety. The factors highlighted above are difficult to tease out through large-N cross-sectional analysis. For example, the boundaries and social significance of different identities are extremely difficult to operationalize (especially *a priori*) across time and space. However, such measurement is crucial for understanding what is taking place. Accordingly, I focus on the case of Côte d'Ivoire to properly examine the topic of demography and its influence on conflict.

Diabolic Demography? The Civil War in Côte d'Ivoire

In 2002, the rebel group *Mouvement Patriotique de Côte d'Ivoire* (MPCI) launched attacks against the Laurent Gbagbo regime. The group stated that it was fighting for the rights of northerners who had been discriminated against by the government, and demanded that the president step down. Within two weeks, the rebels controlled the northern half of the country. The front between the government forces and the rebels corresponded geographically with the north-south divide between Muslims and Christians. However, to better understand the conflict, we need to move beyond simple religious differences. Specifically, this section looks at how demographic shifts in concert with political and economic factors produced converging interests between southern elites and the southern masses. This inspired a discourse justifying exclusion—and later repression—based on cultural identity that eventually set the scene for the emergence of a rebel movement.

Demography: Rapidly Shifting Sands

The ethno-religious demography of Côte d'Ivoire changed dramatically in the decades leading up to the civil war. In 1922, an estimated 100,000 out of 1.6 million (or 6 percent) of people in Côte d'Ivoire were Muslims (Gordon 2005). By contrast, at independence (in 1960), their share of the population had increased rapidly, and Muslims were moving southward to the cocoa-producing areas and the southern cities. By 1998, when the last national census was conducted, Muslims constituted a majority in the north of the country, and approximately 38.6 percent of the total population. This was a significantly larger population than the next largest religious group, Christians, who constituted approximately 29.1 percent of the total (Langer 2005; U.S. State Department 2002).

The most recent shift in favor of Muslims was in part a function of a widening fertility gap between different religions that opened up in the mid-to-late 1990s. In 1994, Muslim fertility was slightly higher than other religious groups, controlling for factors that are common predictors of fertility, such as age, urban versus rural settlement, and education. The coefficient for children born per Muslim women then grew from 0.089 in 1994 to 0.210 in 1998/1999, and the fecundity gap between Muslim and other women was significant at a 1 percent level (Table 17.1).

While fertility was important, the most substantial demographic shift was brought about through decades of large-scale immigration. Immigrants were mainly poor Muslim laborers from neighboring countries. Since 1940, thousands had entered from Burkina Faso (then Upper Volta), and many arrived from Mali, Guinea, and Ghana (Boone 2003). The colonial regime encouraged immigration in order to facilitate the establishment of cocoa plantations; but even after independence, through the 1960s and 1970s, immigrants continued to be welcomed. Indeed, President Felix Houphouët-Boigny gave the migrants considerable rights to land and political participation to encourage people to settle and contribute to the country's booming economy. They soon dominated the labor force in the cocoa plantation sector—75 percent of agricultural workers in 1965 were born abroad (Collett 2006). Muslims also became increasingly numerous in the cities, dominating the informal trading sector.

Table 17.1 Côte d'Ivoire Female Fertility (Number of Children Born)

	1994 Coef. (SE)	1998–1999 Coef. (SE)
Age	.237*** (.002)	.219*** (.003)
Urban	−.431*** (.044)	−.452*** (.070)
Education years	−.082*** (.007)	−.104*** (.008)
Muslim	.089* (.046)	.210*** .210***
Constant	−3.076*** (.076)	−2.841*** (.116)
R^2	.6011	.6223
N	8,092	3,036

Note: *sig. at 10% level, **sig. at 5% level, ***sig. at 1% level. Based on Demographic Health Surveys (DHS) data from www.measuredhs.com

The socioeconomic impact of the population change was readily apparent. Immigrants were critical to the cocoa production, which drove the initial economical success of postindependence Côte d'Ivoire. By the 1970s, they made up a quarter of the total population (Chirot 2006, p. 64).

Although immigration leveled off in the late 1980s and early 1990s, the emerging Muslim fertility advantage continued to tilt the demographic balance in favor of Muslims.[6] In addition, the perception of demographic change may even have been more critical than the actual shifts. By the time conflict broke out, Muslims enjoyed a significant demographic advantage over Christians, whether in terms of group size, geographic distribution, or future growth prospects, and southerners shared a common perception that the Muslim population was rising inexorably relative to Christians. In view of these developments, Launay and Miran (2000, p. 16) issued a stern warning that any attempt to marginalize Islam in favor of Catholicism would be "excessively foolhardy." Nevertheless, the mistake was made and in fact repeated by the regimes that succeeded Houphouët-Boigny after his death in 1993. Their policies were to have dire consequences for Côte d'Ivoire's internal security.

Interests and Identities: Emerging Conflict

By the late 1980s and early 1990s, the immigrants' welcome started to wear thin (Collett 2006). Competition over land and political influence began to intensify. This was due to several factors: (1) a dramatic slump in cocoa prices in the 1980s leading to economic stagnation, (2) a reduction in available virgin forest land for establishing new cocoa plantations, (3) pending regime change as the Houphouët-Boigny era drew to a close, and (4) nascent democratization. On top of this, the demographic balance kept shifting, albeit more slowly, in favor of Muslims and northerners in general. This produced a fear among southern elites of losing power to a candidate with a northern support base and also increased the sense of threat felt by southerners in general as they competed over a shrinking pie of land and jobs. This convergence of fears between the southern elite and masses produced policies that led to a repressive climate for a large share of the population. The policies were justified by a discourse that developed the notion of *ivoirité* (ivoirianness) to distinguish "true" Ivoirians from "foreigners." To highlight how demography mattered in different ways for different groups and how the interests converged and evolved over time, I focus on the processes within and between three distinct audiences: elites, masses, and rebels.

The Strategy of Southern Elites

Southern political elites responded to the demographic shift by raising the specter of a Muslim "invasion." They initiated an autochthony discourse concerning who was truly Ivoirian (i.e., framing belonging based on criteria of being "from the soil"). This emerged out of considerations of voting rights and political power in the context of a growing northern/Muslim population. They urged that citizenship be redefined to encompass only those with ancient roots in the territory, and not to "newcomers" (mostly Muslims), although most Muslims were in fact born in Côte d'Ivoire.

The 1990 elections provided a foretaste of the *ivoirité* discourse when Laurent Gbagbo of the FPI (*le Front Populaire Ivoirien*) party accused Houphouët-Boigny of using northern immigrants as his "electoral cattle" and campaigned on a platform against foreigners' voting rights and their "preponderant" role in the national economy (Marshall-Fratani 2006, p. 22). The main message of the FPI in 1990, therefore, was to stress that the incumbent regime had systematically favored particular ethnic groups—Baoulé and groups from the north—and foreigners (Crook 1997, p. 222). Gbagbo's concerns were primarily political: He was trying to increase his chances in the elections by weakening his competitors. In line with this objective, the FPI press started publishing rumors that Alassane Ouattara (prime minister from 1990–1993), was a foreigner who should not be in office.[7]

The notion of *ivoirité* emerged in 1993/1994 and defined the identity discourse thereafter. This discourse was first created and systematically utilized by President Bédié, the appointed successor to Houphouët-Boigny (Chirot 2006; Toungara 2001). It divided those who were "from the soil" (autochthones), and should therefore possess citizenship rights, from those considered "foreigners" (allochtones) and who therefore should be excluded. The references to autochthones essentially invoke a primordial concept of identity. Cultural fears, which primordialist theorists would predict to be paramount, were in fact secondary to instrumental considerations.

The *ivoirité* discourse can be understood as a strategy of the political elite based on a combination of (1) the strong correspondence between ethnoreligious affiliation and party preference, and (2) a political context in which politics was viewed in essentially clientilistic, zero-sum terms (Chirot 2006). First, the ethnoreligious party system that emerged in Côte d'Ivoire rendered the election outcome predictable to the point of serving as little more than a census. In this type of situation, the power balance between political parties only shifts through demographic change, that is, immigration and/or differential fertility. The only alternative is to manipulate the result by excluding some groups from participating through repressive tactics—or deploying a combination of the two approaches.

Second, since independence, Côte d'Ivoire had been a centralized party-state, where all state resources and prerogatives were based on personal relationships with President Houphouët-Boigny. Consequently, the importance of presidential power provided a strong incentive to use all available means to win elections. The winner-take-all electoral formula interacting with the ethnoreligious party system prompted southern incumbent rulers to launch the *ivoirité* identity discourse—to minimize the northern/Muslim electorate. This was accomplished through legal and bureaucratic electoral barriers and, eventually, through outright intimidation and violent repression.

The first legal step toward an ideology of *ivoirité* was taken in 1994. A new electoral code established by then president Bédié restricted the conditions of eligibility for elected office to those born in Côte d'Ivoire from parents of native birth. This may have been crafted to prevent Alassane Dramane Ouattara, leader of the opposition RDR (*Rassemblement des Républicains*), from running. To delegitimize the RDR, Bédié also described it as "a northern regionalist party with a sinister Muslim agenda" (Collett 2006, p. 623). However, according to Crook (1997, p. 226), the southern leadership had a genuine fear of a growing northern consciousness in the early 1990s. This fear was based on the north's increasing electoral power, as well as an anonymous document circulating in 1992, the *Charter of the Grand North*, which reportedly called for fuller recognition of the Muslim religion, reduction in regional economic inequalities, and end to "Baoulé nepotism" and Akan supremacy.[8]

As the new millennium approached, the *ivoirité*-inspired policies became more violent. In December 1999, General Robert Gueï ousted President Bédié. Although Gueï claimed to be opposed to the ideology of *ivoirité*, he, too, found it a useful tool to justify excluding Ouattara—and thereby retaining power—as the 2000 election approached (Collett 2006). The election itself was marred by violence between RDR and FPI supporters. After the poll, Laurent Gbagbo took office. Thereafter, "foreigners"—including anyone with a northern-sounding name as well as all Muslims—increasingly perceived that their religious/ethnic affiliation made them targets of discrimination and harassment. One of the most frequently cited examples was a program to renew national identity cards. These were needed to work, own land, and vote. Anyone with a Dioula name or Muslim religious affiliation experienced difficulties in obtaining an ID card (Marshall-Fratani 2006), and renewal was delayed for anyone with a "questionable" claim to membership of the Ivoirian nation. Many had their ID cards openly destroyed by police on the streets. Having a northern-sounding name could also lead to outright violent persecution and even death by the security forces or angry mobs of regime sympathizers (Dozon 2001). The incident that received the most attention was what became know as the Yopougon massacre, where in Abidjan in October 2000, gendarmes rounded up 59 Dioula and killed all but two of them (Akindes 2004).

The Role of the Masses

For the majority of northerners, episodes like the ones described above produced an enormous sense of grievance that provided fertile soil for rebel recruitment. Other episodes around the 2000 elections also increased the salience of the division between Christian and Muslim, "true" and "fake" Ivoirian. Mosques were attacked and burned by FPI mobs. In response, churches were attacked by RDR supporters. Attacks on northerners were permitted to continue with impunity, and the police and gendarmes often took an active part in these assaults. For instance, in October 2000, the Aicha Niangon-Sud mosque in Abidjan was attacked by FPI youths. According to Human Rights Watch (2001), the police who were called to protect the mosque arrested the 33 Muslims who remained inside and then stood by while the mosque was ransacked and burned.

For the southern masses, the economic slump caused by the drop in cocoa prices in the late 1980s was the main driver of hostility to "foreigners." Increasing production could not compensate for lower prices, as there was no further virgin land to clear; and with a growing population, jobs were harder to come by. Reserving more resources for "true" Ivoirians while excluding others seemed a tempting solution. The *ivoirité* discourse therefore resonated with the interests of the southern masses. As the discourse played out in the media and on the streets, it contributed to more stereotyped views of the "other" as a threat. "Foreigner" began to be equated with Dioula and Muslim in general (Daddieh 2001, p. 17f). Boundary markers of outsider status included possessing a religion and name in common with those on the other side of the northern border. Muslim identity was also associated with migrant labor (Collett 2006). In other words, the borders and perceived contents of identities changed as southerners increasingly perceived Ivoirian Muslims and immigrants from the north as a monolithic group.

Contrary to primordialist perceptions, the reality of the situation was very different. In fact, the "Grand Nord" was far from unified and homogenous:

It consisted of several distinct ethnic groups with differing religious orientations, different languages, and origins. These intranorthern divisions were downplayed as the north-south dichotomy evolved over time, and as identities metamorphosed from "being permeable to being gradually fixed" (Akindes 2004, p. 30).

Although we know less about the interpretation of identity among the grassroots than we do about elite and state rhetoric, a Pew Global Attitudes Project survey conducted just days before the conflict broke out can shed some light on this. This survey largely supports reports about fear and xenophobia. Seventy-six percent of respondents replied that the state should be more restrictive in controlling the entry of people into the country, and 41 percent concurred that immigration was a "very big problem" in Côte d'Ivoire. Sixty-eight percent of Ivoirian Muslims surveyed felt there were "serious threats to Islam." Many Muslims felt so threatened that they were not opposed to using violent means to defend their faith. A staggering 25 percent believed that suicide bombing could often be justified, and nearly three in four Ivoirian Muslims felt it could be justified on at least some occasions (PEW 2002).

The Response of the Rebels

Despite the *ivoirité* discourse and Muslims' perception that they were being threatened by southerners and the state, the rebel group *Mouvement Patriotique de Côte d'Ivoire* (MPCI) was of mixed religious orientation and did not appeal to a shared Islamic consciousness. Rather, they offered secular grievances such as problems renewing identity cards, being treated like second-class citizens, labeled as foreigners in their own country, or being discriminated against when it came to jobs, positions, and power.

The MPCI did not proclaim a religious identity, nor did it seek to alter the religious orientation of the country or promote northern separatism.[9] In short, there were no attempts to mobilize around religion as primordialist theory would predict. Acknowledging that a religious appeal would likely divide the north and the rebel movement, rebel leaders framed their struggle in terms of a broader set of grievances. This helped rally a wider array of individuals to the cause, but the leaders' motivations were not merely tactical. Indeed, there is little, if any, evidence that key rebel leaders were devout Muslims or perceived of themselves as religious combatants.

As an illustration, rebel leaders "jovially invited the people of Abidjan ... to come and party in Bouaké's night-clubs which throbbed a 'revolutionary beat'" according to an article in *The Economist* in October 2003.[10] In negotiations, the rebels focused on the universal concept of holding free and fair elections open to all, and sought secure citizenship rights for all, including northerners. Furthermore, many of the rebels were Christian. For instance, Guillaume Soro, the main rebel leader, is a Catholic whose political orientation is leftist rather than nationalist or religious. Religion gets little mention in his autobiography (Soro 2005). It seems therefore that southern political elites constructed northerners as monolithically Muslim to rally support for their personal political ambition. Religion was not a genuine motivating force among the rebels.

Is the Devil in the Demography?

The first part of this chapter identified two factors to consider when studying how cultural demography can affect ethnoreligious conflict. First is whether cultural identity constitutes a motive in itself (primordial interpretation), or is dynamic and malleable, and thus can be manipulated by self-interested political entrepreneurs who are the real drivers of conflict (instrumental interpretation). Second, it is important to discriminate between different aspects of cultural demography such as group size, settlement patterns, and their respective variation over time. Existing discussions of the Ivoirian conflict often mention cultural demography as a driving force (e.g., Akindes 2004; Marshall-Fratani 2006; Chirot 2006; Banégas and Losch 2002; Woods 2003). But precisely what role did cultural demography play in the onset of conflict? This Ivoirian case study suggests some answers.

First, in the Ivoirian case, primordial cultural identities do not explain the outbreak of war. In fact, identities were largely created as a product the *ivoirité* discourse and state repression. Second, prior to the emergence of *ivoirité*, northern identity was not defined by religion, nor was it "real" in the sense of possessing a unified culture or striking a "deep emotional chord" in the northern population (Banégas 2006). Instead, it coalesced as a community of shared suffering: a common bond forged in the crucible of exclusion. In other words, the north–south divide was created by the instrumental transformation of identities rather than the politicization of a preexisting cleavage (Collett 2006, p. 628). Finally, the rebels' lack of religious framing or even any emphasis on cultural commonality speaks against a primordial interpretation of the conflict.

Demography played a role in heightening tensions from the early years of independence until the outbreak of war. Nevertheless, the demographic component is neither the most important nor the proximate cause of the conflict. Instead, the impact of demography cuts different ways for different actors, and is mediated by the political and economic context. Demography seems to matter only as a resource that southern elites could draw upon in crafting their strategy in the years leading up to the war. Specifically, the interests of southern elites resounded with the interests of the southern masses. For grassroots southerners, Muslim and northern ethnic settlement patterns in the south, center, and southwest ratcheted up the pressure on their economic interests. Excluding and marginalizing northern immigrants thus proved increasingly tempting for southerners.

The discussion above highlights how the impact of demographic change must be considered in light of other factors, notably the structure of political institutions, democratization, political entrepreneurialism, economic trends, and differential access to resources such as jobs and land. These interactions are pivotal in determining whether demographic shifts trigger large-scale conflict. For instance, the central position of the president as a source of patronage in the Ivoirian polity and the close correspondence between party candidates and ethnoreligious voting blocs raises the electoral stakes. In this context, winning the popular vote for president—a material imperative—is a function of cultural demography. Demography therefore becomes a matter of immense practical importance for the population. Add an economic slump and the opening up of the system to electoral competition, and the scene is set for an identity politics of exclusion. In the Ivoirian case, this sparked countermobilization against the regime and led to a spiral of conflict.

Existing work on demography and conflict often portrays changes in cultural demography as a driver of conflict caused by primordial identity groups clashing over fundamental cultural differences. This study suggests that such is not the case in Côte d'Ivoire. When the cry of retaliation rang in the streets of Abidjan at the onset of the civil war, the rebels were not acting out of religious rage or in defense of the Muslim faith. Rather, they were an ethnically and religiously diverse coalition, branded by the ongoing discourse of *ivoirité* as "foreigners," denied citizenship rights, harassed by the state, and the target of violent attacks.

Demography did, however, matter in that it provided a pretext for state repression. Steady Muslim and northern immigration, higher Muslim fertility rates, and—therefore—an expanding northern electorate threatened southern elites. This spurred the discourse of *ivoirité* and attendant repressive state behavior, which in turn motivated northerners to rebel against the regime. The *ivoirité* discourse and ensuing repression integrated a previously heterogeneous northern population. Therefore, the real devil rests not so much in demography as in the deliberate policies of northern exclusion, initiated by southern elites. In short, the devil is in the discourse and the deeds that follow.

Numerous implications flow from this case study. With regard to theory, it shows that we need to account for demographic changes over time and across space to better understand conflicts. Second, it reveals identity to be dynamic—changing in content and relevance over time depending on the political, economic, and demographic context. This highlights the need to study the interaction effects between different attributes of cultural demography and the economic and political context in which they unfold. Finally, the analysis finds that the priority given to religion in Huntington's thesis and other related work may be problematic. Although on the surface the general predictions of Huntington (1996) appear to hold in Côte d'Ivoire, emphasizing religion in itself provides little analytical leverage in this case. Indeed, it may create a blind spot that distracts us from identifying important cleavages (i.e., class), motivations (i.e., political power and economic gains), and processes (i.e., identity construction).

As for methodology, this study demonstrates the usefulness of case studies for exploring the dynamic and interactive elements of cultural identity and civil conflict. It suggests that we need to move beyond simple dichotomies and *a priori* assumptions about the content, salience, and borders of cultural identities, which tend to dominate large-N studies. In Côte d'Ivoire, identities seem flexible and depend on context. In terms of the attributes of cultural demography, shifts in aggregate numbers, their distribution over time and place, and, importantly, how demography is interpreted and politicized matter for conflict. When conducting large-N analyses, therefore, we should account for such complex interactions and dynamics.

In policy terms, this study provides a salutary reminder that autochthony discourses can be manipulated in ways that may produce violent conflict. This becomes especially dangerous in the context of demographic change and a first-past-the-post, ethnoreligious political system.

In terms of future research, scholars should consider how issues of identity and demography alter as conflicts evolve, and through which means the hardening of identity differentials can be reversed.

Côte d'Ivoire shows the challenges associated with such reversal. After the armed conflict officially ended, the country went through a protracted process of registering voters and deciding on the critical issues of citizenship rights. The elections that, after much delay, were held in November 2010 resulted in an electoral victory for Ouattara, likely reflecting the changed demographic landscape of the country. Yet despite unequivocal declarations by the United Nations, the African Union, the United States, and the European Union confirming Ouattara's electoral victory, Gbagbo refused to accept his electoral defeat.

Gbagbo called on his supporters to defend him, and remained in the capital. Violence broke out, and the result was more than a thousand reported deaths in the post electoral period, human rights violations reportedly committed by both sides, civilian populations displaced, harsh sanctions imposed by the international community, and a protracted stalemate in Abidjan. After several months of escalating fighting, Gbagbo was captured by force, and Ouattara assumed the presidency on 21 May 2011.

For the time ahead, the country will be in a situation of precarious peace. The identity cleavage between northerners and southerners has been solidified through war. The country is therefore still divided along identity lines; the demographic underpinning and legacies of the conflict remain. To consolidate the peace, the new regime must break with the previous divisive identity politics, as it faces the challenging task of uniting a divided nation.

Notes

1. Mouvement Patriotique de Côte d'Ivoire. *Global Policy Forum,* July 14, 2005, by Todd Pitman: http://www.globalpolicy.org/component/content/article/173/30409.html. Accessed 13 August 2009.

2. Phrase from President Bédié's advisors in the Counceil Economic et Sociale in 1998: http://horizon.documentation.ird.fr/exl-doc/pleins_textes/pleins_textes_7/polaf/pdf/078070.pdf. Last accessed 13 August 2009. "Dioula" is commonly used to denote an ethnically diverse group geographically situated in the northern region, whose members are, for historical reasons, Muslim (Akindes 2004, 29).

3. Sells highlights how demography was used to legitimate killings and rape in Bosnia. Dramatically different birth rates "became so heated an issue that Serb nationalists charged Muslims with a premeditated plot to use their higher birthrates to overwhelm and ultimately destroy the Christian Serbs" (Sells 1996, p. 22).

4. This might not be intentional, but follows from the logic applied in the empirical tests.

5. There are some exceptions. Toft (2003) studies whether ethnic groups that are geographically concentrated have a higher risk of war than other groups; and Goldstone (2002) and Toft (2007) examine whether countries with a changing ethnoreligious balance are at heightened

risk of conflict. However, these dynamic studies do not capture changes in settlement patterns or the changing meaning and relevance of different identities over time.

6. However, the figures were also often exaggerated: Sometimes the Muslim population was presented as 45 percent of the population.

7. The instrumental nature of this accusation becomes apparent when we consider the pact between FPI (Gbagbo) and RDR (Ouattara) before the 1995 elections. In March of that year, they struck an agreement to form a united movement, the *Front Républicain* (Crook 1997, p. 229). Previously, in the year preceding Houphouët's death, a rapprochement between the government and FPI was seriously discussed, in spite of Gbagbo's official repeated refusal to accept offers by Ouattara to include the FPI in a government of national unity (Crook 1997, p. 224).

8. The Baoulé are members of the Akan family. Houphouët-Boigny and Bedié are both Baoulé.

9. Two other rebel groups later appeared, the MJP (Movement for Justice and Peace) and the MPIGO (Ivorian Popular Movement of the Great West). The three groups subsequently merged under Soro's leadership, calling themselves *Forces Nouvelles* (the New Forces).

10. The Economist, 2 October 2003. "Côte d'Ivoire's war restarts: Kids with Kalashnikovs." http://www.economist.com/

18

Politics and Demography

A Summary of Critical Relationships

Jack A. Goldstone

THE CHAPTERS IN THIS VOLUME HAVE COVERED A WIDE range of relationships, all of them illustrating the pivotal role that demographic change can play in shaping political identities, conflict, and institutional change. In this conclusion, I briefly highlight several fields of study in which greater attention to demography can help scholars better understand critical trends.

International Relations

Demography has traditionally played an important role in the study of international relations. A number of scholars have pointed out how, throughout history, competition among leading nations has been affected by the relative size of national populations, and their rate of growth. Nazli Choucri and Robert North (1975) have pointed to the critical role of rising population in the European powers provoking the tensions and competition for resources that led to World War I. In general, states with youthful and expanding populations have often been more aggressive, and strong population growth in neighboring states has often led to competition for land and resources that put those states on the path to war (Choucri 1984; Clinton 1973). In addition, larger populations—from that of the North versus the South in the U.S. Civil War, to the populations of the United States and the Soviet Union in World War II, and as superpowers in the cold war era—have often been credited with giving countries major advantages in international competition.

Yet this traditional view is almost obsolete in today's world. International conflicts between states pitting conventional armed forces against each other have become rare, while asymmetric warfare—with local guerilla and insurgent forces fighting against national governments and their allies—has become the major pattern of global conflicts. In asymmetrical warfare, it is not the number of people in the states or militaries that matter, but their distribution and loyalties. Is the population urban or predominantly rural? How concentrated are the populations being protected? How youthful is the population of the country or countries in conflict (important for recruitment of fighters)? How is the population divided in regard to regional, ethnic, and religious affiliations and identities? In short, demographic factors still matter greatly for assessing the risks and likely outcome of international relations and conflicts, but it is not a simple matter of the total populations of combatants, as much as of understanding where the populations are distributed.

Moreover, among the great powers populations are now—unlike in the nineteenth and twentieth centuries—aging and experiencing a slowdown in growth. Even China, due to its one-child policy, has already begun to experience a drop in the number of its military service-age population. Thus, as explored by the chapters in Part II of this volume, the problem to ponder for international relations is not one of how major powers with rising populations will arrange their relationships, but how major powers with stagnant and aging or even shrinking populations will cope with international threats. Where populations are rising—in emerging powers and developing countries such as India, Brazil, Indonesia, Mexico, Turkey, Nigeria, Pakistan, Egypt, Vietnam, the Philippines, and Ethiopia, *each one* of which will have a population nearly as larger or larger than that of Russia by 2050—the critical question for international relations will be what impact these newly significant countries will have on global patterns of geopolitics. At the very least, we seem certainly headed for a multipolar world, with many countries seeking local and regional hegemony and a substantial share in institutions of global governance.

As of 2008, the portion of global GDP produced by four of the five permanent members of the U.N. Security Council—the United States, the Russian Federation, the United Kingdom, and France—has shrunken from 48 percent in 1950 to 35 percent (Maddison 2007, p. 379; World Bank 2009). Given the population slowdown in the developing world, plus a surge in the prime working-age population and education levels in developing countries, it is reasonable to expect faster growth in the latter. If the global economy grows at 3.5 percent per year overall, while that of the United States, Russia, the United Kingdom, and France grows at 2 percent, then by 2050 this quartet's share of global GDP will fall even further, to less than 20 percent. Thus, the key institution for managing international peace is already falling out of balance with the real distribution of economic power in the world, and will fall further out of balance in the coming decades. A similar situation holds for the International Monetary Fund, voting shares in the World Bank, and the other major global institutions established after World War II. It is clear that shifts in international economic and population balances will have to be taken into account in designing a new structure for international institutions, if they are to be seen as legitimate and to remain effective.

International Political Economy

These considerations bring us to a more detailed examination of the role of demography in international political economy—where will the centers of economic growth, of trade and finance, of capital generation and fiscal strength, lie in the future?

Again, demographic factors will play a key role in shaping the answers to these questions. Today's developed nations have dominated the global economy for the last 150 years, roughly since the 1860s and the maturing of the Industrial Revolution. As recently as 1973, Europe (excluding the former U.S.S.R.) produced 29 percent of global GDP, far more than China and India combined, who then produced a mere 8.8 percent of global GDP. But in the last 30 years, this has changed dramatically. By 2003, Europe's share of GDP (in terms of purchasing power) had fallen to 21.1 percent, while the combined share of China and India had soared to 20.6 percent (Maddison 2007, p. 381). Much of this was driven by the "demographic dividend" of Asian countries, which had population distributions focused on the prime earning ages, while Europeans increasingly retired earlier while aging (Bloom, Canning, and Sevilla 2003, p. 39 ff.)

Age distribution has a major effect on economic potential through what is known as the dependency ratio. This is the fraction of the population that is nonworking (mainly children and retirees) and thus dependent on transfers from the working population for their support. Where the dependency ratio is low, most of the population is actively earning, and there is great capacity for saving because expenses on support for children and the elderly are low. However, where the dependency ratio is high—large numbers of children or the elderly requiring support plus investment in schools, teaching, nursing care, and medical support—a smaller portion of the population is generating wealth and a larger portion is consuming it; thus saving is more difficult. One should add that not only is it true that countries with a larger majority of their population in their prime earning years will enjoy a demographic dividend for savings and growth, there is also a difference between dependency ratios driven by large numbers of children, or large numbers of elderly. In countries with lots of children, the expenses of raising, housing, and educating them is an investment for the future, because eventually they will start working and generating wealth themselves. By contrast, in countries with lots of older retired workers, the expenses of their sustenance, housing, and medical care is simply sunk cost, as when they die, all of those expenses will simply have been the consumption of resources, without any role in building future earnings.

In the coming decades, many developing countries will begin, or continue, to enjoy a demographic dividend that consists of increasing numbers of people moving to cities, gaining higher education, and entering their prime earning years. At the same time, today's developed countries will be stagnating and aging, with the numbers of people in the prime earnings age shrinking. Even the United States, considered by far the most demographically healthy of the rich countries, will see its labor force growth (increase in the population aged 15–59) slow so that growth in the years 2000–2050 will be less than one-third the rate it was in 1950–2000 (United Nations Population Division 2011). Thus, the centers of economic growth are likely to shift to the developing countries. Indeed, as we noted in Chapter 2, upwards of three-quarters of all global economic growth in the next four decades will likely come from outside the United States, Europe, and Japan, a sharp reversal of the pattern in most of the twentieth century.

In addition, since the bulk of the world's younger people getting advanced education will be in developing countries, the locus of innovation will likely shift to developing countries as well. Similarly, savings rates will no doubt be far higher in countries enjoying their demographic dividend, due to families entering their prime earning years saving for homes, education, and retirement. Meanwhile, the rich countries, with their aging populations, will have fewer people saving for the future, or for their children, and many more that are dis-saving to fund their retirements. As a result, the global centers of capital accumulation will shift to Asia, the Middle East, Latin America, and even Africa; that is where Europeans and Americans will have to go to seek capital.

Finally, barring some unforeseen technological health care miracle, the richer countries will be saddled with much higher health costs per capita, due to their aging populations, than developing countries. With fewer workers, but many more retirees and elderly, the burdens on state finances due to entitlements will rise much faster in the richer nations. Thus, despite their greater wealth, the rich countries' governments will likely face greater pressures and difficulties than the governments of poorer countries. In the latter, government-backed entitlements are few, while the rapid growth of the economy and of prime workers will make increasing state revenues far easier. Thus—as was dramatically revealed in the response to the Great Recession of 2007–2008—the developing countries may become the site of the fiscally strongest governments, while rich country governments remain hobbled by high entitlements and slow-growing revenues.

In sum, to an even greater degree than one would think from looking at just total population trends, the centers of global economic growth will shift away from the West, and to the emerging and developing economies of Latin America, Africa, the Middle East, and Asia.

In addition, because developing countries will have the bulk of the world's new families, the purchases of new cars and homes, and the most rapid growth in consumer markets, it is likely that consumption and design trends will be driven by trends in developing nations. Just as California became the trend-setter for America due to its rapid growth and its pull for young families in the 1960s and 1970s, so developing countries will become trend-setters for global consumption in the 2000s.

Domestic Political Competition in the Rich Countries

Unfortunately, this shift from leadership in the global economy will likely have a polarizing impact on political competition in the rich countries—trends that are already visibly underway. The Great Recession likely will not be a short-term economic setback followed by a vigorous recovery. The post–World War

II recessions all took place in a context of population growth, generating an inherent demand for housing, consumer goods, and supplying an entry-level workforce on which employers could draw. Today, however, recovery from the Great Recession will take place in the context of low population growth, with aging populations that do not naturally generate a demand for more housing and consumer goods. Demand is more for services—education, health care, insurance, financial planning—which require a small number of highly skilled professionals and large number of lower-paid, entry-level service support personnel. The middle-aged and high-paid workers who produced mass goods and worked in construction will struggle to find work. As a result, high employment and slower growth will likely be long-term trends in most of the developed nations.

The result is a search for someone to blame for this sharp reversal in economic fortunes. Some blame the government; others blame immigrants; still others blame foreign competition. As Gratton's chapter points out, this is a familiar pattern in American history. Whatever the target, the result is politics that become more polarized, bitter, and angry. At the same time, as Frey's chapter in this volume has demonstrated, increases in immigrants and their descendants can tip political alignments in swing voting districts, having a disproportional effect on voting outcomes. This, too, produces angry voters, who blame newcomers for changing the political outcomes in their area.

Global and local demographic changes are thus likely to produce more polarized and volatile politics, with major and sudden swings in the direction of party alignments, and greater difficulties sustaining stable majorities. Even in Japan, which has resisted immigration but has already suffered from economic stagnation for over a decade, and has one of the most rapidly aging populations in the world, the political stability of most of the post–World War II era has evaporated, with an unprecedented number of changes in prime ministers in the last five years.

Both because of the economic slowdown, and because of the pressures to recruit immigrants to fill entry-level workforce positions, the rich countries will also be focused on the politics of immigration for years to come. As the chapters by Coleman and Kaufmann and Skirbekk show, significant changes in the ethnic character of European nations are already underway. Not only who becomes an immigrant, but where immigrants settle and how they vote, will vigorously shape politics in the future.

Differential fertility among various domestic groups will also shape politics. In particular, conservative families tend to have more children, suggesting that strong conservative voting blocs will be maintained and grow—in some cases by deliberate choice and strategy, as Monica Duffy Toft's chapter demonstrates. Even in rich industrialized countries, where there are found competing ethnic or religious groups, differential fertility can shape democratic outcomes, or give rise to preemptive efforts to determine those outcomes, as in Israel and Northern Ireland.

Domestic Conflicts in Developing Countries

The primary source of violence in developing countries is domestic conflicts, whether they take the form of ethnic or secessionist wars, as in Rwanda, Burundi, Sudan, Liberia, and Sierra Leone, or guerrilla and militant extremist insurgencies, as are more common in Latin America and much of the Middle East and South and Southeast Asia.

Here too, demography can tell us much about the pattern of politics. In particular, as the chapters in Parts II and IV of the present volume make clear, there are both direct and indirect effects of population on politics. The direct effects are those of which people are aware—issues of which ethnic groups control political power or sectors of the economy, which groups are favored by the political rules of the game, and how to resolve differences in multiethnic and multireligious societies with histories of conflict. The indirect effects are no less powerful, but people are less aware of them. These are the tendencies, as shown by Madsen's, Cincotta and Doces's, and Urdal's chapters, for societies that are younger and more urbanized to be more violent and less able to consolidate stable democratic regimes. Unfortunately, since for at least the next 20 or 30 years, many parts of the developing world will have very youthful populations and will be experiencing extremely rapid urbanization, we should expect a substantial amount of instability in aspiring democracies, and recurrent outbreaks of ethnic and regional conflicts—unless, of course, the world evolves mechanisms of conflict mediation and intervention that are more successful than those of the past 50 years.

Moreover, simply because of rapidly growing populations in countries that have few surpluses and vulnerable populations, we can expect natural disasters—whether floods or earthquakes or droughts—to affect many more people. When such disasters lead to the displacement and migration of huge numbers of people, to find shelter, work, or new homes, whether they are internally displaced, pour into cities, or cross national borders, enormous efforts are required to head off conflicts between settled groups and newcomers, and to provide humanitarian aid to victims. Whether we are talking about earthquake victims in Haiti, flood victims in Pakistan, or drought victims in eastern Africa, the enormous growth of population in developing nations and vulnerable regions in the past and coming decades inevitably increases the demands for aid and support from local governments and the international community.

Environment and Energy Issues

Finally, we should be carefully attuned, as Richard Matthews's chapter shows, to the likely interactions between population patterns and issues in environment and energy policy. The world's climate will of course be affected by choices we make in power generation and patterns of work and residential locations. In particular, as we have noted, in the coming decades almost all of the world's population growth and most of its economic growth will be in today's developing countries. These countries are seeking to rapidly increase their availability of energy per capita, and are going through a historic shift from being predominantly rural to predominantly urbanized societies.

The demands these changes will make on the world's resources and energy production will be prodigious. China and India are likely to increase their energy production over the next 40 years by an amount equal to the total energy output of the United States today. Whether this occurs through radically new models of energy production, energy use, transit, and work and residential consumption, or through replication of existing rich-world models, will determine the load that the Earth's climate will bear. Nonetheless, we cannot escape or ignore the aspirations of the populations of the developing countries, which will likely increase by 2 billion people, and double the number of middle-class consumers in the world by 2050. Yet as this growth will take place in societies that are generally more crowded and poorer than today's rich countries, it will take urgent global measures in innovation and new incentives to find growth trajectories that do not negatively impact the health and environment of these societies, and the global climate.

Is Demography Destiny?

Critics of demographic analysis often claim that "demography is *not* destiny," noting that we have a choice regarding how to live our lives. They are correct, and simple Malthusian verities that rising population will have specific effects, or inevitably lead to shortages or disasters, have repeatedly been shown to be mistaken. But to admit that demography is not destiny is not to deny its power. Gravity is not destiny either—we have learned to build skyscrapers and airplanes that defy it. Yet we have done so not by ignoring the pervasive effects of gravity but by better measuring and understanding gravity, as well as other forces and how they interact.

The same is true of demography. Changes in global population that are shifting numbers, youth, and urbanization to today's developing countries are powerful forces that we cannot ignore. Similarly, pressures for immigration and the need to cope with aging populations in rich countries are powerful forces as well. If we are to take control of our destiny and shape it, we need to understand how these forces operate, in varied societies around the world, and how they interact. The chapters in this volume make a concerted effort in that direction, and we hope that policymakers and political scientists are assisted in approaching their problems by understanding the inescapable and powerful effects of population on a wide variety of issues in politics.

References

Abbasi-Shavazi, M. J., M. Hossein-Chavoshi, et al. 2007. *Family Change and Continuity in the Islamic Republic of Iran: Birth Control Use Before the First Pregnancy.* Durham, NC: Duke University Press.

Abu-Ayyash, Abdul-Ilah. 1976. "Israeli Regional Planning Policy in the Occupied Territories." *Journal of Palestine Studies* 5(3/4): 83-108.

Abu-Ghaida, Dina, and Stephen Klasen. 2004. "The Economic and Human Development Costs of Missing the Millennium Development Goal on Gender Equity." World Bank. http://siteresources.worldbank.org/EDUCATION/Resources/278200-1099079877269/547664-1099079934475/MDG_Gender_Equity.pdf [Accessed 1 June 2011].

Acemoglu, Daron, S. Johnson, and James A. Robinson. 2001. "The Colonial Origins of Comparative Development: An Empirical Investigation." *American Economic Review* 91(5): 1369-1401.

Acemoglu, Daron, and James A. Robinson. 2006. *Economic Origins of Dictatorship and Democracy.* New York: Cambridge University Press.

Adger, W. 1999. "Social Vulnerability to Climate Change and Extremes in Coastal Vietnam." *World Development* 27(2): 249-269.

Adger, W., N. W. Arnel, and E. L. Tompkins. 2005. "Adapting to Climate Change: Perspectives Across Scales." *Global Environmental Change* 15(2): 75-76.

Adsera, A. 2004. "Marital Fertility and Religion: Recent Changes in Spain," IZA Discussion Paper 1399. Chicago: University of Chicago Population Research Center.

Akindes, Francis. 2004. *The Roots of the Military-Political Crises in Côte d'Ivoire.* Research Report no. 128. Uppsala, Sweden: Nordiska Afrikainstitutet.

Alders, M. 2006. "Forecasting the Population with a Foreign Background in the

Netherlands. *Joint Eurostat-UNECE Work Session on Demographic Projections, Vienna, 21-23 September 2005*. Vienna: Statistics Netherlands Division for Social and Spatial Statistics Department for Statistical Analysis Voorburg.

Anbinder, Tyler. 1994. *Nativism and Slavery*. Oxford, UK: Oxford University Press.

Anwar, M. 1979. *Votes and Policies: Ethnic Minorities and the General Election 1979*. London: Commission for Racial Equality.

Arad, Uzi et al. 2001. "The Herzliya Conference on the Balance of National Strength and Security in Israel." *Journal of Palestine Studies* 31(1): 50-61.

Arreguín-Toft, Ivan. 2005. *How the Weak Win Wars*. Cambridge, UK: Cambridge University Press.

Austin, G. 2008. "Resources, Techniques and Strategies South of the Sahara: Revising the Factor Endowments Perspective on African Economic Development, 1500–2000." *Economic History Review* 61(3): 587-624.

Baguma, R., and A. Ssengendo. 2008. "Growing Population Good, Says Museveni." *The New Vision*, 12 July. http://allafrica.com/stories/200807140448.html [Accessed 10 April 2009].

Balaev, Mikhail. 2009. "The Effects of International Trade on Democracy: A Panel Study of the Post-Soviet World-System." *Sociological Perspectives* 52(3): 337-362.

Bancroft, Hubert Howe. 1887. *The Works of Hubert Howe Bancroft*, Volume XXXVII. *Popular Tribunals*, Vol. II. San Francisco: History Company.

Banégas, Richard. 2006. "Côte d'Ivoire: Patriotism, Ethnonationalism and Other African Modes of Self–Writing." *African Affairs* 105(421): 535-552.

Banégas, Richard, and Bruno Losch. 2002. "*La Côte d'Ivoire au Bord de l'Implosion.*" *Politique Africaine* 87: 139–161.

Bannon, Ian, and Paul Collier, eds. 2003. *Natural Resources and Violent Conflict Options and Actions*. Washington, DC: World Bank.

Barber, Benjamin, 1996. *Jihad Versus McWorld: How Globalism and Tribalism Are Reshaping the World*. New York: Ballantine.

Barnett, Jon, and W. Neil Adger. 2007. "Climate Change, Human Security and Violent Conflict." *Political Geography* 26: 639-655.

Bassock, Motti. 2009. "Israel at 61: Population stands at 7.4 million, 75.5% Jewish," *Ha'aretz*, 27 April. http://www.haaretz.com/hasen/spages/1081532.html.

Bates, R. H. 2008. *When Things Fell Apart: State Failure in Late-Century Africa*. Cambridge, UK: Cambridge University Press.

Baverez, Nicholas. 2003. *La France qui tombe*. Paris: Perrin.

BBC News. 2007. "Israeli Anti-Arab Racism Rises." December 12.

Bely, Mikhail. 2007. "Patriot Babies: Russian Province Holds 'Conception Day.'" *Agence France Presse*, 12 September.

Ben-David, Calev. 2008. "Analyze This: The 'End' of Ethiopian Aliya." *The Jerusalem Post*, 6 August.

Ben-Meir, Alon. 1993. "Israelis and Palestinians: Harsh Demographic Reality and Peace." *Middle East Policy* 2(2): 74-86.

Benoit, Bertrand. 2007. "Baby Boom Times for Germany." *Financial Times* (online at http://www.ft.com).

Berghammer, C., D. Philipov, et al. 2006. "Religiosity and Demographic Events: A Comparative Study of European Countries." Paper delivered at European Population Conference (EPC), Liverpool, UK.

Berman, E., and A. Stepanyan. 2003. "Fertility and Education in Radical Islamic Sects: Evidence from Asia and Africa." Cambridge, MA: National Bureau of Economic Research, www.nber.org/papers.

Berrington, A. 1996. "Marriage Patterns and Inter-Ethnic Unions." Pp. 178-212 in *Ethnicity in the 1991 Census. Volume 1: Demographic Characteristics of the Ethnic Minority Populations.* D. A. Coleman and J. Salt, eds. London: HMSO.

Bilsborrow, R. E., and P. F. DeLargy. 1990. "Land Use, Migration and Natural Resource Deterioration: The Experience of Guatemala and the Sudan." *Population and Development Review* 16 (Supplement): 125-147.

Binswanger, H. P., and K. Deininger. 1997. "Explaining Agricultural and Agrarian Policies in Developing Countries." *Journal of Economic Literature* 35(4): 1958-2005.

Biraben, J. N. 1979. "Essai sur l'Evolution du Nombre des Hommes." *Population* 34(1): 13-25.

Block, Ben. 2009. "UN Raises 'Low' Population Projection for 2050." *Worldchanging* 17 March. http://www.worldchanging.com/archives/009063.html [Accessed 4 June 2011].

Bloemraad, Irene. 2006. "Becoming a Citizen in the United States and Canada: Structured Mobilization and Immigrant Political Incorporation." *Social Forces* 85(2): 667-695.

Bloom, David E., David Canning, and P. Malaney. 2000. "Demographic Change and Economic Growth in Asia." *Population and Development Review* 26 (Supplement): 257-290.

Bloom, David E., David Canning, and Jaypee Sevilla. 2003. *The Demographic Dividend.* Santa Monica, CA: RAND.

Boal, Frederic Wilgar, 1995. *Shaping a City: Belfast in the Late Twentieth Century.* Belfast: Institute of Irish Studies, Queen's University.

Boling, Patricia. 2008. "Demography, Culture and Policy: Understanding Japan's Low Fertility." *Population and Development Review* 34(2): 307-326.

Bongaarts, John. 1997. "The Role of Family Planning Programmes in Contemporary Fertility Transitions." Pp. 422-444 in *The Continuing Demographic Transition.* G.W. Jones et al., eds. Oxford, UK: Clarendon Press.

———. 2008. "Fertility Transitions in Developing Countries: Progress or Stagnation?" Working Paper No. 7. New York: Population Council.

Bookman, Milica Zarkovic. 1997. *The Demographic Struggle for Power: The Political Economy of Demographic Engineering in the Modern World.* London: Frank Cass.

Boone, Catherine. 2003. *Political Topographies of the African State: Territorial Authority and Institutional Choice.* Cambridge, UK: Cambridge University Press.

———. 2007. "Africa's New Territorial Politics: Regionalism and the Open Economy in Côte d'Ivoire." *African Studies Review* 50(1): 59-81.

Bosworth, Barry, and Gary Burtless. 1998. *Aging Societies: The Global Dimension.* Washington, DC: Brookings Institution.

Bradsher, Keith. 2007. "Wages Are on the Rise in China as Young Workers Grow Scarce." *New York Times,* 29 August, p. A1.

Braungart, Richard G. 1984. "Historical and Generational Patterns of Youth Movements: A Global Perspective." *Comparative Social Research* 7: 3-62.

Brennan-Galvin, Ellen. 2002. "Crime and Violence in an Urbanizing World." *Journal of International Affairs* 56: 123-146.

Brett, Rachel, and Irma Specht. 2004. *Young Soldiers: Why They Choose to Fight.* Boulder, CO: Lynne Rienner.

Bronner, Ethan, and Isabel Kershner. 2009. "In 2 West Bank Settlements, Signs of Hope for a Deal." *New York Times,* 26 July. http://www.nytimes.com/2009/07/27/world/middleeast/27settlers.html?ref=global-home.

Brooke, James. 2004. "Japan's New Military Focus: China and North Korea Threats." *New York Times,* 11 December. http://www.nytimes.com/2004/03/05/international/asia/05JAPA.html.

Brooks, David. 2004. "The New Red-Diaper Babies." *New York Times,* 7 December. http://www.nytimes.com/2004/12/07/opinion/07brooks.html?ex=1260162000&en=ebdde83f03fe6d2e&ei=5090.

Brown, Oli, Anne Hammill, and Alec Crawford. 2007. "Climate Change as the 'New' Security Threat: Implications for Africa." *International Affairs* 83: 1141-1154.

Bruce, S. 1998. *Conservative Protestant Politics.* Oxford, UK: Oxford University Press.

———. 2002. *God is Dead.* Oxford, UK: Blackwell.

Buhaug, Halvard, and Scott G. Gates. 2002. "The Geography of Civil War." *Journal of Peace Research* 39(4): 417-433.

Buhaug, Halvard, Nils Petter Gleditsch, and Ole Magnus Theisen. 2008. *The Implications of Climate Change for Armed Conflict.* Washington, DC: World Bank.

Bull, Hedley. 1987. "Population and the Present World Structure." Pp. 74-94 in *Population in an Interacting World.* William Alonso, ed. Cambridge, MA: Harvard University Press.

Burtraw, Dallas, and Thomas Sterner. 2009. "Climate Change Abatement: Not 'Stern' Enough?" 4 April. Resources for the Future: Weekly Policy Commentary. http://www.rff.org/Publications/WPC/Pages/09_04_06_Climate_Change_Abatement.aspx.

Caldwell, C. 2005. "The East in the West." *New York Times Magazine.* 25 September. http://www.nytimes.com/2005/09/25/magazine/25turkey.html [Accessed 17 September 2010].

Calev, Ben-David. 2008. "Analyze This: The 'End' of Ethiopian Aliya." *Jerusalem Post,* 6 August.

Campbell, Kurt M. 2008. *Climatic Cataclysm: The Foreign Policy and National Security Implications of Climate Change.* Washington, DC: Brookings Institute.

Capretta, James C. 2007. *Global Aging and the Sustainability of Public Pension Systems: An Assessment of Reform Efforts in Twelve Developed Countries.* Washington, DC: Center for Strategic and International Studies.

Carlson, Allan, and Paul Mero. 2007. *The Natural Family: A Manifesto.* Dallas, TX: Spence Publishing.

Carothers, Thomas. 2002. "The End of the Transition Paradigm." *Journal of Democracy* 13(1): 5-21.

Cederman, Lars-Erik, Andreas Wimmer, and Brian Min. 2010. "Why Do Ethnic Groups Rebel? New Data and Analysis." *World Politics* 62(1): 87-119.

Census of Ireland, 1861–1911. Database of Irish Historical Statistics, deposited by M.W. Dowling, L.A. Clarkson, L. Kennedy, and E.M. Crawford. Essex: Economic and Social Research Council, 2001. 1901 and 1911 census available online at http://www.census.nationalarchives.ie/.

Census of Northern Ireland, 1926–2001. Northern Ireland Statistics and Research Agency (NISRA). 2001 census data is available at http://www.nisranew.nisra.gov.uk/census/start.html.

Central Bureau of Statistics. 1987. *Special Report.* See *Yedi'ot Aharonot* (Tel Aviv), 6 July.

Central Intelligence Agency. 2001. *Long-Term Global Demographic Trends: Reshaping the Geopolitical Landscape.* Washington, DC: U.S. Central Intelligence Agency.

Chaibong, Hahm. 2008. "South Korea's Miraculous Democracy." *Journal of Democracy* 19(3): 128-142.

Chamie, Joseph. 1977. "Religious Differentials in Fertility: Lebanon, 1971." *Population Studies* 31(2): 365-382.

Chang, Gordon G. 2002. "The Pension Money Is Running Out: Social Security in China." *International Herald Tribune,* 18 July.

Children of Men. 2006. Directed by Alfonso Cuarón. London: Universal Pictures.

Chirot, Daniel. 2006. "The Debacle in Côte d'Ivoire." *Journal of Democracy* 17(2): 63-77.

Choi, S. J. 2009. "Ageing Society Issues in Korea." *Asian Social Work and Policy Review* 3: 63-83.

Choucri, Nazli. 1974. *Population Dynamics and International Violence: Propositions, Insights and Evidence.* Lexington, MA: Lexington Books.

Choucri, Nazli, ed. 1984. *Multidisciplinary Perspectives on Population and Conflict.* Syracuse, NY: Syracuse University Press.

Choucri, Nazli, and Robert C. North. 1975. *Nations in Conflict: National Growth and Industrial Violence.* San Francisco: Freeman.

Christensen, Harold T. 1945–1946. "Factors in the Size and Sex Composition of Families: A Survey of Student Opinion." *Proceedings of the Utah Academy of Sciences, Arts, and Letters* 23: 107-113.

Cincotta, Richard P. 2008. "How Democracies Grow Up." *Foreign Policy* 165: 80-82.

———. 2009. "Half a Chance: Youth Bulges and Transitions to Liberal Democracy." *Environmental Change and Security Program Report* 13: 10-18.

Cincotta, Richard P., Robert Engelman, and Daniele Anastasion. 2003. *The Security Demographic: Population and Civil Conflict after the Cold War.* Washington, DC: Population Action International.

Cincotta, Richard P., and Eric Kaufmann. 2009. "The Changing Face of Israel." *Foreign*

Policy Magazine Web exclusive posted 1 June http://www.foreignpolicy.com/story/cms.php?story_id=4956.

Clapham, C. 2006. "The Political Economy of African Population Change." *Population and Development Review* 32(Supplement): 96-114.

Cleland, J., and L. Lush. 1997. "Population and Policies in Bangladesh, Pakistan." *Forum for Applied Research and Public Policy* 12: 46-50.

Clinton, Richard L., ed. 1973. Population and Politics. Lexington, MA: Lexington Books.

CAN, 2007. *National Security and the Threat of Climate Change.* http://securityandclimate.cna.org/.

Cohen, Lawrence E., and Kenneth C. Land. 1987. "Age Structure and Crime: Symmetry Versus Asymmetry and the Projection of Crime Rates Through the 1990s." *American Sociological Review* 52 (April): 170-183.

Cole, Joshua. 2000. *The Power of Large Numbers: Population, Politics, and Gender in Nineteenth-Century France.* Ithaca, NY: Cornell University Press.

Coleman, David A. 1980. "Some Genetical Inferences from the Marriage System of Reading, Berkshire, and Its Surrounding Area." *Annals of Human Biology* 7(1): 55-76.

———. 2004. "Partner Choice and the Growth of Ethnic Minority Populations." *Bevolking en Gezin* 33(2) (special issue for the 75th Jubilee conference of the Dutch Demographic Society, "*Het huwelijk in de multiculturele samenleving*" [Marriage in multicultural society]): 7-33.

———. 2005. "Europe's Demographic Future: Determinants, Dimensions, and Challenges." Pp. 52-95 in *The Political Economy of Global Population Change: 1950–2050.* Paul Demeny and Geoffrey McNicoll, eds. New York: Population Council.

———. 2006. "Immigration and Ethnic Change in Low-Fertility Countries: A Third Demographic Transition." *Population and Development Review* 32(3): 401-446.

———. 2007. "Ethnic Change in the Populations of the Developed World." British Society for Population Studies Annual Conference. St Andrews, 12 September.

———. 2010. "Projections of the Ethnic Minority Populations of the United Kingdom 2006–2056." *Population and Development Review* 36(3): 441-486.

Coleman, David A., and Sergei Scherbov. 2005. "Immigration and Ethnic Change in Low-Fertility Countries–Towards a New Demographic Transition?" Population Association of America Annual Meeting, Philadelphia, PA, 1 April.

Collett, Moya. 2006. "Ivoirian Identity Constructions: Ethnicity and Nationalism in the Prelude to Civil War." *Nations and Nationalism* 12(4): 613-629.

Collier, Paul. 2000. "Doing Well Out of War: An Economic Perspective." Pp. 91-111 in *Greed & Grievance: Economic Agendas in Civil Wars.* Mats Berdal and David M. Malone, eds. Boulder, CO, and London: Lynne Rienner.

———. 2006. "Economic Causes of Civil Conflict and Their Implications for Policy." In *Leashing the Dogs of War: Conflict Management in a Divided World.* C. A. Crocker, F. O. Hampson, and P. Aall, eds. Washington, DC: U.S. Institute of Peace Press.

———. 2007. *The Bottom Billion.* Oxford, UK: Oxford University Press.

Collier, Paul, and Anke Hoeffler. 2004. "Greed and Grievance in Civil War." *Oxford Economic Papers* 56(4): 563-595.

Collins, R. O. 2008. *A History of Modern Sudan.* Cambridge, UK: Cambridge University Press.

Collins, R. O., and J. M. Burns. 2007. *A History of Sub-Saharan Africa.* Cambridge, UK: Cambridge University Press.

Compton, Paul A., 1976. "Religious Affiliation and Demographic Variability in Northern Ireland." *Institute of British Geographers Transactions* (New Series) 1(4): 433-452.

———. 1982. "The Demographic Dimensions of Integration and Division in Northern Ireland." Pp. 75-104 in *Integration and Division: Geographical Perspectives on the Northern Ireland Problem.* Frederic W. Boal and J. Neville M. Douglas, eds. London and New York: Academic Press.

———. 1991. "The Conflict in Northern Ireland: Demographic and Economic Considerations." Pp. 16-47 in *Economic Dimensions of Ethnic Conflict: International Perspectives.* S. W. R. de S. Samarasinghe and Reed Coughlan, eds. Sri Lanka: International Centre for Ethnic Studies.

Conca, Ken. 2002. "Consumption and Environmentalism in a Global Political Economy." In *Confronting Consumption.* T. Princen, M. Maniates, and K. Conca, eds. Cambridge, MA: MIT Press.

Coolidge, Mary R. 1909. *Chinese Immigration.* New York: Henry Holt.

Copeland, Dale C. 2000. *The Origins of Major War.* Ithaca, NY, and London: Cornell University Press.

COS. 2006. *Key Figures Rotterdam 2006.* Rotterdam, Gemeente Rotterdam, Centrum voor Onderzoek en Statistiek (COS)/ Municipality of Rotterdam, Centre for Research and Statistics. http://www.cos.rotterdam.nl/Rotterdam/Openbaar/Diensten/COS/Publicaties/PDF/KC2006UK.pdf.

Courbage, Youssef, and Philippe Fargues. 1997. *Christians and Jews under Islam.* London: I. B. Tauris.

Crook, Richard C. 1997. "Winning Coalitions and Ethno-Regionalist Politics: The Failure of the Opposition in the 1990 and 1995 Elections in Côte d'Ivoire." *African Affairs* 96: 215-242.

Curtiss, Richard H. 1997. "Year-End Population Statistics Gloss Over Israel's Biggest Problem." *Washington Report on Middle East Affairs* 7(March 15): 38-43.

Daddieh, Cyril K. 2001. "Elections and Ethnic Violence in Côte d'Ivoire: The Unfinished Business of Succession and Democratic Transition." *African Issues* 29(1/2): 14-19.

Dancygier, Rafaela, and E. Saunders. 2006. "A New Electorate? Comparing Preferences and Partisanship Between Immigrants and Natives." *American Journal of Political Science* (October): 964-981.

Daugherty, Helen G., and Kenneth C. W. Kammeyer. 1995. *An Introduction to Population.* 2d ed. New York: Guilford Press.

Dauvergne, Peter. 2008. *Shadows of Consumption.* Cambridge, MA: MIT Press.

Davidman, L., and A. L. Greil. 2007. "Characters in Search of a Script: The Exit Narratives of Formerly Ultra-Orthodox Jews." *Journal for the Scientific Study of Religion* 46(2): 201-216.

Davidson, Lawrence. 1978. "Israeli Reactions to Peace in the Middle East." *Journal of Palestine Studies* 7(4): 34-47.

de Bliokh, Ivan Stanislavovich. 1977. "Population Pressure as a Cause of War." *Population and Development Review* 3(1/2): 129-139. Reprinted excerpts from Volume 5 of *The Future of War from the Point of View of Technology, Economy, and Politics,* St. Petersburg, 1898, translated by Michael Bolysov.

de Tocqueville, Alexis. 1863. *Democracy in America,* 3d ed. Francis Bowen, ed. Cambridge, MA: Sever and Francis.

De Waal, A. 2005. "Who Are the Darfurians? Arab and African Identities, Violence and External Engagement." *African Affairs* 104(415): 181-205.

Defense Data of EDA Participating Member States in 2007. 2007. Brussels: European Defense Agency.

Degler, Carl N. 1964. "American Political Parties and the Rise of the City: An Interpretation." *Journal of American History* 51(1): 41-59.

Dellapergola, Sergio. 1998. "The Global Context of Migration to Israel." Pp. 51-92 in *Immigration to Israel: Sociological Perspectives, Studies of Israeli Society,* Vol 8. Elazar Leshem and Judith T.Shuval, eds. New Brunswick, NJ: Transaction Publishers.

Demeny, Paul. 1999. "Policy Interventions in Response to Below Replacement Fertility." *Population Bulletin of the United Nations* (Special Issue) (40/41): 183-193.

———. 2003. "Population Policy Dilemmas in Europe at the Dawn of the Twenty-First Century." *Population and Development Review* 29(1): 1-28.

Demographic Winter: The Decline of the Human Family. 2008. Directed by Rick Stout. SRB Documentary, LLB.

Desai, R. M., A. Olofsgård, and T. M. Yousef. 2009. "The Logic of Authoritarian Bargains." *Economics and Politics* 21(1): 93-125.

Deudney, Daniel, and Richard Matthew, eds. 1999. *Contested Grounds: Security and Conflict in the New Environmental Politics.* New York: SUNY Press.

Diamond, Jared. 1997. *Guns, Germs, and Steel: The Fates of Human Societies.* New York: W. W. Norton.

———. 2005. *Collapse: How Societies Choose to Fail or Succeed.* New York: Viking Press.

Diamond, Larry J. 1996. "Is the Third Wave Over?" *Journal of Democracy* 7(3): 20-37.

DiCicco, Jonathan M., and Jack S. Levy. 1999. "Power Shifts and Problem Shifts: The Evolution of the Power Transition Research Program." *Journal of Conflict Resolution* 43(6): 675-794.

DMAG 2008. *DMAG Update 19-2008.* GLA Ethnic Group Population Projections Extension to 2031. R2007 PLP Low. London: Data Management and Analysis Group (DMAG), Greater London Authority. http://www.london.gov.uk/gla/publications/factsandfigures/dmag-update-19-2008.pdf.

Dobson, Janet, Alan Latham, and John Salt. 2009. "On the Move—Labor Migration in

Times of Recession." London: Policy Network. http://www.policy-network.org/publications/publications.aspx?id=3194.

Doherty, Paul. 1996. "The Numbers Game: The Demographic Context of Politics." Pp. 199-209 in *Northern Ireland Politics*. A. Aughey and D. Morrow, eds. London: Longman.

Doyle, I. M., and G. Kao. 2004. "'Multiracial' today but 'What' tomorrow? The Malleability of Racial Identification Over Time." Population Association of America Annual Meeting. Boston, April 1–3.

Dozon, Jean-Pierre. 2001. "Post-Prophetism and Post-Houphouëtism in Ivory Coast." *Social Compass* 48(3): 369-385.

Dumont, J. C. and G. Lemaître 2005. *Counting Immigrants and Expatriates in OECD Countries: A New Perspective*. OECD Social, Employment, and Migration Working Papers No. 25. Paris: OECD.

Dunn, Kevin C. 2009. "'Sons of the Soil' and Contemporary State Making: Autochthony, Uncertainty and Political Violence in Africa." *Third World Quarterly* 30(1): 113-127.

Durkheim, E . 1995. *The Elementary Forms of Religious Life*. New York and London: Free Press.

Dyson, Tim. 2005. "On Development, Demography and Climate Change: The End of the World as We Know It?" Conference Paper.

Easterlin, Richard A. 1968. *Population, Labor Force, and Long Swings in Economic Growth: The American Experience*. New York: National Bureau of Economic Research & Columbia University.

———. 1987. "Easterlin Hypothesis." Pp. 1-4 in *The New Palgrave: A Dictionary of Economics*, Vol 2. John Eatwell, Murray Millgate, and Peter Newman, eds, New York: Stockton.

Easterly, W. R., and Levine, R. 1997. "Africa's Growth Tragedy: Policies and Ethnic Divisions." *Quarterly Journal of Economics* 112(4): 1203-1250.

Eberstadt, Nicholas. 2006. "Growing Old the Hard Way: China, Russia, India." *Policy Review* 136. http://www.hoover.org/publications/policyreview/2912391.html [Accessed 28 July 2009].

Ecological Society for Eastern Africa. 2009. "Speech by H. E. Yoweri Kaguta Museveni, President of the Republic of Uganda at the Ecological Society for Eastern Africa (ESEA) Conference, 18 June, Kamapa, Uganda. http://www.ecsea.org/index.php?option=com_content&task=view&id=85&Itemid=3 [Accessed 10 August 2009].

Ediev, D., D. A. Coleman, et al. 2007. "Migration as a Factor in Population Reproduction." *Research Papers of the Vienna Institute of Demography* 1: 57.

Efron, N. J. 2003. *Real Jews: Secular Versus Ultra-Orthodox and the Struggle for Jewish Identity in Israel*. New York: Basic Books.

Ehrlich, Paul R., and David Brower. 1968. *The Population Bomb*. New York: Ballantine Books.

England, Robert Stowe. 2002. *The Macroeconomic Impact of Global Aging: A New Era of Economic Frailty?* Washington, DC: Center for Strategic and International Studies.

———. 2005. *Aging China: The Demographic Challenge to China's Economic Prospects*. Westport, CT: Praeger.

Esty, Daniel C., Jack A. Goldstone, Ted Robert Gurr, Barbara Harff, Marc Levy, Geoffrey D. Dabelko, Pamela T. Surko, and Alan N. Unger. 1998. *State Failure Task Force Report: Phase II Findings*. McLean, VA: Science Applications International Corporation.

European Defense Agency. 2006. *An Initial Long-Term Vision for European Defence Capability and Capacity Needs*. Brussels: European Defense Agency. http://ue.eu.int/ueDocs/cms_Data/docs/pressdata/EN/reports/91135.pdf [Accessed 28 July 2009].

Europe's Demographic Future: Growing Imbalances. 2008. Berlin: Berlin-Institute for Population and Development.

Eurostat. 2008. "Recent Migration Trends." *Statistics in Focus: Population and Social Conditions* 98 (November 18): 11.

Fadul, A. A. 2006. "Natural Resources Management for Sustainable Peace in Darfur." Pp. 33-46 in *Environmental Degradation as a Cause of Conflict in Darfur: Conference Proceedings*. B. O. Saeed, ed.), Addis Ababa, Ethiopia: University for Peace.

Faragher, John Mack, et al. 2003. *Out of Many: History of the American People*, 4th ed. Pearson, NJ.

Fargues, Philippe, 2000. "Protracted National Conflict and Fertility Change Among Palestinians and Israelis." *Population and Development Review* 26(3): 441-482.

———. 2001. "Demographic Islamization: Non-Muslims in Muslim Countries." *SAIS Review* 21(2): 103-116.

Faour, Muhammad. 1989. "Fertility Policy and Family Planning in the Arab Countries." *Studies in Family Planning* 20(5): 254-263.

Fearon, James D. 2004. "Why Do Some Civil Wars Last So Much Longer Than Others?" *Journal of Peace Research* 41(3): 275-301.

———. 2006. "Self-Enforcing Democracy." Working Paper No. 14, Institute of Governmental Studies, University of California, Berkeley.

Fearon, James D., and David D. Laitin. 2003. "Ethnicity, Insurgency, and Civil War." *American Political Science Review* 97(1): 75-90.

———. 2010. "Sons of the Soil, Migrants and Civil War." *World Development* 39(2): 199-211.

Ferrie, Joseph P. 1999. *Yankeys Now: Immigrants in the Antebellum U. S. 1840–1860*. New York: Oxford University Press.

Feuer, Lewis S. 1969. *The Conflict of Generations: The Character and Significance of Student Movements*. London: Heinemann.

Finan, Eileen. 2006. "How Full Is Your Quiver?" *Newsweek*, 13 November. http://www.newsweek.com/id/44652/page/1 [Accessed January 10, 2011].

Finney, Nissa, and Ludi Simpson. 2009. *"Sleepwalking to Segregation": Challenging Myths About Race and Migration*. Bristol, UK: Policy Press.

Foa, Sylvana. 2002. "Battle of the Wombs: The Future's Numbers Game." *The Village Voice*, 2 December. http://www.villagevoice.com/news/0249,foa,40286,1.html.

Fogelman, Aaron S. 1992. "Migrations to the Thirteen British North American Colonies, 1700–1775: New Estimates." *Journal of Interdisciplinary History* 22(4): 691-709.

———. 1998. "From Slaves, Convicts, and Servants to Free Passengers: The Transformation of Immigration in the Era of the American Revolution." *Journal of American History* 85(1): 43-76.

Food and Agriculture Organization (FAO). 2008. *The State of Food Insecurity in the World 2008.* Rome: FAO.

———. 2009. *FAOSTAT.* http://faostat.fao.org/ [Accessed 22 April 2009].

Freedman, Samuel G. 2000. *Jew v. Jew.* New York: Simon & Schuster.

Freedom House. 2008. *Freedom in the World.* New York: Freedom House.

Freeman, Gary P. 1994. "Can Liberal States Control Unwanted Migration?" *Annals of the American Association for Political and Social Sciences* 534: 17-30.

———. 1995. "Modes of Immigration Politics in Liberal Democratic States." *International Migration Review* 29(4): 881-902.

Frejka, T., and C. F. Westoff. 2008. "Religion, Religiousness and Fertility in the U.S. and in Europe." *European Journal of Population-Revue Europeenne De Demographie* 24(1): 5-31.

French, Howard W. 2006. "Rush for Wealth in China's Cities Shatters the Ancient Assurance of Care in Old Age." *New York Times,* 3 November.

Frey, W. H. 1996. "Immigration, Domestic Migration, and Demographic Balkanization in America: New Evidence for the 1990s." *Population and Development Review* 22(4): 741-63.

Friedland, Robert B., and Laura Summer. 2005. *Demography Is Not Destiny, Revisited.* Washington, DC: Center on an Aging Society at Georgetown University.

Friedlander, Dov, and Calvin Goldscheider. 1979. *The Population of Israel.* New York: Columbia University Press.

Friedman, Thomas. 1987. "A Forecast for Israel." *The New York Times,* 19 October.

Fry, R. 2008. *Latino Settlement in the New Century.* Washington, DC: Pew Hispanic Center.

Gallup. 2009. www.gallup.com [Accessed 10 July 2009].

Gallup Brain. 2009. Brain.gallup.com [Accessed 10 July 2009].

Gamm, Gerald H. 1989. *The Making of the New Deal Democrats: Voting Behavior and Realignment in Boston, 1920-1940.* Chicago: University of Chicago Press.

Gellner, E. 1981. *Muslim Society.* Cambridge, UK: Cambridge University Press.

Gemery, Henry A. 2000. "The White Population of the Colonial United States, 1607-1790." Pp. 143-190 in *A Population History of North America.* Michael Robert Haines and Richard Hall, eds. New York: Cambridge University Press.

German Advisory Council on Global Change. 2008. *World in Transition: Climate Change as a Security Risk.* London: Earthscan.

Gerstle, Gary. 2001. *American Crucible.* Princeton, NJ: Princeton University Press.

Geschiere, Peter, and Stephen Jackson. 2006. "Autochthony and the Crisis of Citizenship: Democratization, Decentralization and the Politics of Belonging." *African Studies Review* 49(2): 1-8.

Giddens, Anthony. 2009. *The Politics of Climate Change.* Cambridge, UK: Polity Press.

Gilbar, Gad G., 1997. *Population Dilemmas in the Middle East.* London: Frank Cass.

Girvin, B. 2000. "The Political Culture of Secularisation: European Trends and Comparative Perspectives." Pp. 7-27 in *Religion and Mass Electoral Behaviour in Europe.* D. Broughton and H. M. t. Napel, eds. London: Routledge.

Gleditsch, Nils Petter, Peter Wallensteen, Mikael Eriksson, Margareta Sollenberg, and Håvard Strand. 2002. "Armed Conflict 1946–2001: A New Dataset." *Journal of Peace Research* 39(5): 615-637.

Gleick, Peter. 1989. "The Implications of Global Climate Changes for International Security." *Climate Change* 15: 303-325.

———. 1993. "Water and Conflict: Fresh Water Resources and International Security." *International Security* 18: 79-112.

Glosserman, Brad, and Tomoko Tsunoda. 2009. "Gray Menace." *Foreign Policy* 24 July, http://www.foreignpolicy.com/articles/2009/07/24/japans_coming_crisis_of_age?page=0,1 [Accessed 4 June 2011].

Goldin, Claudia. 1994. "The Political Economy of Immigration Restriction: The United States, 1890–1921." Pp. 223-258 in *The Regulated Economy.* Claudia Goldin and Gary D. Libecap, eds. Chicago: University of Chicago Press.

Goldscheider, Calvin, 2002. *Cultures in Conflict: The Arab-Israeli Conflict.* Westport, CT: Greenwood Press.

Goldstone, Jack A. 1991. *Revolution and Rebellion in the Early Modern World.* Berkeley: University of California Press.

———. 1999. Youth Bulges, Youth Cohorts, and their Contribution to Periods of Rebellion and Revolution. Manuscript, University of California, Davis.

———. 2001a. "Demography, Environment, and Security." Pp. 84-108 in *Environmental Conflict.* Paul F. Diehl and Nils Petter Gleditsch, eds. Boulder, CO: Westview.

———. 2001b. "Demography, Environment, and Security: An Overview." Pp. 38-61 in *Demography and National Security.* Myron Weiner and Sharon Stanton Russell, eds. New York: Berghahn Books.

———. 2002. "Population and Security: How Demographic Change can Lead to Violent Conflict." *Columbia Journal of International Affairs* 56: 245-263.

———. 2008/2009. "Flash Points and Tipping Points: Security Implications of Global Population Changes." *Environmental Change and Security Program Report* 13: 2-9.

———. 2009. "Population Movements and Security." Pp. 5822–5835 in The International Studies Encyclopedia, Vol. IX, Robert A. Denemark, ed. Chichester, West Sussex, UK: Wiley-Blackwell.

———. 2010. "The New Population Bomb: Four Population Megatrends That Will Shape the Global Future." *Foreign Affairs* (Jan/Feb): 31-43.

———. 2012. "Demography: Security Perspectives." In Security and Development in Global Politics: A Critical Comparison. Joanna Spear and Paul D. Williams, eds. Washington, DC: Georgetown University Press.

Gordon, Raymond G., ed. 2005. *Ethnologue: Languages of the World.* 15th ed. Dallas, TX: SIL International.

Goujon, A., V. Skirbekk, et al. 2007. "New Times, Old Beliefs: Investigating the Future of Religions in Austria and Switzerland." Paper Presented at Joint Eurostat/UNECE Work Session on Demographic Projections, Bucharest, 10-12 October. Luxembourg: Office for Official Publications of the European Communities.

Government Actuary's Department 2006. *National population projections 2004-based. Series PP2 No 25. Report Giving Population Projections by Age and Sex for the United Kingdom, Great Britain, and Constituent Countries.* Houndmills, UK: Palgrave Macmillan.

Green, Elliott D. 2007. "Demography, Diversity and Nativism in Contemporary Uganda: Evidence from Uganda." *Nations and Nationalism* 13(4): 717-736.

Green, J. C., L. A. Kellstedt, et al. 2007. "How the Faithful Voted: Religious Communities and the Presidential Vote." Pp. 15-26 in *A Matter of Faith: Religion in the 2004 Presidential Election.* D. E. Campbell, ed. Washington, DC: Brookings Institute.

Gurr, Ted Robert. 1970. *Why Men Rebel.* Princeton, NJ: Princeton University Press.

Guth, J., L. A. Kellstedt, et al. 2006. "Religious Influences in the 2004 Presidential Election." *Presidential Studies Quarterly* 36(2): 223-242.

Haas, Mark L. 2007. "A Geriatric Peace? The Future of U.S. Power in a World of Aging Populations." *International Security* 32(1): 112-147.

———. 2008. "Pax Americana Geriatrica." *Miller-McCune Magazine* August, pp. 30-39.

Habyarimana, J., M. Humphreys, D. N. Posner, and J. M. Weinstein. 2007. "Why Does Ethnic Diversity Undermine Public Goods Provision?" *American Political Science Review* 101(4): 709-726.

Hackett, C. 2008. "Religion and Fertility in The United States: The Influence of Affiliation, Region, and Congregation." PhD diss. University of Texas, Austin.

Hagerty, Barbara Bradley. 2009. "In Quiverfull Movement, Birth Control is Shunned." *Morning Edition,* 25 March, National Public Radio. http://www.npr.org/templates/story/story.php?storyId=102005062.

Hammill, Anne, and Richard Matthew. 2009. *Peacebuilding and Climate Change Adaptation.* Unpublished manuscript.

Handlin, Oscar. 1991. *Boston's Immigrants, 1790–1880.* Cambridge, MA: Harvard University Press.

Harding, Susan. 1994. "Imagining the Last Days: The Politics of Apocalyptic Language." Pp. 57-78 in *Accounting for Fundamentalisms: The Dynamic Character of Movements.* Martin E. Marty and R. Scott Appleby, eds. Chicago: University of Chicago Press.

Hart, Jerome. 2009. "The Kearney-Kalloch Epoch." *The Virtual Museum of the City of San Francisco.* http://www.sfmuseum.net/hist2/kalloch.html.

Hastings, Donald W., Charles H. Reynolds, and Ray R. Canning. 1972. "Mormonism and Birth Planning: the Discrepancy Between Church Authorities, Teachings and Lay Attitudes." *Population Studies* 26(1): 19-28.

Hatton, Timothy J., and Jeffrey G. Williamson. 2008. *Global Migration and the World Economy.* Cambridge, MA: MIT Press.

————. 2009. "Vanishing Third World Emigrants?" Cambridge, MA: National Bureau of Economic Research Working Paper 14785. http://www.nber.org/papers/w14785 [Accessed 22 June 2011].

Haub, Carl, and O. P. Sharma. 2007. *The Future Population of India: A Long-Range Demographic View.* Washington, DC: Population Reference Bureau.

Hauge, Wenche, and Tanja Ellingsen. 1998. "Beyond Environmental Scarcity: Causal Pathways to Conflict." *Journal of Peace Research* 35(3): 299-317.

Heaton, Tim B., and Kristen L. Goodman. 1985. "Religion and Family Formation: A Comparison of Mormons with Catholics and Protestants." *Review of Religious Research* 26(4): 343-359.

Heaton, Tim B., and Sandra Calkins. 1983. "Family Size and Contraceptive Use Among Mormons: 1965-75." *Review of Religious Research* 25(2): 102-113.

Hegre, Håvard, Tanja Ellingsen, Scott Gates, and Nils Petter Gleditsch. 2001. "Toward a Democratic Civil Peace? Democracy, Political Change, and Civil War, 1816–1992." *American Political Science Review* 95: 33-48.

Heinsohn, Gunnar. 2006. *Söhne und Weltmacht: Terror im Aufstieg und Fall der Nationen.* Zurich: Orell Füssli.

Held, David, and Anthony McGrew, David Goldblatt, and Jonathan Perraton. 1999. *Global Transformations: Politics, Economics and Culture.* Stanford, CA: Stanford University Press.

Heller, Peter S. 2003. *Who Will Pay? Coping with Aging Societies, Climate Change, and Other Long-Term Fiscal Challenges.* Washington, DC: International Monetary Fund.

Hepburn, Anthony C. H., 1994. "Long Division and Ethnic Conflict: The Experience of Belfast." Pp. 88-104 in *Managing Divided Cities.* Seamus Dunn, ed. Staffordshire: Ryburn Publishing.

Herbst, J. I. 2000. *States and Power in Africa: Comparative Lessons in Authority and Control.* Princeton, NJ: Princeton University Press.

Heston, Alan, Robert Summers, and Bettina Aten. 2006. "Penn World Table, Version 6.2." Philadelphia: Center for International Comparisons of Production, Income and Prices at the University of Pennsylvania.

Higham, John. 2002. *Strangers in the Land.* New Brunswick, NJ: Rutgers University Press.

Hilgeman, Christin, and Carter T. Butts. 2009. "Women's Employment and Fertility: A Welfare Regime Paradox." *Social Science Research* 38:103-117.

Himalayan News Service. 2009. "Glacier Melt a Looming Threat." 2 September. http://www.thehimalayantimes.com/fullNews.php?headline=Glacier+melting+a+looming+threat&id=MzA4MDM=.

Historical Tables: Budget of the United States Government. 2004. Washington, DC: Office of Management and Budget.

Hobbes, Thomas. 1994 (originals 1651/1658). *Leviathan: with Selected Variants from the Latin Edition of 1658.* Indianapolis: Hackett.

Hochschild, J. 2005. "APSA Presidents Reflect on Political Science: Who Knows What, When, and How?" *Political Science and Politics* 32: 309-334.

————. 2009. *Quiverfull: Inside the Christian Patriarchy Movement.* Boston: Beacon Press.

Kahl, Colin H. 1998. "Population Growth, Environmental Degradation, and State-Sponsored Violence: The Case of Kenya, 1991–93." *International Security* 23: 80-119.

————. 2006. *States, Scarcity, and Civil Strife in the Developing World.* Princeton, NJ and Oxford: Princeton University Press.

Kaplan, Robert D. 1994. "The Coming Anarchy." *Atlantic Monthly* 273: 46.

Karim, M. 2005. "Islamic Teachings on Reproductive Health." Pp. 40-55 in *Islam, the State, and Population.* G. Jones and M. Karim, eds. London, Hurst and Co.ENRfu

Kaufmann, Eric. 2007. "Religion and Politics: The Demographic Imperative." Paper presented at the Annual Meeting of the American Political Science Association, Chicago, August 30–September 2.

Keen, D. 2005. *Conflict and Collusion in Sierra Leone.* Oxford, UK: James Currey.

Kelley, Allen C., and Robert M. Schmidt. 2001. "Economic and Demographic Change: A Synthesis of Models, Findings, and Perspectives." Pp. 67-105 in *Population Matters: Demographic Change, Economic Growth, and Poverty in the Developing World.* Nancy Birdsall, Allen C. Kelley, and Steven W. Sinding, eds. New York: Oxford University Press.

Kennedy, Paul M. 1989. *The Rise and Fall of the Great Powers: Economic Change and Military Conflict from 1500 to 2000.* New York: Vintage.

Kepel, Gilles. 2002. *Jihad: The Trail of Political Islam.* London: Tauris.

Keynes, John Maynard. 1920. *The Economic Consequences of the Peace.* New York: Harcourt, Brace, and Howe.

Keyssar, Alexander. 2001. *The Right to Vote.* New York: Basic Books.

Kihl, Young Wan. 2009. "The Challenges of Democratic Consolidation in South Korea: Post-Election Politics of the Lee Myung-bak Administration." *Korea Observer* 40(2): 233-271.

Kim, Il-Ki. 2000. "Policy Responses to Low Fertility and Population Aging in Korea." Expert Group Meeting on Policy Responses to Population Aging and Population Decline. New York: United Nations Population Division.

Kim, Woosang. 1991. "Alliance Transitions and Great Power War." *American Journal of Political Science* 35(4): 833-850.

Klein, Naomi. 2007. *The Shock Doctrine: The Rise of Disaster Capitalism.* New York: Metropolitan Books.

Korea Institute for Health and Social Affairs. 2007. "National Strategies in Response to Low Fertility and Population Ageing in Korea." www.kihasa.re.kr/html/jsp/lib/download.jsp?bid=203&ano=34 [Accessed 7 August 2009].

Kotlikoff, Larry J., and Scott Burns. 2005. *The Coming Generational Storm: What You Need to Know about America's Economic Future.* Cambridge, MA: MIT Press.

Kraske, Marion. 2008. "Far Right Benefits from Voter Dissatisfaction." *Der Speigel.* http://www.spiegel.de/international/europe/0,1518,581098,00.html [Accessed 2 June 2011].

Krause, Elizabeth L. 2006. "Dangerous Demographies: The Scientific Manufacture of Fear." Briefing no. 36, July. Dorset: The Corner House.

Kulischer, Eugene M. 1948. *Europe on the Move: War and Population Changes, 1917–47.* New York: Columbia University Press.

Kurth, James. 2007. "One-Child Foreign Policy: Lower Birth Rates Will Alter Both Society and Strategy." *American Conservative* 27 August, pp. 6-10.

Kwon, Tai-Hwon. 2003. "Demographic Trends and their Social Implications." *Social Indicators Research*: 19-38, 62, 63.

Laitin, David D. 1994. "The Tower of Babel as a Coordination Game: Political Linguistics in Ghana." *American Political Science Review* 88(3): 622-634.

———. 2007. *Nations, States, and Violence.* Oxford, UK, and New York: Oxford University Press.

Lander, Mark. 2003. "West Europe Is Hard Hit by Strikes over Pensions." *New York Times,* 4 June, p. A9.

Lane, A. T. 1987. *Solidarity or Survival.* New York: Greenwood.

Langer, Arnim. 2005. "Horizontal Inequalities and Violent Group Mobilization in Côte d'Ivoire." *Oxford Development Studies* 33(1): 25-45.

Laqueur, Walter. 2007. *The Last Days of Europe: Epitaph for an Old Continent.* New York: Thomas Dunne Books.

Launay, Robert, and Marie Miran. 2000. "Beyond Mande Mory: Islam and Ethnicity in Côte d'Ivoire." *Paideuma* 46: 63-84.

Leahy, Elizabeth, Robert Engelman, Carolyn Gibb Vogel, Sarah Haddock, and Tod Preston. 2007. *The Shape of Things to Come: Why Age Structure Matters to a Safer, More Equitable World.* Washington, DC: Population Action International.

Leahy Madsen, Elizabeth, Béatrice Daumerie, and Karen Hardee. 2010. *The Effects of Age Structure on Development.* Washington, DC: Population Action International.

Lebanon. *Encyclopædia Britannica.* 2009. Encyclopædia Britannica Online. 9 July. http://www.search.eb.com/eb/article-23374.

Lee, Sam-Sik. 2009. "Low Fertility and Policy Responses in Korea." *Japanese Journal of Population* 7(1): 57-70.

Lehrer, Evelyn L. 2004. "Religion as a Determinant of Economic and Demographic Behavior in the United States." *Population and Development Review* 30(4): 707-726.

Lesthaeghe, R. 2000. "Transnational Islamic Communities in a Multilingual Secular Society." Pp. 1-58 in *Communities and Generations: Turkish and Moroccan Populations in Belgium.* R. Lesthaeghe, ed. Brussels: Centrum voor Bevolkings-en Gezinsstudie (CBGS).

———. 2007. "Second Demographic Transition. *Encyclopedia of Sociology Online.* G. Ritzer, ed. Oxford, UK: Blackwell.

Lesthaeghe, Ron J., and Lisa Neidert. 2006. "The 'Second Demographic Transition' in the U.S.: Spatial Patterns and Correlates." *Population Studies Center Research Report* No. 06-592. Ann Arbor, MI: Population Studies Center.

Leung, Joe C. B. 2006. "Family Support and Community Services for Older Adults in China: Integration and Partnership." Pp. 405-430 in *Handbook of Asian Aging.* Hyunsook Yoon and Jon Hendricks, eds. Amityville, NY: Baywood.

Lewis, Bernard. 1990. "The Roots of Muslim Rage." *Atlantic Monthly,* September. http:// www.theatlantic.com/doc/199009/muslim–rage.

———. 2003. *What Went Wrong? The Clash Between Islam and Modernity in the Middle East.* New York: Perennial.

Lia, Brynjar. 2005. *Globalisation and the Future of Terrorism: Patterns and Predictions.* London and New York: Routledge.

Lievens, J. 1999. "Family-Forming Migration from Turkey and Morocco to Belgium: The Demand for Marriage Partners from the Countries of Origin." *International Migration Review* 33(3): 717-744.

Livi-Bacci, Massimo. 2007. *A Concise History of World Population,* 4th ed. Carl Ipsen, trans. Oxford, UK: Blackwell.

Lombard Street Research Monthly Economic Review. 2003. "Baby Boomers' Poverty Trap." 22 September.

Longman, Phillip. 2004. *The Empty Cradle: How Falling Birthrates Threaten World Prosperity and What to Do About It.* New York: Basic Books.

Lustick, S. Ian. 1999. "Israel as a Non-Arab State: The Political Implications of Mass Immigration of Non-Jews." *Middle East Journal* 53(3): 417-433.

Luttwak, Edward N. 1994. "Where Are the Great Powers? At Home with the Kids." *Foreign Affairs* 73(4): 23-28.

Lutz, Wolfgang, Anne Goujon, K. C. Samir, and Warren Sanderson. 2007. *Reconstruction of Populations by Age, Sex and Level of Educational Attainment for 120 Countries for 1970-2000.* Laxenbourg, Austria: International Institute for Applied Systems Analysis.

Lyons, Francis Stewart Leland. 1971. *Ireland Since the Famine.* London: Weidenfeld and Nicolson.

Maas, Achim, and Dennis Tanzler. 2009. *Regional Security Implications of Climate Change: A Synopsis.* Adelphi Consult.

MacGaffey, W. 1982. "The Policy of National Integration in Zaire." *Journal of Modern African Studies* 20(1): 87-105.

Machunovich, Diane J. 2000. "Relative Cohort Size: Source of a Unifying Theory of Global Fertility Transition?" *Population and Development Review* 26: 236.

Maddison, Angus. 2007. *Contours of the World Economy, 1–2030 A.D.* Oxford, UK: Oxford University Press.

Magnus, George. 2009. *The Age of Aging: How Demographics are Changing the Global Economy and Our World.* Singapore: John Wiley & Sons.

Mamdani, M. 1996. *Citizen and Subject: Contemporary Africa and the Legacy of Late Colonialism.* Princeton, NJ: Princeton University Press.

———. 2009. *Saviors and Survivors: Darfur, Politics and the War on Terror.* New York: Pantheon.

Manger, L. 2006. "Resource Conflict as a Factor in the Darfur Crisis in Sudan." Paper presented at the Conference on The Frontiers of Land Issues: Embeddedness of Rights and Public Policies, Montpellier, VT, 17-19 May.

Marshall, Montgomery G., and Keith Jaggers. 2009. "Polity IV Project, Political Regime Characteristics and Transitions, 1800–2007: Dataset Users' Manual." Fairfax, VA: Center for Systemic Peace, George Mason University.

Marshall-Fratani, Ruth. 2006. "The War of 'Who Is Who': Autochthony, Nationalism, and Citizenship in the Ivoirian Crisis." *African Studies Review* 49(2): 9-43.

Martin, D. 2001. *Pentecostalism: The World Their Parish.* Oxford, UK: Blackwell.

Martis, Kenneth, ed. 1982. *The Historical Atlas of Political Parties in the United States Congress, 1789–1989.* New York: Macmillan.

———. 1989. *The Historical Atlas of United States Congressional Districts, 1789–1983.* New York: Macmillan.

Masalha, Nur. 1992. *Expulsion of the Palestinians: The Concept of "Transfer" in Zionist Political Thought, 1882–1948.* Institute for Palestine Studies.

Matthew, Richard, Jon Barnett, Bryan McDonald, and Karen O'Brien. 2009. *Global Environmental Change and Human Security.* Cambridge, MA: MIT Press.

Matthew, Richard, Mark Halle, and Jason Switzer, eds. 2002. *Conserving the Peace: Resources, Livelihoods, and Security.* Geneva and Winnipeg: IISD Press.

McCann, J. 1995. *People of the Plow: An Agricultural History of Ethiopia, 1800–1990.* Madison, WI: University of Wisconsin Press.

McFarlane, Deborah R., and Kenneth J. Meier. 2001. *The Politics of Fertility Control.* New York: Chatham House.

McGarry, John, and Brendan O'Leary. 2009. "Power Shared After the Death of Thousands." Chapter 1 in *Consociational Theory: McGarry & O'Leary and the Northern Ireland Conflict.* Rupert Taylor, ed. New York: Routledge.

McGray, H., et al. 2007. *Weathering the Storm, Options for Framing Adaptation and Development.* Washington, DC: World Resources Institute.

McNeill, J. R. 2008. "Can History Help Us With Global Warming?" Pp. 26-48 in *Climatic Cataclysm: The Foreign Policy and National Security Implications of Climate Change.* Kurt M. Campbell, ed. Washington, DC: Brookings Institute.

McNeill, William H. 1982. *The Pursuit of Power: Technology, Armed Force, and Society Since A.D. 1000.* Chicago: University of Chicago Press.

———. 1990. *Population and Politics Since 1750.* Charlottesville: University Press of Virginia.

McQuillan, Kevin. 2004. "When Does Religion Influence Fertility?" *Population and Development Review* 30(1): 25-56.

McTernan, Oliver. 2003. *Violence in God's Name: Religion in an Age of Conflict.* Maryknoll, NY: Orbis.

Meadows, Donella H., Dennis I. Meadows, Jorgen Randers, and William W. Behrens III. 1972. *The Limits to Growth.* New York: Universe Books.

Mearsheimer, John J. 2001 *The Tragedy of Great Power Politics.* New York: W. W. Norton.

Menon, Jayant, and Anna Melendez-Nakamura. 2009. "Aging in Asia: Trends, Impacts and Responses." In Working Paper Series on Regional Economic Integration. Manila, Philippines: Asian Development Bank.

Mesquida, Christian G., and Neil I. Wiener. 1999. "Male Age Composition and the Severity of Conflicts." *Politics in the Life Sciences* 18(2): 181-189.

Meszaros, A. 1999. "The Gypsy population in Hungary in the 1990s (*Romske obyvatelstvo v Madarsku v 90. letech)*" [in Czech with English abstract.] *Demografie* 41(2): 120-137.

Michalopoulos, S. 2008. "The Origins of Ethnolinguistic Diversity: Theory and Evidence." Unpublished working paper. Department of Economics, Tufts University.

Miguel, E. 2004. "Tribe or Nation? Nation Building and Public Goods in Kenya versus Tanzania." *World Politics* 56(3): 327-362.

Miller, Kerby. 1985. *Emigrants and Exiles.* New York: Oxford University Press.

Mink, Gwendolyn. 1990. *Old Labor and New Immigrants.* Ithaca, NY: Cornell University Press.

Moller, Herbert. 1968. "Youth as a Force in the Modern World." *Comparative Studies in Society and History* 10: 237-260.

Moore, J. L., L. Manne, T. Brooks, N. D. Burgess, R. Davies, C. Rahbek, et al. 2002. "The Distribution of Cultural and Biological Diversity in Africa." Proceedings of the Royal Society of London 269(1501): 1645-1653.

Morgan, S. Philip. 2003. "Is Low Fertility a Twenty-First Century Demographic Crisis?" *Demography* 40(4): 589-603.

Morgenthau, Hans J. 1948. *Politics Among Nations.* New York: Alfred A. Knopf.

Morland, P. 2009. "Defusing the Demographic Scare." *Ha'aretz,* June 2.

Munson, Z. 2001. "Islamic Mobilization: Social Movement Theory and the Egyptian Muslim Brotherhood." *Sociological Quarterly* 42(4): 487-510.

Musser, A. Milton. 1904. "Race Suicide—Infanticide, Prolicide, Leprocide vs. Children—Letters to Messrs. Joseph Smith and William H. Kelley." Salt Lake City, UT: Privately published pamphlet.

Mwenda, A. 2007. "Personalizing Power in Uganda." *Journal of Democracy* 18(3): 23-37.

Myers, Norman. 1993. *Ultimate Security: The Environmental Basis of Political Stability.* New York: W. W. Norton.

Myrskylä, M., H. Kohler, and F. C. Billari. 2009. "Advances in Development Reverse Fertility Declines." *Nature* 460(6): 741-743.

National Institute of Population and Social Security Research. 2003. *Population Statistics of Japan 2003.* Tokyo: National Institute of Population and Social Security Research.

National Intelligence Council (NIC). 2004. *Mapping the Global Future.* Washington, DC: Government Printing Office.

———. 2006. "Rethinking Democracy Promotion Efforts." *PDBM-2006-11.* Washington, DC: Office of the Director of National Intelligence.

New York Times. 1994. "Israelis Fear a Return of Displaced Arabs." 7 May 1994, p. 3.

Nichiporuk, Brian. 2000. *The Security Dynamics of Demographic Factors.* Santa Monica, CA: RAND.

———. 2005. *Alternative Futures and Army Force Planning: Implications for the Future Force Era.* Santa Monica, CA: RAND.

NIS News Bulletin. 2009. "Immigrants Nearly in Majority in Rotterdam." http://www.nisnews.nl/public/050509_1.htm [Accessed 28 May 2011].

Norris, P., and R. Inglehart. 2004. *Sacred and Secular: Religion and Politics Worldwide.* Cambridge, UK: Cambridge University Press.

Nunis, Doyce B., Jr., ed. 1967. "The Demagogue and the Demographer: Correspondence of Denis Kearney and Lord Bryce." *Pacific Historical Review* 36(2): 269–288.

Nunn, N. 2008. "The Long-Term Effects of Africa's Slave Trade." *Quarterly Journal of Economics* 123(1): 139-176.

O'Gorman, Thomas. 1895. *A History of the Catholic Church in the United States.* New York: Christian Literature Company.

O'Neill, Brian C., F. Landis MacKellar, and Wolfgang Lutz. 2001. *Population and Climate Change.* Cambridge, UK: Cambridge University Press.

O'Neill, Terence. 1972. *The Autobiography of Terence O'Neill.* London: Rupert Hart-Davis.

Obama, Barack. 2009. "Remarks on Health Care." *MarketWatch,* 11 June.

O'Brien, K., and R. Leichenko. 2000. "Double Exposure: Assessing the Impacts of Climate Change Within the Context of Economic Globalisation." *Global Environmental Change* 10: 221-232.

Oeuvres de Bossuet, Vol. 1. 1841. Paris: Firmin Didot Frères.

Oeuvres de Frédéric le Grand, Vol. 4. 1846. Berlin: Rodolphe Decker.

Office of the Prime Minister, France. 2006. First National Conference on Public Finance. Paris: Office of the Prime Minister. http://www.archives.premier-ministre.gouv.fr/villepin/en/information/latest_news_97/1st_national_conference_on_55114.html [Accessed 28 July 2009].

ONS. 2008. *Birth Statistics. Review by the National Statistician on Births and Family Building in England and Wales, 2007.* Series FM1 No. 36. London: The Stationery Office.

ONS. 2009. *2008-based National Population Projections.* London: Office for National Statistics.

Organization for Economic Cooperation and Development (OECD). 2005. Employment Outlook: Statistical Annex. 2005. OECD.

———. 2006. *Live Longer, Work Longer.* Paris: OECD.

———. 2007. "Average Effective Age of Retirement in 1970-2007 in OECD Countries." Paris: OECD. http://www.oecd.org/dataoecd/3/1/39371913.xls [Accessed 28 July 2009].

———. 2009. "Taxes on the Average Worker in OECD Factbook 2009" Paris: OECD. http://fiordiliji.sourceoecd.org/pdf/factbook2009/302009011e-10-04-02.pdf [Accessed 28 July 2009].

Organski, A. F. K. 1958. *World Politics.* New York: Alfred A. Knopf.

Oum, Young Rae. 2003. "Beyond a Strong State and Docile Women: Reproductive Choices, State Policy and Skewed Sex Ratio in South Korea." *International Feminist Journal of Politics* 5(3): 420-446.

Overbeek, Johannes. 1974. *History of Population Theories.* Rotterdam: Rotterdam University Press.

OXFAM. 2008. *Climate Wrongs and Human Rights: Putting People at the Heart of Climate Change Policy.* OXFAM Briefing Paper 117: London: OXFAM.

Parkanova, Vlasta. 2009. "A Role to Play." European Defense Agency Bulletin no. 10 (February 2009), pp. 8-9.

Patterson, H., and Eric Kaufmann. 2007. *Unionism and Orangeism in Northern Ireland Since 1945.* Manchester, UK: Manchester University Press.

People's Republic of China. 2004a. *Social Security White Paper of China.* Beijing: State Council Information Office. http://unpan1.un.org/intradoc/groups/public/documents/APCITY/UNPAN019944.pdf [Accessed 28 July 2009].

———. 2004b. Chapter IV: Defense Expenditure and Defense Assets in *PRC: 2004 White Paper on National Defense* [Online] Beijing: State Council Information Office. Available at: http://www.fas.org/nuke/guide/china/doctrine/natdef2004.html [Accessed 28 July 2009].

"Personal Robots to Monitor Elderly Vital Signs." 2009. *Emailwire.com* 15 June. http://www.emailwire.com/release/23732-Personal-Robots-to-Monitor-Elderly-Vital-Signs.html..

Peterson, Peter G. 1999. *Gray Dawn: How the Coming Age Wave Will Transform America—and the World.* New York: Times Books.

Pew Forum on Religion & Public Life. 2009. *Mapping the Global Muslim Population: A Report on the Size and Distribution of the World's Muslim Population.* Washington, DC: Pew Research Center.

———. 2011. "The Future of the Global Muslim Population 2010-2030" 27 January. http://pewforum.org/The-Future-of-the-Global-Muslim-Population.aspx [Accessed 31 May 2011].

Pew Hispanic Center. 2008. *Latinos Account for Half of U.S. Population Growth Since 2000.*

Pew Research Center. 2002. *What the World Thinks in 2002.* Washington, DC: Pew Research Center.

Phillips, Kevin. 2003. *William McKinley.* New York: Henry Holt.

Philpott, D. 2007. "Explaining the Political Ambivalence of Religion." *American Political Science Review* 101(3): 505-525.

Platt, L., L. Simpson, et al. 2005. "Stability and Change in Ethnic Groups in England and Wales." *Population Trends* 121: 35–46.

Platt, Lucinda. 2009. *Ethnicity and Family: Relationships Within and Between Ethnic Groups.* Institute for Social and Economic Research.

Polity IV Project. 2008. *Polity IV Project: Political Regime Characteristics and Transitions, 1800-2007.* Arlington, VA: Center for Systemic Peace and George Mason University.

PollingReport.Com 2009. www.pollingreport.com.

Poole, Michael A., ed., 1983. "The Demography of Violence." Pp. 151-180 in *Northern Ireland: The Background to the Conflict.* Belfast: Appletree Press.

Population Action International. 2009. "The Importance of Population for Climate Change Challenges and Solutions." Fact Sheet 37. Washington, DC.

Portugese, Jacqueline. 1998. *Fertility Policy in Israel: The Politics of Religion, Gender, and Nation.* Westport, CT: Praeger.

Posen, Barry R. 2003. "Command of the Commons: The Military Foundation of U.S. Hegemony." *International Security* 28(1): 5-46.

Posner, Daniel. 2004. "The Political Salience of Cultural Difference: Why Chewas and Tumbukas Are Allies in Zambia and Adversaries in Malawi," *American Political Science Review* 98(4): 529-545.

Pottier, J. 2006. "Roadblock Ethnography: Negotiating Humanitarian Access in Ituri, Eastern DR Congo, 1999-2004." *Africa: Journal of the International African Institute* 76(2): 151-179.

Poulain, M., N. Perrin, et al. 2006. *Towards Harmonised European Statistics on European Migration (THESIM).* Louvain la Neuve, France : Universitaires de Louvain Presses.

PovertyNet. 2004. "Dramatic Decline in Global Poverty, but Progress Uneven." 23 April. http://web.worldbank.org/WBSITE/EXTERNAL/TOPICS/EXTPOVERTY/0,,cont entMDK:20195240~pagePK:148956~piPK:216618~theSitePK:336992,00.html.

Pride, Mary. 1985. *The Way Home: Beyond Feminism, Back to Reality.* Wheaton, IL: Crossway Books.

Przeworski, Adam, Michael E. Alvarez, José Antonio Cheibub, and Fernando Limongi. 2000. *Democracy and Development: Political Institutions and Well-Being in the World, 1950–1990.* Cambridge, UK: Cambridge University Press.

Purvis, Thomas L. 1984. "The European Ancestry of the United States Population, 1790: A Symposium." *William and Mary Quarterly* 41(1): 85.

Raleigh, Clionadh, and Henrik Urdal. 2007. "Climate Change, Environmental Degradation and Armed Conflict." *Political Geography* 26(6): 674-694.

Raynaut, C. 1988. "Aspects of the Problem of Land Concentration in Niger." Pp. 221-242 in *Land and Society in Contemporary Africa.* R. E. Downs and S. P. Reyna, eds. Hanover, NH: University Press of New England.

Reiss, Bob, 2001. *The Coming Storm: Extreme Weather and Our Terrifying Future.* New York: Hyperion.

Republic of Korea.1994. *An Overview of National Family Planning Program in Korea.* Prepared for the International Conference on Population and Development, Cairo, Egypt. Seoul: Republic of Korea.

Republic of Uganda, Ministry of Finance, Planning and Economic Development. 2004. *Poverty Eradication Action Plan 2004/5-2007/8.* Kampala: Ministry of Finance, Planning and Economic Development.

———. 2008. *National Population Policy for Social Transformation and Sustainable Development.* Kampala: Population Secretariat.

Reuters. 2006. "Ahmadinejad Urges Iranians To Have More Kids." 22 October. http://www.msnbc.msn.com/id/10663272/ns/world_news-mideast_n_africa/t/ahmadine-jad-urges-iranians-have-more-kids/ [Accessed 2 June 2011].

Reuveny, Rafael, and Quan Li. 2003. "Economic Openness, Democracy, and Income Inequality." *Comparative Political Studies* 36(5): 575-601.

Reynal-Querol, Marta. 2002. "Ethnicity, Political Systems, and Civil Wars." *Journal of Conflict Resolution* 46(1): 29–54.

Richardson, Gary. 2005. "The Origins of Anti-Immigrant Sentiments: Evidence from the Heartland in the Age of Mass Migration." *Topics in Economic Analysis & Policy* 5(1): 1-46.

Romaniuk, A. 1980. "Increase in Natural Fertility During the Early Stages of Modernization: Evidence from an African Case Study, Zaire." *Population Studies* 34(2): 293-310.

Roper Center for Public Opinion Research. 2009. http://www.ropercenter.uconn.edu.

Rosen, James E., and Shanti R. Conly. 1996. *Pakistan's Population Program: The Challenge Ahead.* Washington, DC: Population Action International.

Rosenthal, Elisabeth. 2006. "European Union's Plunging Birthrates Spread Eastward." *New York Times,* 4 September, p. A3.

Ross, Michael L. 2001. "Does Oil Hinder Democracy?" *World Politics* 53: 325-361.

Rouhana, Nadim N., and Nimber Sultany. 2003. "Redrawing the Boundaries of Citizenship: Israel's New Hegemony." *Journal of Palestine Studies* 33(1): 5-22.

Ruggles, Steven. 2009. *Integrated Public Use Microdata Series: Version 4.0* [Machine-readable database]. Minneapolis: Minnesota Population Center.

Sachs, Jeffrey, 2005. "Climate Change and War." http://www.tompaine.com/print/climate_change_and_war.

SAIC (Science Applications International Corporation). 1995. *Final Report of the State Failure Task Force.* Washington, DC: Science Applications International Corp. and U.S. Agency for International Development.

Salehi-Isfahani, Djavad, and Daniel Egel. 2008. *Youth Exclusion in Iran: The State of Education, Employment and Family Formation.* Washington, DC: Brookings Institution. http://www.shababinclusion.org/section/publications.

Salehi-Isfahani, Djavad, and Navtej Dhillon. 2008. *Stalled Youth Transitions in the Middle East: A Framework for Policy Reform.* Washington, DC: Brookings Institution. http://www.shababinclusion.org/section/publications.

Salt, J. 2000. "Trafficking and Human Smuggling: A European Perspective." *International Migration* 38(3): 31-54.

———. 2005. *Current Trends in International Migration in Europe.* Strasburg, Germany: Council of Europe.

Salt, J., A. Singleton, et al. 1994. *Europe's International Migrants. Data Sources, Patterns and Trends.* London: HMSO.

Sambanis, Nicholas. 2002. "A Review of Recent Advances and Future Directions in the Quantitative Literature on Civil War." *Defense and Peace Economics* 13: 224.

Saving, Thomas R. 2007. "Medicare Meltdown." *Wall Street Journal,* 9 May, p. A17.

Scheidel, Walter. 2006. "Sex and Empire: A Darwinian Perspective." Princeton/Stanford Working Papers in Classics no. 050603. Princeton, NJ: Princeton University.

Schirrmacher, Frank. 2006. *Minimum: Vom Vergehen und Neuentstehen unserer Gemeinschaft.* Munich: Blessing.

Schmitter, Phillippe C. 1980. *Speculations About the Prospective Demise of Authoritarian Regimes and Its Possible Consequences*. Washington, DC: Woodrow Wilson Center.

Sciubba, Jennifer Dabbs. 2008. *The Politics of Population Aging in Germany, Italy, and Japan*. PhD diss. Department of Government and Politics, University of Maryland. College Park: University of Maryland.

Scott, Rachel. 2004. *Birthing God's Mighty Warriors*. Longwood, FL: Xulon Press.

Sedgh, Gilda, Stanley Henshaw, Susheela Singh, Elisabeth Ahman, and Iqbal Shah. 2007. "Induced Abortion: Estimated Rates and Trends Worldwide." *Lancet* 370(9595): 1338-1345.

Sells, Michael. 1996. *The Bridge Betrayed: Religion and Genocide in Bosnia*. Berkeley: University of California Press.

Settlements in Focus. 2005. *Peace Now*. May. http://www.peacenow.org.il/site/en/peace.asp?pi=62&docid=1294.

Shapiro, D. 1995. "Population Growth, Changing Agricultural Practices and Environmental Degradation in Zaire." *Population and Environment* 16(3): 221-236.

Shuttleworth, Ian. 1992. "Population change in Northern Ireland, 1981–1991: Preliminary Results of the 1991 Census of population." *Irish Geography* 25(1): 83-88.

Simon, Rita J., and Susan H. Alexander. 1993. *The Ambivalent Welcome: Print Media, Public Opinion, and Immigration*. Ann Arbor: University of Michigan.

Sinn, Hans Werner. 2007. *Can Germany be Saved?: The Malaise of the World's First Welfare State*. Cambridge, MA: MIT Press.

Skeldon, R. 2008. "International Migration as a Tool in Development Policy: A Passing Phase?" *Population and Development Review* 34(1): 1-18.

Skirbekk, Vegard. 2008. "Age and Productivity Potential: A New Approach Based on Ability Levels and Industry-Wide Task Demand." *Population and Development Review* 34(suppl.): 191-207.

———. 2009. "Human Fertility and Survival Across Space and Time." Working paper. Laxenburg, Austria: IIASA World Population Program.

Skirbekk, Vegard, Eric Kaufmann, and Anne Goujon. 2010. "Secularism, Fundamentalism or Catholicism?" *Journal for the Scientific Study of Religion* 49(2): 293-310.

Slaughter, Anne-Marie. 2009. "America's Edge: Power in the Networked Century." *Foreign Affairs* 88(1).

Smith, Dan, and Janna Vivekananda. 2007. "A Climate of Conflict: The Links Between Climate Change, Peace and War." International Alert. http://www.international-alert.org/pdf/A_Climate_Of_Conflict.pdf.

Smith, Dan. 2009. Personal blog. 16 June. http://dansmithsblog.com/2009/06/16/climate-conflict-peacebuilding-and-adaptation-a-need-for-leaps-and-links/.

Smith, Kerri. 2008. *The Population Problem. Nature Reports. Climate Change*. Vol. 2. http://www.nature.com/reports/climatechange.

Snyder, Scott. 2009. "Lee Myung-bak's Foreign Policy: A 250-day Assessment." *Korean Journal of Defense Analysis* 21(1): 85-102.

Sobotka, Tomas. 2009. Presentation to Conference on Fertility Decline, Cambridge, UK, July.

Social Security Administration. 2004. "International Update: Recent Developments in Foreign Public and Private Pensions." Washington, DC: Social Security Administration Office of Policy. http://www.socialsecurity.gov/policy/docs/progdesc/intl_update/2004-10/2004-10.html [Accessed 28 July 2009].

Soffer, Arnon. 1986. "Lebanon: Where Demography is the Core of Politics and Life." *Middle Eastern Studies* 22,(2).

———. 1987. "The Arabs of Israel." University of Haifa: Van Leer Institution.

———. 1988. "The Demographic Jinni: The End of the Zionist Dream?" *Ha'aretz*, 2 August, p. 4.

———. 2000. "Israel-2020–Demographic Perspectives and Ecological and Political Implications." Pp. 64-66 in *Israel 2000*. M.S. Aharoni, ed. Kefar Saba: Miksam.

Soro, Guillaume. 2005. *Pourquoi je suis devenu un rebelle: La Côte d'Ivoire au bord du gouffre.* [Why I Became a Rebel: Côte d'Ivoire on the Brink]. Paris: Hachette.

Sorokin, Pitrim A. 1937. *Social and Cultural Dynamics.* New York: American Book Co.

Spengler, Joseph J. 1979. *France Faces Depopulation: Postlude Edition, 1936–1976.* Durham, NC: Duke University Press.

Spengler, O. 1918. *Der Untergang des Abendlandes.* Munich: Beck.

Sprout, Harold, and Margaret Sprout. 1945. *Foundations of National Power.* Princeton, NJ: Princeton University Press.

Stangeland, Charles E. 1904. *Pre-Malthusian Doctrines of Population: A Study in the History of Economic Theory.* New York: Sentry Press.

Stark, L., and H. P. Kohler. 2002. "The Debate over Low Fertility in the Popular Press: A Cross-National Comparison, 1998–1999." *Population Research and Policy Review* 21(6): 535-574.

Stark, R. 1996. *The Rise of Christianity: A Sociologist Reconsiders History.* Princeton, NJ: Princeton University Press.

Statistics Norway. 2008. *Projection of the Immigrant population 2008–2060.* Oslo: Statistics Norway.

Statistics Sweden. 2004. *Sveriges framtida befolkning 2004-2050. reviderad befolkningsprognos från SCB.* [Population projections 2004-2050: revised projections from Statistics Sweden] BE 18 SM 0401. Stockholm: Sveriges Officiella Statistik. Statistik Meddelanden.

Steinmann, G., and M. Jäger. 2000. "Immigration and Integration: Non-linear Dynamics of Minorities." *Journal of Mathematical Population Studies* 9(1): 65-82.

Stern, Nicholas. 2006. "The Economics of Climate Change." Available at http://www.hm-treasury.gov.uk/independent_reviews/stern_review_economics_climate_chamnge/stern_review_report.cfm.

Steyn, M. 2006. *America Alone: The End of the World As We Know It.* Washington, DC: Regnery.

Stites, Elizabeth, Darlington Akabwai, Dyan Mazurana, and Priscilla Ateyo. 2007.

Angering Akuju: Survival and Suffering in Karamoja. Medford, MA: Feinstein International Center.

Surkyn, J., and R. Lesthaeghe. 2004. "Value Orientations and the Second Demographic Transition (STD) in Northern, Western and Southern Europe: An Update." *Demographic Research* Special Collection 3: Article 3.

Suzuki, Toro. 2008. "Korea's Strong Familism and Lowest-Low Fertility." *International Journal of Japanese Sociology* 2008(17): 30-41.

Swift, Mike, and Sean Webby. 2008. "Latino and Black Voters Push Anti-Gay Marriage Referendum." *San Jose Mercury News* 5 November. http://www.thelatinojournal. com/2008/11/latino-and-black-voters-push-anti-gay.html [Accessed March 2009].

Tainter, Joseph A. 1988. *The Collapse of Complex Societies.* Cambridge, UK: Cambridge University Press.

Takayama, Noriyuki. 2002. "Pension Reform of PRC: Incentives, Governance, and Policy Options." Paper prepared for the Fifth Anniversary Conference on Challenges and the New Agenda for the People's Republic of China, Asian Development Bank. Tokyo, Japan, 5–6 December.

Tammen, Ronald L., Jacek Kugler, Douglas Lemke, Allan C. Stam III, Mark Abdollahian, Carole Alsharabati, Brian Efird, and A. F. K. Organski. 2000. *Power Transitions: Strategies for the 21st Century.* New York: Chatham House.

Taylor, C. 2007. *A Secular Age.* Cambridge, MA: Belknap Press.

Teitelbaum, Michael S., and Jay M. Winter. 1985. *The Fear of Population Decline.* London: Academic Press.

The Economist. 2009. "Fertility and Living Standards: Go Forth and Multiply a Lot Less; Lower Fertility is Changing the World for the Better." 31 October, pp. 15-17.

The Times. 2008. "Leading geneticist Steve Jones says human evolution is over." October 7.

The Herzliya Conference on the Balance of National Strength and Security in Israel. 2001. *Journal of Palestine Studies* 31(1): 50-61.

"The Quarterly Poll." 1947. *The Public Opinion Quarterly* 11: 476.

Tichenor, Daniel J. 2002. *Dividing Lines.* Princeton, NJ: Princeton University Press.

Tir, Jarosalv, and Paul F. Diehl. 1998. "Demographic Pressure and Interstate Conflict: Linking Population Growth and Density to Militarized Disputes and Wars, 1930–89." *Journal of Peace Research* Special Issue on Environmental Conflict 35(3): 319-339.

Toft, Monica Duffy. 2002. "Differential Demographic Growth in Multinational States: Israel's Two-Front War." *Journal of International Affairs* 56(1): 71-94.

———. 2003. *The Geography of Ethnic Violence.* Princeton, NJ: Princeton University Press.

———. 2007a. "Getting Religion? The Puzzling Case of Islam and Civil War." *International Security* 4(31): 97-131.

———. 2007b. "Population Shifts and Civil War: A Test of Power Transition Theory." *International Interactions* 33(3): 243-269.

Toungara, Jeanne M. 2001. "Francophone Africa in Flux: Ethnicity and Political Crisis in Côte d'Ivoire." *Journal of Democracy* 12(3): 63-72.

Toynbee, Arnold J. 1924. *Greek Civilization and Character: The Self-Revelation of Ancient Greek Society.* New York: E. P. Dutton.

Tsui, Amy Ong. 2001. "Population Policies and Family Planning Programs in Asia's Rapidly Developing Economies." In *Population Change and Economic Development in East Asia.* A. Mason, ed. Stanford, CA: Stanford University Press.

Tucker, Rufus. 1923. "Old Americans in 1920." *Quarterly Journal of Economics* 37(4): 755-761.

Turner, David, Claudio Giorno, Alain De Serres, Ann Vourc'h, and Peter Richardson. 1998. "The Macroeconomic Implications of Aging in a Global Context." Working Paper No. 193. Paris: Economics Department OECD.

U.S. Census Bureau. 2008. *United States Population Projections by Age, Sex, Race and Hispanic Origin: July 1, 2000–2050.* Washington, DC: U.S. Bureau of the Census.

———. 2011. International Data Base website: http://www.census.gov/ipc/www/idb/country.php [Accessed 4 June 2011].

U.S. Congress. 1917. *Congressional Record.* 64th Cong., 2d. sess. Vol. 54, 2456-2457.

———. 1921. *Congressional Record.* 66th Cong., 3d sess. Vol. 60, 286-287.

———. House. 1891. *Report of the Select Committee on Immigration and Naturalization, 1891 ... and Testimony Taken by the Committee on Immigration of the Senate and ... Under Concurrent Resolution of March 12, 1890,* 51st Cong., 2nd sess., 15 January 1891, H. Rept. 3472 (Serial 2886).

U.S. Department of Homeland Security. 2009. *2008 Yearbook of Immigration Statistics.* Washington DC, US Department of Homeland Security, Office of Immigration Statistics. http://www.dhs.gov/xlibrary/assets/statistics/yearbook/2008/ois_yb_2008.pdf.

U.S. State Department. 2002. *International Religious Freedom Report 2002.* http://www.state.gov/g/drl/rls/irf/2002/.

Ueda, Reed. 1982. "Naturalization and Citizenship." Pp. 106-154 in *Immigration.* R. Easterlin, D. Ward, W. Bernard, and R. Ueda, eds. Cambridge, MA: Harvard University Press.

Uganda Bureau of Statistics (UBOS) and Macro International Inc. 2007. *Uganda Demographic and Health Survey 2006.* Kampala, Uganda, and Calverton, MD: UBOS and Macro International.

Ulfelder, Jay, and Michael Lustik. 2007. "Modeling Transitions to and from Democracy." *Democratization* 14(3): 351-387.

United Nations Development Programme (UNDP). 2002. *The Arab Human Development Report 2002.* New York: UNDP.

United Nations Environment Program. 2009. *From Conflict to Peacebuilding: The Role of Natural Resources and the Environment.* Geneva: UNEP.

United Nations Population Division. 2000. *Replacement Migration: Is It a Solution to Declining and Aging Populations?* New York: United Nations Population Division. http://www.un.org/esa/population/publications/migration/migration.htm [Accessed 28 July 2009].

———. 2007. *World Population Prospects: The 2006 Revision.* New York: United Nations Population Division.

———. 2008. *World Contraceptive Use 2007.* New York: United Nations Population Division.

———. 2009. *World Population Prospects: The 2008 Revision.* New York: United Nations Population Division.

———. 2011. *World Population Prospects: The 2010 Revision.* New York: United Nations Population Division.

University of California. 2009. Historical Labor Statistics Project. http://eh.net/databases/labor/.

Uppsala Conflict Data Program (UCDP) and Centre for the Study of Civil Wars, International Peace Research Institute (PRIO). 2008. *UCDP/PRIO Armed Conflict Dataset,* Version 4 2008.

Urdal, Henrik. 2004. *The Devil in Demographics: The Effect of Youth Bulges on Domestic Armed Conflict, 1950–2000.* Social Development Papers. 14 July. Washington, DC: World Bank.

———. 2006. "A Clash of Generations? Youth Bulges and Political Violence." *International Studies Quarterly* 50(3): 607-629.

———. 2007. "The Demographics of Political Violence: Youth Bulges, Insecurity and Conflict." Pp. 90-100 in Too Poor for Peace? Global Poverty, Conflict and Security in the 21st Century. Lael Brainard and Derek Chollet, eds. Washington, DC: Brookings Institution.

———. 2008. *Demographic Aspects of Climate Change, Environmental Degradation and Armed Conflict.* United Nations Expert Group Meeting on Population Distribution, Urbanizatioin, Internal Migration and Development.

Vanhanen, T. 1999 "Domestic Ethnic Conflict and Ethnic Nepotism: A Comparative Analysis." *Journal of Peace Research* 36(1): 55-73.

"Vladimir Putin on Raising Russia's Birth Rate." 2006. *Population and Development Review* 32 (2): 385-389.

Vlassenroot, K., and C. Huggins. 2005. "Land, Migration and Conflict in Eastern DRC." Pp. 115-195 in *From the Ground Up: Land Rights, Conflict and Peace in Sub-Saharan Africa.* C. Huggins and J. Clover, eds. Pretoria, South Africa: Institute for Security Studies.

Voss-Hubbard, Mark. 2002. *Beyond Party.* Baltimore, MD: Johns Hopkins University Press.

Vought, Hans P. 2004. *The Bully Pulpit and the Melting Pot.* Macon, GA: Mercer University Press.

Wakabi, Wairagala. 2006. "Population Growth Continues to Drive Up Poverty in Uganda." *Lancet* 367: 558.

Wang, Gabe T. 1999. *China's Population: Problems, Thoughts, and Policies.* Brookfield, VT: Ashgate.

Wapner, Paul, and Richard Matthew. 2009. "The Humanity of Global Environmental Ethics." *Journal of Environment and Development* 18: 203-222.

Waters, M. C. 1990. *Ethnic Options: Choosing Identities in America.* Berkeley: University of California Press.

Wattenberg, Ben. 1987. *The Birth Dearth.* New York: Pharos Books.

———. 2004. *Fewer: How the New Demography of Depopulation Will Shape Our Future.* Chicago: Ivan R. Dee.

Weigel, George. 2005. *The Cube and the Cathedral: Europe, America, and Politics Without God.* New York: Basic Books.

Weiner, Myron. 1978. *Sons of the Soil: Migration and Ethnic Conflict in India.* Princeton, NJ: Princeton University Press.

Weiner, Myron, and Michael S. Teitelbaum. 2001. *Political Demography and Demographic Engineering.* New York: Bergahn Books.

Weiner, Myron, and Sharon Stanton Russell, eds. 2001. *Demography and Security.* Oxford: Berghahn.

Westoff, C. F., and E. Jones. 1979. "The End of 'Catholic' Fertility." *Demography* 16(2): 209-217.

Westoff, C. F. and T. Frejka. 2007. "Religiousness and Fertility Among European Muslims." *Population and Development Review* 33(4): 785-809.

White Paper on German Security Policy and the Future of the Bundeswehr. 2006. Berlin: German Federal Ministry of Defense.

White, Aoife. 2006. "EU: Germany Must Stick to Spending Cuts to Reduce Budget Deficit by End of 2007." Associated Press, 1 March.

Wickham, C. R. 2002. *Mobilizing Islam, Religion, Activism and Political Change in Egypt.* New York: Columbia University Press.

Williamson, Jeffrey G. 2001. "Demographic Change, Economic Growth, and Inequality." Pp.106-136 in *Population Matters: Demographic Change, Economic Growth, and Poverty in the Developing World.* Nancy Birdsall, Allen C. Kelley, and Steven W. Sinding, eds. New York: Oxford University Press.

Wimmer, Andreas. 2007. "The Making and Unmaking of Ethnic Boundaries: Toward a Comparative Theory." Working paper. New Haven, CT: Yale Center for Comparative Research.

Winckler, Onn. 2002. "The Demographic Dilemma of the Arab World: The Employment Aspect." *Journal of Contemporary History* 37: 621.

———.2005. *Arab Political Demography.* Brighton, UK and Portland, OR: Sussex Academic Press.

Wisconsin Bureau of Labor and Industrial Statistics. 1888. Third Biennial Report, 1887–1888. Madison, WI: Democrat Printing Co.

Wise, Y. 2007. "Majority of Jews Will Be Ultra-Orthodox by 2050." University of Manchester press release 23 July. http://www.manchester.ac.uk/aboutus/news/archive/list/item/?id=2932&year=2007&month=07.

Wong, Carolyn. 2006. *Lobbying for Inclusion.* Stanford, CA: Stanford University Press.

Woods, Dwayne. 2003. "The Tragedy of the Cocoa Pod: Rent-Seeking, Land and Ethnic Conflict in Ivory Coast." *Journal of Modern African Studies* 41: 641–655.

Woolley, John, and Gerhard Peters. 2011. *The American Presidency Project.* http://www.presidency.ucsb.edu/index.php. [Accessed 10 May 2011].

World Bank. 1994. *Averting the Old Age Crisis: Policies to Protect the Old and Promote Growth.* New York: Oxford University Press.

———. 2007a. Global Economic Prospects 2007: Managing the Next Wave of Globalization. Washington, DC: World Bank.

———. 2007b. "Uganda Grapples with Youth Unemployment as WDR 2007 Is Launched." http://go.worldbank.org/FTO3IRJZ30 [Accessed 5 August 2009].

———. 2008. *Governance Matters 2008.* Washington, DC: World Bank.

———. 2009. *World Development Indicators.* http://web.worldbank.org/WBSITE/EX-TERNAL/DATASTATISTICS/0,,contentMDK:0398986~menuPK:64133163~pagePK:64133150~piPK:64133175~theSitePK:239419,00html [Accessed 29 June 2009].

World Patent Report: A Statistical Review. 2008. Geneva, Switzerland: World Intellectual Property Organization.

World Population Data Sheet. 2008. Washington, DC: Population Reference Bureau.

Wriggins, W. Howard, and James F. Guyot, eds. 1973. "Demographic Change and Politics: An Introduction." Pp. 1-29 in *Population, Politics and the Future of Southern Asia.* New York: Columbia University Press.

Wyman, Mark. 1993. *Round-Trip to America.* Ithaca, NY: Cornell University Press.

Wynn, Gerald, 2009. "Climate Change Forces New Migration Response." Reuters. 10 June. http://www.reuters.com/article/environmentNews/idUSTRE55928W20090610

Xinhua General News Service. 2005. "Japanese Government Approves Smaller FY2006 Budget." 24 December.

Yavuz, S. 2005. "Fertility Transition and the Progression to Third Birth in Turkey." *MPIDR Working Papers.*

Yomiuri Shimbun. 2003. "Savings Rate Slides as Population Ages." 29 October, p. 8.

Yonah, Yossi. 2004. "Israel's Immigration Policies: The Twofold Face of the 'Demographic Threat.'" *Social Identities* 10(2): 195-218.

Young, Brigham. 1856. *Journal of Discourses,* Vol. 4, No. 4 (21 Sept. 1856), p. 56.

Young, M. C. 1976. *The Politics of Cultural Pluralism.* Madison: University of Wisconsin Press.

Zakaria, Fareed. 2001. "The Roots of Rage." *Newsweek* 138: 24.

Zeidel, Robert Frederic. 1986. *The Literacy Test for Immigrants.* PhD diss., Marquette University, Milwaukee, WI.

Zertal, Idith, and Akiva Eldar. 2005. *Lords of the Land: The War Over Israel's Settlements in the Occupied Territories, 1967–2007.* Vivian Eden, trans. New York: Nation Books.

———. 2007. "Settler Population 1972-2005." Foundation for Middle East Peace, (data for West Bank and Gaza Strip).

Zuberi, T., A. Sibanda, A. Bawah, and A. Noumbissi. 2003. "Population and African Society." *Annual Review of Sociology* 29: 465-486.

Zureik, Elia. 2003. "Demography and Transfer: Israel's Road to Nowhere." *Third World Quarterly* 24(4): 619-630.

Index

About the Contributors

Richard P. Cincotta is demographer-in-residence at the Stimson Center in Washington, DC. He was formerly director of Demographic and Social Science Programs in the Long Range Analysis Unit of the (U.S.) National Intelligence Council (NIC). His research focuses on the course of the demographic transition and on trends in human migration, and he has studied their relationships to natural resource dynamics, human health, regime type, and the onset of civil conflict. His findings on demographic topics have been published in *Foreign Policy, Current History, Nature,* and *Science,* and he contributed to the NIC's global analysis, *Global Trends 2025: A Transformed World* (2009). Dr. Cincotta has more than five years of overseas field research experience, including projects in China, India, and Morocco, and another six years of overseas military and professional experience elsewhere.

David Coleman is professor of demography at Oxford University. Between 1985 and 1987 he worked for the British government as the Special Adviser to the Home Secretary, and then to the Ministers of Housing and of the Environment. His research interests include the comparative demographic trends in the industrial world; the future of fertility, the demographic consequences of migration and the demography of ethnic minorities. He has published over one hundred papers and eight books including *The State of Population Theory: Forward from Malthus* (ed. with R. S. Schofield, 1986), *The British Population: Patterns, Trends, and Processes* (with J. Salt, 1992, Oxford University Press),

International Migration: Regional Responses and Processes (ed. with M. Macura, 1994), and *Europe's Population in the 1990s* (ed. 1996, Oxford University Press). He has been joint editor of the *European Journal of Population* (Paris), and in 2001 was elected to the Council of the International Union for the Scientific Study of Population. He is a fellow of St. John's College and a lecturer at St. Catherine's College.

Jennifer Dabbs Sciubba is an assistant professor in the International Studies department at Rhodes College in Memphis, Tennessee. Her teaching and research examine the various security challenges and opportunities posed by trends in the environment, population, disease, and globalization. Dr. Sciubba has studied at the Max Planck Institute for Demographic Research in Rostock, Germany, and was formerly a demographics consultant to the Office of the Secretary of Defense (Policy) in Arlington, VA. Her latest book is *The Future Faces of War: Population and National Security* (Praeger/ABC-CLIO 2011). She received her PhD and MA from the University of Maryland and her BA from Agnes Scott College.

John Doces is assistant professor of political economy and public policy at Bucknell University. His teaching and research interests are in the political economy of development including population studies. His research has been published in *International Interactions, Polity,* and *Swiss Political Science Review.* Doces is also U.S. Director of the Ugandan-based Kigezi Healthcare Foundation where he manages a child malnutrition center in Kabale, Uganda. He holds an MA in economics and a PhD in political economy from the University of Southern California.

Monica Duffy Toft is associate professor of public policy at Harvard University's John F. Kennedy School of Government. Her research interests include international relations, religion, nationalism and ethnic conflict, civil and interstate wars, and the relationship between demography and political violence. Professor Toft is the author of *The Geography of Ethnic Conflict: Identity, Interests, and Territory* (Princeton, 2003), *Securing the Peace: The Durable Settlement of Civil Wars* (Princeton, 2010), and *God's Century: Resurgent Religion and Global Politics* (Norton, 2011). Professor Toft is director of the Belfer Center's Initiative on Religion in International Affairs, which was established with a generous grant from the Henry Luce Foundation.

William H. Frey is a demographer and sociologist specializing in U.S. population issues. He is currently a senior fellow with the Metropolitan Policy Program at the Brookings Institution in Washington, DC and Research Professor at the

University of Michigan's Institute for Social Research. Frey has authored well over one hundred publications relating to migration, population redistribution, and the demography of metropolitan areas. His books include Regional and Metropolitan Growth and Decline in the U.S. (with Alden Speare Jr., 1988, Russell Sage) and America By the Numbers: A Fieldguide to the U.S. Population (with Bill Abresch and Jonathan Yeasting, The New Press, 2001). He has contributed to the 1995 President's National Urban Policy Report, to HUD's State of the Cities 2000 report, to the Russell Sage Foundation's Census research series in 1980 and 1990, and has been consultant to the U.S. Census Bureau on migration research and publications.

Jack A. Goldstone is Hazel Professor and director of the Center for Global Policy at George Mason University, and a senior fellow at the Mercatus Center. He is the author of *Revolution and Rebellion in the Early Modern World* (California, 1981) and editor of *The Encyclopedia of Political Revolutions* (Congressional Quarterly, 1998). He has received the Distinguished Contribution to Scholarship award of the American Sociological Association, the Momigliano Prize of the Historical Society, and fellowships from the ACLS and the MacArthur Foundation. He recently published *Why Europe? The Rise of the West in World History* (McGraw-Hill, 2008) and is working on *A Peculiar Path: The Rise of the West and the Origins of Modern Economic Growth 1500–1800* (forthcoming from Harvard University Press). His article "The New Population Bomb," presenting the international security implications of global population change, appeared in the January 2010 issue of *Foreign Affairs*.

Brian Gratton is professor in the Department of History at Arizona State University. Under grants from the National Institutes of Health, he has examined the history of a variety of ethnic groups in the United States from 1850 to 2000. Fulbright Fellowships in Spain and Ecuador led to publications on Ecuadorian emigration to the United States and Europe. He served as a Russell Sage Fellow in New York City, writing on immigration, assimilation, and immigration policy. Professor Gratton's most recent work has appeared in the *Journal of American Ethnic History,* the *Journal of Interdisciplinary History,* the *Journal of Ethnic and Migration Studies,* and *Historical Statistics of the United States.*

Elliott D. Green is lecturer in development studies in the Department of International Development, London School of Economics, where he teaches courses on poverty and African development. He holds degrees from Princeton University (BA) and the London School of Economics (MSc, PhD). His research on ethnic politics and conflict in Africa has been published in such journals as *Comparative Politics, International Studies Quarterly, Perspectives on Politics,* and *Studies in Comparative International Development.*

Mark L. Haas is associate professor of political science at Duquesne University in Pittsburgh. He is the author of *The Ideological Origins of Great Power Politics, 1789–1989* (Cornell University Press, 2005) and *The Clash of Ideologies: Middle Eastern Politics and American Security* (Oxford University Press, 2012), and co-editor (with David Lesch) of *The Middle East and the United States: History, Politics, and Ideologies* (5th edition, Westview Press, 2011). Haas's scholarly articles and essays have appeared in *International Security, International Organization,* the *Boston Globe,* the *Washington Post,* and the *Pittsburgh Post-Gazette,* as well as other journals. Haas has received research support from the Olin Institute for Strategic Studies and the Belfer Center for Science and International Affairs (both at Harvard University), the Earhart Foundation, the Institute for the Study of World Politics, and Duquesne's Wimmer Foundation, Faculty Development Fund, and Presidential Scholarships. Haas is currently writing a book that examines the effects of global population aging on the future of American power.

Neil Howe is a senior associate with the Global Aging Initiative at the Center for Strategic and International Studies (CSIS). He is also cofounder of LifeCourse Associates, a marketing, human resources, and strategic planning consultancy serving corporate, government, and nonprofit clients. An historian, economist, and demographer, he writes and speaks frequently on the aging of the population, long-term fiscal policy, and generations in history. His coauthored books include *On Borrowed Time* (1988), *Generations* (Morrow, 1991), *13th-Gen* (Vintage, 1993), *The Fourth Turning* (Broadway, 1997), and *Millennials Rising* (Vintage, 2000). He holds graduate degrees in history and economics from Yale University.

Richard Jackson is a senior fellow at the Center for Strategic and International Studies (CSIS), where he directs the Global Aging Initiative, a research program that explores the economic, social, and geopolitical implications of the aging population in the United States and around the world. He is also a senior adviser to the Concord Coalition. Jackson is the author of numerous policy studies, including *The Global Aging Preparedness Index* (CSIS, 2010), *The Graying of the Great Powers* (CSIS, 2008), *Long-Term Immigration Projection Methods: Current Practice and How to Improve It* (CSIS, 2006), and *The Graying of the Middle Kingdom* (CSIS/Prudential Financial, 2004). He regularly speaks on long-term demographic and economic issues and is widely quoted in the national and international media. He holds a BA in classics from SUNY at Albany and a PhD in history from Yale University.

Eric P. Kaufmann is professor of politics at Birkbeck College, University of London. He is the author of *Shall the Religious Inherit the Earth*: *Demography and Politics in the Twenty-First Century* (Profile, 2011), *The Rise and Fall of Anglo-America* (Harvard, 2004), *The Orange Order* (Oxford, 2007), co-author of *Unionism and Orangeism in Northern Ireland Since 1945* (Manchester, 2007), and editor of *Rethinking Ethnicity: Majority Groups and Dominant Minorities* (Routledge, 2004). He is also an editor of the journal *Nations & Nationalism*. He has written on religion and demography in academic journals as well as for *Newsweek International, Foreign Policy,* and *Prospect* magazines. He recently finished co-editing a book with W. Bradford Wilcox entitled *Whither the Child: Causes and Consequences of Low Fertility* (Paradigm, 2012).

Elizabeth Leahy Madsen was until recently a senior research associate at Population Action International (PAI) in Washington, DC, and is currently an independent consultant. Her research has focused on the relationship between population dynamics and broader development issues, including vulnerability to conflict. She is the primary author of the 2007 PAI publication, *The Shape of Things to Come: Why Age Structure Matters to a Safer, More Equitable World.* Her work has been published by the Council on Foreign Relations, Environmental Change and Security Program at the Woodrow Wilson Center, International Encyclopedia of Public Health (Elsevier), and U.S. Army Corps of Engineers. She received her BA from Knox College and her MA in international affairs from the George Washington University.

Christian Leuprecht is associate professor of political science and economics at the Royal Military College of Canada. He is also cross-appointed to the Department of Political Studies and the School of Policy Studies at Queen's University, where he is a fellow of the Institute of Intergovernmental Relations, the Queen's Centre for International and Defense Policy, and the Chair in Defense Management Studies. He has been the Bicentennial Visiting Associate Professor in Canadian Studies at Yale University (2009–2010), and a research fellow at the Austrian Institute for European and Security Policy (since 2010). His recent publications include *Europe without Soldiers? Recruitment and Retention across the Armed Forces of Europe* (McGill-Queen's University Press, 2011), *Defending Democracy and Security Diversity* (Routledge, 2010), and *Mission Critical: Smaller Democracies' Role in Global Stability Operations* (McGill-Queen's University Press, 2010).

Richard Matthew is director of the Center for Unconventional Security Affairs and professor of international and environmental politics in the Schools of Social Ecology and Social Science at the University of California at Irvine. He is also the Senior Fellow for Security at the International Institute for Sustainable Development (IISD); a member of the World Conservation Union's Commission on Environmental, Economic, and Social Policy; and a member of the UNEP Expert Group on Conflict and Peacebuilding. Recent books and co-edited volumes include *Contested Grounds: Security and Conflict in the New Environmental Politics* (SUNY Press, 1999), *Dichotomy of Power: Nation versus State in World Politics* (Lexington, 2002), *Conserving the Peace: Resources, Livelihoods, and Security* (IISD, 2002), *Reframing the Agenda: The Impact of NGO and Middle Power Cooperation in International Security Policy* (Praeger, 2003), and *Landmines and Human Security: International Relations and War's Hidden Legacy* (SUNY Press, 2004).

Ragnhild Nordås is a senior researcher at the Centre for the Study of Civil War at the International Peace Research Institute, Oslo (PRIO). She has been an International Security Program Predoctoral Fellow for 2008–2010 in the Initiative on Religion in International Affairs at Harvard's Kennedy School of Government and a visiting researcher at the Kroc Institute for International Peace Studies at the University of Notre Dame. Nordås is a member of the editorial committee of the *Journal of Peace Research,* and her work has been published in *International Studies Quarterly* and *Political Geography.*

Vegard Skirbekk is the leader of the Age and Cohort Change (ACC) Project at IIASA in Austria, supported by a "Starting Grant" from the European Research Council. Dr. Skirbekk investigates trends in global population developments; demographic change by religion; the demography of religion and conflict; the age and gender distribution of human capital, skills, and work performance focusing on life cycle and cohort changes; and how to improve senior workers' skills and capacities—an issue of paramount importance for many countries coping with challenges of an aging population. He also studies the impact of generational and life cycle variation on societal values and belief structures, considering cohort and life cycle changes, migration, fertility differences, and intrafamilial transmissions. Another key research interest is the determinants of childbearing in a low fertility Asian/European context. He has published in leading academic journals, including *Science, Demography,* and *Population and Development Review.*

Henrik Urdal is Senior Researcher at the Peace Research Institute, Oslo (PRIO), and Research Fellow at the Kennedy School of Government, Harvard University. He is editor of the international bi-monthly *Journal of Peace Research*. His research has been published in such leading journals as *International Studies Quarterly, Journal of Conflict Resolution, Journal of Development Studies, Journal of Peace Research*, and *Political Geography*. Urdal was co-editor of a special issue of the *Journal of Peace Research* on "The Demography of Conflict and Violence" (2005), and of an edited volume on "The Demography of Armed Conflict" (Springer, 2006). Urdal's research interests include the security implications of population change, climate change, and conflict; and the demographic consequences of armed conflict.